A MANUAL

OF

ANCIENT HISTORY.

BY

M. E. THALHEIMER,

FORMERLY TEACHER OF HISTORY AND COMPOSITION IN THE PACKER COLLEGIATE INSTITUTE, BROOKLYN, N. Y.

WILSON, HINKLE & CO.,

137 WALNUT ST., CINCINNATI. 28 BOND ST., NEW YORK.

ELECTROTYPED AT THE FRANKLIN TYPE FOUNDRY, CINCINNATI.

PREFACE.

SEVERAL causes have lately augmented both the means and the motives for a more thorough study of History. Modern criticism, no longer accepting primitive traditions, venal eulogiums, partisan pamphlets, and highly wrought romances as equal and trustworthy evidence, merely because of their age, is teaching us to sift the testimony of ancient authors, to ascertain the sources and relative value of their information, and to discern those special aims which may determine the light in which their works should be viewed. The geographical surveys of recent travelers have thrown a flood of new light upon ancient events; and, above all, the inscriptions discovered and deciphered within half a century, have set before us the great actors of old times, speaking in their own persons from the walls of palaces and tombs.

Nor is the new knowledge of little value. If we look familiarly into the daily life of our fellow-men thousands of years ago, it is to find them toiling at the same problems which perplex us; suffering the same conflict of passion and principle; failing, it may be, for our warning, or winning for our encouragement; in any case, reaching results which ought to prevent our repeating their mistakes. The national questions which fill our newspapers were discussed long ago in the Grove, the Agora, and the Forum; the relative advantages of government by the many and the few, were wrought out to a demonstration in the states and colonies of Greece; and no man whose vote, no woman whose influence, may sway in ever so small a degree the destinies of our Republic, can afford to be ignorant of what has already been so wisely and fully accomplished.

Present tasks can only be clearly seen and worthily performed in the light of long experience; and that liberal acquaintance with History which, under a monarchical government, might safely be left as an ornament and privilege to the few, is here the duty of the many.

The present work aims merely to afford a brief though accurate outline of the results of the labors of NIEBUHR, BUNSEN, ARNOLD, MOMMSEN, RAWLINSON, and others — results which have never, so far as we know, been embraced in any American school-book, but which within a few years have greatly increased the treasures of historical literature. While it may have been impossible, within our limits, to reproduce the full and life-like outlines in which they have portrayed the characters of ancient times, we have sought, with their aid, at least to ascertain the limits of fact and fable. With but few exceptions, and those clearly stated as such, we have introduced no narrative which can reasonably be doubted.

The writer is more confident of justice of aim than of completeness of attainment. No one can so acutely feel the imperfections of a work like this, as the one who has labored at every point to avoid or to remove them; to compress the greatest amount of truth into the fewest words, and while reducing the scale, to preserve a just proportion in the details. To hundreds of former pupils, who have never been forgotten in this labor of love, and to the kind judgment of fellow-teachers — some of whom well know that effort has not been spared, even where ability may have failed — this Manual is respectfully submitted.

BROOKLYN, N. Y., *April*, 1872.

CONTENTS.

INTRODUCTION.

BOOK I.

Asiatic and African Nations, from the Dispersion at Babel to the Rise of the Persian Empire.

PART I.—THE ASIATIC NATIONS.

PART II.—THE AFRICAN NATIONS.

BOOK II.

The Persian Empire, from the Rise of Cyrus to the Fall of Darius.

BOOK III.

Grecian States and Colonies, from their Earliest Period to the Accession of Alexander the Great.

First Period.

Second Period.

Third Period.

BOOK IV.

History of the Macedonian Empire, and the Kingdoms formed from it, until their Conquest by the Romans.

First Period.

SECOND PERIOD.

THIRD PERIOD.

BOOK V.

History of Rome, from the Earliest Times to the Fall of the Western Empire.

INTRODUCTION.

SOURCES AND DIVISIONS OF HISTORY.

1. THE former inhabitants of our world are known to us by three kinds of evidence: (1) Written Records; (2) Architectural Monuments; (3) Fragmentary Remains.

2. Of these the first alone can be considered as true sources of History, though the latter afford its most interesting and valuable illustrations. Several races of men have disappeared from the globe, leaving no records inscribed either upon stone or parchment. Their existence and character can only be inferred from fragments of their weapons, ornaments, and household utensils found in their tombs or among the ruins of their habitations. Such were the Lake-dwellers of Switzerland, and the unknown authors of the shell-mounds of Denmark and India, the tumuli of Britain, and the earthworks of the Mississippi Valley.

3. The magnificent temples and palaces of Egypt, Assyria, and India have only afforded materials of history since the patient diligence of oriental scholars has succeeded in deciphering the inscriptions which they bore. Within a few years they have added immeasurably to our knowledge of primeval times, and explained in a wonderful manner the brief allusions of the Bible.

4. The oldest existing books are the Hebrew Scriptures, which alone* of ancient writings describe the preparation of the earth for the abode of man; his creation and primeval innocence; the entrance of Sin into the world, and the promise of Redemption; the first probation, and the almost total destruction of the human race by a flood; the vain attempt of Noah's descendants to avert similar punishment in future by building a "city and

---

*Scattered traditions of the same events have been found in several nations. The most remarkable were in the writings of Berosus (see note, p. 18), who, to his account of the Creation, added that the monstrous living creatures which had floated in the darkness of the primeval ocean perished at the appearance of light. These must have been the pre-adamite animals which Geology has made known to us only within the present century. Berosus describes a deluge, from which only righteous men were saved.

tower whose top should reach unto heaven," and their consequent dispersion. The Bible lays the foundation of all subsequent history by sketching the division of the human race into its three great families, and describing their earliest migrations.

5. The family of SHEM, which was appointed to guard the true primeval faith, remained near the original home in south-western Asia. Of the descendants of HAM, a part settled in the valleys of the Tigris and Euphrates, and built the great cities of Nineveh and Babylon; while the rest spread along the eastern and southern shores of the Mediterranean, and became the founders of the Egyptian Empire. The children of JAPHETH constituted the Indo-Germanic, or Aryan race, which was divided into two great branches. One, moving eastward, settled the table-lands of Iran and the fertile valleys of northern India; the other, traveling westward along the Euxine and Propontis, occupied the islands of the Ægean Sea, and the peninsulas of Greece and Italy. By successive migrations they overspread all Europe.

6. Our First Book treats of the Hamitic and Semitic empires. With the rise of the Medo-Persian monarchy, the Aryan race came upon the scene, and it has ever since occupied the largest place in History. The *Hamitic* nations were distinguished by their material grandeur, as exemplified by the enormous masses of stone employed in their architecture, and even in their sculpture; the *Semitic*, by their religious enthusiasm; the *Indo-Germanic*, by their intellectual activity, as exhibited in the highest forms of art, literature, and political organization.

7. History is divided into three great portions or periods: Ancient, Mediæval, and Modern.

Ancient History narrates the succession of empires which ruled Asia, Africa, and Europe, until the Roman dominion in Italy was overthrown by northern barbarians, A. D. 476.

Mediæval History begins with the establishment of a German kingdom in Gaul, and ends with the close of the fifteenth century, when the revival of ancient learning, the multiplication of printed books, and the expansion of ideas by the discovery of a new continent, occasioned great mental activity, and led to the Modern Era, in which we live.

8. Ancient History may be divided into five books:

I. History of the Asiatic and African nations, from the earliest times to the foundation of the Persian Empire, B. C. 558.

II. History of the Persian Empire, from the accession of Cyrus the Great to the death of Darius Codomannus, B. C. 558—330.

III. History of the States and Colonies of Greece, from their earliest period to the accession of Alexander of Macedon, B. C. 336.

IV. History of the Macedonian Empire, and the kingdoms formed from it, until their conquest by the Romans.

V. History of Rome from its foundation to the fall of the Western Empire, A. D. 476.

9. In the study of events, the two circumstances of time and place constantly demand our attention. Accordingly, CHRONOLOGY and GEOGRAPHY have been called the two eyes of History. It is only by the use of both that we can gain a complete and life-like impression of events.

10. For the want of the former, a large portion of the life of man upon the globe can be but imperfectly known. There is no detailed record of the ages that preceded the Deluge and Dispersion; and even after those great crises, long periods are covered only by vague traditions. We have no complete chronology for the Hebrews before the building of Solomon's Temple, B. C. 1004; for the Babylonians before Nabonassar, B. C. 748; or for the Greeks before the first Olympiad, B. C. 776. When its system of computation was settled, each nation selected its own era from which to date events; but we reduce all to our common reckoning of time before and after the Birth of Christ.

11. The study of GEOGRAPHY is more intimately connected with that of History than may at first appear. The growth and character of nations are greatly influenced, if not determined, by soil and climate, the position of mountains, and the course of rivers.

NOTE.—It is recommended to Teachers that the Geographical sections which precede Parts 1 and 2 of Book I, Book III, and Book V, be read aloud in the class, each pupil having his or her eye upon the map, and pronouncing the name of each locality mentioned, *only when it is found.* By this means the names will become familiar, and questions upon the peculiarities of each country can be afterward combined with the lessons.

Pupils are strongly urged to study History with the map before them; if possible, even a larger and fuller map than can be given in this book. Any little effort which this may cost, will be more than repaid in the ease with which the lesson will be remembered, when the places where events have occurred are clearly in the mind.

BOOK I.

NATIONS OF ASIA AND AFRICA FROM THE DISPERSION AT BABEL TO THE FOUNDATION OF THE PERSIAN EMPIRE.

B. C. (ABOUT) 2700-558.

PART I. ASIATIC NATIONS.

VIEW OF THE GEOGRAPHY OF ASIA.

12. ASIA, the largest division of the Eastern Hemisphere, possesses the greatest variety of soil, climate, and products. Its central and principal portion is a vast table-land, surrounded by the highest mountain chains in the world, on whose northern, eastern, and southern inclinations great rivers have their rise. Of these, the best known to the ancients were the Tigris and Euphra′tes, the Indus, Etyman′der, Arius, Oxus, Jaxar′tes, and Jordan.

13. NORTHERN ASIA, north of the great table-land and the Altai range, is a low, grassy plain, destitute of trees, and unproductive, but intersected by many rivers abounding in fish. It was known to the Greeks under the general name of Scythia. From the most ancient times to the present, it has been inhabited by wandering tribes, who subsisted mainly upon the milk and flesh of their animals.

14. CENTRAL ASIA, lying between the Altai on the north, and the Elburz, Hindu Kûsh, and Himala′ya Mountains on the south, has little connection with ancient History. Three countries in its western part are of some importance: *Choras′mia*, between the Caspian and the Sea of Aral; *Sogdia′na* to the east, and *Bac′tria* to the south of that province. The modern Sam′arcand is Maracan′da, the ancient capital of Sogdiana. Bactra, now Balkh, was probably the first great city of the Aryan race.

15. SOUTHERN ASIA may be divided into eastern and western sections by the Indus River. The eastern portion was scarcely known to the

Persians, Greeks, and Romans; and materials are yet lacking for its authentic history: the western, on the contrary, was the scene of the earliest and most important events.

16. South-western Asia may be considered in three portions: (1) Asia Minor, or the peninsula of Anato′lia; (2) The table-land eastward to the Indus, including the mountains of Arme′nia; (3) The lowland south of this plateau, extending from the base of the mountains to the Erythræ′an Sea.

17. Asia Minor, in the earliest period, contained the following countries: Phry′gia and Cappado′cia, on its central table-land, divided from each other by the river Ha′lys; Bithy′nia and Paphlago′nia on the coast of the Euxine; Mysia, Lydia, and Caria, on that of the Æge′an; Lycia, Pamphyl′ia, and Cilic′ia, on the borders of the Mediterranean. It possessed many important islands: Proconne′sus, in the Propon′tis; Ten′edos, Les′bos, Chi′os, Sa′mos, and Rhodes, in the Ægean; and Cy′prus, in the Levant′.

18. *Phrygia* was a grazing country, celebrated from the earliest times for its breed of sheep, whose fleece was of wonderful fineness, and black as the plumage of the raven. The Ango′ra goat and the rabbit of the same region were likewise famed for the fineness of their hair. *Cappadocia* was inhabited by the White Syrians, so called because they were of fairer complexion than those of the south. The richest portion of Asia Minor lay upon the coast of the Ægean; and of the three provinces, *Lydia*, the central, was most distinguished for wealth, elegance, and luxury. The Lydians were the first who coined money. The River Pacto′lus brought from the recesses of Mt. Tmolus a rich supply of gold, which was washed from its sands in the streets of Sardis, the capital.

19. The Grecian colonies, which, at a later period, covered the coasts of Asia Minor, will be found described in Book III.* This peninsula was the field of many wars between the nations of Europe and Asia. From its intermediate position, it was always the prize of the conqueror; and after the earliest period of history, it was never occupied by any kingdom of great extent or of long duration.

20. The highlands of south-western Asia contained seventeen countries, of which only the most important will here be named. *Arme′nia* has been called the Switzerland of Western Asia. Its highest mountain is Ar′arat, 17,000 feet above the sea-level. From this elevated region the Tigris and Euphrates take their course to the Persian Gulf; the Halys to the Euxine; the Arax′es and the Cyrus to the Caspian Sea. *Colchis* lay east of the Euxine, upon one of the great highways of ancient traffic. It was celebrated, in very early times, for its trade in linen. *Media* was a mountainous region, extending from the Araxes to the Caspian Gates. *Persia*

---

* See Book III, §§ 35-37, 84-86.

lay between Media and the Persian Gulf. Its southern portion is a sandy plain, rendered almost desert in summer by a hot, pestilential wind from the Steppes of Kerman. Farther from the sea, the country rises into terraces, covered with rich and well-watered pastures, and abounding in pleasant fruits. The climate of this region is delightful; but it soon changes, toward the north, into that of a sterile mountain tract, chilled by snows, which cover the peaks even in summer, and affording only a scanty pasturage to flocks of sheep.

21. The lowland plain of south-western Asia comprised Syr′ia, Arabia, Assyr′ia, Susia′na, and Babylo′nia. *Syria* occupied the whole eastern coast of the Mediterranean, and consisted of three distinct parts: (1) Syria Proper had for its chief river the Oron′tes, which flowed between the parallel mountain ranges of Lebanon and Anti-Lebanon. (2) Phœni′cia comprised the narrow strip of coast between Lebanon and the sea. (3) Palestine, south of Phœnicia, had for its river the Jordan, and for its principal mountains Hermon and Carmel. Syria becomes less fertile as it recedes from the mountains, and merges at last into a desert, with no traces of cities or of settled habitations. Yet even this sandy waste is varied by a few fertile spots. The site of Palmy′ra, "Queen of the Desert," may be discerned even now in her magnificent ruins. In more prosperous days she afforded entertainment to caravans on their way from India to the coast of the Mediterranean.

22. *Arabia* is a vast extent of country south and east of Syria, lying between the Red Sea and the Persian Gulf. Though more than one-fourth the size of Europe, it was of little importance in ancient times; for its usually rocky or sandy soil sustained few inhabitants, and afforded little material for commerce.

Assyria Proper lay east of the Tigris and west of the Median Mountains. The great empire which bore that name varied in extent under different monarchs, and the name of Assyria is often applied to all the territory between the Zagros Mountains and the Mediterranean Sea. The region between the two great rivers and north of Babylonia was called by the Greeks *Mesopota′mia*. It differed from the more southerly province in being richly wooded: the forests near the Euphrates more than once supplied materials for a fleet to Roman emperors in later times.

Susiana lay along the Tigris, south-east of Assyria. It was crossed by numerous rivers, and was very rich in grain. Its only important city was Susa, its capital.

23. *Babylonia* comprised the great alluvial plain between the lower waters of the Tigris and Euphrates, and sometimes included the country south of the latter river, on the borders of Arabia Deserta, which is better known as *Chaldæ′a*. When the snows melt upon the mountains of Armenia, both rivers, but especially the Euphrates, become suddenly swollen, and tend to overflow their banks. In fighting against this aggression of Nature, the Babylonians early developed that energy of mind which made their country the first abode of Eastern civilization. The net-work of canals which covered the country served the three purposes of internal traffic, defense, and irrigation. Immense lakes were dug or enlarged for the preservation of surplus waters; and the earth thrown out of these excavations formed dykes along the banks of the rivers. The fertile plain, so thoroughly watered, produced enormous quantities of grain, the farmer being rewarded with never less than two hundred fold the seed sown, and in favorable seasons, with three hundred fold. We shall not be surprised, therefore, to learn that Babylonia was, from the earliest times, the seat of populous cities, crowded with the products of human industry, and that its people long constituted the leading state of Western Asia. Though the plain of Babylonia afforded neither wood nor stone for building, Nature had provided for human habitations a supply of excellent clay for brick, and wells of bitumen which served for mortar. (Gen. xi: 3.)

24. SOUTH-EASTERN ASIA. *India* extends from the Indus eastward to the boundaries of China, being bounded on the south by the Indian Ocean, and on the north by the Himala′yas, from whose snowy heights many great rivers descend to fertilize the plains. The richness of the soil fits it for the abode of a swarming population; and roads, temples, and other structures, dating from a very remote period, attest the skill and industry of the people. Herod′otus * names them as the greatest and wealthiest of nations, though he had not seen them. It was only in the fifth century before Christ that the Indian peninsulas became distinctly known to the Greeks; and it was two centuries later, in the invasion by Alexander, that the remarkable features of the country were first described to the Western world by eye-witnesses. "Wool-bearing trees" were mentioned as a most peculiar production; for cotton, as well as sugar, was first produced in India. The pearl fisheries, however, of the eastern coast, the diamonds of Golcon′da, the rubies of Mysore′, as well as the abundant gold of the river-beds, the aromatic woods of the forests, and the fine fabrics of cotton, silk, and wool, for which India was already famous, † drew the merchants of Phœnicia at a much earlier period to the banks of the Indus.

25. *China* was even less known than India to the inhabitants of the ancient world. The province of Se′rica, which formed the north-western

---

* Herodotus, the Father of History, was a Greek of Halicarnassus, a Doric city in Caria, and was born B. C. 484. He collected the materials for his works by extensive travels and laborious research.

† Our word "shawl" belongs to the Sanskrit, the oldest known language of India, showing that "India shawls" have been objects of luxury and commerce from the earliest ages.

corner of what is now the Chinese Empire, was visited, however, by Babylonian and Phœnician merchants, for its most peculiar product, silk. The extreme reserve of the Chinese in their dealings with foreigners, may already be observed in the account given by Herodotus of their trade with the neighboring Scythians. The Sericans deposited their bales of wool or silk in a solitary building called the Stone Tower. The merchants then approached, deposited beside the goods a sum which they were willing to pay, and retired out of sight. The Sericans returned, and, if satisfied with the bargain, took away the money, leaving the goods; but if they considered the payment insufficient, they took away the goods and left the money. The Chinese have always been remarkable for their patient and thorough tillage of the soil. Chin-nong, their fourth emperor, invented the plow; and for thousands of years custom required each monarch, among the ceremonies of his coronation, to guide a plow around a field, thus paying due honor to agriculture, as the art most essential to the civilization, or, rather, to the very existence of a state.

CHALDÆAN MONARCHY.

26. After the dispersion of other descendants of Noah from Babel,* Nimrod, grandson of Ham, remained near the scene of their discomfiture, and established a kingdom south of the Euphrates, at the head of the Persian Gulf. The unfinished tower was converted into a temple, other buildings sprang from the clay of the plain, and thus Nimrod became the founder of Babylon, though its grandeur and magnificent adornments date from a later period. Nimrod owed his supremacy to the personal strength and prowess which distinguished him as a "mighty hunter before the Lord." In the early years after the Flood, it is probable that wild beasts multiplied so as to threaten the extinction of the human race, and the chief of men in the gratitude and allegiance of his fellows was he who reduced their numbers. Nimrod founded not only Babylon, but E′rech, or O′rchoë, Ac′cad, and Cal′neh. The Chaldæans continued to be notable builders; and vast structures of brick cemented with bitumen, each brick bearing the monarch's or the architect's name, still attest, though in ruins, their enterprise and skill. They manufactured, also, delicate fabrics of wool, and possessed the arts of working in metals and engraving on gems in very high perfection. Astronomy began to be studied in very early times, and the observations were carefully recorded. The name of Chaldæan became equivalent to that of seer or philosopher.

27. The names of fifteen or sixteen kings have been deciphered upon

---

* See p. 10, and Gen. xi: 1–9.

the earliest monuments of the country, but we possess no records of their reigns. It is sufficient to remember the dynasties, or royal families, which, according to Bero'sus,* ruled in Chaldæa from about two thousand years before Christ to the beginning of connected chronology.

1. A Chaldæan Dynasty, from about 2000 to 1543 B. C. The only known kings are Nimrod and Chedorlao'mer.

2. An Arabian Dynasty, from about 1543 to 1298 B. C.

3. A Dynasty of forty-five kings, probably Assyrian, from 1298 to 772 B. C.

4. The Reign of Pul, from 772 to 747 B. C.

During the first and last of these periods, the country was flourishing and free; during the second, it seems to have been subject to its neighbors in the south-west; and, during the third, it was absorbed into the great Assyrian Empire, as a tributary kingdom, if not merely as a province.

ASSYRIAN MONARCHY.

28. At a very early period a kingdom was established upon the Tigris, which expanded later into a vast empire. Of its earliest records only the names of three or four kings remain to us; but the quadrangular mounds which cover the sites of cities and palaces, and the rude sculptures found by excavation upon their walls, show the industry of a large and luxurious population. The history of Assyria may be divided into three periods:

I. From unknown commencement of the monarchy to the Conquest of Babylon, about 1250 B. C.

II. From Conquest of Babylon to Accession of Tiglath-pileser II, 745 B. C.

III. From Accession of Tiglath-pileser to Fall of Nineveh, 625 B. C.

One king of the FIRST PERIOD, Shalmaneser I, is known to have made war among the Armenian Mountains, and to have established cities in the conquered territory.

B. C. 1270.

29. SECOND PERIOD, B. C. 1250–745. About the middle of the thirteenth century B. C., Tiglathi-nin conquered Babylon. A hundred and twenty years later, a still greater monarch, Tiglath-pileser I, extended his conquests eastward into the Persian mountains, and westward to the borders of Syria. After the warlike reign of his son,

B. C. 1130.

* Berosus, a learned Babylonian, wrote a history of his own and neighboring countries in three books, which are unfortunately lost. He drew his information from records kept in the temple of Belus, from popular traditions, and in part, probably, from the Jewish Scriptures. Fragments have been preserved to us by later writers. He lived from the reign of Alexander, 356–323 B. C., to that of Antiochus II, 261–246 B. C.

Assyria was probably weakened and depressed for two hundred years, since no records have been found. From the year 909 B. C., the chronology becomes exact, and the materials for history abundant. As′shur-nazir-pal I carried on wars in Persia, Babylonia, Armenia, and Syria, and captured the principal Phœnician towns. He built a great palace at Ca′lah, which he made his capital. His son, Shalmane′ser II, continued his father's conquests, and made war in Lower Syria against Benha′dad, Haza′el, and A′hab.

B. C. 1100–909.

B. C. 886–858.

B. C. 858–823.

30. B. C. 810–781. I′va-lush (Hu-likh-khus IV) extended his empire both eastward and westward in twenty-six campaigns. He married Sam′-mura′mit (Semi′ramis), heiress of Babylonia, and exercised, either in her right or by conquest, royal authority over that country. No name is more celebrated in Oriental history than that of Semiramis; but it is probable that most of the wonderful works ascribed to her are purely fabulous. The importance of the real Sammuramit, who is the only princess mentioned in Assyrian annals, perhaps gave rise to fanciful legends concerning a queen who, ruling in her own right, conquered Egypt and part of Ethiopia, and invaded India with an army of more than a million of men. This mythical heroine ended her career by flying away in the form of a dove. It became customary to ascribe all buildings and other public works whose origin was unknown, to Semiramis; the date of her reign was fixed at about 2200 B. C.; and she was said to have been the wife of Ninus, an equally mythical person, the reputed founder of Nineveh.

31. Asshur-danin-il II was less warlike than his ancestors. The time of his reign is ascertained by an eclipse of the sun, which the inscriptions place in his ninth year, and which astronomers know to have occurred June 15, 763 B. C. After Asshur-likh-khus, the following king, the dynasty was ended with a revolution. Nabonas′sar, of Babylon, not only made himself independent, but gained a brief supremacy over Assyria. The Assyrians, during the Second Period, made great advances in literature and arts. The annals of each reign were either cut in stone or impressed upon a duplicate series of bricks, to guard against destruction either by fire or water. If fire destroyed the burnt bricks, it would only harden the dried; and if the latter were dissolved by water, the former would remain uninjured. Engraved columns were erected in all the countries under Assyrian rule.

B. C. 771–753.

B. C. 753–745.

32. THIRD PERIOD, B. C. 745–625. Tiglath-pileser II was the founder of the New or Lower Assyrian Empire, which he established by active and successful warfare. He conquered Damascus, Samaria, Tyre, the Philistines, and the Arabians of the Sinaitic peninsula; carried away captives from the eastern and northern tribes of Israel, and took tribute from the king of Judah. (2 Kings xv: 29; xvi: 7–9.)

B. C. 745–727.

Shalmaneser IV conquered Phœnicia, but was defeated in a naval assault upon Tyre. His successor, Sargon, took Samaria, which had revolted, and carried its people captive to his newly conquered provinces of Media and Gauzanitis. He filled their places with Babylonians, whose king, Merodach-baladan, he had captured, B. C. 709. An interesting inscription of Sargon relates his reception of tribute from seven kings of Cyprus, "who have fixed their abode in the middle of the sea of the setting sun." The city and palace of Khor′sabad′ were entirely the work of Sargon. The palace was covered with sculptures within and without; it was ornamented with enameled bricks, arranged in elegant and tasteful patterns, and was approached by noble flights of steps through splendid porticos. In this "palace of incomparable splendor, which he had built for the abode of his royalty," are found Sargon's own descriptions of the glories of his reign. "I imposed tribute on Pharaoh, of Egypt; on Tsamsi, Queen of Arabia; on Ithamar, the Sabæan, in gold, spices, horses, and camels." Among the spoils of the Babylonian king, he enumerates his golden tiara, scepter, throne and parasol, and silver chariot. In the old age of Sargon, Merodach-baladan recovered his throne, and the Assyrian king was murdered in a conspiracy.

33. His son, Sennach′erib, reëstablished Assyrian power at the eastern and western extremities of his empire. He defeated Merodach-baladan, and placed first an Assyrian viceroy, and afterward his own son, Assarana′dius, upon the Babylonian throne. He quelled a revolt of the Phœnician cities, and extorted tribute from most of the kings in Syria. He gained a great battle at El′tekeh, in Palestine, against the kings of Egypt and Ethiopia, and captured all the "fenced cities of Judah." (2 Kings xviii: 13.) In a second expedition against Palestine and Egypt, 185,000 of his soldiers were destroyed in a single night, near Pelusium, as a judgment for his impious boasting. (2 Kings xix: 35, 36.) On his return to Nineveh, two of his sons conspired against him and slew him, and E′sarhad′don, another son, obtained the crown. His reign (B. C. 680-667) was signalized by many conquests. He defeated Tir′hakeh, king of Egypt, and broke up his kingdom into petty states. He completed the colonization of Samaria with people from Babylonia, Susiana, and Persia. His royal residence was alternately at Nineveh and Babylon.

B. C. 705-680.

34. Under As′shur-ba′ni-pal, son of Esarhaddon, Assyria attained her greatest power and glory. He reconquered Egypt, which had rallied under Tirhakeh, overran Asia Minor, and imposed a tribute upon Gyges, king of Lydia. He subdued most of Armenia, reduced Susiana to a mere province of Babylonia, and exacted obedience from many Arabian tribes. He built the grandest of all the Assyrian

B. C. 667-647.

COURT OF SARGON'S PALACE, AT KHORSABAD.

palaces, cultivated music and the arts, and established a sort of royal library at Nineveh.

35. The reign of his son, Asshur-emid-ilin, called Saracus by the Greeks, was overwhelmed with disasters. A horde of barbarians, from the plains of Scythia, invaded the empire, and before it could recover from the shock, it was rent by a double revolt of Media on the north, and Babylonia on the south. Nabopolassar, the Babylonian, had been general of the armies of Saracus; but finding himself stronger than his master, he made an alliance with Cyax'ares, king of the Medes, in concert with whom he besieged and captured Nineveh. The Assyrian monarch perished in the flames of his palace, and the two conquerors divided his dominions between them. Thus ended the Assyrian Empire, B. C. 625.

B. C. 647–625.

36. The Third Period was the Golden Age of Assyrian Art. The sculptured marbles which have been brought from the palaces of Sargon, Sennacherib, and Asshur-bani-pal, show a skill and genius in the carving which remind us of the Greeks. A few may be seen in collections of colleges and other learned societies in this country. The most magnificent specimens are in the British Museum, the Louvre at Paris, and the Oriental Museum at Berlin. During the same period the sciences of geography and astronomy were cultivated with great diligence; studies in language and history occupied multitudes of learned men; and modern scholars, as they decipher the long-buried memorials, are filled with admiration of the mental activity which characterized the times of the Lower Empire of Assyria.

Kings of Assyria.

For the First and more than half the Second Period, the names are discontinuous and dates unknown. We begin, therefore, with the era of ascertained chronology.

Kings of the Second Period.

Asshur-danin-il I	died	B. C.	909.
Hu-likh-khus III	reigned	"	909–889.
Tiglathi-nin II	"	"	889–886.
Asshur-nasir-pal I	"	"	886–858.
Shalmaneser II	"	"	858–823.
Shamas-iva	"	"	823–810.
Hu-likh-khus IV	"	"	810–781.
Shalmaneser III	"	"	781–771.
Asshur-danin-il II	"	"	771–753.
Asshur-likh-khus	"	"	753–745.

Kings of the Third Period.

Tiglath-pileser II, usurper,* . . .	B. C.	745–727.
Shalmaneser IV, ...	"	727–721.
Sargon, usurper, ...	"	721–705.
Sennacherib, ...	"	705–680.
Esarhaddon, ...	"	680–667.
Asshur-bani-pal, ... about	"	667–647.
Asshur-emid-ilin, ...	"	647–625.

RECAPITULATION.

A kingdom of mighty hunters and great builders is founded by Nimrod, B. C. 2000. Chaldæa becomes subject, first to Arabian, then to Assyrian invaders, but is made independent by Pul, B. C. 772. The Assyrian monarchy absorbs the Chaldæan, and extends itself from Syria to the Persian mountains. After two hundred years' depression, its records become authentic B. C. 909. Iva-lush and Sammuramit reign jointly over greatly increased territories. The Lower Empire is established by Tiglath-pileser II, whose dominion reaches the Mediterranean. Sargon records many conquests in his palace at Khorsabad. Sennacherib recaptures Babylon and gains victories over Egypt and Palestine. The Assyrian Empire is increased by Esarhaddon, and culminates under Asshur-bani-pal, only to be overthrown in the next reign by a Scythian invasion and a revolt of Media and Babylonia.

MEDIAN MONARCHY.

37. Little is known of the Medes before the invasion of their country by Shalmaneser II, B. C. 830, and its partial conquest by Sargon,† in 710. They had some importance, however, in the earliest times after the Deluge, for Berosus tells us that a Median dynasty governed Babylon during that period. The country was doubtless divided among petty chieftains, whose rivalries prevented its becoming great or famous in the view of foreign nations.

---

* The student's memory may be aided by some explanation of the long names of the Assyrian kings. They resemble the Hebrew in their composition; and, as in that language, each may form a complete sentence. Of the two, three, or four distinct words which always compose a royal appellation, one is usually the name of a divinity. Thus, Tiglathi-nin = "Worship be to Nin" (the Assyrian Hercules); Tiglath-pileser = "Worship be to the Son of Zira;" Sargon = "The King is established;" Esar-haddon = "Asshur has given a brother."

In Babylonian names, Nebo, Merodach, Bel, and Nergal correspond to Asshur, Sin, and Shamas in Assyrian. Thus, Abed-nego (for Nebo) is the "Servant of Nebo;" Nebuchadnezzar means "Nebo protect my race," or "Nebo is the protector of landmarks;" Nabopolassar = "Nebo protect my son"—the exact equivalent of Asshur-nasir-pal in the Assyrian Dynasty of the Second Period.

† See § 32.

38. About 740 B. C., according to Herodotus, the Medes revolted from Assyria, and chose for their king Dei′oces, whose integrity as a judge had marked him as fittest for supreme command. He built the city of Ecbat′-ana, which he fortified with seven concentric circles of stone, the innermost being gilded so that its battlements shone like gold. Here Deioces established a severely ceremonious etiquette, making up for his want of hereditary rank by all the external tokens of the divinity that "doth hedge a king." No courtier was permitted to laugh in his presence, or to approach him without the profoundest expressions of reverence. Either his real dignity of character or these stately ceremonials had such effect, that he enjoyed a prosperous reign of fifty-three years. Though Deioces is described by Herodotus as King of the Medes, it is probable that he was ruler only of a single tribe, and that a great part of his story is merely imaginary.

39. The true history of the Median kingdom dates from B. C. 650, when Phraor′tes was on the throne. This king, who is called the son of Deioces, extended his authority over the Persians, and formed that close connection of the Medo-Persian tribes which was never to be dissolved. The supremacy was soon gained by the latter nation. The double kingdom was seen by Daniel in his vision, under the form of a ram, one of whose horns was higher than the other, and "the higher came up last." (Daniel viii: 3, 20.) Phraor′tes, reinforced by the Persians, made many conquests in Upper Asia. He was killed in a war against the last king of Assyria, B. C. 633.

40. Determined to avenge his father's death, Cyaxares renewed the war with Assyria. He was called off to resist a most formidable incursion of barbarians from the north of the Caucasus. These Scythians became masters of Western Asia, and their insolent dominion is said to have lasted twenty-eight years. A band of the nomads were received into the service of Cyaxares as huntsmen. According to Herodotus, they returned one day empty-handed from the chase; and upon the king's expressing his displeasure, their ferocious temper burst all bounds. They served up to him, instead of game, the flesh of one of the Median boys who had been placed with them to learn their language and the use of the bow, and then fled to the court of the King of Lydia. This circumstance led to a war between Alyat′tes and Cyaxares, which continued five years without any decisive result. It was terminated by an eclipse of the sun occurring in the midst of a battle. The two kings hastened to make peace; and the treaty, which fixed the boundary of their two empires at the River Halys, was confirmed by the marriage of the son of Cyaxares with the daughter of Alyattes. The Scythian oppressions were ended by a general massacre of the barbarians, who, by a secretly concerted plan, had been invited to banquets and made drunken with wine.

41. Cyaxares now resumed his plans against Assyria. In alliance with Nabopolassar, of Babylon, he was able to capture Nineveh, overthrow the empire, and render Media a leading power in Asia. The successful wars of Cyaxares secured for himself and his son nearly half a century of peace, during which the Medes rapidly adopted the luxurious habits of the nations they had conquered. The court of Ecbatana became as magnificent as that of Nineveh had been when at the height of its grandeur. The courtiers delighted in silken garments of scarlet and purple, with collars and bracelets of gold, and the same precious metal adorned the harness of their horses. Reminiscences of the old barbaric life remained in an excessive fondness for hunting, which was indulged either in the parks about the capital, or in the open country, where lions, leopards, bears, wild boars, stags, and antelopes still abounded. The great wooden palace, covered with plates of gold and silver, as well as other buildings of the capital, showed a barbarous fondness for costly materials, rather than grandeur of architectural ideas. The Magi, a priestly caste, had great influence in the Median court. The education of each young king was confided to them, and they continued throughout his life to be his most confidential counselors.

42. B. C. 593. Cyaxares died after a reign of forty years. His son, Asty′ages, reigned thirty-five years in friendly and peaceful alliance with the kings of Lydia and Babylon. Little is known of him except the events connected with his fall, and these will be found related in the history of Cyrus, Book II.

KNOWN KINGS OF MEDIA.

Phraortes	died	B. C.	633.
Cyaxares	reigned	"	633–593.
Astyages	"	"	593–558.

NOTE.—It is impossible to reconcile the chronology of the reign of Cyaxares with *all* the ancient accounts. If the Scythian invasion occurred *after* the beginning of his reign, continued twenty-eight years, and ended before the Fall of Nineveh, it is easy to see that the date of the latter event must have been later than is given in the text. The French school of Orientalists place it, in fact, B. C. 606, and the accession of Cyaxares in 634. The English school, with Sir H. Rawlinson at their head, give the dates which we have adopted.

BABYLONIAN MONARCHY.

43. For nearly five hundred years, Babylon had been governed by Assyrian viceroys, when Nabonassar (747 B. C.) threw off the yoke, and established an independent kingdom. He destroyed the humiliating records of former servitude, and began a new era from which Babylonian time was afterward reckoned.

44. Merodach-baladan, the fifth king of this line, sent an embassy to Hezekiah, king of Judah, to congratulate him upon his recovery from illness, and to inquire concerning an extraordinary phenomenon connected with his restoration. (Isaiah xxxviii: 7, 8; xxxix: 1.) This shows that the Babylonians were no less alert for astronomical observations than their predecessors, the Chaldæans. In fact, the brilliant clearness of their heavens early led the inhabitants of this region to a study of the stars. The sky was mapped out in constellations, and the fixed stars were catalogued; time was measured by sun-dials, and other astronomical instruments were invented by the Babylonians. B. C. 721-709.

45. The same Merodach-baladan was taken captive by Sargon, king of Assyria, and held for six years, while an Assyrian viceroy occupied his throne. He escaped and resumed his government, but was again dethroned by Sennacherib, son of Sargon. The kingdom remained in a troubled state, usually ruled by Assyrians, but seeking independence, until Esarhaddon, son of Sennacherib, conquered Babylon, built himself a palace, and reigned alternately at that city and at Nineveh. B. C. 680-667. His son, Sa′os-duchi′nus, governed Babylon as viceroy for twenty years, and was succeeded by Cinnelada′nus, another Assyrian, who ruled twenty-two years. B. C. 667-647. B. C. 647-625.

46. B. C. 625. SECOND PERIOD. Nabopolas′sar, a Babylonian general, took occasion, from the misfortunes of the Assyrian Empire, to end the long subjection of his people. He allied himself with Cyaxares, the Median king, to besiege Nineveh and overthrow the empire. In the subsequent division of spoils, he received Susiana, the Euphrates Valley, and the whole of Syria, and erected a new empire, whose history is among the most brilliant of ancient times. The extension of his dominions westward brought him in collision with a powerful neighbor, Pha′raoh-ne′choh, of Egypt, who actually subdued the Syrian provinces, and held them a few years. But Nabopolassar sent his still more powerful son, Nebuchadnez′zar, who chastised the Egyptian king in the battle of Car′chemish, and wrested from him the stolen provinces. He also besieged Jerusalem, and returned to Babylon laden with the treasures of the temple and palace of Solomon. He brought in his train Jehoi′akim, king of Judah, and several young persons of the royal family, among whom was the prophet Daniel. B. C. 625-604. B. C. 608. B. C. 605.

47. During his son's campaign, Nabopolassar had died at Babylon, and the victorious prince was immediately acknowledged as king. Nebuchadnezzar made subsequent wars in Phœnicia, Palestine, and Egypt, and established an empire which extended westward to the Mediterranean Sea. He deposed the king of Egypt, and placed Amasis upon the throne as his deputy. Zedeki′ah, who had been elevated B. C. 604-561.

to the throne of Judah, rebelled against Babylon, and Nebuchadnezzar set out in person to punish his treachery. He besieged Jerusalem eighteen months, and captured Zedekiah, who, with true Eastern cruelty, was compelled to see his two sons murdered before his eyes were put out, and he was carried in chains to Babylon. In a later war, Nebuzar-adan, general of the armies of Nebuchadnezzar, destroyed Jerusalem, burned the temple and palaces, and carried the remnant of the people to Babylon. The strong and wealthy city of Tyre revolted, and resisted for thirteen years the power of the great king, but at length submitted, and all Phœnicia remained under the Babylonian yoke. B. C. 585.

48. The active mind of Nebuchadnezzar, absorbed in schemes of conquest, began to be visited by dreams, in one of which the series of great empires which were yet to arise in the east was distinctly foreshadowed. Of all the wise men of the court, Daniel alone was enabled to interpret the vision; and his spiritual insight, together with the singular elevation and purity of his character, gained him the affectionate confidence of the king. (Read Daniel ii.)

49. The reign of Nebuchadnezzar was illustrated by grand public works. His wife, a Median princess, sighed for her native mountains, and was disgusted with the flatness of the Babylonian plain, the greatest in the ancient world. To gratify her, the elevated—rather than "hanging"—gardens were created. Arches were raised on arches in continuous series until they overtopped the walls of Babylon, and stairways led from terrace to terrace. The whole structure of masonry was overlaid with soil sufficient to nourish the largest trees, which, by means of hydraulic engines, were supplied from the river with abundant moisture. In the midst of these groves stood the royal winter residence; for a retreat, which in other climates would be most suitable for a summer habitation, was here reserved for those cooler months in which alone man can live in the open air. This first great work of landscape gardening which history describes, comprised a charming variety of hills and forests, rivers, cascades, and fountains, and was adorned with the loveliest flowers the East could afford.

50. The same king surrounded the city with walls of burnt brick, two hundred cubits high and fifty in thickness, which, together with the gardens, were reckoned among the Seven Wonders of the World. During his reign and that of his son-in-law, Nabona′dius, the whole country was enriched by works of public utility: canals, reservoirs, and sluices were multiplied, and the shores of the Persian Gulf were improved by means of piers and embankments.

51. Owing to these encouragements, as well as to her fortunate position midway between the Indus and the Mediterranean, with the Gulf and the two great rivers for natural highways, Babylon was thronged with the merchants of all nations, and her commerce embraced the known world.

Manufactures, also, were numerous and famous. The cotton fabrics of the towns on the Tigris and Euphrates were unsurpassed for fineness of quality and brilliancy of color; and carpets, which were in great demand among the luxurious Orientals, were nowhere produced in such magnificence as in the looms of Babylon.

52. It is not strange that the pride of Nebuchadnezzar was kindled by the magnificence of his capital. As he walked upon the summit of his new palace, and looked down upon the swarming multitudes who owed their prosperity to his protection and fostering care, he said, "Is not this great Babylon, that *I* have built for the house of the kingdom by the might of my power, and for the honor of my majesty?" At that moment the humiliation foretold in a previous dream, interpreted by Daniel, came upon him. We can not better describe the manner of the judgment than in the king's own words (Daniel iv: 31–37):

"While the word was in the king's mouth, there fell a voice from heaven, saying, O King Nebuchadnezzar, to thee it is spoken; The kingdom is departed from thee. And they shall drive thee from men, and thy dwelling shall be with the beasts of the field: they shall make thee to eat grass as oxen, and seven times shall pass over thee, until thou know that the Most High ruleth in the kingdom of men, and giveth it to whomsoever he will. The same hour was the thing fulfilled upon Nebuchadnezzar: and he was driven from men, and did eat grass as oxen, and his body was wet with the dew of heaven, till his hairs were grown like eagles' feathers, and his nails like birds' claws. And at the end of the days, I, Nebuchadnezzar, lifted up mine eyes unto heaven, and mine understanding returned unto me, and I blessed the Most High, and I praised and honored him that liveth forever, whose dominion is an everlasting dominion, and his kingdom is from generation to generation. . . . . At the same time my reason returned unto me; and for the glory of my kingdom, mine honor and brightness returned unto me; and my counselors and my lords sought unto me; and I was established in my kingdom, and excellent majesty was added unto me. Now I, Nebuchadnezzar, praise and extol and honor the King of heaven, all whose works are truth, and his ways judgment: and those that walk in pride he is able to abase."

53. The immediate successors of Nebuchadnezzar were not his equals in character or talent. Evil-merodach, his son, was murdered after a reign of two years by Nereglis′sar, his sister's husband. B. C. 561-559. This prince was advanced in years when he ascended the throne, having been already a chief officer of the crown thirty years before at the siege of Jerusalem. B. C. 559-555. He reigned but four years, and was succeeded by his son, La′borosoar′chod. The young king was murdered, after only nine months' reign, by Nabona′dius, who became the last king of Babylon. The usurper strengthened his title by marrying a daughter of Nebuchadnezzar—probably the widow of Nereglissar—and afterward by associating their son Belshaz′zar with him in the government. He also sought security in foreign alliances. He fortified his capital by river walls, and constructed water-works in connection with the river above the city, by which the whole plain north and west could be flooded to prevent the approach of an enemy.

B. C. 555–538.

54. A new power was indeed arising in the East, against which the three older but feebler monarchies, Babylonia, Lydia, and Egypt, found it necessary to combine their forces. After the conquest of Lydia, and the extension of the Persian Empire to the Ægean Sea, Nabonadius had still fifteen years for preparation. He improved the time by laying up enormous quantities of food in Babylon; and felt confident that, though the country might be overrun, the strong walls of Nebuchadnezzar would enable him cheerfully to defy his foe. On the approach of Cyrus he resolved to risk one battle; but in this he was defeated, and compelled to take refuge in Bor′sippa. His son Belshazzar, being left in Babylon, indulged in a false assurance of safety. Cyrus, by diverting the course of the Euphrates, opened a way for his army into the heart of the city, and the court was surprised in the midst of a drunken revel, unprepared for resistance. The young prince, unrecognized in the confusion, was slain at the gate of his palace. Nabonadius, broken by the loss of his capital and his son, surrendered himself a prisoner; and the dominion of the East passed to the Medo-Persian race. Babylon became the second city of the empire, and the Persian court resided there the greater portion of the year.

RECAPITULATION.

Deioces, the first reputed king of Media, built and adorned Ecbatana. Phraortes united the Medes and Persians into one powerful kingdom. In the reign of Cyaxares, the Scythians ruled Western Asia twenty-eight years. After their expulsion, Cyaxares, in alliance with the Babylonian viceroy, overthrew the Assyrian Empire, divided its territories with his ally, and raised his own dominion to a high degree of wealth. His son Astyages reigned peacefully thirty-five years.

Babylon, under Nabonassar, became independent of Assyria, B. C. 747. Merodach-baladan, the fifth native king, was twice deposed, by Sargon and Sennacherib, and the country again remained forty-two years under Assyrian rule. It was delivered by Nabopolassar, whose still more powerful son, Nebuchadnezzar, gained great victories over the kings of Judah and Egypt, replacing the latter with viceroys of his own, and transporting the former, with the princes, nobles, and sacred treasures of Jerusalem, to Babylon. By a thirteen years' siege, Tyre was subdued and all Phœnicia conquered. From visions interpreted by Daniel, Nebuchadnezzar learned the future rise and fall of Asiatic empires. He constructed the Hanging Gardens, the walls of Babylon, and many other public works. His pride was punished by seven years' degradation. Evil-merodach was murdered by Nereglissar, who after four years bequeathed his crown to Laborosoarchod. Nabonadius obtained the throne by violence, and in concert with his son Belshazzar, tried to protect his dominions against Cyrus; but Babylon was taken and the empire overthrown, B. C. 538.

KINGDOMS OF ASIA MINOR.

55. The Anatolian peninsula, divided by its mountain chains into several sections, was occupied from very ancient times by different nations nearly equal in power. Of these, the PHRYGIANS were probably the earliest settlers, and at one time occupied the whole peninsula. Successive immigrations from the east and west pressed them inward from the coast, but they still had the advantage of a large and fertile territory. They were a brave but rather brutal race, chiefly occupied with agriculture, and especially the raising of the vine.

56. The Phrygians came from the mountains of Armenia, whence they brought a tradition of the Flood, and of the resting of the ark on Mount Ararat. They were accustomed, in primitive times, to hollow their habitations out of the rock of the Anatolian hills, and many of these rock cities may be found in all parts of Asia Minor. Before the time of Homer, however, they had well-built towns and a flourishing commerce.

57. Their religion consisted of many dark and mysterious rites, some of which were afterward copied by the Greeks. The worship of Cyb′ele, and of Saba′zius, god of the vine, was accompanied by the wildest music and dances. The capital of Phrygia was Gor′dium, on the Sanga′rius. The kings were alternately called Gor′dias and Mi′das, but we have no chronological lists. Phrygia became a province of Lydia B. C. 560.

58. In later times LYDIA became the greatest kingdom in Asia Minor, both in wealth and power, absorbing in its dominion the whole peninsula, except Lycia, Cilicia, and Cappadocia. Three dynasties successively bore rule: the *Atyadæ*, before 1200 B. C.; the *Heraclidæ*, for the next 505 years; and the *Mermnadæ*, from B. C. 694 until 546, when Crœsus, the last and greatest monarch, was conquered by the Persians. The name of this king has become proverbial from his enormous wealth. When associated with his father as crown prince, he was visited by Solon of Athens, who looked on all the splendor of the court with the coolness of a philosopher. Annoyed by his indifference, the prince asked Solon who, of all the men he had encountered in his travels, seemed to him the happiest. To his astonishment, the wise man named two persons in comparatively humble stations, but the one of whom was blessed with dutiful children, and the other had died a triumphant and glorious death. The vanity of Crœsus could no longer abstain from a direct effort to extort a compliment. He asked if Solon did not consider him a happy man. The philosopher gravely replied that, such were the vicissitudes of life, no man, in his opinion, could safely be pronounced happy until his life was ended.

59. Crœsus extended his power over not only the whole Anatolian peninsula, but the Greek islands both of the Ægean and Ionian seas. He made an alliance with Sparta, Egypt, and Babylon to resist the growing empire of Cyrus; but his precautions were ineffectual; he was defeated and made prisoner. He is said to have been bound upon a funeral pile, or altar, near the gate of his capital, when he recalled with anguish of heart the words of the Athenian sage, and three times uttered his name, "Solon, Solon, Solon!" Cyrus, who was regarding the scene with curiosity, ordered his interpreters to inquire what god or man he had thus invoked in his distress. The captive king replied that it was the name of a man with whom he wished that every monarch might be acquainted; and described the visit and conversation of the serene philosopher who had remained undazzled by his splendor. The conqueror was inspired with a more generous emotion by the remembrance that he, too, was mortal; he caused Crœsus to be released and to dwell with him as a friend.

Kings of Lydia.

Of the First and Second Dynasties, the names are only partially known, and dates are wanting.

Atyadæ:	*Heraclidæ, last six:*	*Mermnadæ:*		
Manes,	Adyattes I,	Gyges,	B. C.	694–678.
Atys,	Ardys,	Ardys,	"	678–629.
Lydus,	Adyattes II,	Sadyattes,	"	629–617.
Meles.	Meles,	Alyattes,	"	617–560.
	Myrsus,	Crœsus,	"	560–546.
	Candaules.			

PHŒNICIA.

60. The small strip of land between Mount Lebanon and the sea was more important to the ancient world than its size would indicate. Here arose the first great commercial cities, and Phœnician vessels wove a web of peaceful intercourse between the nations of Asia, Africa, and Europe.

61. Sidon was probably the most ancient, and until B. C. 1050, the most flourishing, of all the Phœnician communities. About that year the Philistines of Askalon gained a victory over Sidon, and the exiled inhabitants took refuge in the rival city of Tyre. Henceforth the daughter surpassed the mother in wealth and power. When Herodotus visited Tyre, he found a temple of Hercules which claimed to be 2,300 years old. This would give Tyre an antiquity of 2,750 years B. C.

62. Other chief cities of Phœnicia were Bery′tus (Beirût), Byb′lus, Tri′polis, and Ara′dus. Each with its surrounding territory made an independent state. Occasionally in times of danger they formed themselves into a league, under the direction of the most powerful; but the name Phœnicia applies merely to territory, not to a single well organized state, nor even to a permanent confederacy. Each city was ruled by its king, but a strong priestly influence and a powerful aristocracy, either of birth or wealth, restrained the despotic inclinations of the monarch.

63. The commerce of the Phœnician cities had no rival in the earlier centuries of their prosperity. Their trading stations sprang up rapidly along the coasts and upon the islands of the Mediterranean; and even beyond the Pillars of Hercules, their city of Gades (Kadesh), the modern Cadiz, looked out upon the Atlantic. These remote colonies were only starting points from which voyages were made into still more distant regions. Merchantmen from Cadiz explored the western coasts of Africa and Europe. From the stations on the Red Sea, trading vessels were fitted out for India and Ceylon.

64. At a later period, the Greeks absorbed the commerce of the Euxine and the Ægean, while Carthage claimed her share in the Western Mediterranean and the Atlantic. By this time, however, Western Asia was more tranquil under the later Assyrian and Babylonian monarchs; and the wealth of Babylon attracted merchant trains from Tyre across the Syrian Desert by way of Tadmor. Other caravans moved northward, and exchanged the products of Phœnician industry for the horses, mules, slaves, and copper utensils of Armenia and Cappadocia. A friendly intercourse was always maintained with Jerusalem, and a land-traffic with the Red Sea, which was frequented by Phœnician fleets. Gold from Ophir, pearls and diamonds from Eastern India and Ceylon, silver from Spain, linen embroidery from Egypt, apes from Western Africa, tin from the British Isles, and amber from the Baltic, might be found in the cargoes of Tyrian vessels.

65. The Phœnicians in general were merchants, rather than manufacturers; but their bronzes and vessels in gold and silver, as well as other works in metal, had a high repute. They claimed the invention of glass, which they manufactured into many articles of use and ornament. But the most famous of their products was the "Tyrian purple," which they obtained in minute drops from the two shell-fish, the *buccinum* and *murex*, and by means of which they gave a high value to their fabrics of wool.

66. About the time of Pygma′lion, the warlike expeditions of Shalmaneser II overpowered the Phœnician towns, and for more than two hundred years they remained tributary to the Assyrian Empire. Frequent but usually vain attempts were made, during the latter half of this period, to throw off the yoke. With the fall of Nineveh it is probable that Phœnicia became independent.

67. B. C. 608. It was soon reduced, however, by Necho of Egypt, who added all Syria to his dominions, and held Phœnicia dependent until he himself was conquered by Nebuchadnezzar (B. C. 605) at Carchemish.

The captive cities were only transferred to a new master; but, in 598, Tyre revolted against the Babylonian, and sustained a siege of thirteen years. When at length she was compelled to submit, the conqueror found no plunder to reward the extreme severity of his labors, for the inhabitants had secretly removed their treasures to an island half a mile distant, where New Tyre soon excelled the splendor of the Old.

68. Phœnicia remained subject to Babylon until that power was overcome by the new empire of Cyrus the Great. The local government was carried on by native kings or judges, who paid tribute to the Babylonian king.

69. The religion of the Phœnicians was degraded by many cruel and uncleanly rites. Their chief divinities, Baal and Astar′te, or Ashtaroth, represented the sun and moon. Baal was worshiped in groves on high places, sometimes, like the Ammonian Moloch, with burnt-offerings of human beings; always with wild, fanatical rites, his votaries crying aloud and cutting themselves with knives. Melcarth, the Tyrian Hercules, was worshiped only at Tyre and her colonies. His symbol was an ever-burning fire, and he probably shared with Baal the character of a sun-god. The marine deities were of especial importance to these commercial cities. Chief of these were Posi′don, Ne′reus, and Pontus. Of lower rank, but not less constantly remembered, were the little Cabi′ri, whose images formed the figure-heads of Phœnician ships. The seat of their worship was at Berytus.

70. The Phœnicians were less idolatrous than the Egyptians, Greeks, or Romans; for their temples contained either no visible image of their deities, or only a rude symbol like the conical stone which was held to represent Astarte.

Kings of Tyre.

First Period.

Abibaal, partly contemporary with David in Israel.		
Hiram, his son, friend of David and Solomon, .	B. C	1025–991.
Balea′zar, ...	"	991–984.
Abdastar′tus, ...	"	984–975.
One of his assassins, whose name is unknown, .	"	975–963.
Astartus, ...	"	963–951.
Aser′ymus, his brother, ...	"	951–942.
Phales, another brother, who murdered Aserymus,	"	942–941.
Ethba′al,* high priest of Astarte, ...	"	941–909.
Bade′zor, his son, ...	"	909–903.

* His daughter Jezebel became the wife of Ahab, king of Israel. His reign is marked in Phœnician annals by a drought which extended throughout Syria.

Matgen, son of Badezor and father of Dido, . . .	B. C.	903–871.
Pygmalion, brother of Dido, ...	"	871–824.

For 227 years Tyre remained tributary to the Eastern Monarchies, and we have no list of her native rulers.

Second Period.

Ethbaal II, contemporary with Nebuchadnezzar,	B. C.	597–573.
Baal, ...	"	573–563.
Ec′niba′al, judge for three months, ...	"	563.
Chel′bes, judge ten months, ...	"	563–562.
Abba′rus, judge three months, ...	"	562.
Mytgon and Gerastar′tus, judges five years, . .	"	562–557.
Bala′tor, king, ...	"	557–556.
Merbal, king, ...	"	556–552.
Hiram, king, ...	"	552–532.

SYRIA.

71. Syria Proper was divided between several states, of which the most important in ancient times was Damascus, with its territory, a fertile country between Anti-Lebanon and the Syrian Desert. Beside this were the northern Hittites, whose chief city was Carchemish; the southern Hittites, in the region of the Dead Sea; the Pate′na on the lower, and Hamath on the upper Orontes.

72. Damascus, on the Abana, is among the oldest cities in the world. It resisted the conquering arms of David and Solomon, who, with this exception, reigned over all the land between the Jordan and the Euphrates; and it continued to be a hostile and formidable neighbor to the Hebrew monarchy, until Jews, Israelites, and Syrians were all alike overwhelmed by the growth of the Assyrian Empire.

Kings of Damascus.

Hădad,	contemporary with	David,	about B. C.	1040.
Rezon,	"	Solomon,	"	1000.
Tab-rimmon,	"	Abijah,	"	960–950.
Ben-hadad I,	"	Baasha and Asa,	"	950–920.
Ben-hadad II,	"	Ahab,	"	900.
Hazael,	"	Jehu and Shalmaneser II,	"	850.
Ben-hadad III,	"	Jehoahaz,	"	840.
Unknown until Rezin,	"	Ahaz of Judah,	"	745–732.

JUDÆA.

73. The history of the Hebrew race is better known to us than that of any other people equally ancient, because it has been carefully preserved in the sacred writings. The separation of this race for its peculiar and important part in the world's history, began with the call of Abraham from his home, near the Euphrates, to the more western country on the Mediterranean, which was promised to himself and his descendants. The story of his sons and grandsons, before and during their residence in Egypt, belongs, however, to family rather than national history. Their numbers increased until they became objects of apprehension to the Egyptians, who tried to break their spirit by servitude. At length, Moses grew up under the fostering care of Pharaoh himself; and after a forty years' retirement in the deserts of Midian, adding the dignity of age and lonely meditation to the "learning of the Egyptians," he became the liberator and law-giver of his people.

74. The history of the Jewish nation begins with the night of their exodus from Egypt. The people were mustered according to their tribes, which bore the names of the twelve sons of Jacob, the grandson of Abraham. The sons of Joseph, however, received each a portion and gave their names to the two tribes of Ephraim and Manas′seh. The family of Jacob went into Egypt numbering sixty-seven persons; it went out numbering 603,550 warriors, not counting the Levites, who were exempted from military duty that they might have charge of the tabernacle and the vessels used in worship.

75. After long marches and countermarches through the Arabian desert — needful to arouse the spirit of a free people from the cowed and groveling habits of the slave, as well as to counteract the long example of idolatry by direct Divine revelation of a pure and spiritual worship — the Israelites were led into the land promised to Abraham, which lay chiefly between the Jordan and the sea. Two and a half of the twelve tribes — Reuben, Gad, and the half tribe of Manasseh — preferred the fertile pastures east of the Jordan; and on condition of aiding their brethren in the conquest of their more westerly territory, received their allotted portion there.

76. Moses, their great leader through the desert, died outside the Promised Land, and was buried in the land of Moab. His lieutenant, Joshua, conquered Palestine and divided it among the tribes. The inhabitants of Gibeon hastened to make peace with the invaders by a stratagem. Though their falsehood was soon discovered, Joshua was faithful to his oath already taken, and the Gibeonites escaped the usual fate of extermination pronounced upon the inhabitants of Canaan, by becoming servants and tributaries to the Hebrews.

77. The kings of Palestine now assembled their forces to besiege the traitor city, in revenge for its alliance with the strangers. Joshua hastened to its assistance, and in the great battle of Beth-horon defeated, routed, and destroyed the armies of the five kings. This conflict decided the possession of central and southern Palestine. Jabin, "king of Canaan," still made a stand in his fortress of Hazor, in the north. The conquered kings had probably been in some degree dependent on him as their superior, if not their sovereign. He now mustered all the tribes which had not fallen under the sword of the Israelites, and encountered Joshua at the waters of Merom. The Canaanites had horses and chariots; the Hebrews were on foot, but their victory was as complete and decisive as at Beth-horon. Hazor was taken and burnt, and its king beheaded.

78. The nomads of the forty years in the desert now became a settled, civilized, and agricultural people. Shiloh was the first permanent sanctuary; there the tabernacle constructed in the desert was set up, and became the shrine of the national worship.

79. Jewish History is properly divided into three periods:

I. From the Exodus to the establishment of the Monarchy, B. C. 1650–1095.

II. From the accession of Saul to the separation into two kingdoms, B. C. 1095–975.

III. From the separation of the kingdoms to the Captivity at Babylon, B. C. 975–586.

80. During the First Period the government of the Hebrews was a simple theocracy, direction for all important movements being received through the high priest from God himself. The rulers, from Moses down, claimed no honors of royalty, but led the nation in war and judged it in peace by general consent. They were designated to their office at once by revelation from heaven, and by some special fitness in character or person which was readily perceived. Thus the zeal and courage of Gideon, the lofty spirit of Deb′orah, the strength of Samson, rendered them most fit for command in the special emergencies at which they arose. The "Judge" usually appeared at some time of danger or calamity, when the people would gladly welcome any deliverer; and his power, once conferred, lasted during his life.

After his death a long interval usually occurred, during which "every man did that which was right in his own eyes," until a new invasion by Philis′tines, Ammonites, or Zidonians called for a new leader. The chronology of this period is very uncertain, as the sacred writers only incidentally mention the time of events, and their records are not always continuous. The system of chronology was not settled until a later period. We have given in the list the dates which seem most probable.

RULERS AND JUDGES OF ISRAEL.

Moses,	about B. C.	1650–1610.
Joshua,	"	1610–1595.
Interregnum 30 years,	"	1595–1565.
Servitude under Chushan-rishathaim,	"	1565–1557.
Othniel,	"	1557–1517.
Interregnum 5 years,	"	1517–1512.
Servitude under Eglon, king of Moab,	"	1512–1494.
Ehud, (during his and the following reign, Shamgar, the land had rest 80 years.)	"	1494–1414.
Servitude under Jabin, king of Canaan, 20 yrs.,	"	1414–1394.
Deborah. (Land had rest 40 years.)	"	1394–1354.
Servitude under Midian 7 years,	"	1354–1347.
Gideon,	"	1347–1307.
Abimelech, king,	"	1307–1304.
Interregnum 5 years,	"	1304–1299.
Tola,	"	1299–1276.
Jair,	"	1276–1254.
Interregnum about 5 years,	"	1254–1249.
Servitude under Ammon 18 years,	"	1249–1231.
Jephthah,	"	1231–1225.
Ibzan,	"	1225–1218.
Elon,	"	1218–1208.
Abdon,	"	1208–1200.
Interregnum about 5 years,	"	1200–1195.
Servitude under the Philistines 40 years,	"	1195–1155.
Samson, in south-western Palestine, during the last 20 years of the above,	"	1175–1155.
Eli, high priest and judge,	"	1155–1115.
Samuel, last of the judges,	"	1115–1095.

81. SECOND PERIOD. The Israelites at length became dissatisfied with the irregular nature of their government, and demanded a king. In compliance with their wishes, Saul, the son of Kish, a young Benjamite distinguished by beauty and loftiness of stature, was chosen by Divine command, and anointed by Samuel, their aged prophet and judge.

82. He found the country in nearly the same condition in which Joshua had left it. The people were farmers and shepherds; none were wealthy; even the king had "no court, no palace, no extraordinary retinue; he was still little more than leader in war and judge in peace." The country was still ravaged by Ammonites on one side, and Philistines on the other; and under the recent incursions of the latter, the Israelites had become so weak that they had no weapons nor armor, nor even any workers in iron. (1 Samuel xiii: 19, 20.)

83. Saul first defeated the Ammonites, who had overrun Gilead from the east; then turned upon the Philistines, and humbled them in the battle of Michmash, so that they were driven to defend themselves at home, instead of invading Israel, until near the close of his reign. He waged war also against the Am′alekites, Mo′abites, E′domites, and the Syrians of Zobah, and "delivered Israel out of the hand of them that spoiled them."

84. He forfeited the favor of God by disobedience, and David, his future son-in-law, was anointed king. Jonathan, the son of Saul, was a firm friend and protector of David against the jealous rage of his father. Even the king himself, in his better moods, was moved to admiration and affection by the heroic character of David.

85. In Saul's declining years, the Philistines, under A′chish, king of Gath, again invaded the country, and defeated the Israelites at Mount Gilboa. Saul and all but one of his sons fell in the battle. Ishbo′sheth, the surviving son, was acknowledged king in Gilead, and ruled all the tribes except Judah for seven years. But David was crowned in Hebron, and reigned over his own tribe until the death of Ishbosheth, when he became ruler of the whole nation.

86. He conquered Jerusalem from the Jeb′usites, made it his capital, and established a kingly court such as Israel had never known. The ark of the covenant was removed from its temporary abode at Kirjathje′arim, and Jerusalem became henceforth the Holy City, the seat of the national religion as well as of the government.

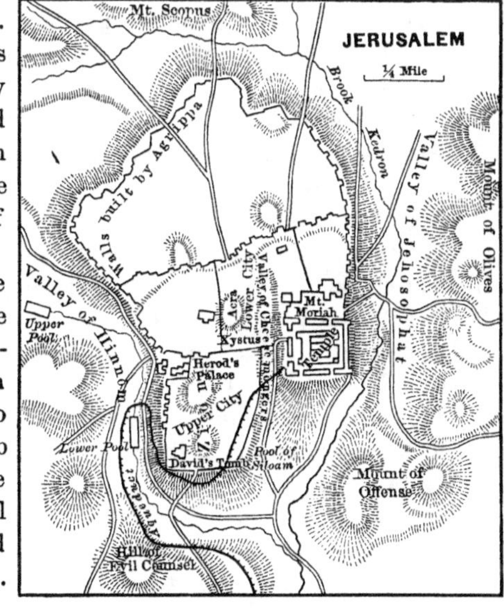

87. The wars of David were still more victorious than those of Saul, and the empire of Israel was now extended from the borders of the Red Sea to those of the Euphrates. Moab was rendered tributary, the Philistines punished, and all the Syrian tribes east and north of Palestine subdued. (2 Samuel viii.)

88. Great as was the military glory of David, his fame with later times is derived from his psalms and songs. He was the first great poet of Israel, and perhaps the earliest in the world. The freshness of the pastures and mountain-sides among which his youth was passed, the assurance of Divine protection amid the singular and romantic incidents of his varied career, the enlargement of his horizon of thought with the magnificent dominion which was added to him in later life, all gave a richness and depth to his experience, which were reproduced in sacred melody, and found their fitting place in the temple service; and every form of Jewish and Christian worship since his time has been enriched by the poetry of David.

89. This great hero and poet was not exempt from common human sins and follies, and the only disasters of his reign sprang directly from his errors. The consequences of his plurality of wives, in the jealousies which arose between the different families of princes, distracted his old age with a succession of crimes and sorrows. His sons Ab′salom and Adoni′jah at different times plotted against him and assumed the crown. Both were punished for their treason, the one by death in battle, the other by the sentence of Solomon after his father's death.

90. Solomon, the favorite son of David, succeeded to a peaceful kingdom. All the neighboring nations acknowledged his dignity, and the king of Egypt gave him his daughter in marriage. The Israelites were now the dominant race in Syria. Many monarchs were tributary to the great king, and the court of Jerusalem rivaled in its splendors those of Nineveh and Memphis.

B. C. 1015.

91. Commerce received a great impulse both from the enterprise and the luxury of the king. Hiram, king of Tyre, was a firm friend of Solomon, as he had been of David his father. Cedars were brought from the forests of Lebanon for the construction of a palace and temple. Through his alliance with Hiram, Solomon was admitted to a share in Tyrian trade; and by the influence of Pharaoh, his father-in-law, he gained from the Edomites the port of Ezion-ge′ber, on the Red Sea, where he caused a great fleet of merchant vessels to be constructed. Through these different channels of commerce, the rarest products of Europe, Asia, and Africa were poured into Jerusalem. Gold and precious stones, sandal-wood and spices from India, silver from Spain, ivory from Africa, added to the luxury of the court. Horses from Egypt, now first introduced into Palestine, filled the royal stables. By tribute as well as trade, a constant stream of gold and silver flowed into Palestine.

92. The greatest work of Solomon was the Temple on Mount Moriah, which became the permanent abode of the ark of the covenant, and the holy place toward which the prayers of Israelites, though scattered throughout the world, have ever turned. The temple precincts included apartments for the priests, and towers for defense, so that it has been said that the various purposes of forum, fortress, university, and sanctuary were here combined in one great national building. The superior skill of the

Phœnicians in working in wood and metal, was enlisted by Solomon in the service of the temple. Hiram, the chief architect and sculptor, was half Tyrian, half Israelite, and his genius was held in equal reverence by the two kings who claimed his allegiance. More than seven years were occupied in the building of the temple. The Feast of the Dedication drew together a vast concourse of people from both extremities of the land — "from Hamath to the River of Egypt." And so important is this event as a turning point in the history of the Jews, that it constitutes the beginning of their connected record of months and years.

93. The early days of Solomon were distinguished by all the virtues which could adorn a prince. In humble consciousness of the greatness of the duties assigned him, and the insufficiency of his powers, he chose wisdom rather than long life or riches or great dominion, and he was rewarded by the possession of even that which he had not asked. His wisdom became greater than that of all the philosophers of the East; his knowledge of natural history, improved by the collections of rare plants and curious animals which he gathered from all parts of the world, was considered miraculous. (1 Kings iii : 5–15; iv : 29–34.)

94. But prosperity corrupted his character. He introduced the licentious luxury of an Oriental court into the Holy City of David, and even encouraged the degrading rites of heathen worship. His commerce enriched himself, not his people. His enormous and expensive court was sustained by the most exhausting taxes. The great public works which he carried on withdrew vast numbers of men from the tillage of the soil, and thus lessened the national resources.

95. The glory of Solomon dazzled the people and silenced their complaints, but on the accession of his son the smothered discontent broke forth. Rehobo′am, instead of soothing his subjects by needed reforms, incensed them by his haughty refusal to lighten their burdens. (1 Kings xii : 13, 14.) The greater number of the people immediately revolted, under the lead of Jerobo′am, who established a rival sovereignty over the Ten Tribes, henceforth to be known as the Kingdom of Israel. The two tribes of Judah and Benjamin remained loyal to the house of David.

B. C. 975.

KINGS OF THE UNITED MONARCHY.

Saul, ...	B. C.	1095–1055.
David at Hebron, and Ishbosheth at Mahanaim,	"	1055–1048.
David, over all Israel, ...	"	1048–1015.
Solomon, ...	"	1015–975.

96. THIRD PERIOD. The Kingdom of Israel had the more extensive and fertile territory, and its population was double that of Judah. It extended from the borders of Damascus to within ten miles of Jerusalem; included the whole territory east of the Jordan, and held Moab as a tributary. But it had no capital equal in strength, beauty, or sacred associations to Jerusalem. The government was fixed first at She′chem, then at Tir′zah, then at Sama′ria.

97. Its first king, Jeroboam, in order to break the strongest tie which bound the people to the house of David, made golden calves for idols, and set up sanctuaries in Bethel and Dan, saying, "It is too much for you to go up to Jerusalem; behold thy gods, O Israel, which brought thee up out of the land of Egypt!" A new priesthood was appointed in opposition to that of Aaron, and many Levites and other faithful adherents of the old religion emigrated into the kingdom of Judah.

98. The people too readily fell into the snare. A succession of prophets, gifted with wonderful powers, strove to keep alive the true worship; but the poison of idolatry had entered so deeply into the national life, that it was ready to fall upon the first assault from without. In the time of Elijah, only seven thousand were left who had not "bowed the knee unto Baal;" and even these were unknown to the prophet, being compelled by persecution to conceal their religion.

99. The kings of Israel belonged to nine different families, of which only two, those of Omri and Jehu, held the throne any considerable time. Almost all the nineteen kings had short reigns, and eight died by violence. The kingdom was frequently distracted by wars with Judah, Damascus, and Assyria. Jeroboam was aided in his war with Judah by his friend and patron in days of exile, Shishak, king of Egypt. Nadab, son of Jeroboam, was murdered by Baasha, who made himself king. This monarch began to build the fortress of Ramah, by which he intended to hold the Jewish frontier, but was compelled to desist by Ben-hadad, of Syria, who thus testified his friendship for Asa, king of Judah.

100. Ahab, of the house of Omri, allied himself with Ethbaal, king of Tyre, by marrying his daughter Jez′ebel; and the arts of this wicked and idolatrous princess brought the kingdom to its lowest pitch of corruption. Her schemes were resisted by Elijah the Tishbite, one of the greatest of the prophets, who, in a memorable encounter on Mount Carmel, led the people to reäffirm their faith in Jehovah and exterminate the priests of Baal. (1 Kings xviii: 17–40.) The evil influence of Jezebel and the Tyrian idolatry were not removed from Israel until she herself and her son Jehoram had been murdered by order of Jehu, a captain of the guard, who became first of a new dynasty of kings. Jehu lost all his territories east of the Jordan in war with Hazael, of Damascus, and paid tribute, at least on one occasion, to Asshur-nazir-pal, of Assyria.* His son Jehoahaz also lost cities to the Syrian king; but Joash, the grandson of Jehu, revived the

* See p. 19.

Israelite conquests. He defeated Ben-hadad, son of Hazael, and won back part of the conquered territory. His son, Jeroboam II, had the longest and most prosperous reign in the annals of the Ten Tribes. He not only regained all the former possessions of Israel, but captured Hamath and Damascus. But this was the end of Israelite prosperity. Two short reigns followed, each ended by an assassination, and then Men′ahem of Tirzah made a vain attempt to renew the glories of Jeroboam II by an expedition to the Euphrates. He captured Thapsacus, but drew upon himself the vengeance of Pul, king of Chaldæa, who invaded his dominions and made Menahem his vassal.

101. In the later years of Israelite history, Tiglath-pileser, king of Assyria, desolated the country east of the Jordan, and threatened the extinction of the kingdom. Hosh′ea, the last king, acknowledged his dependence upon the Assyrian Empire, and agreed to pay tribute; but he afterward strengthened himself by an alliance with Egypt, and revolted against his master. Shalmaneser came to chastise this defection, and besieged Samaria two years. At length it fell, and the disgraceful annals of the Israelite kingdom came to an end.

102. According to the despotic custom of Eastern monarchs, the people were transported to Media and the provinces of Assyria; and for a time the country was so desolate that wild beasts multiplied in the cities. People were afterward brought from Babylon and the surrounding country to take the places of the former inhabitants.

KINGS OF ISRAEL.

Jeroboam,	B. C.	975–954.
Nadab,	"	954–953.
Baasha,	"	953–930.
Elah,	"	930–929.
Zimri, slew Elah and reigned 7 days,	"	929.
Omri, captain of the host under Elah,	"	929–918.
Ahab,	"	918–897.
Ahaziah,	"	897–896.
Jehoram,	"	896–884.
Jehu,	"	884–856.
Jehoahaz,	"	856–839.
Joash,	"	839–823.
Jeroboam II,	"	823–772.
Zechariah, reigned 6 months,	"	772.
Shallum, murdered Zechariah and was himself murdered,	"	772.
Menahem,	"	772–762.
Pekahiah,	"	762–760.
Pekah,	"	760–730.
Hoshea,	"	730–721.

103. The Kingdom of Judah began its separate existence at the same time with that of revolted Israel, but survived it 135 years. It consisted of the two entire tribes of Judah and Benjamin, with numerous refugees from the other ten, who were willing to sacrifice home and landed possessions for their faith. The people were thus closely bound together by their common interest in the marvelous traditions of the past and hopes for the future.

104. Notwithstanding danger from numerous enemies, situated as it was on the direct road between the two great rival empires of Egypt and Assyria, this little kingdom maintained its existence during nearly four centuries; and, unlike Israel, was governed during all that time by kings of one family, the house of David.

The first king, Rehoboam, saw his capital seized and plundered by Shi′shak, king of Egypt, and had to maintain a constant warfare with the revolted tribes. Abijam, his son, gained a great victory over Jeroboam, by which he recovered the ancient sanctuary of Bethel and many other towns. Asa was attacked both by the Israelites on the north and the Egyptians on the south, but defended himself victoriously from both. With all the remaining treasures of the temple and palace, he secured the alliance of Ben-hadad, king of Damascus, who, by attacking the northern cities of Israel, drew Baasha away from building the fortress of Ramah. The stones and timbers which Baasha had collected were carried away, by order of Asa, to his own cities of Geba in Benjamin, and Mizpeh in Judah.

105. Jehosh′aphat, son of Asa, allied himself with Ahab, king of Israel, whom he assisted in his Syrian wars. This ill-fated alliance brought the poison of Tyrian idolatry into the kingdom of Judah. In the reign of Jehoram, who married the daughter of Ahab, Jerusalem was captured by Philistines and Arabs. His son, Ahaziah, while visiting his Israelitish kindred, was involved in the destruction of the house of Ahab; and after his death his mother, Athali′ah, a true daughter of Jezebel, murdered all her grandchildren but one, usurped the throne for six years, and replaced the worship of Jehovah with that of Baal. But Jehoi′ada, the high priest, revolted against her, placed her grandson, Joash, on the throne, and kept the kingdom clear, so long as he lived, from the taint of idolatry.

106. Amaziah, the son of Joash, captured Pe′tra from the Edomites, but lost his own capital to the king of Israel, who carried away all its treasures. Azariah, his son, conquered the Philistines and the Arabs, and reëstablished on the Red Sea the port of Elath, which had fallen into decay since the days of Solomon. During a long and prosperous reign he strengthened the defenses of Jerusalem, reorganized his army, and improved the tillage of the country. But he presumed upon his dignity and the excellence of his former conduct to encroach upon the office of the priests, and was punished by a sudden leprosy, which separated him from human society the rest of his days. In the reign of Ahaz, his grandson, Jerusalem was besieged by the kings of Israel and Syria, who carried away from Judah two hundred thousand captives. Ahaz invoked the aid of Tiglath-pileser, king of Assyria, and became his tributary. The Assyrian conquered Damascus, and thus relieved Jerusalem. Ahaz filled the cities of Judah with altars of false gods, and left his kingdom more deeply stained than ever with idolatry.

107. Hezekiah, his son, delivered the land from foreign dominion and from heathen superstitions. He became for a time tributary to Sennacherib, but afterward revolted and made an alliance with Egypt. During a second invasion, the army of Sennacherib was destroyed and his designs abandoned; but the kingdom of Judah continued to be dependent upon the empire.

108. Manasseh, the son of Hezekiah, brought back all the evil which his father had expelled. Even the temple at Jerusalem was profaned by idols and their altars, and the Law disappeared from the sight and memory of the people, while those who tried to remain faithful to the God of their fathers were violently persecuted. In the midst of this impiety, Manasseh fell into disgrace with the Assyrian king, who suspected him of an intention to revolt. He was carried captive to Babylon, where he had leisure to reflect upon his sins and their punishment. On his return to Jerusalem, he confessed and forsook his errors, and wrought a religious reformation in his kingdom.

109. His son Amon restored idolatry; but his life and reign were speedily ended by a conspiracy of his servants, who slew him in his own house.

The assassins were punished with death, and Josiah, the rightful heir, ascended the throne at the age of eight years. He devoted himself with pious zeal and energy to the cleansing of his kingdom from the traces of heathen worship; carved and molten images and altars were ground to powder and strewn over the graves of those who had officiated in the sacrilegious rites. The king journeyed in person not only through the cities of Judah, but through the whole desolate land of Israel, as far as the borders of Naphtali and the upper waters of the Jordan, that he might witness the extermination of idolatry. This part of his work being completed, he returned to Jerusalem to repair the Temple of Solomon, which had fallen into ruins, and restore, in all its original solemnity, the worship of Jehovah.

110. In the progress of repairs an inestimable manuscript was found, being no less than the "Book of the Law of the Lord, given by the hand of Moses." These sacred writings had been so long lost, that even the king and the priests were ignorant of the curses that had been pronounced upon idolatry. The tender conscience of the king was overwhelmed with distress as he read the pure and perfect Law, which presented so stern a contrast with the morals of the people; but he was comforted with the promise that he should be gathered to his grave in peace before the calamities which the Law foretold, and the sins of Judah had deserved, should come upon the kingdom. In the eighteenth year of Josiah's reign a grand passover was held, to which all the inhabitants of the northern kingdom who remained from the captivity were invited. This great religious festival, which signalized the birth of the nation and its first deliverance, had not been kept with equal solemnity since the days of Samuel the prophet. The entire manuscript lately discovered was read aloud by the king himself in the hearing of all the people, and the whole assembly swore to renew and maintain the covenant made of old with their fathers.

111. The end of Josiah's reign was marked by two great calamities. A

B. C. 634-632. wild horde of Scythians,* from the northern steppes, swept over the land, carrying off flocks and herds. They advanced as far as As′calon, on the south-western coast, where they plundered the temple of Astarte, and were then induced to retire by the bribes of the king of Egypt. One trace of their incursion remained a thousand years, in the new name of the old city Bethshan, on the plain of Esdrae′lon. It was named by the Greeks Scythopolis, or the city of the Scythians. This was the first eruption of northern barbarians upon the old and civilized nations of southern Asia and Europe. Later events in the same series will occupy a large portion of our history.

112. The other and greater calamity of Josiah's reign arose from a different quarter. Necho, king of Egypt, had become alarmed by the growth of Babylonian power, and was marching northward with a great army. Though in no way the object of his hostility, Josiah imprudently went forth to meet him, hoping to arrest his progress in the plain of Esdraelon.

B. C. 609. The battle of Megid′do followed, and Josiah was slain. Never had so great a sorrow befallen the Jewish people. The prophet Jeremiah, a friend and companion of Josiah from his youth, bewailed the nation's loss in his most bitter "Lamentation": "The breath of our nostrils, the anointed of the Lord, was taken in their pits, of whom we said, Under his shadow we shall live among the heathen." For more than a hundred years the anniversary of the fatal day was observed as a time of mourning in every family.

113. In the reign of Jehoiakim, son of Josiah, Nebuchadnezzar, prince of Babylon, gained a great victory † over Necho, and extended his father's kingdom to the frontier of Egypt. Jehoiakim submitted to be absorbed into the empire, but afterward revolted and was put to death.

Jehoiachin, his son, was made king; but, three months after his accession, was carried captive to Babylon. Zedeki′ah, reigning at Jerusalem,

---

* See § 40, p. 23.

† The battle of Carchemish. See p. 25.

rebelled and allied himself with Apries, king of Egypt. Upon this, the ever active Nebuchadnezzar laid siege to the revolted city. In the second year it was taken and destroyed; the king and the whole nation, with the treasures of the temple and palace, were conveyed to Babylon, and the history of the Jews ceased for seventy years.

Kings of Judah.

Rehoboam, ...	B. C. 975–958.
Abijam, ...	" 958–956.
Asa, ...	" 956–916.
Jehoshaphat, ...	" 916–892.
Jehoram, ...	" 892–885.
Ahaziah, slain by Jehu after 1 year, ...	" 885–884.
Athaliah, murders her grandchildren and reigns,	" 884–878.
Joash, son of Ahaziah, ...	" 878–838.
Amaziah, ...	" 838–809.
Azariah, or Uzziah, ...	" 809–757.
Jotham, ...	" 757–742.
Ahaz, ...	" 742–726.
Hezekiah, ...	" 726–697.
Manasseh, ...	" 697–642.
Amon, ...	" 642–640.
Josiah, ...	" 640–609.
Jehoahaz, dethroned by Necho after 3 months, .	" 609.
Jehoiakim, tributary to Necho 4 years, ...	" 609–598.
Jehoiachin, ...	" 598–597.
Zedekiah, ...	" 597–586.

RECAPITULATION.

The Phrygians, earliest settlers of Asia Minor, were active in tillage and trade, and zealous in their peculiar religion. Lydia afterward became the chief power in the peninsula. At the end of three dynasties, it had reached its greatest glory under Crœsus, when it was conquered by Cyrus, and became a province of Persia, B. C. 546.

The first great commercial communities in the world were the Phœnician cities, of which Sidon and Tyre were the chief; their trade extending by sea from Britain to Ceylon, and by land to the interior of three continents. Tyrian dyes, and vessels of gold, silver, bronze, and glass were celebrated. Phœnicia was subject four hundred years to the Assyrian Empire, and became independent at its fall, only to pass under the power of Necho of Egypt, and, in turn, to be subdued by Nebuchadnezzar of Babylon. Baal, Astarte, Melcarth, and the marine deities were objects of Phœnician worship.

Syria Proper was divided into five states, of which Damascus was the oldest and most important.

The Hebrew nation began its existence under the rule of Moses, who led his people forth from Egypt, and through the Arabian Desert, in a journey of forty years. Joshua conquered Palestine by the two decisive battles of Beth-horon and the waters of Merom, and divided the land among the twelve tribes. Judges ruled Israel nearly six hundred years.

Saul, being anointed as king, subdued the enemies of the Jews; but, becoming disobedient, he was slain in battle, and David became king, first of Judah, and afterward of all Israel. He made Jerusalem his capital, and extended his dominion over Syria and Moab, and eastward to the Euphrates. His sacred songs are the source of his enduring fame. Solomon inherited the kingdom, which he enriched by commerce and adorned with magnificent public works, both for sacred and secular uses. The Dedication of the Temple is the great era in Hebrew chronology. The wisdom of Solomon was widely famed, but the luxury of his court exhausted his kingdom, and on the accession of Rehoboam ten tribes revolted, only Judah and Benjamin remaining to the house of David.

Jeroboam fixed his capital at Shechem, and the shrines of his false gods at Bethel and Dan. In spite of the faithful warnings of the prophets, the kingdom of Israel became idolatrous. The nineteen kings who ruled B. C. 975–721 belonged to nine different families. Ahab and Jezebel persecuted true believers and established Tyrian idolatry; but their race was exterminated and Jehu became king. The Ten Tribes reached their greatest power and wealth under Jeroboam II. In the reign of Menahem they became subject to Pul, of Chaldæa. A revolt of Hoshea against Assyria led to the capture of Samaria, and the captivity of both king and people.

The kingdom of Judah, with a smaller territory, had a people more united in faith and loyalty, and was ruled four hundred years by descendants of David. Jehoshaphat made a close alliance with Ahab, which brought many calamities upon Judah. In the reign of Jehoram, Jerusalem was taken by Arabs and Philistines; and after the death of Ahaziah, Athaliah, daughter of Jezebel, usurped the throne. Joash, her grandson, was protected and crowned by Jehoiada, the high priest. The prosperity of Judah was restored by the conquests and efficient policy of Azariah. Ahaz became tributary to Tiglath-pileser, of Assyria, and degraded his kingdom with idolatry. Hezekiah resisted both the religion and the supremacy of the heathen. Manasseh was carried captive to Babylon, and on his return reformed his administration. Josiah cleansed the land from marks of idolatry, rebuilt the Temple, discovered the Book of the Law, and renewed the celebration of the Passover. The Scythians invaded Palestine. Josiah was slain in the battle of Megiddo, and his sons became vassals of Egypt. Nebuchadnezzar subdued both Egypt and Palestine, captured Jerusalem, and transported two successive kings and the mass of the people to Babylon.

QUESTIONS FOR REVIEW.

BOOK I.—PART I.

1. What are the sources of historical information? . . . . §§ 1–4.
2. Describe the character and movements of the three families of the sons of Noah. . . . . 5, 6.
3. Into what periods may history be divided? . . . . 7, 8.
4. Name six primeval monarchies in Western Asia. . . . . . .
5. What were the distinguishing features of the Chaldæan Monarchy? . 26.
6. Name the principal Assyrian kings of the Second Period. . . . 29–31.
7. Who was Semiramis? . . . . 30.
8. Describe the founder of the Lower Assyrian Empire. . . . . . 32.
9. What memorials exist of Sargon? . . . . 32.
10. Describe the career of Sennacherib. . . . . 33.

11. What was the condition of Assyria under Asshur-bani-pal? . . . § 34.
12. What under his son? . . . . 35.
13. What was the early history of Media? . . . . 37, 38.
14. What of Phraortes? . . . . 39.
15. Describe the reign of Cyaxares. . . . . 40, 41.
16. The character of the Babylonians. . . . . 43, 44.
17. The career of Merodach-baladan. . . . . 45.
18. The empire of Nabopolassar. . . . . 46.
19. The conquests and reverses of the greatest Babylonian monarch. . . . . 47–52.
20. The decline and fall of Babylon. . . . . 53, 54.
21. Relate the whole history of Lydia. . . . . 58, 59.
22. Describe the Phœnician cities and their commerce. . . . . . . 61–64.
23. To what four kingdoms were they successively subject? . . . . . 66–68.
24. Describe the religion of the Phœnicians. . . . . 69, 70.
25. What were the divisions of Syria Proper? . . . . 71, 72.
26. Describe the rise of the Jewish nation. . . . . 73, 74.
27. Their conquest of Palestine. . . . . 76, 77.
28. Their government during the First Period. . . . . 80.
29. The reign of Saul. . . . . 81–83.
30. The conquests and character of David. . . . . 84–89.
31. The acts and wisdom of Solomon. . . . . 90–94.
32. What changes occurred at his death? . . . . 95.
33. Compare the two kingdoms. . . . . 96–100, 105, 106.
34. What was the policy of Jeroboam? . . . . 97, 98.
35. Describe the reign of Ahab. . . . . 101.
36. What kings of Israel had dealing with Assyria? . . . . . . 100, 101.
37. Mention three kings of Judah who had wars with Israel. . . . 104.
38. Three in alliance with Israel. . . . . 105.
39. Describe the reign of Azariah; of Ahaz, Hezekiah, Manasseh. . . . 106–108.
40. The events of Josiah's reign. . . . . 109–112.
41. The relations of three kings with Babylon, ... 113.

PART II. AFRICAN NATIONS.

GEOGRAPHICAL OUTLINE OF AFRICA.

114. The continent of Africa differs in many important respects from that of Asia. The latter, extending into three zones, has its greatest extent in the most favored of all, the North Temperate. Africa is almost wholly within the tropics, only a small portion of its northern and southern extremities entering the two temperate zones, where their climate is most nearly torrid. Asia has the loftiest mountains on the globe, from which flow great rivers spreading fertility and affording every means of navigation. Africa has but two great rivers, the Nile and the Niger, and but few mountains of remarkable elevation.

115. Africa is thus the hottest, driest, and least accessible of the continents. One-fifth of its surface is covered by the great sea of sand which stretches from the Atlantic nearly to the Red Sea. Much of the interior consists of marshes and impenetrable forests, haunted only by wild beasts and unfit for human habitation. With the exception of a very few favored portions, Africa is therefore unsuited to the growth of great states; and it is only through two of these, Egypt and Carthage, that it claims an important part in ancient history.

116. Northern Africa alone was known to the ancients, and its features were well marked and peculiar. Close along the Mediterranean lay a narrow strip of fertile land, watered by short streams which descended from the Atlas range. These mountains formed a rocky and scantily inhabited region to the southward, though producing in certain portions abundance of dates. Next came the Great Desert, varied only by a few small and scattered oases, where springs of water nourished a rich vegetation. South of the Sahara was a fertile inland country, near whose large rivers and lakes were cities and a numerous population; but these central African states were only visited by an occasional caravan which crossed the desert from the north, and had no political connection with the rest of the world.

117. In the western portion of Northern Africa, the mountains rise more gradually by a series of natural terraces from the sea, and the fertile country here attains a width of two hundred miles. This well watered, fruitful, and comparatively healthful region, is one of the most favored on the globe. In ancient times it was one vast corn-field from the Atlas to the Mediterranean. Here the native kingdom of Maurita′nia flourished;

and after it was subdued by the Romans, the same fertile fields afforded bread to the rest of the civilized world.

118. Eastward from Mauritania the plain becomes narrower, the rivers fewer, and the soil less fertile, so that no great state, even if it had originated there, could have long maintained itself. The north-eastern corner of the continent, however, is the richest and most valuable of all the lands it contains. This is owing to the great river which, rising in the highlands of Abyssin′ia, and fed by the perpetual rains of Equatorial Africa, rolls its vast body of waters from south to north, through a valley three thousand miles in length. Every year in June it begins to rise; from August to December it overflows the country, and deposits a soil so rich that the farmer has only to cast his grain upon the retiring waters, and abundant harvests spring up without further tillage.

119. The soil of Egypt was called by its inhabitants the "Gift of the Nile." In a climate almost without rain, this country without its river would, indeed, have been only a ravine in the rocky and sandy desert; as barren as Sahara itself. The prosperity of the year was, from the earliest times, accurately measured by the Nilometers at Mem′phis and Elephan′-tine. If the water rose less than eighteen feet, famine ensued; a rise of from eighteen to twenty-four feet betokened moderate harvests; twenty-seven feet were considered "a good Nile;" a flood of thirty feet was ruinous, for, in such a case, houses were undermined, cattle swept away, the land rendered too spongy for the following seed-time, the labor of the farmer was delayed, and often fevers were bred by the stagnant and lingering waters. Usually, however, the Nile was the great benefactor of the Egyptians, and was considered a fit emblem of the creating and preserving Osi′ris. Its waters were carefully distributed by canals and regulated by dykes. During the inundation, the country appeared like a great inland lake girdled by mountains. Lower Egypt, or the Delta, was compared by Herodotus to the Grecian Archipelago, dotted with villages which appeared like white islands above the expanse of waters.

120. Lower Egypt is a vast plain; Upper Egypt a narrowing valley. The fertile portion of the latter occupies only a part of the space between the Lib′yan Desert and the sea. In its widest part it is less than eleven, in its narrowest only five miles in width; and in some places the granite or limestone cliff springs directly from the river. Being so well fitted to support a numerous people, the whole valley of the Nile, through Nubia and Abyssinia as well as Egypt, was very early colonized from the opposite shores of Asia. The hair, features, and form of the skull represented in the human figures on the monuments, prove the dominant race in these countries to have been of the same great family with the people on the neighboring peninsula of Arabia.

121. Before the conquests of the Persians, Northern Africa was divided between five nations: the Egyptians, Ethiopians, Phœnicians, Libyans, and Greeks.

122. The ETHIOPIANS occupied the Nile Valley above Egypt, including what is now known as Abyssinia. The great plateau between the head-waters of the Nile and the Red Sea is rendered fertile by frequent and abundant rains; and the many streams which descend from it to the Nile cause in part the yearly overflow which fertilizes Egypt. Mer′oë was the chief city of the Ethiopians. Some learned men have supposed its monuments of architecture and sculpture to be even older than those of Egypt.

123. Arabian traditions say that the inhabitants of the northern coasts of Africa were descendants of the Canaanites whom the Children of Israel drove out of Palestine. As late as the fourth century after Christ, two pillars of white marble near Tangier still bore the inscription in Phœnician characters: "We are they that fled from before the face of the robber Joshua, the son of Nun." Whether or not this legend expressed a historical fact, it expressed the wide-spread belief of the people; and it is well known by other evidence that the African coasts of the Mediterranean were very early dotted with PHŒNICIAN settlements, such as the two Hip′pos, U′tica, Tu′nes, Hadrume′tum, Lep′tis, and greatest of all, though among the latest, Carthage.

124. The LIBYANS occupied a greater portion of Northern Africa than any other nation, extending from the borders of Egypt to the Atlantic Ocean, and from the Great Desert, with the exception of the foreign settlements on the coast, to the Mediterranean Sea. They had, however, comparatively little power, consisting chiefly as they did of wandering tribes, destitute of settled government or fixed habitations. In the western and more fertile portion, certain tribes of Libyans cultivated the soil and became more nearly civilized; but these were soon subjected to the growing power of the Phœnician colonies.

125. The GREEKS possessed a colony on that point of Northern Africa which approached most nearly to their own peninsula. They founded Cyre′ne about B. C. 630, and Barca about seventy years later. They had also a colony at Naucra′tis in Egypt, and probably upon the greater oasis. The history of these Grecian settlements will be found in Book III.

HISTORY OF EGYPT.

PERIODS.

I.	The Old Empire, from earliest times to	B. C. 1900.
II.	Middle Empire, or that of the Shepherd Kings,	" 1900–1525.
III.	The New Empire,	" 1525–525.

126. From the island of Elephantine to the sea, a distance of 526 miles, the Nile Valley was occupied by EGYPT, a monarchy the most ancient, with a history among the most wonderful in the world. While other nations may be watched in their progress from ignorance and rudeness to whatever art they have possessed, Egypt appears in the earliest morning light of history "already skillful, erudite, and strong." Some of her buildings are older than the Migration of Abraham, but the oldest of them show a skill in the quarrying, transporting, carving, and joining of stone which modern architects admire but can not surpass.

127. FIRST PERIOD. The early Egyptians believed that there had been a time when their ancestors were savages and cannibals, dwelling in caves in those ridges of sandstone which border the Nile Valley on the east; and that their greatest benefactors were Osiris and Isis, who elevated them into a devout and civilized nation, eating bread, drinking wine and beer, and planting the olive. The worship of Osiris and Isis, therefore, became prevalent throughout Egypt, while the several cities and provinces had each its own local divinities. According to Manetho, a native historian of later times,* gods, spirits, demigods, and *manes*, or the souls of men, were the first rulers of Egypt. This is merely an ancient way of saying that the earliest history of Egypt, as of most other countries, is shrouded in ignorance and fabulous conjecture.

128. Instead of commencing its existence as a united kingdom, Egypt consisted at first of a number of scattered *nomes*, or petty states, each having for its nucleus a temple and a numerous establishment of priests. Fifty-three of these nomes are mentioned by one historian, thirty-six by another. As one became more powerful, it sometimes swallowed up its neighbors, and grew into a kingdom which embraced a large portion or even the whole of the country.

129. The first mortal king of Mis′raim, the "double land," was Menes, of This. His inheritance was in Upper Egypt, but by his talents and exploits he made himself master of the Lower, and selected there a site for his new capital. For this purpose he drained a marshy tract which at certain seasons had been overflowed by the Nile, made a dyke to confine the river within its regular channel, and on the reclaimed ground built the city of Memphis. Menes may therefore be considered as the founder of the empire.

130. Athothes (Thoth), his son and successor, was skilled in medicine and wrote works on anatomy. Of the six following kings in regular descent who form this dynasty little is known, and it is even possible that they belong rather to tradition than to ascertained history. After the two Thoths came Mnevis, or Uenephes, who bore the name of the Sacred Calf of Heliopolis. He is said, nevertheless, to have been a high-minded, in-

* He lived in the reign of Ptolemy I, B. C. 323–283.

telligent man, and the most affable prince on record. He built the pyramid of Koko'me, whose site can not now be identified. During his reign there was famine in Egypt.

131. The Third Dynasty reigned at Memphis; its founder was Sesorcheres the Giant. The third king, Sesonchosis, was a wise and peaceful monarch, who advanced the three arts of writing, medicine, and architecture, and was celebrated by a grateful people in hymns and ballads as among their greatest benefactors. He introduced the fashion of building with hewn stones, previous structures having been made either of rough, irregular stones or of brick. He was known to the Greeks as the "peaceful Sesostris," while the two later monarchs who bore this name were great warriors and conquerors.

132. His son, Sasychis (Mares-sesorcheres), was a celebrated law-giver. He is said to have organized the worship of the gods, and to have invented geometry and astronomy. He also made that singular law by which a debtor might give his father's mummy as security for a debt. If the money was not paid, neither the debtor nor his father could ever rest in the family sepulcher, and this was considered the greatest possible disgrace.

133. The monumental and more certain history begins with the Second, Fourth, and Fifth Dynasties of Manetho, which reigned simultaneously in Lower, Middle, and Upper Egypt. Of these the Fourth Dynasty, reigning at Memphis, was most powerful, the others being in some degree dependent. Proofs of its greatness are found in the vast structures of stone which overspread Middle Egypt between the Libyan Mountains and the Nile; for the Fourth Dynasty may be remembered as that of the pyramid-builders.

B. C. 2440.

134. The name of Soris, the first of the family, has been found upon the northern pyramid of Abousîr. Suphis I, or Shufu, was the Cheops of Herodotus, and is regarded as the builder of the Great Pyramid. His brother, Suphis II, or Nou-shufu, had part in this work. He reigned jointly with Suphis I, and alone, after his death, for three years. These two kings were oppressors of the people and despisers of the gods. They crushed the former by the severe toils involved in their public works, and ordered the temples of the latter to be closed and their worship to cease.

135. Mencheres the Holy, son of Suphis I, had, like his father, a reign of sixty-three years, but differed from him in being a good and humane sovereign. He re-opened the temples which his father had closed, restored religious ceremonies of sacrifice and praise, and put an end to the oppressive labors. He was therefore much venerated by the people, and was the subject of many ballads and hymns. The four remaining kings of the Fourth Dynasty are known to us only by names and dates. The family included eight kings in all, and the probable aggregate of their reigns is 220 years.

136. The kings of the Second Dynasty ruling Middle Egypt from This or Abydus, and those of the Fifth ruling Upper Egypt from the Isle of Elephantine, were probably related by blood to the powerful sovereigns of Lower Egypt, and the tombs of all three families are found in the neighborhood of Memphis. The structure of the Pyramids shows great advancement in science and the mechanical arts. Each is placed so as exactly to face the cardinal points, and the Great Pyramid is precisely upon the 30th parallel of latitude. The wonderful accuracy of the latter in its astronomical adjustments, has led a few profound scholars * of the present day to believe that it could only have been built by Divine revelation; not by the Egyptians, but by a people led from Asia for the purpose, the object being to establish a perfectly trustworthy system of weights and measures.

137. The Arabian copper-mines of the Sinaitic peninsula were worked under the direction of the Pyramid kings. At this period the arts had reached their highest perfection. Drawing, † sculpture, and writing, as well as modes of living and general civilization, were much the same as fifteen centuries later.

138. B. C. 2220. While a sixth royal family succeeded the pyramid-builders at Memphis, the second and fifth continued to reign at This and Elephantis, while two more arose at Heracleop′olis and Thebes; so that Egypt was now divided into five separate kingdoms, the Theban becoming gradually the most powerful. Thus weakened by division, and perhaps exhausted by the great architectural works which had withdrawn the people from the practice of arms, the country easily became the prey of nomad tribes from the neighboring regions of Syria and Arabia. These were called Hyk′sos, or Shepherd Kings. They entered Lower Egypt from the north-east, and soon became masters of the country from Memphis to the sea.

139. Second Period. B. C. 1900–1525. Native dynasties continued for a time to reign in Middle and Upper Egypt; and even in the heart of the Delta a new kingdom sprang up at Xo′is, which maintained itself during the whole time that the Shepherds were in the land. A large number of the enslaved Egyptians continued to cultivate the soil, paying tribute to the conquerors; and, in time, the example of their good order may have mollified the fierce invaders. The latter built themselves a strongly fortified camp, Ava′ris, in the eastern portion of the Delta, near the later city of Pelusium.

---

* See "Our Inheritance in the Great Pyramid," by Prof. Piazzi Smyth.

† See § 187.

140. At the same period with the invasion, a Twelfth Egyptian Dynasty, the Osortasidæ, arose at Thebes, and became one of the most powerful tribes of native rulers. They obtained paramount authority over the kingdoms of Elephantine and Heracleopolis, held the Sinaitic Peninsula, and extended their victorious arms into Arabia and Ethiopia. Sesortasen I ruled all Upper Egypt. Under the second and third sovereigns of that name the kingdom reached its highest prosperity. The third Sesortasen enriched the country by many canals, and left monuments of his power at Senneh, near the southern border of the empire, which still excite the wonder of travelers. The largest edifice and the most useful work in Egypt were executed by his successor, Ammenemes III. The first was the Labyrinth in the Faioom, which Herodotus visited, and declared that it surpassed all human works. It contained three thousand rooms; fifteen hundred of these were under ground, and contained the mummies of kings and of the sacred crocodiles. The walls of the fifteen hundred upper apartments were of solid stone, entirely covered with sculpture. The other work of Ammenemes was the Lake Moëris. This was a natural reservoir formed near a bend of the Nile; but he so improved it by art as to retain and carefully distribute the gifts of the river, and thus insure the fruitfulness of the province.

141. A weaker race succeeded, and the calamities of Lower Egypt were now extended throughout the land. The Hyksos advanced to the southward, and the fugitive kings of Thebes sought refuge in Ethiopia. With the exception of the Xoites, intrenched in the marshes of the Delta, all Egypt became for a time subject to the Shepherds. They burned cities, destroyed temples, and made slaves of all the people whom they did not put to death. Two native dynasties reigned at Memphis, and one at Heracleopolis, but they were tributary to the conquerors.

142. Some have supposed that the Pyramids were erected by these Shepherd Kings. But the best authorities describe the race as rude, ignorant, and destitute of arts, as compared with the Egyptians, either before or after their invasion; and after the long deluge of barbarism was swept back, we find religion, language, and art—kept, doubtless, and cultivated in seclusion by the learned class—precisely as they were before the interruption. The absence of records during this period would alone prove the lack of learning in the ruling race. Baron Bunsen supposes the Hyksos to have been identical with the Philistines of Palestine. Some of them took refuge in Crete when they were driven out of Egypt, and re-appeared in Palestine from the west about the same time that the Israelites entered it from the east. In any case, a gap of nearly four hundred years occurs in Egyptian history between the old and the new empires, during which the Holy City of Thebes was in the hands of barbarians, the annals ceased, and the names of the kings, either native or foreign, are for the most part unknown.

143. Third Period. B. C. 1525–525. After their long humiliation, the people of Egypt rallied for a great national revolt, under the Theban king Amo′sis, and drove the invaders, after a hard-fought contest, from their soil. Now came the brightest period of Egyptian history. Amosis was rewarded with the undivided sovereignty, and became the founder of the Eighteenth Dynasty. Memphis was made the imperial capital. Many temples were repaired, as we may learn from memoranda preserved in the quarries of Syene and the Upper Nile. Aahmes, the wife of Amosis, bears the surname Nefru-ari, "the good, glorious woman," and seems to have been held in the highest honor ever ascribed to a queen. She was a Theban princess of Ethiopian blood, and probably had many provinces for her dowry. Amosis died B. C. 1499.

144. For eight hundred years Egypt continued a single, consolidated kingdom. During this time art obtained its highest perfection; the great temple-palaces of Thebes were built; numerous obelisks, "fingers of the sun," pointed heavenward; and the people, who had long groaned under a cruel servitude, enjoyed, under the Eighteenth, Nineteenth, and Twentieth Dynasties, the protection of a mild and well-organized government.

145. It may be feared that the Egyptians wreaked upon a captive nation within their own borders their resentment against their late oppressors. The Hebrews grew and multiplied in Egypt, and their lives were made bitter with hard bondage. Many of the vast brick constructions of the Eighteenth and Nineteenth Dynasties may have been erected by the captive Hebrews, who are expressly said to have built the two treasure cities, Pithom and Raamses.

146. Royal women were treated with higher respect in Egypt than in any other ancient monarchy. Thothmes I, the third king of the Eighteenth Dynasty, was succeeded by his daughter, Mesphra or Amen-set, who reigned as regent for her younger brother, Thothmes II. He died a minor, and she held the same office, or, perhaps, reigned jointly with her next younger brother, Thothmes III; but not with his cordial consent, for when she, too, died, after a regency of twenty-two years, he caused her name and image to be effaced from all the sculptures in which they had appeared together.

147. B. C. 1461–1414. This king, Thothmes III, is distinguished not more for his foreign wars than for the magnificent palaces and temples which he built at Karnac, Thebes, Memphis, Heliopolis, Coptos, and other places. Hardly an ancient city in Egypt or Nubia is unmarked by remains of his edifices. The history of his twelve successive campaigns is recorded in sculpture upon the walls of his palace at Thebes. He drove the Hyksos from their last stronghold, Ava′ris, where they had been shut up since the days of his father. The two obelisks near Alexandria, which some Roman wit called Cleopa′tra's Needles, bear the name of this king. His military expeditions extended both to the north and south; inscriptions on his monuments declare that he took tribute from Nineveh, Hit (or Is), and Babylon.

148. His grandson, Thothmes IV, caused the carving of the great Sphinx
B. C. 1400–1364. near the Pyramids. Amunoph III, his successor, was a great and powerful monarch. He adorned the country by magnificent buildings, and improved its agriculture by the construction of tanks or reservoirs to regulate irrigation. The two *Colossi* near Thebes, one of which is known as the vocal Memnon, date from his reign; but the Amenophe′um, of which they were ornaments, is now in ruins. Amunoph maintained the warlike fame of his ancestors by expeditions into all the countries invaded by Thothmes III. He is styled upon his monuments, "Pacificator of Egypt and Tamer of the Libyan Shepherds." He built the gorgeous palace of Luxor, which he connected with the temple at Karnac by an avenue of a thousand sphinxes. He made a similar avenue also at Thebes, lined with colossal sitting statues of the cat-headed goddess Pasht (Bubastis).

149. B. C. 1364–1327. In the reign of Horus, his son, the nation was distracted by many claimants for the crown, most of whom were princes or princesses of the blood royal. Horus outlived his rivals and destroyed their monuments. He had successful foreign wars in Africa, and made
B. C. 1327–1324. additions to the palaces at Karnac and Luxor. With the next king, Rathotis (or Resitot), the Eighteenth Dynasty ended.

150. B. C. 1324–1322. Rameses I, founder of the Nineteenth Dynasty, was descended from the first two kings of the eighteenth. His son, Seti, inherited all the national hatred toward the Syrian invaders, and "avenged the shame of Egypt on Asia." He reconquered Syria, which had revolted some forty years earlier, and carried his victorious arms as far as the borders of Cilicia and the banks of the Euphrates. He built the great Hall at Karnac — in which the whole Cathedral of Notre Dame, at Paris, could stand without touching either walls or ceiling — and his tomb is the most beautiful of all the sepulchers of the kings.

151. B. C. 1311–1245. Rameses II, the Great, reigned sixty-six years; and his achievements in war and peace fill a large space in the records of his time, in which fact and fiction are often intermingled by his flatterers. During his father's life-time, he began his military career by subduing both Libya and Arabia. His ambition being thus inflamed, he had no sooner succeeded to the throne than he resolved upon the conquest of the world. He provided for the security of his kingdom during his absence, by re-dividing the country into thirty-six nomes and appointing a governor for each. He then equipped an immense

FIGURE OF AMUNOPH III, NEAR THEBES.

Called by the Greeks the Vocal Memnon. It was 47 feet in height, or 53 feet including the pedestal.

To face p

army, which is said to have included 600,000 foot, 24,000 horse, and 27,000 war chariots. Having conquered Ethiopia, Rameses made a fleet of four hundred vessels, the first which any Egyptian king had possessed, and sailing down the Red Sea to the Arabian, continued his voyage as far as India. He returned only to make fresh preparations, and lead another great army eastward beyond the Ganges, and onward till he reached a new ocean. Columns were every-where erected recording the victories of the monarch, and lauding the courage or shaming the cowardice of those who had encountered him.

152. Returning from his Asiatic conquests, Rameses entered Europe and subdued the Thracians; then, after nine years absence, during which he had covered himself with the glory of innumerable easy victories, he reëntered Egypt. He brought with him a long train of captives, whom he intended to employ upon the architectural works which he had already projected. Among the most celebrated are the Rock Temples of Ipsambul, in Nubia, whose sides are covered with bas-reliefs representing the victories of Sesostris; the Ramesse′um, or Memnonium, at Thebes; and additions to the palace at Karnac. He built, also, a wall near the eastern frontier of Egypt, from Pelusium to Heliopolis, and, perhaps, even as far as Sye′ne, to prevent future invasions from Arabia. More monuments exist of Rameses II than of any other Pharaoh; but the strength of the New Empire was exhausted by these extraordinary efforts in war and building. The king tormented both his subjects and his captives, using them merely as instruments of his passion for military and architectural display. It was this king who drove the Israelites to desperation by his inhuman oppressions, especially by commanding every male child to be drowned in the Nile. (Exodus i: 8–14, 22.)

153. In the great hall of Abydus, or This, Rameses is represented as offering sacrifice to fifty-two kings of his own race, he himself, in a glorified form, being of the number. The sculpture is explained by an inscription: "A libation to the Lords of the West, by the offerings of their son, the king Rameses, in his abode." The reply of the royal divinities is as follows: "The speech of the Lords of the West, to their son the Creator and Avenger, the Lord of the World, the Sun who conquers in truth. We ourselves elevate our arms to receive thy offerings, and all other good and pure things in thy palace. We are renewed and perpetuated in the paintings of thy house," etc.

154. The son of Rameses II, Menephthah, or Amenephthes, was the Pharaoh of the Exodus. The escaping Israelites passed along the bank of the canal made by the Great King, and thus were supplied with water for their multitude both of men and beasts. By the dates always found upon Egyptian buildings, we learn that architectural labors ceased for twenty years; and this contrast to the former activity affords an interesting coincidence with the Scriptural narrative. Josephus,* also, quotes from Manetho a tradition, that the son of the great Rameses was overthrown by a revolt, under Osarsiph (Moses), of a race of lepers who had been grievously oppressed by him; and that he fled into Ethiopia with his son, then only five years old, who, thirteen years later, recovered the kingdom as Sethos II. To express their contempt for their former captives, the Egyptian historians always refer to the Israelites as lepers. With Seti, or Sethos II, the house of the great Rameses became extinct.

155. B. C. 1219. Rameses III, the first of the Twentieth Dynasty, maintained extensive wars, both by sea and land. His four sons all bore his name and came successively to the throne, but there are no great events to signalize their reigns. Six or seven kings of the same name followed, and the family ended about B. C. 1085.

156. During this period Egypt rapidly declined, as well in intellectual as military power. Her foreign enterprises ceased; no additions were made to the magnificent buildings of former ages; and sculpture and painting, instead of deriving new life from the study of Nature, were compelled to copy the old set forms or confine themselves to dull and meaningless imitations.

157. The Twenty-first Dynasty was a priestly race, whose capital was Ta′nis, or Zo′an, in Lower Egypt, but who were supreme throughout the country. They wore sacerdotal robes, and called themselves High Priests of Amun. One of them gave his daughter in marriage to Solomon. (1 Kings iii: 1; ix: 16.) The seven kings of this dynasty had usually short reigns, marked by few events. B. C. 1085–990.

158. B. C. 993–972. Sheshonk, or Shishak, the founder of the Twenty-second Dynasty, revived the military power of the nation. He married the daughter of Pisham II, the last king of the Tanite race, and took upon himself, also, the title of High Priest of Amun, but beyond this there are no signs of priesthood in this line. Bubastis, in the Delta, was the seat of his government. It was to him that Jerobo′am fled when plotting to make himself king of Israel; and Shishak afterward made an expedition against Judæa for the purpose of confirming Jeroboam on his throne.
B. C. 972.
He plundered Jerusalem and received the submission of Rehoboam. Osorkon II, the fourth king of this dynasty, and an Ethiopian prince, was probably the Zerah of Scripture, who invaded
B. C. 956–933.
Syria, and was defeated by Asa, king of Judah, in the battle of Mareshah. (2 Chron. xiv: 9–14.)

* Josephus was a Jewish historian, born A. D. 37, the son of a priest, and descended by his mother's side from the same royal family with the Herods. His greatest work is his "Jewish Antiquities," in twenty books. The history begins at the Creation of the World, and ends A. D. 66, with the Revolt of the Jews against the Romans.

159. At the expiration of this line in the person of Takelot II, about B. C. 847, a rival family sprang up at Tanis, forming the Twenty-third Dynasty. It comprised only four kings, none of whom were famous. B. C. 847–758.

160. B. C. 758–714. The Twenty-fourth Dynasty consisted of one king, Boccho′ris. He fixed the government at Sa′ïs, another city of the Delta, and was widely famed for the wisdom and justice of his administration. In the latter half of this period, Sabaco, the Ethiopian, overran the country and reduced the Saïte monarch to a mere vassal. Bocchoris, attempting to revolt, was captured and burned to death, after a reign of forty-four years.

B. C. 730.

161. Sabaco I, having subdued Egypt, established the Twenty-fifth Dynasty. He fought with the king of Assyria for the dominion of western Asia, but was defeated by Sargon in the battle of Raphia, B. C. 718. Assyrian influence became predominant in the Delta, while the power of the Ethiopian was undisturbed only in Upper Egypt. The second king of this family was also named Sabaco. The third and last, Tir′hakeh, was the greatest of the line. He maintained war successively with three Assyrian monarchs. The first, Sennacherib, was overthrown * B. C. 698. His son, Esarhaddon, was successful for a time in breaking Lower Egypt into a number of tributary provinces. Tirhakeh recovered his power and reunited his kingdom; but after two years' war with Asshur-bani-pal, the next king of Assyria, he was obliged to abdicate in favor of his son. The son was expelled, and Egypt was divided for thirty years into many petty kingdoms, which remained subject to Assyria until the death of the conqueror.

B. C. 690–665.

162. For the Egyptians this was merely a change of foreign rulers. Their patriotism had long been declining, and their native army had lost its fame and valor from the time when the kings of the Twenty-second Dynasty intrusted the national defense to foreigners. The military caste became degraded, and the crown even attempted to deprive the soldiers of their lands. Egypt had become in some degree a naval power, and a commercial class had arisen to rival the soldiers and farmers.

163. About 630 B. C., the Assyrians had to concentrate their forces at home in resistance to the Scythians; and Psammet′ichus, one of the native viceroys whom they had set up in Egypt, seized the opportunity to throw off their yoke. The great Assyrian Empire was now falling under the Median and Babylonian revolt, and its power ceased to be felt in distant provinces. Psammetichus gained victories over his brother viceroys, and established the Twenty-sixth Dynasty over all Egypt. He was an enlightened monarch, and during his reign art and science received a new impulse.

---

* See § 33.

164. Having overcome the dodecarchy by means of his Greek and Tyrian auxiliaries, he settled these foreign troops in permanent camps, the latter near Memphis, the former near the Pelusiac branch of the Nile. His native soldiery were so incensed by being thus superseded by foreign mercenaries, that many deserted and took up their residence in Ethiopia. So many foreigners of all classes now flocked to the ports of Egypt, that a new caste of dragomans, or interpreters, arose. Psammetichus caused his own son to be instructed in Greek learning, a sure sign that the barriers which had hitherto separated the intellectual life of Egypt from the rest of the world were now broken down.

165. Those northern barbarians who had terrified the Assyrians had now overrun Palestine and threatened an invasion of Egypt; but the messengers of Psammetichus met them at Ascalon with bribes which induced them to return.

166. B. C. 610–594. In the reign of Necho, son of Psammetichus, the navy and commerce of Egypt were greatly increased, and Africa was for the first time circumnavigated by an Egyptian fleet. This expedition sailed by way of the Red Sea. Twice the seamen landed, encamped, sowed grain, and waited for a harvest. Having reaped their crop, they again set sail, and in the third year arrived in Egypt by way of the Mediterranean. The foreign conquests of Necho may even be compared with those of the great Rameses, for he enlarged his dominions by all the
B. C. 605. country between Egypt and the Euphrates. But he met a stronger foe in Nebuchadnezzar, and when he fled from the field of Car′chemish all his Asiatic conquests fell into the hands of the great Babylonian.

167. B. C. 588–569. His grandson, Apries, the Pharaoh-hophra of Scripture, resumed the warlike schemes of Necho. He besieged Sidon, fought a naval battle with Tyre, and made an unsuccessful alliance with
B. C. 569–525. Zedekiah, king of Judah, against Nebuchadnezzar. He was deposed, and his successor, Ama′sis, held his crown at first as a tributary to the Babylonian. He afterward made himself independent; and many monuments throughout Egypt bear witness to his liberal encouragement of the arts, while his foreign policy enriched the country. He was on friendly terms with Greece and her colonies, and many Greek merchants settled in Egypt.

168. Alarmed by the increasing power of Persia, he sought to strengthen himself by alliances with Crœsus of Lydia, and Polycrates of Samos. The precaution was ineffectual, but Amasis did not live to see the ruin of his country. Cambyses, king of Persia, was already on his march at the head of a great army, when Psammen′itus, son of Amasis, succeeded to the throne of Egypt. The new king hastened to meet the invader at Pelusium, but was defeated and compelled to shut himself up in Memphis, his capital, where the Persians now advanced to besiege him. The city was taken and its king made captive, after a reign of only six months. A little later he was put to death; and the Kingdom of Egypt, after a thousand years of independent existence, became a mere province of the Persian Empire, B. C. 525.

RECAPITULATION.

At a very early period Egypt was highly civilized, but not united, for it consisted of many independent nomes governed by priests. Menes built Memphis, and founded the Empire of Upper and Lower Egypt, which was ruled by twenty-six dynasties before the Persian Conquest. Sesorcheres founded the Third Dynasty; Sesonchosis patronized all the arts, and his son improved the laws and worship. The Fourth Dynasty built many pyramids, while the Second and Fifth reigned as dependents in This and Elephantine. Egypt was afterward divided into five kingdoms, and became subject to the Hyksos from Asia, who enslaved the people, and after a time subdued the whole country, except Xois in the Delta. During the early part of their invasion, the Twelfth Dynasty reigned at Thebes in great power and splendor.

B. C. 1525, Amosis led a revolt which expelled the Hyksos, and founded the Eighteenth Dynasty at Memphis. Several queens were highly honored. The people were prosperous, but the captive Hebrews were oppressed. Thothmes III built many palaces; Seti re-conquered Syria; and his son, Rameses the Great, gained victories in Europe, Asia, and Africa. In the reign of Menephthah, the Israelites were led out of Egypt by Moses. Under the Twentieth Dynasty, the art, enterprise, and power of Egypt declined. The Twenty-first Dynasty was composed of priests; the Twenty-second, of soldiers. The Twenty-fourth was overthrown by Sabaco the Ethiopian; the Twenty-fifth, which he founded, was, in turn, reduced by the Assyrians. After thirty years' subjection, Egypt was delivered and united by Psammetichus, with the aid of foreign troops. Necho, his son, was successful in many naval and military enterprises, but was defeated at last by Nebuchadnezzar, in the battle of Carchemish. Apries was deposed by the same king, and Amasis came to the throne as a viceroy of Babylon. His son, Psammenitus, was conquered by Cambyses, and Egypt became a Persian province.

RELIGION OF EGYPT.

169. The religion of the ancient Egyptians was a perplexing mixture of grand conceptions and degrading superstitions. No other ancient people had so firm an assurance of immortality, or felt its motives so intimately affecting their daily life; yet no other carried its idolatries to so debasing and ridiculous an extreme. The contradiction is partly solved if we remember two distinctions: the first applying chiefly to the ancient and heathen world, between the religion of priests and people; the second every-where existing, even in the One True Faith, between theory and practice—between ideal teaching and the personal character of those who receive it.

170. The sacred books of the Egyptians contained the system adopted by the priests. Their fundamental doctrine was that God is one, unrepresented, invisible. But as God acts upon the world, his various attributes or modes of manifestation were represented in various forms. As the Creator, he was Phtha; as the Revealer, he was Am′un; as the Benefactor and the Judge of men, he was Osiris; and so on through an endless list of primary, secondary, and tertiary characters, which to the uneducated became so many separate divinities. Some portion of his divine life was even supposed to reside in plants and animals, which were accordingly cherished and worshiped by the ignorant. For what to the wise were merely symbols, to the people became distinct objects of adoration; and the Egyptian priests, like all other heathen philosophers, disdained to spread abroad the light which they possessed. They despised the common people, whom they judged incapable of apprehending the sacred mysteries, and taught them only those convenient doctrines which would render them submissive to kingly and priestly authority.

171. The people, then, believed in eight gods of the first order, twelve of the second, and seven of the third; but each of these was worshiped under many titles, or as connected with different places. Isis was, therefore, surnamed Myriônyma, or "with ten thousand names." The sun and the moon were admitted to their worship; the former as representing the life-giving power of the deity, the latter as the regulator of time and the messenger of heaven. The moon was figured as the Ibis-headed Thoth, who corresponds to the Greek Hermes, the god of letters and recorder of all human actions.

172. A principle of evil was worshiped, in very early times, under the name of Seth, the Satan of Egyptian mythology. He was figured on a monument as instructing a king in the use of a bow. Sin is elsewhere represented as a great serpent, the enemy of gods and men, slain by the spear of Horus, the child of Isis. It seems impossible to doubt that the Egyptians had preserved some traditions of the promises made to Eve. At a later period the worship of the evil principle was abolished, and the square-eared images of Seth were chiseled off from the monuments.

173. The most interesting article of Egyptian mythology is the appearance of Osiris on earth for the benefit of mankind, under the title of Manifestor of Goodness and Truth; his death by the malice of the evil one; his burial and resurrection, and his office as judge of the dead. In every part of Egypt, and during all periods of its history, Osiris was regarded as the great arbiter of the future state.

174. In the earliest times human sacrifices were practiced, as is proved by the Sacrificial Seal which was accustomed to be affixed to the victim, and copies of which are frequently found in the tombs. It represents a kneeling human figure, bound, and awaiting the descent of the knife which glitters in the hand of a priest. But the practice was abolished by Amosis (B. C. 1525–1499), who ordered an equal number of waxen effigies to be offered instead of the human victims.

175. The worship of animals was the most revolting feature of Egyptian ceremonies. Throughout Egypt the ox, dog, cat, ibis, hawk, and the fishes lepidotus and oxyrrynchus were held sacred. Beside these there were innumerable local idolatries. Men′des worshiped the goat; Heracleop′-olis, the ichneumon; Cynop′olis, the dog; Lycop′olis, the wolf; A′thribis, the shrew-mouse; Sa′ïs and Thebes, the sheep; Babylon near Memphis the ape, etc. Still more honored were the bull Apis, at Memphis; the calf Mne′vis, at Heliopolis; and the crocodiles of Om′bos and Arsin′oë. These were tended in their stalls by priests, and worshiped by the people with profound reverence. Apis, the living symbol of Osiris, passed his days in an Apeum attached to the Serapeum at Memphis. When he died he was embalmed, and buried in so magnificent a manner that the persons in charge of the ceremony were often ruined by the expense. He was supposed to be the son of the moon, and was known by a white triangle or square on his black forehead, the figure of a vulture on his back, and of a beetle under his tongue. He was never allowed to live more than twenty-five years. If he seemed likely to survive this period, he was drowned in the sacred fountain, and another Apis was sought. The chemistry of the priests had already produced the required white spots in the black hair of some young calf, and the candidate was never sought in vain. At the annual rising of the Nile, a seven-days' feast was held in honor of Osiris.

176. Difference of worship sometimes led to bitter enmities between the several nomes. Thus, at Ombos the crocodile was worshiped, while at Ten′tyra it was hunted and abhorred; the ram-headed Am′un was an object of adoration at Thebes, and the sheep was a sacred animal, while the goat was killed for food; in Men′des the goat was worshiped and the sheep was eaten. The Lycopol′ites also ate mutton in compliment to the wolves, which they venerated.

177. If we turn from the trivial rites to the moral effects of the Egyptian faith, we find more to respect. The rewards and punishments of a future life were powerful incitements to right dealing in the present. At death all became equal: the king or the highest pontiff equally with the lowest swine-herd must be acquitted by the judges before his body was permitted to pass the sacred lake and be buried with his fathers. Every nome had its sacred lake, across which all funeral processions passed on their way to the city of the dead. On the side nearest the abodes of the living, have been found the remains of multitudes who failed to pass the ordeal, and whose bodies were ignominiously returned to their friends, to be disposed of in the speediest manner.

178. Beside the earthly tribunal of forty-two judges, who decided the fate of the body, it was believed that the soul must pass before the divine judgment-seat before it could enter the abodes of the blessed. The Book of the Dead—the only one yet discovered of the forty-two sacred books of the Egyptians—contains a description of the trial of a departed soul. It is represented on its long journey as occupied with prayers and confessions. Forty-two gods occupy the judgment-seat. Osiris presides; and before him are the scales, in one of which the statue of perfect Justice is placed; in the other, the heart of the deceased. The soul of the dead stands watching the balance, while Horus examines the plummet indicating which way the beam preponderates; and Thoth, the Justifier, records the sentence. If this is favorable, the soul receives a mark or seal, "Justified."

179. The temples of Egypt are the grandest architectural monuments in the world. That of Am′un, in a rich oasis twenty days' journey from Thebes, was one of the most famous of ancient oracles Near it, in a grove of palms, rose a hot spring, the Fountain of the Sun, whose bubbling and smoking were supposed to be tokens of the divine presence. The oasis was a resting-place for caravans which passed between Egypt and the interior regions of Nigritia or Soudan; and many rich offerings were placed in the temple by merchants, thankful to have so nearly escaped the perils of the desert, or anxious to gain the favor of Amun for their journey just begun.

180. The Egyptians were divided into castes, or ranks, distinguished by occupations. These have been variously numbered from three to seven. The priests stood highest, the soldiers next; below these were husbandmen, who may be divided into gardeners, boatmen, artisans of various kinds, and shepherds, the latter including goat-herds and swine-herds, which last were considered lowest of all.

181. The land, at least under the new empire, belonged exclusively to the king, the priests, and the soldiers. In the time when Joseph the Hebrew was prime minister, all other proprietors surrendered their lands to the crown,* retaining possession of them only on condition of paying a yearly rent of one-fifth of the produce.

182. The king was the representative of deity, and thus the head not only of the government but of the religion of the state. His title, Phrah (Pharaoh), signifying the Sun, pronounced him the emblem of the god of light. It was his right and office to preside over the sacrifice and pour out libations to the gods.

183. On account of his great responsibilities, the king of Egypt was allowed less freedom in personal habits than the meanest of his subjects. The sacred books contained minute regulations for his food, drink, and dress, and the employment of his time. No indulgence of any kind was permitted to be carried to excess. No slave or hireling was allowed to

* See Genesis xlvii: 18-26.

hold office about his person, lest he should imbibe ideas unworthy of a prince; but noblemen of the highest rank were alone privileged to attend him. The ritual of every morning's worship chanted the virtues of former kings, and reminded him of his own duties. After death his body was placed in an open court, where all his subjects might come with accusations; and if his conduct in life was proved to have been unworthy his high station, he was forever excluded from the sepulcher of his fathers.

184. The priestly order possessed great power in the state, and, so far as the sovereign was concerned, we can not deny that they used it well. They were remarkable for their simple and temperate habits of living. So careful were they that the body should "sit lightly upon the soul," that they took food only of the plainest quality and limited amount, abstaining from many articles, such as fish, mutton, swine's flesh, beans, peas, garlic, leeks, and onions, which were in use among the common people. They bathed twice a day and twice during the night—some of the more strict, in water that had been tasted by their sacred bird, the ibis, that they might have undoubted evidence of its cleanliness. By this example of abstinence, purity, and humility, as well as by their reputation for learning, the Egyptian priests established almost unlimited control over the people. Their knowledge of physical science enabled them, by optical illusions and other tricks, to excite the terror and superstitious awe of their ignorant spectators. Nor did their reputed power end with this life, for they could refuse to any man the passport to the "outer world," which alone could secure his eternal happiness.

185. The science of medicine was cultivated by the priests in even the remotest ages. The universal practice of embalming was exercised by physicians, and this enabled them to study the effects of various diseases, by examination of the body after death. Asiatic monarchs sent to Egypt for their physicians, and the prolific soil of the Nile Valley supplied drugs for all the world. To this day, the characters used by apothecaries to denote drams and grains are Egyptian ciphers as adopted by the Arabs.

186. The soldiers, when not engaged in service either in foreign wars, in garrisons, or at court, were settled on their own lands. These were situated chiefly east of the Nile or in the Delta, since it was in these quarters that the country was most exposed to hostile invasions. Each soldier was allotted about six acres of land, free from all tax or tribute. From its proceeds he defrayed the expense of his own arms and equipment.

187. Upon the walls of their tombs are found vivid delineations of the daily life of the Egyptians. Their industries, such as glass-blowing, linen-weaving, rope-making, etc., as well as their common recreations of hunting, fishing, ball-playing, wrestling, and domestic scenes, as in the entertainment of company, are all represented in sculpture or paintings upon the walls of Thebes or Beni-hassan. Dolls and other toys of children are found in the tombs; and it is evident that the Egyptians had so familiarized the idea of death as to have rid themselves of the gloomy and painful associations with which it is often surrounded. The body, after being prepared for the tomb, was returned to the house of its abode, where it was kept never less than thirty days, and sometimes even a year, feasts being given in its honor, and it being always present in the company of guests. From the moment when the forty-two judges had pronounced their favorable verdict on the border of the lake, the lamentations of the funeral train were changed into songs of triumph, and the deceased was congratulated on his admission to the glorified company of the friends of Osiris.

CARTHAGE.

188. About 850 B. C., Dido, sister of Pygmalion, king of Tyre, having been cruelly wronged by her brother in the murder of her husband, Acer′bas, resolved to escape from his dominions and establish a new empire. Accompanied by some Tyrian nobles who were dissatisfied with the rule of Pygmalion, she sailed in a fleet laden with the treasures of her husband, and came to anchor at length in a bay on the northern coast of Africa, about six miles north of the modern Tunis.

189. The Libyan natives, who knew the value of commerce and the wealth of Phœnician colonies, were inclined to be friendly; but their first transaction with the new settlers promised advantages only to one side. Dido proposed to lease from them as much land as could be covered with a bullock's hide. The yearly ground-rent being settled, she then ordered the hide to be cut into the thinnest possible strips, and thus surrounded a large portion of land, on which she built the fortress of Byr′sa. The colony prospered, however, and was strengthened by the alliance of Utica and other Tyrian settlements on the same coast. By similar arrangements with the Libyans, the queen obtained permission to build the town of CARTHAGE, which became the seat of a great commercial empire.

190. As the New City* rose to a high degree of power and wealth, Hiar′bas, a neighboring king, sent to demand a marriage with Dido, threatening war in case of refusal. The queen seemed to consent for the benefit of her state; but at the end of three months' preparation, she ascended a funeral pile upon which sacrifices had been offered to the shades of Acer′-bas, and declaring to her people that she was going to her husband, as

* The Phœnician name of Carthage signified the New City, distinguishing it either from the neighboring Utica, whose name meant the Old City, or from Byrsa, the first fortress of Dido. When New Carthage (Carthagena) was built upon the coast of Spain, the original settlement began to be called by the Romans *Carthago Vetus*, which is as if we should say "Old Newtown."

they had desired, plunged a sword into her breast. Dido continued to be worshiped as a divinity in Carthage as long as the city existed.

191. So far our story is mixed with fable, though containing, doubtless, a large proportion of truth. What we certainly know is, that the latest colony of Tyre soon became the most powerful; that it grew by the alliance and immigration of the neighboring Libyans, as well as of its sister colonies; and that it gained in wealth by the destruction* of its parent city in the Babylonian wars. While the Levantine commerce of Tyre fell to the Greeks, that of the West was naturally inherited by the Carthaginians. B. C. 585.

192. The African tribes, to whom the colonists were at first compelled to pay tribute for the slight foot-hold they possessed, became at length totally subjugated. They cultivated their lands for the benefit of Carthage, and might at any time be forced to contribute half their movable wealth to her treasury, and all their young men to her armies. The Phœnician settlements gradually formed themselves into a confederacy, of which Carthage was the head, though she possessed no authority beyond the natural leadership of the most powerful. Her dominions extended westward to the Pillars of Hercules, and down the African coast to the end of the Atlas range; on the east her boundaries were fixed, after a long contest with the Greek city of Cyre′ne, at the bottom of the Great Syrtis, or gulf, which indents the northern shore.

193. Not content with her continental domains, Carthage gained possession of most of the islands of the western Mediterranean. The coast of Sicily was already dotted with Phœnician trading stations. These came under the control of Carthage; and though out-rivaled in prosperity by the free cities of the Greeks, especially Agrigen′tum and Syr′acuse, the western portion of the island long remained a valuable possession. The Balearic Islands were occupied by Carthaginian troops. Sardinia was conquered by a long and severe conflict, and became a most important station for the trade with Western Europe. Settlements were established in Corsica and Spain, while, in the Atlantic, the islands of Madeira and the Canaries were early subdued.

194. These conquests were made chiefly by means of foreign mercenaries drawn both from Europe and Africa. South and west of Carthage were the barbarous but usually friendly tribes of Numid′ia and Mauritania; and her merchants in their journeys had frequent dealings with the warlike races of Spain, Gaul, and northern Italy. It is said that the Carthaginians mingled these various nations in their armies in such a manner that difference of language might prevent their plotting together.

195. The navy of Carthage was of great importance in protecting her

---

* See § 47.

commerce from the swarms of pirates which infested the Mediterranean. The galleys were propelled by oars in the hands of slaves, but the officers and sailors were usually native Carthaginians. With these land and naval forces, Carthage became for several centuries undisputed mistress of the central and western Mediterranean.

196. Toward the middle of the sixth century B. C., a great commercial rival appeared in the western waters. The Greeks had begun their system of colonization; had opened a trade with Tartes'sus, multiplied their settlements in Sicily and Corsica, and built Massil'ia near the mouth of the Rhone. Near the close of our First Period, the two powers came into fierce collision, and the Grecian fleet was destroyed by that of Carthage, aided by her

B. C. 509. Etruscan allies. At the same time Rome, which had grown powerful under her kings, became free by their expulsion; and the Carthaginians, hitherto on friendly terms with the Italians, made a treaty of alliance with the new Republic which was to prove their most unrelenting foe.

197. The government of Carthage, under the forms of a republic, was really an aristocracy of wealth. The two chief officers were the Suffe'tes, who at first, like the Hebrew rulers from Joshua to Samuel, led the people in war and judged them in peace. In later times their office became exclusively civil, and generals were appointed for military command. The Suffetes were elected only from certain families, and probably for life.

198. Next came the Council of several hundreds of citizens, from which committees of five were chosen to administer the various departments of state. At a later period, when the house of Mago had risen to a degree of military power which was thought to endanger the public safety, a Council of One Hundred was added to these, before which all generals returning from war were obliged to present themselves and render an account of their actions. So severe were the judgments of this tribunal, that an unsuccessful general often preferred suicide upon the field of battle to meeting their awards. With the two judges and the two high priests, this council constituted the Supreme Court of the Republic.

199. The larger Council, or Senate, received foreign embassadors, deliberated upon all matters of state, and decided questions of war or peace, with a certain deference to the authority of the Suffetes. If the judges and the senate could not agree, appeal was made to the people.

200. The religion of Carthage was the same as that of Tyre, with the addition of the worship of two or three Grecian divinities, whom the Carthaginians thought it necessary to appease by sacrifices after destroying their temples in Sicily. Every army was accompanied by a prophet or diviner, without whose direction nothing could be done. Generals frequently offered sacrifices, even during the progress of a battle. There was no hereditary priesthood, as in Egypt, but the priestly offices were filled by the highest persons in the state, sometimes even by the sons of the kings or judges. In every new settlement a sanctuary was erected, that the religion of the mother country might grow together with her government and commerce. Every year a fleet left Carthage, laden with rich offerings and bearing a solemn embassy to the shrine of the Tyrian Hercules. The human sacrifices and other hideous rites of Phœnician worship prevailed at Carthage; and though these features were somewhat softened by advancing civilization, we shall find traces enough, in future pages of her history, of that cruelty which makes so dark a blemish in the character of the whole race.

201. The trade of Carthage was carried on both by land and sea. Her caravans crossed the Great Desert by routes still traveled, and exchanged the products of northern countries for those of Upper Egypt, Ethiopia, Fezzan, and, perhaps, the far interior regions of Nigri′tia. The manufactures of Carthage included fine cloths, hardware, pottery, and harness of leather; but beside the exchange of her own products, she possessed almost exclusively the carrying-trade between the nations of Africa and western Europe.

202. The ships of Carthage penetrated all the then known seas; and though confined to coast navigation, they explored the Atlantic from Norway to the Cape of Good Hope. Hanno, the son of Hamil′car, conducted sixty ships bearing 30,000 colonists to the western shores of Africa, where he planted a chain of six colonies between the Straits and the island of Cer′ne. He then went southward with some of his ships as far as the River Gambia, and visited the Gold Coast, with which his countrymen thenceforth carried on a regular traffic. On his return he placed an inscription, commemorative of this voyage, on a brazen tablet in the temple of Kro′nos, at Carthage. Himilco, his brother, led another expedition the same year to the western coast of Europe, but of this the history is lost.

203. These extensive voyages in the interest of trade brought the products of the world into the Carthaginian markets. There might be seen muslins from Malta; oil and wine from Italy; wax and honey from Corsica; iron from Elba; gold, silver, and iron from Spain; tin from Cornwall and the Scilly Isles; amber from the Baltic; gold, ivory, and slaves from Senegam′bia.

204. While commerce was so abundant a source of wealth, agriculture was the favorite pursuit of nobles and people. The fertile soil of Libya yielded a hundred-fold to the farmer. So fond were wealthy Carthaginians of the healthful toils of the field, that one of their great men wrote a work, in twenty-eight volumes, on methods of husbandry; and this alone, of all the treasures of their literature, was thought by their Roman conquerors worthy of preservation.

205. We have slightly anticipated the course of events, in order to present a connected account of the government, religion, and trade of Carthage. Of her wars with the Sicilian Greeks, from the disastrous defeat of Hamilcar at Him′era, B. C. 480, to the peace of B. C. 304, we have no space for the details. The final period of Carthaginian history, comprising the Roman wars and the destruction of the city, will be found in Book V.

RECAPITULATION.

Carthage, a colony of Tyre, became sovereign of the shores and islands of the western Mediterranean, a rival of Greece, and an ally of Rome. Her army and navy were largely composed of European and African mercenaries. Her government was republican, with two judges at its head, foreign affairs being transacted by a council of citizens. Religious ceremonies claimed a large share of attention, both in war and peace. Commerce extended by land to the interior of Africa; by sea, from the Baltic to the Indian Ocean; and products of all the world filled the Carthaginian markets. Agriculture was a favorite employment with nobles and common people.

QUESTIONS FOR REVIEW.

Book I.—Part II.

1. What is remarkable in the early history of Egypt? . . . . . . §§ 126–128.
2. Describe the first monarch of the united empire. . . . . . . 129.
3. His successors in the same dynasty. . . . . 130.
4. How many dynasties before the Persian Conquest? . . . . . . 163.
5. Describe the kings of the Third Dynasty. . . . . 131, 132.
6. The Pyramid-builders. . . . . 133–135.
7. What dynasties were subject to the fourth? . . . . 136.
8. Describe the divisions of Egypt and their consequences. . . . 138, 139.
9. The monuments of the Twelfth Dynasty. . . . . . . 140.
10. The dominion and character of the Hyksos. . . . . 141, 142.
11. The rise of the New Empire. . . . . 143.
12. The family of Thothmes I. . . . . 146, 147.
13. Name the remaining kings of the Eighteenth Dynasty. . . . 148, 149.
14. Who founded the Nineteenth Dynasty? . . . . 150.
15. Describe its second and third kings. . . . . 150–152.
16. The Exodus of the Hebrews. . . . . 154.
17. Egypt under the Twentieth Dynasty. . . . . 155, 156.
18. What connections of Egyptian and Hebrew history under the Twenty-first and Twenty-second Dynasties? . . . . . . 157, 158.
19. Who constituted the Twenty-fourth Dynasty? . . . . 160.
20. Tell the history of the Twenty-fifth Dynasty. . . . . 161.
21. What was the condition of Egypt after the fall of Tirhakeh? . . 162.
22. What led to the rise of the Twenty-sixth Dynasty? . . . . . . 163.
23. What was the foreign policy of Psammetichus? . . . . . . 164.
24. What naval enterprise in the reign of Necho? . . . . 166.
25. Describe the reigns of Apries and Amasis. . . . . 167.
26. The theory and practice of Egyptian religion. . . . . 169, 170.

27. What were the objects of worship? . . . . §§ 171, 172, 175.
28. Describe the twofold judgment of the dead. . . . . 177, 178.
29. Into what ranks were Egyptians divided? . . . . 180.
30. Who owned the land? . . . . 181.
31. Describe the dignities and duties of the king. . . . . 182, 183.
32. The life and power of the priests. . . . . 184.
33. Their medical practice. . . . . 185.
34. The tombs, and honors paid to the dead. . . . . . . 187.
35. Give the traditional account of the founding of Carthage. . . . 188, 189.
36. Describe the causes of its prosperity. . . . . 191.
37. The extent of its dominion. . . . . 192, 193.
38. Its army and navy. . . . . 194, 195.
39. What war and what alliance in the sixth century? . . . . . . 196.
40. Describe the government of Carthage. . . . . 197–199.
41. Its religion. . . . . 200.
42. Its trade by land and sea. . . . . 201–203.
43. What was the favorite pursuit of the Carthaginians? . . . . . 204.

BOOK II.

The Persian Empire from the Rise of Cyrus to the Fall of Darius.

B. C. 558-330.

1. About 650 B. C., a warlike people, from the highlands east of the Caspian, took possession of the hilly country north of the Persian Gulf. They belonged, like the Medes, to the Aryan or Indo-Germanic family, and were distinguished by a more hardy, simple, and virtuous character, and a purer faith, from the luxurious inhabitants of the Babylonian plains. The nation, as it soon became constituted, consisted of ten tribes, of whom four continued nomadic, three settled to the cultivation of the soil, and three bore arms for the general defense. Of these the Pasar′-gadae were preëminent, and formed the nobility of Persia, holding all high offices in the army and about the court.

2. The first king, Achae′menes, was a Pasargadian, and from him all subsequent Persian kings were descended. For the first hundred years of its history, Persia was dependent upon the neighboring kingdom of Media. But a little after the middle of the sixth century before Christ, a revolution under Cy′rus reversed the relations of the Medo-Persian monarchy, and prepared the foundations of a great empire which was to reach beyond the Nile and the Hellespont on the west, and the Indus on the east.

3. Cyrus spent many of his early years at the court of Asty′ages, his maternal grandfather, in the seven-walled city of Ecbat′ana.* The brave, athletic youth, accustomed to hardy sports and simple fare, despised the wine and dainty food, the painted faces and silken garments of the Median nobles. He saw that their strength was wasted by luxury, and that in case of a collision they would be no match for his warlike countrymen. At the same time, a party of the younger Medes gathered around Cyrus, preferring his manly virtues to the effeminate pomp and cruel tyranny of their king, and impatient for the time when he should be their ruler.

* See Book I, §§ 38, 41.

4. When all was ready, the Persian prince rallied his countrymen and persuaded them to become independent of the Medes. Astyages raised an B. C. 558. army to quell the revolt, but when the two forces met at Pasar′gadæ, the greater part of the Medes went over to the Persian side. In a second battle Astyages was made prisoner, and the sovereignty of Media remained to the conqueror.

5. The reign of Cyrus was full of warlike enterprises. By the time he had subdued the Median cities, Crœsus,* king of Lydia, had become alarmed by his rapidly increasing power, and had stirred up Egypt, Babylon, and the Greeks to oppose it. He crossed the Ha′lys, and encountered the army of Cyrus near Sino′pe, in Cappado′cia. Neither party gained a victory; but Crœsus, finding his numbers inferior, drew back toward his capital, thinking to spend the winter in renewed preparations. B. C. 546. Cyrus pursued him to the gates of Sardis, and defeated him in a decisive battle. The city was taken, and Crœsus owed his life to the mercy of his conqueror. His kingdom, which comprised all Asia Minor west of the Halys, was added to the Persian Empire.

6. The monarchs of Asia had three methods of maintaining their dominion over the countries they had conquered: 1. A large standing army was kept upon the soil, at the cost of the vanquished. 2. In case of revolt, whole nations were sometimes transported over a distance of thousands of miles, usually to the islands of the Persian Gulf or the Indian Ocean, while their places were filled by emigrants whose loyalty was assured. 3. A more injurious, though apparently more indulgent policy, compelled a warlike people to adopt luxurious and effeminate manners. Such was the treatment of the Lydians, by the advice of their captive king. Crœsus was now the trusted counselor of Cyrus. With a view to save his people from the miseries of transportation, he suggested that they should be deprived of their arms, compelled to clothe themselves in soft apparel, and to train their youth in habits of gaming and drinking, thus rendering them forever incapable of disturbing the dominion of their conquerors. From a brave, warlike, and industrious race, the Lydians were transformed into indolent pleasure-seekers, and their country remained a submissive province of the empire of Cyrus.

7. Capture of Babylon. Leaving Harpagus to complete the conquest of the Asiatic Greeks, Cyrus turned to the east, where he aimed at the greater glory of subduing Assyria. Nabonadius,† the Babylonian king, believed that the walls of his capital were proof against assault; but he was defeated, and the great city became the prey of the conqueror. The writings of Daniel, who was resident at the court of Nabonadius, and a

---

* See Book I, § 59.

† See Book I, §§ 53, 54.

witness of the overthrow of his kingdom, inform us that Dari′us the Median took Babylon, being about sixty-two years old. It is probable that Darius was another name of Astyages himself, who, being deprived of his own kingdom, was compensated by the government of the most magnificent city of the East. His arbitrary decrees concerning Daniel and his accusers accord well with the character of Astyages.

8. Return of the Jews. It will be remembered that the Jews were now captives in Babylonia, where they had remained seventy years, since the destruction of their Holy City by Nebuchadnez′zar. Cyrus, who, like the Hebrews, was a believer in One God, found their pure religion an agreeable contrast to the corrupt and degrading rites of the Babylonians. He may have been moved by the prophecies of Isaiah, uttered nearly two centuries before, and those of Jeremiah at the time of the Captivity. (Isaiah xliv: 28, and xlv: 1–5; Jeremiah xxv: 12, and xxviii: 11.) He may also have had more selfish motives for favoring the Jews, in his designs upon Egypt, thinking it an advantage to have a friendly people established in the fortresses of Judah. In any case, he fulfilled the prophecies by giving orders for the return of the Israelites to their own land, and for the rebuilding of the Temple at Jerusalem. The 5,400 golden and silver vessels of the House of the Lord were brought forth from the Babylonian treasury and delivered to the prince of Judah, who received the Persian title Sheshbaz′zar, corresponding to the modern Pasha′. Few of the original captives had survived, like Daniel, to witness the return; but a company of fifty thousand, men, women, and children, were soon collected from their settlements on the Euphrates and the Persian Gulf, and moving toward their own land. (Read Ezra i, and ii: 1, 64, 65, 68–70.) On their arrival, the altar was immediately set up, the great festivals reëstablished, a grant of cedars from the forests of Lebanon obtained, and preparations made for rebuilding the Temple.

9. Cyrus never accomplished in person his designs upon Egypt. He extended his conquests westward to the borders of Macedonia, and eastward to the Indus. Some of the conquered countries were left under the control of their native kings; some received Persian rulers. All were made tributary, but the proportion of their tribute was not fixed. The organization of this vast dominion was left to the successors of Cyrus.

10. His last expedition was against the Massa′getæ, a tribe which dwelt east of the Sea of Aral. The barbarians who roamed over these great northern plains had become formidable foes to the civilized empires of the south, but they were so thoroughly subdued by Cyrus that they troubled Persia no more for two hundred years. The victor, however, lost his life in a battle with Tom′yris, their queen, and the government and extension of his empire were left to the care of his son Camby′ses.

B. C. 529.

11. In departing for his Scythian campaign, Cyrus had left his young cousin Dari′us in Persia, the satrapy of his father, Hystas′pes. The night after crossing the Arax′es, he dreamed that he saw Darius with wings on his shoulders, the one overshadowing Asia, and the other Europe. The time and the region were fruitful in dreams, and this had a remarkable fulfillment.

12. Reign of Cambyses. B. C. 529–522. Without the ability of his father, Cambyses inherited his warlike ambition, and soon proceeded to execute the plans of African conquest long cherished by Cyrus. He was a man of violent passions, which his unlimited power left without their just restraint, and many of his acts are more like those of a willful and ignorant child than of a reasonable man.

13. Egypt, now governed by Ama′sis, was the only part of the Babylonian dominion which had not yielded to Cyrus. Amasis had begun his reign as viceroy of Nebuchadnezzar, but during the decline of the empire he had become independent. Cambyses prepared for his Egyptian campaign by the conquest of Phœnicia and Cyprus, the two naval powers of western Asia. He then marched into Egypt with a great force of Persians and Greeks. Amasis had recently died, but his son Psammen′itus awaited the invader near the Pelusiac mouth of the Nile. A single battle decided the fate of Egypt. Psammenitus was defeated, and with his surviving followers shut himself up in Memphis. The siege was short, and at its termination all Egypt submitted to Cambyses, who assumed the full dignity of the Pharaohs as "Lord of the Upper and Lower Countries." The neighboring Libyans and the two Greek cities, Cyre′ne and Barca, also sent in their submission and offered gifts.

14. Cambyses now meditated three expeditions: one by sea against the great commercial empire of Carthage; one against the Ammonians of the desert; and a third against the long-lived Ethiopians,* whose country was reputed to be rich in gold. The first was abandoned, because the Phœnicians refused to serve against one of their own colonies. To the last-named people Cambyses sent an embassy of the Ich′thyoph′agi, who lived upon the borders of the Red Sea and understood their language. These were charged to carry presents to the Macrobian king, and assure him that the Persian monarch desired his friendship. The Ethiopian replied in plain terms: "Neither has the king of Persia sent you because he valued my

* The *Macro′bii*, so called by the Greeks because they were reputed to live 120 years or more, were a tribe of extraordinary strength and stature dwelling southward from Egypt. Some suppose them to have been ancestors of the Somauli, near Cape Guardafui, while others place them on the left bank of the Nile, in what is now Nubia. Their prisoners were said to be fettered with golden chains, because gold with them was more abundant and cheaper than iron. The bodies of their dead were inclosed in columns of glass or crystal.

alliance, nor do you speak the truth, for you are come as spies of my kingdom. Nor is he a just man; for if he were just, he would not desire any land but his own, nor would he reduce people to servitude who have done him no harm. However, give him this bow, and say these words to him: The king of the Ethiopians advises the king of the Persians, when his Persians can thus easily draw a bow of this size, then to make war upon the long-lived Ethiopians with a more numerous army; but until that time let him thank the gods, who have not inspired the sons of the Ethiopians with a desire of adding another land to their own."

15. When Cambyses heard the reply of the Ethiopian he was enraged, and without the usual military forethought to provide magazines of food, he instantly put his army in motion. Arriving at Thebes, he sent off a detachment of 50,000 men to destroy the temple and oracle of Amun * in the Oasis. This army was buried in the sands of the desert, without even beholding Ammo′nium. The main army of Cambyses was almost equally unfortunate. Before a fifth part of its journey was completed its provisions were spent. The beasts of burden were then eaten, and life was supported a little longer by herbs gathered from the soil. But when they reached the desert, both food and water failed, and the wretched men were reduced to eating certain of their comrades chosen by lot. By this time even the rage of the king was exhausted, and he consented to turn back; but he arrived at Memphis with a small portion of the host which had gone forth with him upon this ill-concerted enterprise.

16. He found the Memphians keeping a joyous festival in honor of the god Apis, who had just reäppeared. † The Persian was in ill humor from his recent disasters, and chose to believe that the Egyptians were rejoicing in his misfortunes. He ordered the new Apis to be brought into his presence. When the animal appeared, he drew his dagger and pierced it in the thigh; then, laughing loudly, exclaimed: "Ye blockheads, are there such gods as this, consisting of blood and flesh, and sensible of steel? This, truly, is a god worthy of the Egyptians!" He commanded his officers to scourge the priests and kill all the people who were found feasting. The Egyptians believed that Cambyses was instantly smitten with insanity as a punishment for this sacrilege. A reason may be found for his contemptuous treatment of Apis in that Persian hatred of idolatry which led him to shatter even the colossal images of the kings before many temples, and caused him to be regarded by ancient travelers as the great iconoclast of Egypt.

17. The mad career of Cambyses was near its end. Before leaving Persia, he had caused the secret assassination of his younger brother,

---

* See Book I, § 179.

† See Book I, § 175.

Bar′des, or, as the Greek historians called him, Smerdis, to whom their father had left the government of several provinces. He was about to leave Egypt, when a report arrived that Smerdis had revolted against him. The king now suspected that he had been betrayed by the too faithful messenger whom he had sent to kill his brother. The leader of the revolt, however, was neither of royal nor Persian blood. Goma′tes, a Magian, had been left by Cambyses steward of his palace at Susa. This man conspired with his order throughout the empire for a rising of the Medes against the Persians, and for the suppression of the reformed religion which the latter had brought in. Happening to resemble the younger son of Cyrus, he boldly announced to the people that Smerdis, brother of Cambyses, claimed their obedience. The story appeared credible, for the death of the prince had purposely been kept secret, so that nearly all the world, except Praxas′pes and his master, supposed him to be still alive.

18. Cambyses was already in Syria when he received a herald who demanded the obedience of the army to Smerdis, son of Cyrus. Caught in his own toils, the king lamented in vain that for foolish jealousy he had murdered the only man who could have exposed the fraud, and who might have been the best support and defender of his throne. Overcome with grief and shame, he sprang on horseback to begin his journey to Persia, but in the act his sword was unsheathed and entered his side, inflicting a mortal wound. He lingered three weeks, during which time he showed more reason than in all his life before. He confessed and bewailed the murder of his brother, and besought the Persian nobles to conquer the deceitful Magus and bestow the kingdom on one more worthy. He had neither son nor brother to succeed him. He had reigned seven years and five months.

19. Reign of the Pseudo-Smerdis. B. C. 522–521. As it is the just punishment of liars not to be believed even when they speak the truth, Cambyses' last confession was commonly supposed to be the most artful transaction of his life. The nobles, who had no knowledge of the death of Smerdis, believed that it was he indeed who was reigning at Susa, and that his brother had invented the story of the Magus to make his dethronement more certain. The pretended king lived in great seclusion, never quitting his palace, and permitting the various members of his household no intercourse with their relations. All orders were issued by his prime minister. He closed the Zoroastrian temples, restored the Magian priesthood, and ordered the discontinuance of the rebuilding at Jerusalem. (Read Ezra iv: 17–24.) These religious changes, such as no Achæmenian prince could have favored, began to awaken suspicions. Seven great princes of the royal race, having learned by a spy within the palace that the pretended monarch was only a Magian whom Cyrus had deprived of his ears, formed a league to dethrone him. Their bold attack was successful; the Magus was pursued into Media, and slain after a reign of eight months; and Dari′us Hystas′pes,* one of the seven conspirators, was eventually chosen to be king.

20. Reign of Darius I. B. C. 521–486. The first years of Darius were disturbed by rebellions which shook his throne to its foundation. No fewer than eleven satrapies were successively in revolt. The most important was that of Babylon, which for twenty months defied all the efforts of the great king to reduce it. At length Zop′yrus, son of one of the conspirators who had raised Darius to the throne, invented an ingenious though revolting scheme. He cut off his own nose and ears, applied the scourge to his shoulders until they were stained with blood, and having agreed with the king upon his further conduct, deserted to the Babylonians. To them he represented that the king had treated him with such cruel indignity that he burned for revenge. His wounds added plausibility to his story; he was received into the confidence of the rebels, and on the tenth day he was intrusted with the command of a sallying party which was to repulse an attack of the Persians.

Darius had been advised to send to the Semi′ramis Gate a body of those troops whom he could best spare: a thousand of them were cut to pieces. In a second sortie led by Zopyrus, two thousand Persians were slain; in a third, four thousand. This slaughter of seven thousand of his countrymen removed from the minds of the Babylonians all doubt of the truth of Zopyrus. The keys of the city were committed to his care, and the preparation for his treachery was now complete. During a concerted assault by the Persians, he opened the gates to Darius, who proceeded to take signal vengeance for the long defiance of his power. The reckless sacrifice of human life in this transaction shows how the habit of unlimited power had impaired the disposition of Darius, which was naturally merciful.

21. To guard against future disturbances, Darius now endeavored to give a more thorough and efficient organization to the great empire, which Cyrus and Cambyses had built up. He divided the whole territory into twenty satrapies, or provinces, and imposed upon each a tribute according to its wealth. The native kings whom Cyrus had left upon their thrones were all swept away, and a Persian governor, usually connected by blood or marriage with the great king, was placed over each province. Order within and safety from without were secured by standing armies of Medes or Persians, posted at convenient stations throughout the empire. Royal roads were constructed and a system of couriers arranged, by which the court received constant and swift intelligence of all that occurred in the provinces.

---

* See § 11. Also, Darius's own account of the imposture of the Magus, p. 87.

22. To prevent revolt, an elaborate system of checks was instituted, which left the satrap little power of independent action. In this earlier and stronger period of the consolidated empire, the satrap exercised only the civil government, the military being wielded by generals and commandants of garrisons, while, in Persia at least, the judicial power resided in judges appointed directly by the king. Beside these constitutional checks upon the satrap, there were in every province the "king's eyes" and the "king's ears," in the persons of royal secretaries attached to his court, whose duty it was to communicate secretly and constantly with the sovereign, and to keep him informed of every occurrence within their respective districts.

The slightest suspicion of revolt communicated to the king by these spies, was sufficient to bring an order for the death of the satrap. This order was addressed to his guards, who instantly executed it by hewing him down with their sabers. Each province, moreover, was liable every moment to a sudden visit from the king or his commissioner, who examined the satrap's accounts, heard the grievances of his subjects, and either deprived an unjust ruler of his place, or noted a wise, upright, and beneficent one for promotion to greater honor. The satrap, on a smaller scale, affected the same magnificence of living as the great king himself. Each had his "paradises," or pleasure-gardens, attached to numerous palaces. The satrap of Babylon had a daily revenue of nearly two bushels of coined silver; his stables contained nearly seventeen thousand steeds, and the income from four towns barely sufficed for the maintenance of his dogs.

23. The court of Susa surpassed all this display of wealth as much as the sun surpasses the planets. Fifteen thousand persons fed daily at the king's table. The royal journeys were of necessity confined to the wealthier portion of the empire, for in the poorer provinces such a visitation would have produced a famine. The king seldom appeared in public, and the approach to his presence was guarded by long lines of officers, each of whom had his appointed station, from the ministers of highest rank who stood in the audience-chamber, to the humblest attendant who waited at the gate.

24. The royal retinue included a numerous army, divided according to its nationalities into corps of 10,000 each. Of these the most celebrated were the Persian "Immortals," so called because their number was always exactly maintained. If an "Immortal" died, a well-trained member of a reserve-corps was ready to take his place. They were chosen from all the nation for their strength, stature, and fine personal appearance. Their armor was resplendent with silver and gold, and on the march or in battle they were always near the person of the king. The royal secretaries, or scribes, formed another important part of the retinue of the court. They

FIGURE OF A GOOD ANGEL—PERHAPS SRAOSHA.

wrote down every word that fell from the monarch's lips, especially his commands, which, once uttered, could never be recalled. (Esther viii : 8; Daniel vi : 8, 12, 15.)

RECAPITULATION.

Persia, having been for a century subject to the Medes, became independent under Cyrus, who also conquered Lydia and Babylonia, liberated the Jews, and founded a great empire reaching from Macedonia to India. He died in war with the Scythians, and the African expedition was left to Cambyses, his son. This king conquered Egypt, but his attempts against Ethiopia and the temple of Amun resulted only in disaster. His contempt for Egyptian idolatry was, according to the priests, punished with madness. A revolt in the name of Smerdis, whom he had murdered, placed a Magian upon the throne, and effected a reaction against the Persian reformation. The Magian was dethroned by Darius Hystaspes, who became the great organizer of the empire of Cyrus. Twenty satrapies took the place of the conquered kingdoms. A system of royal roads, couriers, and spies kept the whole dominion within the reach and beneath the eye of the king, who was surrounded by a multitude of officials and protected by a numerous army, the Persian Immortals having precedence in rank.

PERSIAN RELIGION.

25. The Persians held the reformed religion taught by Zo′roas′ter, a great law-giver and prophet, who appeared in the Medo-Bactrian kingdom long before* the birth of Cyrus. In every part of the East, the belief in One God, and the pure and simple worship which the human family had learned in its original home, had become overlaid by false mythologies and superstitious rites. The teachings of Zoroaster divided the Aryan family into its two Asiatic branches, which have ever since remained distinct. The Hindus retained their sensuous Nature-worship, of which In′dra (storm and thunder), Mith′ra (sunlight), Va′yu (wind), Agni (fire), Arama′ti (earth), and Soma (the intoxicating principle in liquids), were the chief objects. Zoroaster was led, either by reason or divine revelation, to a purer faith. He taught the supremacy of a Living Creator, a person, and not merely a power, whom he called Ahu′rô-Mazdâo, or Or′mazd. The name has been differently rendered, the Divine Much-Giving, the Creator of Life, or the Living Creator of All. Ormazd was believed to bestow not merely earthly good, but the most precious spiritual gifts—truth, devotion, the "good mind," and everlasting joy.

26. It has been seen that Cyrus regarded the God of the Hebrews as the object of his own worship (Ezra i: 1–4); and the Jewish prophets recognize the same identity in their description of Cyrus (Isaiah xlv: 1–5). Both nations had a profound hatred of idolatry. No image of any kind was seen in the Persian temples. Both believed in the ministration of angels. The throne of Ormazd was surrounded by six princes of light,

---

* He was probably contemporary with Abraham.

and beneath them were innumerable hosts of warriors and messengers, who passed to and fro defending the right and exterminating wrong. Chief of these was Serosh, or Srao′sha, "the serene, the strong," general-in-chief of the armies of Ormazd. He never slept, but continually guarded the earth with his drawn sword, especially after sunset, when demons had greatest power. At their death, he conducted the souls of the just to the presence of Ormazd, assisting them to pass the narrow bridge, from which the wicked fell into the abyss below.

27. A later development of the doctrines of Zoroaster was that dualism which divided the universe into a Kingdom of Light and a Kingdom of Darkness. The latter was ruled by Ahriman′, the source of all impurity and pain, assisted by his seven superior *devas*, or princes of evil; and the whole world was a battle-ground between the two armies of spirits, good and bad. If Ormazd created a paradise, Ahriman sent into it a venomous serpent. All poisonous plants, reptiles, and insects, all sickness, poverty, plague, war, famine, and earthquakes, all unbelief, witchcraft, and deadly sins were the work of Ahriman; and the world, which should have been "very good," was thus made the scene of suffering. Every object, living or inanimate, belonged to one or the other kingdom; and it was the duty of the servant of Ormazd to foster every thing holy and destroy every thing evil and impure. Agriculture was especially favored by Zoroaster, as promoting beautiful and healthful growths, and conquering blight, mildew, famine, and all destructive influences. It was the firm belief of all devout Zoroastrians that the Kingdom of Darkness would at length be overthrown, and the Kingdom of Light fill the universe.

28. Religion of the Medes. The Magianism of the Medes, at the time of their conquest by Cyrus, was a third form of Aryan belief, modified by contact with the barbarous Scythians. It was a peculiar form of Nature-worship, of which the four physical elements (so regarded), fire, air, earth, and water, were the objects. Fire, as the most energetic, was the chief. This system was wholly dependent on priest-craft; the Magi, or priestly caste, one of the seven Median tribes, were alone permitted to offer prayers and sacrifices. The Zoroastrians abhorred this doctrine as the work of devas, to supplant the pure principles which the race had received, in the beginning, from Ormazd himself. Darius in his inscriptions describes the usurpation of Goma′tes the Magian as the period when "the lie" prevailed. During the Magophonia, or yearly festival, which celebrated the suppression of this revolt, no Magian dared stir abroad for fear of death.

But with increased power and luxury came a change in the national religion. The showy cer′emonies of Magianism were better suited to the pomp of an Eastern court than the simple and spiritual worship of the Zoroastrians. A reconciliation was probably begun in the reign of Darius, and completed in that of Artaxerx′es Longim′anus. The Magians accepted the essential doctrines of Zoroaster, and were permitted, in turn, to introduce a part of their own symbolism and priestly rites into the national worship. They kept the sacred fire in the temples, fed it with costly woods, and never suffered it to be blown with human breath. At the rising of the sun they chanted sacred hymns to the Lord and Giver of Light. One of them waked the king each morning with the words, "Rise, sire, and think upon the duties which Ormazd has commanded you to perform." The whole religious ceremonial of the court was committed to their care. They alone possessed the sacred liturgies by which Ormazd was to be addressed; and it was believed that through them God revealed his will, either in the interpretation of dreams or by the motion of the stars.

29. Except that of the Hebrews, the Persian faith was the purest monotheism of the East. But its benefits were chiefly confined to the princely and noble caste, while with them its influence was neutralized in a great measure by the corruptions of the court. Polygamy was the fatal weakness of the Persian as of all other Eastern monarchies. The furious enmities of rival princesses filled the palace with discord, and often stained it with the darkest crimes. The hardy Persian mountaineers who had won the victories of Cyrus, whose simple but noble education taught them only "to ride the horse, to draw the bow, and to speak the truth," adopted the slavish manners of the races they had conquered, learned to dissemble and prostrate themselves before the face of a mortal, and became the splendid but often useless ornaments of an extravagant court.

30. Indian Conquests. The first great expedition of Darius was against the Punjab′, or Five Rivers of Western India. The imperial revenues were increased one-third by the acquisition of this rich gold-tract, and a lucrative commerce now sprang up between the banks of the Indus and the shores of the Persian Gulf.

31. Scythian Campaign. The next enterprise of Darius was against the Scythians of Central Europe, between the Don and the Danube. His design was to avenge the Scythian devastations of Media and Upper Asia a century before, and to terrify the barbarians into future good behavior by a display of his power; perhaps also to open a way into Greece by the conquest of the Thracian tribes. The whole army and navy of the empire, consisting of not less than 700,000 land soldiers and 600 ships, assembled at the Thracian Bosphorus, which they crossed by a bridge of boats constructed by Ionian engineers. The naval force was furnished wholly by the Greeks of the Ægean.

32. Sending his fleet through the Black Sea into the Danube, with orders to make a bridge of boats two days' journey from its mouth, Darius marched through Thrace, receiving or compelling the submission of its tribes, and adding their young men to his army. Arriving at the

Danube, he crossed the bridge and gave orders to the Greeks to remain and guard it sixty days; if in that time he did not return, they might conclude that he had gone to Media by another route. The details of the great king's operations north of the Danube are unknown to history. There were no great cities to take; the wandering Scythians destroyed their scanty harvests, stopped their wells, removed their families northward to places of security, and drew the invader after them into the depths of their forests or uninhabited deserts.

Unable to bring his enemy to battle, and seeing his army reduced to great distress for want of food and water, Darius was compelled to retreat by the way he had come. The sixty days were more than elapsed when a Scythian force, which had been watching his movements, hastened to the Danube by a shorter route, urging the Ionians, who were still on guard, to destroy the bridge and leave Darius to perish, like Cyrus, in the northern deserts. The Greeks of Asia might thus have gained their freedom without a blow; but the tyrants who commanded the fleet had interests of their own quite separate from those of their people. Histiæ'us of Mile'tus urged upon his fellow-despots that their power must fall with that of Darius, being sustained by him against the popular will. His arguments prevailed, and the great king, arriving in the darkness of midnight, closely pursued by the Scythians, was able to repass the river in safety.

33. Histiæus was rewarded by a grant of land on the river Stry'mon, including the town of Myrci'nus, for the site of a colony. With its fertile soil, ample forests, convenience for commerce, and neighboring mines of gold and silver, this new domain immediately attracted settlers and became an important maritime station. Its rapid growth, indeed, excited the fears of Darius, lest its owner might become too powerful for a vassal, and interpose a barrier between himself and the Greeks. He sent for Histiæus, whom he treated with every mark of respect, and pretending that he could not do without his valuable counsels, kept him constantly within reach at the court of Susa. Histiæus, resolved to break his golden chains at any cost, sent a singular epistle to his cousin, Aristag'oras, whom he had left as his lieutenant at Miletus, commanding him to stir up a revolt among the Asiatic Greeks.

34. The Ionian cities, extending ninety miles along the coast in an almost unbroken line of magnificent quays, warehouses, and dwellings, were so important to the empire, on account of the fleets which they could furnish, that they had been left in greater freedom than any other conquered territory. Instead of satraps, they were governed by their own magistrates — either a single tyrant in each city or a council of nobles, called an oligarchy — but always in the Persian interest. The European Greeks were stirred by a desire to liberate their brethren in Asia, and this afforded a constant pretext for a Persian war. The forces of Athens and Ere′tria were now added to those of Aristagoras, who had, moreover, strengthened his cause by abdicating his tyranny, and aiding the other cities to assume the same free and popular government which he established at Miletus. The tyrants were every-where expelled, and the people sprang to arms.

From Eph′esus the united forces marched up the valley of the Cay′ster, and swiftly crossing the mountains, took Sardis by surprise. The city was easily captured, but Ar′apher′nes, the satrap, retired with a strong garrison to the castle, which, from its inaccessible rock, defied assault. A spark falling on the light reeds which formed the roofs of Sardis set fire to the town, and the invaders were compelled to retire. They were pursued and defeated with great loss by Artaphernes, in the battle of Ephesus. The Athenians now withdrew, but the war went on with undiminished spirit. The inhabitants of Cyprus, the Carians and Caunians of the south-western corner of the peninsula made common cause with the Ionian, Æo′lian, and Hellespontine Greeks; Byzantium was taken, and the whole coast from the Thracian Bosphorus to the Gulf of Issus was for the moment free from Persian dominion. The brave Carians, though twice defeated with great loss, were victorious in a third battle, where a son-in-law of Darius was slain. But the power of the great king was at length triumphant. The fleet of the Ionians was defeated near Miletus, and the vengeance of the Persians was concentrated on this devoted city, the leader of the rebellion. After a long blockade, it was taken by storm in the sixth year of the revolt.

35. The honor of the great king was now engaged to the punishment of those European Greeks who had intermeddled between himself and his subjects. It was the first time that the Athenians had come to the notice of Darius. He inquired who and what sort of men they were, and being told, he seized his bow and shot an arrow into the air, crying aloud, "O Supreme God, grant that I may avenge myself on the Athenians!" From that time a servant was instructed to say to him three times every day as he sat at table, "Sire, remember the Athenians!"

36. In the spring of 492 B. C., a great force was intrusted for this purpose to Mardo′nius, son-in-law of Darius. Its immediate design failed, for the fleet was shattered at Mount Athos, and the army nearly destroyed by the Brygians, a Thracian tribe. Thasos, however, was captured, and Macedonia was subjected to Persia.

37. B. C. 490. A second great expedition, two years later, was conducted by Datis, accompanied by Artaphernes, son of the former satrap of that name, and nephew of the king. Having passed the sea, they fell first upon Eretria, which was taken by treachery, its temples burnt, and its inhabitants bound in chains for transportation to Asia. The first decisive trial of strength between Persia and the western Greeks took place at Mar'athon, in Attica. The Persians numbered 100,000 men, the Greeks but little more than 10,000. The Medo-Persian troops had hitherto been considered invincible; but that magnificent soldiery was now, to a certain extent, replaced by unwilling conscripts from conquered tribes, who marched, dug, or fought under the lash of overseers. Miltiades, who, as prince of the Chersonesus, had served in the Persian armies, well knew this element of weakness, and it was with just confidence in the superiority of his free Athenians that he gave orders for the battle.

38. In the center, where the native Persians fought, they gained the advantage, and pursued the Athenians up one or two of the valleys which surround the base of Mount Kotro'ni; but, at the same time, both the right and left of the Asiatics were defeated by the Greeks, who, instead of pursuing, united their forces on the field to the relief of their center, and thus gained a complete victory. The Persians fled to their ships, now fiercely followed by the Greeks, and a still more furious contest ensued at the water's edge. The Athenians sought to fire the fleet, but seven galleys only were destroyed; the rest, with the shattered remains of the army, made good their escape.

39. The Persian commander did not lose his spirit in defeat. Encouraged by a preconcerted signal of the partisans of Hip'pias, he sailed immediately around Attica, hoping to surprise Athens in the absence of its defenders. But Miltiades, too, had seen the glittering shield raised upon a mountaintop, and guessed its meaning. Leaving Aristi'des with one tribe to guard the spoils of the battle-field, he led his army by a rapid night-march across the country to Athens. When Datis, the next morning, having doubled the point of Su'nium, sailed up the Athenian harbor, he saw upon the heights above the city the same victorious troops from whom his men had fled the evening before. He made no attempt to land, but sailed away with his Eretrian prisoners to the coasts of Asia.

Silver Daric of Darius I, enlarged one-half.

40. Rather angered than dismayed by these failures, Darius prepared to lead in person a still greater expedition against the Greeks. But a revolt in Egypt first diverted his attention, and his death, in the following year, gave the free states of Europe time to complete their preparations for defense. B. C. 486.

41. Many works and trophies of Darius remain in various parts of his empire. He was the first king who coined money in Persia. The golden and silver *darics* circulated not only throughout the empire but in Greece. The most interesting memorials are the two records in his own words of the events of his reign, engraven upon his tomb at Nakshi-rus′tam, and upon the great rock-tablet of Behistûn′. The latter is of the greater length; it consists of five columns, each containing from sixteen to nineteen paragraphs, written in three languages, Persian, Babylonian, and Scythic, or Tartar. These trilingual inscriptions, embracing the three great families of human speech, Aryan, Semitic, and Turanian, almost justify the claim made by Darius to universal empire.

NOTE.—A specimen of the style of the great king may be of interest to the scholar. It should be stated that the Behistun cliff forms part of the Zagros mountain range between Babylon and Ecbatana. This great natural table of stone, which seems to have been expressly fitted for enduring records, is 1,700 feet in perpendicular height, and bears four sets of sculptures, one of which is ascribed to Semiramis. The inscription of Darius is most important. It has been deciphered within a few years, with wonderful learning, industry, and patience, by Col. Sir Henry Rawlinson, of the British army. For many years after its existence was known, it was considered inaccessible, as it was 300 feet from the foot of the perpendicular wall, and it was necessary for the explorer to be drawn up with ropes by a windlass placed at the summit. Even when a copy was thus made, with great risk and inconvenience, the work was only begun, for the arrow-headed (cuneiform) characters in which the Persian language was written were as yet but partly understood. These difficulties have now been surmounted, and the common student can read the words of "Darius the King." The whole inscription, in Persian and English, may be found in Rawlinson's Herodotus, Vol. II, Appendix. A few of the shorter paragraphs are here subjoined:

I. 8. "Says Darius the King: Within these countries the man who was good, him have I right well cherished. Whoever was evil, him have I utterly rooted out. By the grace of Ormazd, these are the countries by which my laws have been observed." ......

I. 11. "Says Darius the King: Afterward there was a man, a Magian, named Gomates...... He thus lied to the state: 'I am Bardes, the son of Cyrus, the brother of Cambyses.' Then the whole state became rebellious...... He seized the empire. Afterward Cambyses, unable to endure, died."

I. 13. "Says Darius the King: There was not a man, neither Persian nor Median, nor any one of our family, who would dispossess that Gomates the Magian of the crown. The state feared him exceedingly. He slew many people who had known the old Bardes; for that reason he slew them, 'lest they should recognize me that I am not Bardes, the son of Cyrus.' No one dared say any thing concerning Gomates the Magian until I arrived. Then I prayed to Ormazd; Ormazd brought help to me. On the 10th day of the month Bagayadish, then it was, with the help of my faithful men, that I slew that Gomates the Magian and those who were his chief followers. The fort named Sictachotès, in the district of Media called Nisæa, there I slew him. I dispossessed him of the empire; I became king. Ormazd granted me the scepter."

I. 14. "Says Darius the King: The empire which had been taken away from our family, that I recovered. I established it in its place. As it was before, so I made it. The temples which Gomates the Magian had destroyed I rebuilt. The sacred offices of the state, both the religious chants and the worship, I restored to the people, which Gomates the Magian had deprived them of...... By the grace of Ormazd I did this."

RECAPITULATION.

Persian monotheism differed essentially from the Nature-worship of the Hindus and the element-worship of the Medes; but under Darius and his successors the Magi gained exclusive control of religious rites, and luxury destroyed the manly virtues of the people. Darius conquered western India, and invaded European Scythia, but without result. His detention of Histiæus led to a six years' revolt of all the Greeks of Asia Minor, aided by the Athenians and Eretrians. He failed in his first retaliatory enterprise against the European Greeks; and, in the second, the great decisive battle of Marathon ended in the overthrow of the Persians. The death of Darius postponed the Grecian wars.

REIGN OF XERXES I.

42. Xer′xes, the Ahasue′rus of the Book of Esther, succeeded to his father's dominions, instead of Artabaza′nes, his elder brother, who had been born before Darius's accession to the throne. His first care was the crushing of the Egyptian revolt. This was accomplished in the second year of his reign; a severer servitude was imposed, and his brother Achae′menes remained as his viceroy in the Valley of the Nile. The Babylonians attempted an insurrection, but dearly paid for their rashness with all the treasure of their temples.

B. C. 486–465.

43. In the third year of his reign,* the king convened his satraps and generals, "the nobles and princes of the provinces," at Susa, to deliberate concerning the invasion of Greece. In their presence he detailed the motives of ambition and revenge which urged him against a people which had dared to defy his power, and declared his intention to march through Europe, from one end to the other, and make of all its lands one country. He believed that, the Greeks once conquered, no people in the world could stand against him, and thus the sun would no longer shine upon any land beyond his own. He concluded by commanding each general to make ready his forces, assuring them that he who appeared upon the appointed day with the most effective troop should receive the rewards most precious to every Persian.

44. During four years all Asia, from the docks of Sidon and Tyre to the banks of the Indus, rang with notes of preparation. All races and tribes of the vast empire sent men and material. The maritime nations furnished the largest fleet which the Mediterranean had yet seen. The Phœnicians and Egyptians were charged with the construction of a double bridge of boats over the Hellespont, from Aby′dus, on the Asiatic, to a point between Sestus and Mad′ytus, on the European side of the strait.

* See Esther i: 1–4.

After this work was completed, a violent storm broke it to pieces and threw the shattered fragments upon the shore. The king, unused to being thwarted in any of his designs, caused the engineers to be beheaded, the sea scourged, and a pair of fetters, as a hint of the required submission, thrown into the offending waters. A new bridge, or, rather, pair of bridges, was now formed with still greater care. Two lines of ships, anchored at stem and stern, were united each by six great cables, which reached from shore to shore. They supported a platform of wood, which was covered with earth and protected by a balustrade.

45. Another body of men, working under the lash of Persian overseers, were employed three years in cutting a canal from the Strymonic to the Singitic Gulf, to sever Mount Athos from the mainland, and thus enable the fleet to avoid the strong and shifting currents and high seas which prevailed around the peninsula. Immense stores of provisions, collected from all parts of the empire, were deposited at suitable intervals along the line of march.

46. The rendezvous of the troops was at Crital′la, in Cappadocia, whence they were moved forward to Sardis. In the autumn of 481 B. C., Xerxes arrived at the latter capital, and early in the following spring set his vast army in motion toward the Hellespont. Near the person of the king were the ten thousand Immortals, whose entire armor glittered with gold. He was preceded by the Chariot of the Sun, in which no mortal dared seat himself, drawn by eight snow-white horses.

47. At Abydus the king surveyed, from his throne of white marble elevated upon a hill, the countless multitudes which thronged the plain, and the myriads of sails that studded the Hellespont. The momentary pride that swelled his breast, with the consciousness that he was supreme lord of all that host, gave way to a more worthy emotion as he reflected that the whole life of those myriads upon earth was almost as transitory as their passage of the bridge, which lay before him, connecting the known with the unknown continent. Early the next morning perfumes were burnt and myrtle boughs strewn upon the bridges, while the army awaited in silence the rising of the sun. When it appeared, Xerxes, with head uncovered—excelling, not only in rank, but in strength, stature, and beauty, all his host—poured a libation into the sea, praying, meanwhile, with his face toward the rising orb, that no disaster might befall his arms until he had penetrated to the uttermost boundaries of Europe. Having prayed, he cast the golden cup and a Persian cimeter into the sea, and gave a signal for the army to march.

48. So numerous was the host that, marching day and night without intermission, and goaded by the whip, it occupied seven days in crossing the straits by the two bridges. On the Thracian plain of Doris′cus, near the sea, the army was drawn up for a final review. The land force consisted of forty-six nations. According to Herodotus, who gathered his information by most careful inquiry of persons who were present, the foot soldiers numbered 1,700,000; the war-chariots and camels, 20,000; the horse, 80,000. The fleet consisted of 1,207 triremes, and 3,000 smaller vessels, carrying in all 517,610 men. Beside this actual fighting force, we must suppose an equal number of slaves, attendants, and the crews of provision ships, making a total of more than five millions of human beings.

49. Several rivers were dried in giving drink to this multitude, while their food, even the scanty allowance of Asiatic slaves, amounted to 662,000 bushels of flour each day; but the excellent commissariat of Xerxes, which had been organizing for seven years, was not at fault. On the march from Doriscus toward Greece, the king, still within his own empire, received further accessions from Thracian, Macedonian, and other European tribes, so that his fighting force at Thermop′ylae amounted to 2,640,000 men. Various cities along the route had been commanded to furnish each one meal for the army; and although they had spent years in preparation, some were ruined by the expense.*

50. Meanwhile the Greeks had not been idle. The ten years since the battle of Marathon had been employed in active drilling of forces, by sea and land. Each state furnished its quota; and though but a handful compared with the myriads of invaders, they had the strength, derived from patriotism and high discipline, to oppose the mere material mass and weight of the Persian host. It was mind against matter.

51. Abandoning the defense of Thessaly, which was open by too many

B. C. 480.

avenues to the Persians, the little army of Leon′idas, king of Sparta, had made a resolute stand at Thermopylæ, a narrow pass between Mount Œta and the sea. The whole force amounted to only 6,000 men, of whom but 300 were Spartans. Xerxes waited several days upon the Trachinian plain, expecting that this little band would melt away from mere terror at the sight of his vast numbers. At length he sent the Median cavalry to force a passage. They were repulsed with loss. The Immortals made the same attempt with no better success. At this point, Ephial′tes, a Malian, offered for a large reward to show the invaders a mountain-path by which they could reach the rear of the Spartan camp. The Phocian guards of this path were overpowered. Leonidas learned that he was betrayed, and declaring that he and his Spartans must remain at their post, dismissed all the rest of his army except the Thespians and Thebans. Then, before the body of Persians who were crossing the mountain, under lead of the traitor, could attack him from behind, he threw himself upon the enemy in front, resolving to exact as dear a ven-

* One of these repasts cost half a million of dollars.

geance as possible. Many of the Persian host fell beneath the Spartan swords, many were trodden to death by their own multitudes, and many were forced into the sea. Leonidas soon fell, and the contest for his body inspired his men with new fury. Having recovered it, they placed their backs against a wall of stone and fought until every man was slain.

52. During the same days several battles were fought at sea between the Greek and Persian fleets. No decisive advantage was gained by either side, but the result was most disheartening to the Persians, who had been most confident of success. The elements, too, had neither been scourged nor scolded into good behavior; a terrible hurricane raged three days and nights upon the coast of Magnesia, tearing the ships from their moorings and dashing them against the cliffs. At least four hundred ships of war were thus destroyed, beside a countless number of transports with their stores and treasures. Another squadron of two hundred vessels, which had been sent around Eubœa to cut off the retreat of the Greeks, perished, in a sudden tempest, upon the rocks. The Grecian commanders were unable to profit by these advantages, for the defeat at Thermopylæ compelled them to withdraw from Artemis′ium to provide for the safety of Attica and the Peloponnesus.

53. By the death of the Spartan three hundred, the gates of Greece were thrown open, and the hosts of Asia poured through, wasting the country with fire and sword. At Pano′peus a detachment was sent to plunder the temple of Apollo at Delphi, while Xerxes led his main army through Bœo′tia. On the march he received the submission of all the people except the Platæans and Thespians, who, rather than yield to an invader, abandoned their cities to be burnt. Before his arrival at Athens, the chief object of his revenge, the king heard of the total defeat of his Delphian expedition. According to Greek tradition, no mortal hand turned back the invaders, but Apollo himself hurled down great rocks and crags upon their heads, in the dark ravines of Parnassus, and thus defended his sanctuary.

54. Athens was a deserted city. All the fighting men were with the fleet, while women, children, and infirm persons had been removed to Salamis, Ægi′na, or Trœze′ne. The conqueror stormed the citadel, plundered and burnt the temples, and sent word to Susa that Athens had shared the fate of Sardis. B. C. 480.

55. Xerxes now resolved upon a decisive naval battle in the Saronic Gulf. The Grecian fleet had assembled off Salamis, to the number of 378 vessels, while the Persians numbered 1,200. A throne was erected on the mainland, upon the slope of Mount Ægaleos, from which the great king beheld the struggle which was to end his dreams of conquest. The Persian fleet occupied the channel between Salamis and the coast of Attica. Their vast numbers, crowded into so narrow a space, were a fatal disadvantage to themselves, for they could only come near the Greeks by small detachments; while the latter, more accustomed to those waters, drove their brazen-pointed prows into the sides of the Persians, advancing and retiring with wonderful dexterity and surety of aim. Feeling the eye of their king upon them, the Persians fought with desperate bravery. The battle lasted all day; when night fell, Xerxes saw his forces scattered or destroyed, and instead of renewing the battle, resolved to seek his own safety in retreat.

56. Mardonius engaged to complete the conquest of Greece with 300,000 men. The fleet was ordered to the Hellespont, and the king with the remainder of his forces set out for home. His magazines had been exhausted, and during this forced retreat many died of hunger. Forty-five days after his departure from Attica he arrived at the Hellespont, and finding his second bridge of boats destroyed, returned to Asia by ship. He entered Sardis at the end of the year 480, humbled and depressed, only eight months from the time when he left it full of vain hopes of subduing the western world.

57. The operations of Mardonius will be more fully detailed in the History of Greece;* a mere outline is here presented. Wintering in Thessaly, he sought by magnificent promises to detach the Athenians from the Greek interests. Diplomacy failing, his army was at once poured into Attica, filling Athens, whose inhabitants had taken refuge again at Salamis. He destroyed the beautiful city by fire, completing the destruction which Xerxes had begun. Then finding that the Greeks were concentrating their forces at the Isthmus, he retired into Bœotia, where, in September, 479, the great battle of Platæ′a was fought. Mardonius was slain and his forces routed with terrible carnage. The last remnant of the Persian fleet was similarly routed at Myc′ale, on the opposite side of the Ægean, and the deliverance of Europe was complete. No Persian army henceforth trod the soil of European Greece, and for twelve years no Persian sail appeared in the Ægean.

58. Having spent his own best strength and that of his empire in this disastrous war, Xerxes made no further effort for military glory, but gave himself up to luxurious indolence. The highest rewards were offered to him who could invent a new pleasure. His subjects followed the example of their king; the empire was weakened by licentiousness and distracted by violence. It was only a fitting close to such a reign, when, at the end of twenty years, Xerxes was murdered by Artaba′nus, the captain of his guard, and Aspami′tres, his chamberlain.

59. Reign of Artaxerxes I. B. C. 465–425. The assassins placed upon the throne the youngest son of their victim, Artaxerxes Longimanus,

---

* See pp. 142–144.

or the Long-Handed. The eldest son, Darius, was executed on a false charge of having murdered his father. The second, Hystas′pes, claimed the crown, but was defeated and slain in battle. The crimes of the real assassins were proved against them, and they were punished with death. Artaxerxes enjoyed an undisputed reign of forty years, during which the power of the empire declined, notwithstanding his beneficent efforts to promote the interests of his people.

60. Egyptian Revolt. In the early part of his reign Egypt revolted under I′narus, son of Psammet′ichus, who was aided by the Athenians. Achaemenes, brother of the king, was sent with a great army to punish the rebellion; but he was defeated and slain by the hand of Inarus in the battle of Papre′mis, and a vast number of Persians perished. The remainder of the army were shut up in the White Castle at Memphis, and suffered a siege of three years. A new force, led by Megaby′zus, was more successful: Memphis was relieved, Inarus taken, and the Athenian fleet destroyed. Amyrtæ′us, the ally of Inarus, held out six years longer in the marshes of the Delta, until, by the intervention of Athens, peace was made. The Persians were defeated with great loss off Salamis, in Cyprus, and consented to very humiliating terms. They engaged not to visit with fleet or army the western shores of Asia Minor, but to respect the independence of the Asiatic Greeks. Even the leader of the revolt was punished only by the loss of his principality.

B. C. 460.

B. C. 455.

61. Contrary to the solemn agreement of Megabyzus, Inarus, after five years at the Persian court, was given up, with fifty Athenian companions, to the vengeance of the queen-mother, and suffered a barbarous death for having slain Achaemenes. Disgusted by this violation of his honor, Megabyzus stirred up a revolt in his province of Syria. He was the greatest general in the empire, and the success of his operations against the forces sent to subdue him, so alarmed his master that he was permitted to dictate his own terms of peace. The intercessions of his wife, Am′ytis, sister of the king, aided much in his reconciliation; but the example was ruinous to the strict organization of the provinces which Darius had introduced. The tendencies to decay now acted with greater and greater rapidity.

62. In the seventh year of Artaxerxes' reign, a new migration of Jews was led from Babylon by Ezra, a man of priestly lineage and high in favor at the Persian court. Laden with contributions from the Jews of Babylonia, he arrived in Jerusalem with great treasures for the completion of the temple, and for the reëstablishment of civil government throughout the country. He found that the people had allied themselves with the neighboring tribes by marriage, and insisted on the immediate dismissal of all heathen members from Jewish households.

63. The defeat of the Persians at Cyprus, 449 B. C., operated to a certain degree in favor of the Jews; for all the maritime ports of the empire having been ceded, the natural fortress of Zion, commanding the roads between Egypt and the capital, became of great importance. Hitherto the Persian monarchs had forbidden Jerusalem to be fortified, but in the twentieth year of Artaxerxes' reign, Nehemi'ah, the Jewish cup-bearer of the great king, received a commission to rebuild its walls. He moved with great celerity and secrecy, for the neighboring Samaritans, Ammonites, and Arabians, no longer awed, as formerly, by a decree of the empire, violently opposed the work. Laboring by night, with tools in one hand and weapons in the other, the Jews of every rank gave themselves so zealously to the task, that in fifty-two days Jerusalem was inclosed by walls and towers strong enough to defy her foes. (Nehemiah i–v : 16.)

Meanwhile Ezra, relieved from the civil command, labored at his great work, the collection and editing of the Sacred Books. During the captivity many writings had been lost, among them the Book of Jasher, that of "The Wars of the Lord," the writings of Gad and Iddo, the prophets, and the works of Solomon on Natural History. The sacred books which remained were arranged in three great divisions: the Law, the Prophets, and the Hagiographa; the latter including Job, the Psalms, and Proverbs, Ecclesiastes, Canticles, Ruth, Daniel, and the Chronicles. The Books of Malachi, Ezra, Nehemiah, and Esther were afterward added, and the canon closed.

64. On the departure of Nehemiah the old disorders returned. Ezra died; the high priest allied himself with the deadliest enemy of the Jewish faith, Tobi'ah the Ammonite, to whom he gave lodgings in the temple. The Sabbath was broken; Tyrian traders sold their merchandise in the gates of Jerusalem on the Holy Day. Nehemiah returned with the power of a satrap, and with his usual skill reformed these abuses. He expelled Manasseh, who had now become high priest, because he had married a daughter of Sanballat the Horonite. The pagan father-in-law hereupon built a rival temple on the summit of Mount Gerizim, of which Manasseh became high priest. The bitter hatred arising from this schism continued for centuries, and did not cease even with the destruction of the temple at Jerusalem, A. D. 70. "The Jews had no dealings with the Samaritans." From the time of the division there was no more intermingling of pagan elements in the religion and customs of Judæa. The Hebrews became not only the most rigidly monotheistic, but, in spite of their later wanderings, the most nearly isolated of all the nations.

65. XERXES II. Artaxerxes died B. C. 425, and was succeeded by his son, Xerxes II. After a reign of only forty-five days, the young king was assassinated by his half-brother, Sogdia'nus; and the funeral train of his father was overtaken, on its way to the royal tombs at Persepolis, by his own.

66. SOGDIANUS. B. C. 425, 424. The murderer enjoyed the fruits of his crime but little more than half a year. Another half-brother, O′chus, revolted with the satraps of Egypt and Armenia and the general of the royal cavalry. Sogdianus was deposed and put to death.

67. DARIUS II. B. C. 424–405. Ochus, ascending the throne, took the name of Darius, to which the Greeks added the contemptuous surname No′thus. This prince spent the nineteen years of his reign under the control of his wife, Parysa′tis, who surpassed her mother, Amas′tris, in wickedness and cruelty. The empire, meanwhile, was shaken by continual revolts, and the means that were taken to quell them compromised instead of confirming the integrity of the nation. Promises were made which were never intended to be kept, for the purpose of leading on the rebellious satraps to their destruction; and the tools of these falsehoods, instead of resenting, like Megabyzus, the loss of their honor, gladly accepted the spoils of their victims. The precautions of Darius I were disregarded; civil and military powers were combined in the same person, and two or three countries were often united under the rule of one satrap. These great governments, descending often from father to son, became more like independent kingdoms than provinces of the empire.

68. The Medes, after more than a century of submission to Persian rule, attempted to free themselves, B. C. 408, but were defeated. The Egyptians, being more distant, were more successful. Always the most discontented of the Persian provinces, their opposition was even more a matter of religion than of patriotism, and was constantly fomented by the priests. Under two successive dynasties of native kings, they were now able to maintain their independence nearly sixty years. B. C. 405–346.

69. While the empire was undergoing these losses, it gained a great advantage in the recovery of the Greek cities of Asia Minor. The Athenians and Spartans had been wasting their forces against each other in the Peloponnesian war (B. C. 431–404), which, more than any regard to their engagements, had interrupted their hostile attempts against Persia. The power of Athens was now broken by disasters in Sicily; and the Lydian satrap, Tissapher′nes, seized the occasion to cultivate the alliance of Sparta, and aid the Athenian colonies, Lesbos, Chios, and Erythræ, in their intended revolt. Pharnaba′zus, satrap of the Hellespontine provinces, pursued the same course; and through the rivalry of the two Greek states, their ancient enemy gained undisputed possession of "all Asia."

Cyrus, the younger son of the king, becoming satrap of Phrygia, Lydia, and Cappadocia, used his wealth and power without reserve to aid the Lacedemonians and humble the Athenians. He declared to Lysan′der, the Spartan admiral, that if it were needful he would sell his very throne, or coin it into money, to meet the expenses of the war. This liberality had another cause than friendship. The Spartans were esteemed the best soldiers in the world, and Cyrus was preparing for a bold and difficult movement in which he wanted their assistance.

70. This young prince had been "born in the purple," while his elder brother had been born before their father's accession to the throne. With this pretext, which had availed in the case of Xerxes I, his mother, Parysatis, whose favorite he was, strove in vain to persuade Darius to name him his successor in the empire. Cyrus assumed royal state in his province; and though naturally haughty and cruel, he managed to gain the affection of his courtiers by his amiable manners, while his more brilliant qualities commanded their admiration. Darius, alarmed by his son's unbounded ambition, recalled him to the capital, which he reached only in time to witness his father's death and his brother's accession to the throne.

71. B. C. 405–359. ARTAXERXES II was called Mnemon, for his wonderful memory. His first royal act was to cast his brother into prison, upon a report, probably too well founded, that he was plotting against the life of the king. Cyrus was condemned to die, but his mother, who had instigated the plot, plead for him with such effect, that Artaxerxes not only spared his life, but sent him back to his satrapy. If Cyrus was ambitious and rebellious before, he had now the additional motive of revenge urging him to dethrone his brother and reign in his stead. He raised an army of Greek mercenaries, for a pretended expedition against the robbers of Pisid'ia, and set out from Sardis in the spring of 401.

Artaxerxes was informed of his movements by Tissaphernes, and was well prepared to meet him. The Greeks learned the real object of their march too late to draw back. The army passed through Phrygia and Cilicia, entered Syria by the mountain-passes near Issus, crossed the Euphrates at Thap'sacus, and advanced to the plain of Cunax'a, about fifty-seven miles from Babylon. Here he encountered a royal army at least four times as numerous as his own. The Greeks sustained their ancient renown by utterly routing the Asiatics who were opposed to them; but Cyrus, rashly penetrating to the Persian center, where his brother commanded in person, was stricken down by one of the royal guard. He had already wounded the king. Artaxerxes commanded his head and traitorous right hand to be cut off, and his fate ended the battle.

B. C. 401.

72. The Grecian auxiliaries who had been entrapped into the war by Cyrus now found themselves in a perilous position. Their Persian allies were scattered; they were in the heart of an unknown and hostile country, two thousand miles from home, and surrounded by the victorious army of Artaxerxes. The wily Tissaphernes, who had been rewarded with the dominions of Cyrus, detained them nearly a month by false pretenses of negotiation; and having led them as far as the head-waters of the Tigris, gained possession of all their officers, whom he caused to be put to death.

At this crisis, the Athenian Xen′ophon, who had accompanied the army of Cyrus, though not as a soldier, called together the principal Greeks at midnight, and urged the election of new officers who should lead them back to their native land. The suggestion was adopted; five generals were chosen, of whom Xenophon was one, and by break of day the army had been mustered for its homeward march.

Here began the Retreat of the Ten Thousand, celebrated in the annals of war as, perhaps, the most remarkable instance of an enterprise conducted against prodigious obstacles, with perfect coolness, valor, and success. Tissaphernes with his army hung upon their rear, hostile barbarians were in front, and to the fatigues of the march were added the perils of frequent battles. Their course lay over the table-lands of Armenia, where many perished in the freezing north winds, or were blinded by the unusual glare of snow. The survivors pressed on with indomitable spirit, until, ascending a mountain south of Treb′izond, they beheld, far away to the north-west, the dark waters of the Euxine. Their greatest perils were now over; a joyous cry, "The sea! the sea!" arose from the front rank and was quickly caught up by those behind. Officers and soldiers embraced each other with tears of joy; and all united to erect upon this happy lookout a monument of the trophies collected during their wearisome journey.

73. By their part in the rebellion of Cyrus, however involuntary, the Spartans had given unpardonable offense to Artaxerxes, and they resolved to be the first movers in the war which must ensue. Securing the services of the Ten Thousand, they attacked the Persians in Asia Minor with a success which promised a speedy end to their dominion. But Persia had grown wiser since the days of Xerxes, and fought the Greeks not so much with her unwieldy masses of troops as with subtle intrigue. By means of skillful emissaries well supplied with gold, she brought about a league between the secondary states of Greece — Argos, Corinth, Athens, and Thebes — which at once overbalanced the power of Sparta. Persian ships had part in the battle of Cnidus, by which the confederates gained the dominion of the sea. B. C. 394. Sparta was reduced to accepting the humiliating peace of Antal′cidas, by which the Asiatic Greeks were left under the control of Persia, and the great king gained an authoritative voice in all quarrels between the Grecian states. B. C. 387.

74. Artaxerxes was haunted by the desire to restore the empire to its greatest extent under Darius Hystaspes. He reöccupied Samos, which he intended as a stepping-stone to the rest of the Greek islands; and sent a great expedition into Egypt under the joint command of Iphic′rates, an Athenian, and Pharnabazus, a Persian general. This enterprise failed, partly through the jealousies of the two commanders; and the failure hastened a revolt in the western satrapies, which came near to overturn the empire. Egypt now retaliated, and attempted to revive her ancient glories by the conquest of Syria and Phœnicia. But these movements were defeated by management and gold, and Artaxerxes left his dominion with nearly the same boundaries which it had at the beginning of his reign.

75. Reign of Artaxerxes III. B. C. 359–338. The death of Artaxerxes II was followed by the usual crimes and atrocities which attended a change upon the Persian throne. His youngest son, Ochus, seized the crown after the murder of his eldest and the suicide of his second brother. He assumed the name of Artaxerxes III, and by his energy and spirit did much to retrieve the failing prosperity of the empire. He did not, however, abate the inherent sources of its weakness in the corruptions of the court. Family affection had been replaced by jealousy and hatred. The first act of Ochus was the extermination of his own royal race, in order that no rival might remain to dispute his throne. His more ambitious enterprises were delayed by a revolt of Artabazus in Asia Minor, which was abetted by Athens and Thebes. The defeated satrap fled to Philip of Macedon, whose ready protection and Ochus's retaliatory measures led to the most important results. These will be detailed in Book IV.

76. About B. C. 351, Ochus was ready to attempt the subjugation of Egypt. He was defeated in his first campaign, and retired into Persia to recruit his forces. This retreat was the signal for innumerable revolts. Phœnicia placed herself under the independent government of the king of Sidon; Cyprus set up nine native sovereigns; in Asia Minor a dozen separate kingdoms were asserted, if not established. But the spirit of Artaxerxes III was equal to the occasion. He raised a second armament, hired ten thousand Greek mercenaries, and proceeded in person to war against Phœnicia and Egypt. Sidon was taken and Phœnicia subdued. Mentor the Rhodian, who, in the service of the king of Egypt was aiding the Sidonians, went over to the Persians with four thousand Greeks. Egypt was then invaded with more success. Nectanebo was defeated and expelled, and his country again reduced to a Persian satrapy.

77. Most of the later victories of Artaxerxes were due to the valor of his Greek auxiliaries, or to the treachery or incapacity of his opponents. After the reëstablishment of his government, he abandoned himself to the pleasures of his palace, while the control of affairs rested exclusively with Bago′as, his minister, and Mentor, his general. The people were only reminded from time to time of his existence by some unusually bloody mandate. Whatever hope might have been inspired by his really great abilities, was disappointed at once by his unscrupulous violence and indolent self-indulgence. He died of poison by the hand of Bagoas, B. C. 338.

78. Arses. B. C. 338–336. The perfidious minister destroyed not merely the king himself, but all the royal princes except Ar′ses, the youngest, whom he placed upon the throne, believing that, as a mere boy, he would be subservient to his control. After two years he was alarmed by some signs of independent character in his pupil, and added Arses to the number of his victims. He now conferred the sovereignty upon Darius Codoman′nus, a grandson of Darius II, whom he regarded as a friend, but who commenced his reign by an act of summary justice, in the execution of the wretch to whom he owed his crown. B. C. 336.

79. Reign of Darius III. B. C. 336–331. As has often happened in the world's history, one of the best of the Persian kings had to bear the results of the tyrannies of his predecessors. Darius was not more distinguished for his personal beauty than for the uprightness and benevolence of his character; and as satrap of Armenia, before his accession to the throne, he had won great applause both for his bravery as a soldier and his skill as a general. But the Greeks, whose reasons for hostility against the Persians had been two hundred years accumulating, had now, at last, a leader more ambitious than Xerxes, and more able than Cyrus. Already, before Darius had mounted the throne, Alexander the Great had succeeded his father in Macedon, had been appointed general-in-chief of all the Greek forces, and had commenced his movement against Asia.

80. The Persian monarch despised the presumption of an inexperienced boy, and made no effort, by aiding the European enemies of Alexander, to crush the new foe in his cradle. The satraps and generals shared the confidence of their master, and though a large force was collected in Mysia, no serious opposition was made to his passage of the Hellespont. In B. C. 334, Alexander with his 35,000 Greeks crossed the strait which had been passed by Xerxes, with his five millions, less than 150 years before. The Greek army was scarcely more inferior to the Persian in number than superior in efficiency. It was composed of veteran troops in the highest possible state of equipment and discipline, and every man was filled with enthusiastic devotion to his leader and confidence of success.

Memnon, a brother of Mentor the Rhodian, with the satraps Spithrida′tes and Arsi′tes, commanded the Persians in Asia Minor. Their first collision with Alexander was in the attempt to prevent his passage of the Grani′cus, a little Mysian river which flows into the Propon′tis. They were totally defeated, and Alexander, advancing southward, subdued, or rather liberated all the cities of the western coast without long delay. Halicarnas′sus, under the command of Memnon, made an obstinate resistance, and it was only at the end of autumn that it surrendered. Memnon then resolved to carry the war into Greece. He gathered a large fleet and captured many islands in the Ægean; but his death at Mytile′ne relieved Alexander of the most able of his opponents.

81. The king of Macedon wintered at Gor′dium, where he cut or untied the celebrated knot, which an ancient prophecy had declared could never be loosened except by the conqueror of Asia. With fresh reinforcements from Greece, he commenced his second campaign, in the spring of 333, by marching through Cappadocia and Cilicia to the gates of Syria. Darius met him, in the narrow plain of Issus, with an army of half a million men. Hemmed in between the mountains, the river, and the sea, the Persian horsemen could not act, and their immense numbers were rather an incumbrance than an advantage. Darius was defeated and fled across the Euphrates. His mother, wife, and children fell into the hands of the conqueror, who treated them with the utmost delicacy and respect.

82. B. C. 333–331. The conquests of Syria, Phœnicia, and Egypt, which Alexander now accomplished in less than two years, will be described in the Macedonian history. In the spring of 331, he retraced his triumphant march through Syria, crossed the Euphrates at Thapsacus, traversed Mesopotamia, and met Darius again on the great Assyrian plain east of the Tigris. The Persian king had spent the twenty months which had intervened since the battle of Issus in mustering the entire force of his empire. The ground was carefully selected as most favorable to the movements of cavalry, and as giving him the full advantage of his superior numbers. A large space was leveled and hardened with rollers for the evolutions of the scythe-armed chariots. An important part of the infantry was formed of the brave and hardy mountaineers of Afghanistan, Bokhara, Khiva, and Thibet; and the cavalry, of the ancestors of the modern Kurds and Turcomans, a race always distinguished for bold and skillful horsemanship. A brigade of Greek auxiliaries was alone considered able to withstand the charge of Alexander's phalanx. Altogether the forces of Darius numbered more than a million of men, and they surpassed all former general levies of the Persians in the efficient discipline which enabled them to act together as one body.

83. The Macedonian phalanx, which formed the center of Alexander's army, was the most effective body of heavy-armed troops known to ancient tactics. The men were placed sixteen deep, armed with the *sarissa*, or long pike, twenty-four feet in length. When set for action, the spear-heads of the first six ranks projected from the front. In receiving a charge, the shield of each man, held over the head with the left arm, overlapped that of his neighbor; so that the entire body resembled a monster clothed in the shell of a tortoise and the bristles of a porcupine. So long as it held together, the phalanx was invincible. Whether it advanced its vast weight upon an enemy like a solid wall of steel bristling with spear-points, or, kneeling, with each pike planted in the ground, awaited the attack, few dared to encounter it.

84. Battle of Arbela. On the morning of the 1st of October, B. C. 331, the two great forces met upon the plain of Gaugame′la. Alexander fought at the head of his cavalry, on the right of his army. Darius, in the Persian center, animated his men both by word and example. Both sides fought with wonderful bravery, but the perfect discipline of the Macedonians gained at length a complete victory. The Persian war-chariots, which, with long scythes extending from their wheels, were intended to make great havoc among the Greek horse, were rendered useless by a detachment of light-armed troops trained for the purpose, who, first wounding horses and drivers with their javelins, ran beside the horses and cut the traces or seized the reins, while the few which reached the Macedonian front were allowed to pass between files which opened to receive them, and were easily captured in the rear. Five brigades of the phalanx bore down the Greek mercenaries who were opposed to them, and penetrated to the Persian center, where Darius commanded in person. The king's charioteer was killed by a javelin; he himself mounted a fleet horse and galloped from the field.

Elsewhere the issue of the day was much more doubtful for Alexander; but the news of Darius's flight disheartened his officers, and spurred the Macedonians, who were outnumbered and almost overpowered, to fresh exertions. A party of Persian and Indian horsemen, who were plundering the Macedonian camp, were put to flight by a reserve corps of the phalanx. The fugitive king, followed at length by his whole army, directed his course to the city of Arbe′la, twenty miles distant, where his military treasures were deposited. The river Ly′cus lay in their way, crossed only by a narrow bridge, and the number of Persians drowned in this rapid stream exceeded even those who had perished upon the battle-field.

85. The next day Alexander arrived at Arbela and took possession of its treasures. The Persian king, unhappily for himself, had escaped a generous conqueror only to fall into the hands of his treacherous satrap Bes′sus. This man had led a division of the Persian army in the battle of Arbela, but finding his master's fortunes ruined, had plotted with some fellow-officers to seize his person, and either put him to death or deliver him to Alexander, hoping thus to gain for themselves important commands. Loaded with chains, the unhappy king was carried away by his servants in their flight toward Hyrca′nia; but Alexander's troops pressed them closely, and finding escape impossible, they mortally wounded their captive and left him by the road-side to die.

The former lord of Asia was indebted to a Macedonian soldier, who brought him a cup of cold water, for the last act of attendance. He assured the man that his inability to reward this service added bitterness to his dying moments; but commended him to Alexander, whose generosity he himself had proved, and who would not fail to honor this his last request. The conqueror came up while the lifeless remains of Darius still lay by the road-side. Deeply moved, he threw his own royal mantle over the body of his foe, and ordered that a magnificent procession should convey the last of the Persian kings to the tomb of his fathers. In the battle of Arbela the Persian empire fell. The reduction of the provinces occupied the few remaining years of Alexander's life; but their submission was certain from the moment when the forces of Asia were put to flight and their monarch was a captive.

RECAPITULATION.

Xerxes, having re-conquered Egypt and laid all his empire under contribution, led into Europe the largest army which the world has seen. He gained the pass of Thermopylæ by treachery, but his fleet was shattered by storms and utterly defeated at Salamis. The war ended, the following year, in the overthrow of Mardonius at Platæa, and the destruction of a Persian fleet and army at Mycale. The forty years' reign of Artaxerxes Longimanus began the decline of the empire. A fresh immigration of liberated Jews re-fortified Jerusalem, and the books of the Old Testament were for the first time collected and arranged. The feud with the Samaritans was perpetuated by their building a rival temple on Mount Gerizim. In the reign of Darius II many provinces revolted, and Egypt remained independent sixty years. Upon the death of Darius, his younger son Cyrus, with the aid of 10,000 Spartan mercenaries, made war upon his brother Artaxerxes Mnemon, but he was defeated and slain at Cunaxa. A general war followed, in which Sparta was humbled by the combined forces of Persia and the minor states of Greece, and the treaty of Antalcidas made the great king arbiter in Grecian affairs. Artaxerxes III, having murdered all his kindred, re-conquered Syria, Phœnicia, and Egypt. He was destroyed, with all his children, by Bagoas, his minister, who conferred the sovereignty on Darius Codomannus. This last of the Achaemenidæ was defeated by Alexander the Great at Issus, and finally at Arbela; and all the dominions of Persia became parts of the Macedonian Empire.

QUESTIONS FOR REVIEW.

Book II.

1. Who and what were the Persians? . . . . § 1.
2. What were their relations with the Medes? . . Book I, 39; Book II, 2.
3. What led to the revolution in the Medo-Persian dominion? . . . . 3, 4.
4. Describe the wars of Cyrus. . . . . 5, 7, 9.
5. His treatment of the Lydians. . . . . 6.
6. What led to the return of the Jews? . . . . 8.
7. What was the character of Cambyses? . . . . 12.
8. Describe his Egyptian campaign. . . . . 13.
9. His operations beyond Egypt. . . . . 14, 15.
10. His behavior at Memphis. . . . . 16.
11. The Magian revolt. . . . . 17.
12. The last days of Cambyses. . . . . 18.
13. The reign and dethronement of the false Smerdis. . . . 19.
14. The revolts against Darius Hystaspes. . . . . 20.
15. His system of government. . . . . 21, 22.
16. His court and retinue. . . . . 23, 24.
17. Compare the religious systems of the Persians, Hindus, and Medes. . 25–28.
18. What causes of corruption in the Persian court? . . . . 29.

19. Describe the wars of Darius I. . . . . §§ 30–32.
20. The causes and incidents of the Ionian revolt. . . . . . 33, 34.
21. The Persian measures of revenge against the Athenians. . 35–40.
22. The memorials of Darius Hystaspes. . . . . . 41 and Note.
23. Describe the beginning of Xerxes' reign. . . . . 42, 43.
24. His preparations against Greece. . . . . 44–46.
25. The passage of the Hellespont. . . . . 47.
26. The magnitude of the army. . . . . 48, 49.
27. The first battle with the Greeks. . . . . 51.
28. The disasters by sea. . . . . 52.
29. What occurred at Delphi? At Athens? At Salamis? . . . . . . 53–55.
30. Describe the retreat of Xerxes, and his subsequent career. . . . 56, 58.
31. The operations of Mardonius in Greece. . . . . 57.
32. The accession of Artaxerxes Longimanus. . . . . . . 59.
33. The revolts during his reign. . . . . 60, 61.
34. The affairs of the Jews under Artaxerxes. . . . . . . 62–64.
35. Who were the next three kings? . . . . 65–67.
36. What was the condition of the kingdom under Darius II? . . . 67, 68.
37. Describe the enterprise of Cyrus the younger. . . . . 69–71.
38. Its results to the Greeks. . . . . 72, 73.
39. The reign of Artaxerxes Mnemon. . . . . 74.
40. The reign of Artaxerxes III. . . . . 75–77.
41. Who succeeded him? . . . . 78.
42. What was the character of Darius III? . . . . 79.
43. Compare the armies of Alexander and Darius. . . . . 80, 82, 83.
44. Describe the battles of Issus and Arbela. . . . . 81, 84.
45. The fate of Darius. . . . . 85.
46. How long had the Persian Empire continued?
47. How many kings, commencing with Cyrus?
48. What was its greatest extent, described by boundaries?
49. What is meant by a *satrapy?*

BOOK III.

Grecian States and Colonies from their Earliest Period to the Accession of Alexander the Great.

GEOGRAPHICAL OUTLINE OF GREECE.

1. Of the three peninsulas which extend southward into the Mediterranean, the most easterly was first settled, and became the seat of the highest civilization which the ancient world could boast. Its southern portion only was occupied by Greece, which extended from the 40th parallel southward to the 36th. Continental Greece never equaled in size the state of Ohio. Its greatest length, from Mount Olym′pus to Cape Tæn′arum, was 250 miles; and its greatest breadth, from Actium to Marathon, was but 180. Yet this little space was divided into twenty-four separate countries, each of which was politically independent of all the rest.

2. The most peculiar trait of the Grecian peninsula is the great extent of its coast as compared with its area. It is almost cut into three distinct portions by deep indentations of the sea, northern Greece being separated from the central portion by the Ambra′cian and Ma′lian, and central Greece from the Peloponnesus by the Corinth′ian and Saron′ic gulfs. A country thus surrounded and penetrated by water, of necessity became maritime. The islands of the Ægean afforded easy stepping-stones from Europe to Asia. Opposite, on the south, was one of the most fertile portions of Africa; and, on the west, the Italian peninsula was only thirty miles distant at the narrowest portion of the channel.

3. The northern boundary of Greece is the Cambu′nian range, which crosses the peninsula from east to west. About midway between the two seas, this range is intersected by that of Pin′dus, which runs from north to south, like the Ap′ennines of Italy. This lofty chain sends off a branch toward the eastern coast, which, running parallel to the Cambunian at a distance of sixty miles, incloses the beautiful plain of Thes′saly. West of Mount Pindus is Epi′rus, a rough and mountainous country inhabited by various tribes, some Greek, some barbarian. Its ridges, running north and south, were alternated with well-watered valleys. Through the most easterly of these flows the Achelo′us, the largest river in Greece. Near its source were the sacred oaks of Dodo′na, in the rustling of whose leaves the voice of the supreme divinity was believed to be heard.

4. Central Greece was occupied by eleven states: At′tica, Meg′aris, Bœo′tia, Malis, Ænia′nia, eastern and western Locris, Phocis, Doris, Æto′lia, and Ac′arna′nia. Between Ætolia and Doris, Mount Pindus divides into two branches. One of these runs south-easterly into Attica, and comprises the noted summits of Parnas′sus, Hel′icon, Cithæ′ron, and Hymet′tus; the other turns to the southward, and reaches the sea near the entrance of the Corinthian Gulf.

Attica is a triangular peninsula, having two sides washed by the sea and its base united to the land. Protected by its mountain barriers of Cithæron and Par′nes, it suffered less from war in early times than other parts of the country; and the olive, its chief production, became for all ages a symbol of peace.

5. Southern Greece contained eleven countries: Cor′inth, Sicyo′nia, Acha′ia, E′lis, Arca′dia, Messe′nia, Laco′nia, Ar′golis, Epidau′ria, Trœze′nia, and Hermi′onis.

The territory of Corinth occupied the isthmus between the Corinthian and Saronic gulfs; and by its two ports, Lechæ′um and Cen′chreae, carried on an extensive commerce both with the eastern and western seas. Thus admirably situated, Corinth, the chief city, was noted for its wealth even in the time of Homer.

Sicyonia was considered the oldest state in Greece, and Argolis next. The ruins of Tir′yns and Myce′næ, in the latter, existed long before the beginning of authentic history.

Elis was the Holy Land of the Helle′nes. Every foot of its territory was sacred to Zeus, and it was sacrilege to bear arms within its limits. Thus it was at peace when all Greece beside was at war; and though its wealth surpassed that of all the neighboring states, its capital remained unwalled.

Arcadia, the Switzerland of the Peloponnesus, was the only Grecian state without a sea-coast. Its wild, precipitous rocks were clothed in gloomy forests, and buried during a great part of the year in fogs and snows. Its people were rustic and illiterate; they worshiped Pan, the god of shepherds and hunters, but if they returned empty-handed from the chase, they expressed their disgust by pricking or scourging his image.

Messenia occupied the south-western corner of Greece, and encircled a gulf to which it gave its name. Laconia embraced the other two promontories in which the Peloponnesus terminates, together with a larger tract to the northward. It consisted mainly of a long valley bounded by two high ranges, whence it was sometimes called *Hollow* La′cedæ′mon. Down the center of the vale flowed the Euro′tas, whose sources were in the steep recesses of Mount Tay′getus. Sparta, the capital, was the only important town. It lay on the Eurotas about twenty miles from the sea, inclosed by an amphitheater of mountains which shut out cooling winds and concentrated the sun's rays, so as to produce intense heat in summer.

6. Although the name of Greece is now strictly limited to the peninsula which we have described, it was often more generally applied by the ancients to all the homes and colonies of the Hellenic race. The south of Italy was long known as *Mag′na Græ′cia;* the eastern shores of the Ægean constituted Asiatic Greece, and the cities of Cyrene in Africa, Syracuse in Sicily, and Massilia in southern France, were all, to the Greeks, equally essential parts of Hellas. The description of the numerous and important colonies belongs to a later period. A few of the islands more immediately belonging to Greece will alone be mentioned here.

7. Chief of these was Eubœ′a, the great breakwater of the eastern coast, which extended a distance of 100 miles in length and 15 in width. Nearly as important, though smaller, was Corcy′ra, on the western coast; and south of it lay Paxos, Leuca′dia, Ith′aca, Cephalle′nia, and Zacyn′thus. On the south were the Œnus′sæ and the important island of Cythe′ra. On the east, among others were Hy′drea, Ægina, and Salamis. Besides these littoral, or coast, islands there were, in the northern Ægean, Lemnos, Imbros, Thasos, and Samothra′ce; in the central, the Cyc′lades; and, in the southern, the large island of Crete.

HISTORY OF GREECE.

Periods.

I. Traditional and Fabulous History, from the earliest times to the Dorian Migrations, about B. C. 1100.

II. Authentic History, from the Dorian Migrations to the beginning of the Persian wars, B. C. 1100–500.

III. From the beginning of the Persian wars to the victory of Philip of Macedon at Chæronea, B. C. 500–336.

8. First Period. The name of Greece was unknown to the Greeks, who called their country *Hellas* and themselves *Helle′nes.* But the Romans, having probably made their first acquaintance with the people of that peninsula through the *Grai′koi,* a tribe who inhabited the coast nearest Italy, applied their name to the whole Hellenic race. A more ancient name, *Pelas′gia,* was derived from the earliest known inhabitants of the country—a widely extended people, who may be traced by the remains of their massive architecture in various parts of Italy as well as Greece. The *Pelasgi* were among the first of the Indo-Germanic family to migrate from Asia to Europe.

9. By conquest or influence, the Hellenes very early acquired the control of their neighbors, and spread their name, language, and customs over the whole peninsula. They were then regarded as consisting of four tribes, the Dorians, Achæ'ans, Æo'lians, and Ionians; but the last two, if not all four, were probably members of the earlier race.

10. Though of the same family with the Medes, Persians, Bactrians, and the Brahmins of India, the Greeks had no tradition of a migration from Asia, but believed that their ancestors had sprung from the ground. They, however, acknowledged themselves indebted, for some important elements of their civilization, to immigrants from foreign lands. *Ce'crops*, a native of Sais in Egypt, was said to have founded Athens, and to have established its religious rites. The citadel bore, from him, the name Cecro'pia in later times. Better authorities make Cecrops a Pelasgian hero. *Da'naus*, another reputed Egyptian, was believed to have founded Argos, having fled to Greece with his fifty daughters. To him the tribe of the Da'nai traced their name, which Homer sometimes applied to all the Greeks; but the story is evidently a fable.

Pe'lops was said to have come from Phrygia, and by means of his great wealth to have gained the kingdom of Mycenæ. The whole peninsula south of the Corinthian Gulf bore his name, being called Peloponnesus. A fourth tradition which describes the settlement of the Phœnician *Cad'mus* at Thebes, in Bœotia, rests upon better evidence. He is said to have introduced the use of letters, the art of mining, and the culture of the vine. It is certain that the Greek alphabet was derived from the Phœnician; and Cadmus may be regarded, in this elementary sense, as the founder of European literature. The fortress of Thebes was called, from him, Cadme'a.

11. The earliest period of Grecian history is called the Heroic Age. In later times, poets and sculptors loved to celebrate its leaders as a nobler race than themselves, ranking between gods and men; differing from the former by being subject to death, but surpassing the latter both in strength of body and greatness of mind. The innumerable exploits of the Heroes must be read rather in Mythology than History. The three who had the strongest hold in the belief, and influence upon the character of the people, were Hercules, the great national hero; The'seus, the hero of Attica; and Minos, king of Crete.

The "Twelve Labors of Hercules" represent the struggle of Man with Nature, both in the destruction of physical evil and the acquisition of wealth and power. To understand his reputed history, we must bear in mind that, in that early age, lions as well as other savage beasts were still numerous in southern Europe; that large tracts were covered by undrained marshes and impenetrable forests; and that a wild, aboriginal race of men, more dangerous than the beasts, haunted land and sea as robbers and pirates.

12. Theseus was the civilizer of Attica. He established a constitutional government, and instituted the two great festivals, the Panathenæa * and Synoikia, in honor of the patron goddess of Athens. The Isthmian Games, in honor of Neptune, were also traced to him.

13. Minos, king of Crete, was regarded by the Greeks as the first great law-giver, and thus a principal founder of civilization and social order. After his death he was believed to be one of the judges of souls in Hades. It is worth noticing that the traditional law-givers of many nations have borne similar names; and Menu in India, Menes in Egypt, Manis in Lydia, Minos in Crete, and Mannus in Germany may all be mythical names for *Man* the Thinker, as distinguished from the savage.

14. Of the many remarkable enterprises of the Grecian heroes, the last and greatest was the Siege of Troy. Zeus, † pitying the earth — so says the fable — for the swarming multitudes she was compelled to sustain, resolved to send discord among men that they might destroy each other. The occasion of war was found in the wrong inflicted upon Menelaus, king of Sparta, by Paris, son of Priam, king of Troy. All the Greek princes, resenting the injury, assembled their forces from the extremities of Hellas — from Mount Olympus to the islands of Ithaca, Crete, and Rhodes — and crossing the Ægean under the command of Agamem′non, spent ten years in the siege of Troy. The story of the tenth year must be read in the Iliad of Homer. ‡ It is impossible to separate the historical from the poetical part in his spirited narration. Some historians have assigned a definite period to the siege, while others have doubted whether Troy, as described by Homer, ever existed.

B. C. 1194.

B. C. 1184.

15. Though much doubt may be felt as to the character of their heroes and events, the poems of Homer give us a true picture of the government and manners of the Greeks at this early age. From them we learn that each of the petty states had its own king, who was the father, the judge, the general, and the priest of his people. He was supposed to be of divine descent and appointment. But unlike the blind believers in "divine right" in modern times, the Greeks demanded that their kings should prove themselves superior to common men in valor, wisdom, and greatness of soul. If thus shown to be sons of the gods, they received unquestioning obedience.

16. A council of nobles surrounded the king and aided him by their advice. The people were often assembled to witness the discussions in the council and the administration of justice, as well as to hear the intentions of the king; but in this early age they had no voice in the proceedings. The nobles, like the king, were descended from the gods, and were distinguished by their great estates, vast wealth, and numerous slaves.

* See note, p. 128. † See §§ 23, 25. ‡ See note, p. 110.

17. The Greeks of the Heroic Age were distinguished by strong domestic attachments, generous hospitality, and a high sense of moral obligation. Every stranger was welcomed and supplied with the best cheer before he was asked his name or errand. If he came to seek protection, the family were under a still stronger obligation to receive him, even if he were an enemy; for Zeus had no mercy on him who turned away from the prayer of a suppliant.

18. The manners of the age were simple and homely. The sons of the gods cooked their own dinners, and were proud of their skill in so doing. Ulysses built his bed-chamber and constructed his raft, beside being an excellent plowman and reaper. The high-born ladies, in like manner, carded and spun the wool of their husbands' sheep, and wove it into clothing for themselves and their families; while their daughters brought water from the wells, or assisted the slaves to wash garments in the river.

19. Though simple, these people were not uncivilized. They lived in fortified towns, adorned by palaces and temples. The palaces of the nobles were ornamented with vases of gold, silver, and bronze, and hung with rich Tyrian draperies. The warriors were protected by highly wrought and richly embellished armor. Agriculture was highly honored. Wheat, flax, wine, and oil were the chief productions.

20. The arts of sculpture and design had already made some progress. Poetry was cultivated by minstrels, who wandered from place to place singing songs of their own composition, and were sure of an honorable welcome in every palace. In this way, doubtless, the blind Homer* related the brave deeds done before the walls of Troy, and praised the heroes of that epoch in the houses of their descendants.

21. The religion of the Greeks had some of its first elements in common with that of the Hindus. Zeus, the king of gods and men, who reigned upon the snowy summit of Olympus, was doubtless the same conception with Dyaus′, the Bright Ether or Serene Heaven of the Brahmin worship. But as the forces of Nature were the objects of adoration, each system borrowed its distinctive features from those of the country in which it was developed, and that of the Greeks became incomparably the more delicate and refined. The Asiatic origin of their faith was recognized by the Greeks themselves, in the fable that Zeus had brought Euro′pa, daughter of Age′-nor (the same with Canaan), in her early youth, across the Hellespont and

---

* Homer was an Asiatic Greek who lived probably about B. C. 850. Seven cities claimed the honor of his birth, which ancient critics commonly accorded to Chios, and modern, to Smyrna. Many legends describe his sorrowful and changeful life, shadowed by poverty and blindness; but we can be sure of little except that he was the author of some of the earliest and yet greatest poems in the world's literature.

through Thrace. An old tradition said that the people of the ante-Hellenic age worshiped all the gods, but gave names to none; a mystical expression of the truth that the Greeks, like most other ancient people, had descended from the worship of One God to the belief in many.

Watching with keen eyes the various and apparently conflicting operations of Nature, the Greeks, unaided by revelation, were led to believe in many distinct and sometimes hostile gods; for their science, as imperfect as their religion, had not yet arrived at a perception of unity beneath the apparent variety, nor taught them that all forces may be resolved into one. Hence we read of conflicts and jealousies among the divine inhabitants of Olympus, of which the most ignorant child should be ashamed. In more enlightened ages, philosophers severely censured this ascription of unworthy passions to the gods, and taught that they should only be conceived as serene, beneficent, and superior to human excitements.

22. Much of the mythology of the Greeks belonged merely to poetry, and had no religious character whatever. Many stories of the gods may be explained by the familiar appearances of nature. E′os, the dawn, was the sister of He′lios, the sun, and Sele′ne, the moon. She dwelt upon the banks of Ocean, in a golden-gated palace, whence she issued each morning to announce to gods and men the approach of her greater brother. She was the mother of the Winds and of the Morning Star. I′ris was the messenger of the gods. The many-colored rainbow was the road over which she traveled, and which vanished, when she no longer needed it, as suddenly as it had appeared.

23. The twelve who constituted the Olympian Council were Zeus, the supreme; Posi′don, the god of the sea; Apollo, the sun-god, and patron of music, poetry, and eloquence; A′res, the god of war; Hephæs′tus, of fire and the useful arts; Her′mes, the herald of the gods, and promoter of commerce and wealth; Hera, the great goddess of Nature; Athe′na, the favorite daughter of Zeus, and patroness of all wisdom, civilization, and art; Ar′temis, the goddess of the moon or of hunting; Aphrodi′te, of beauty and love; Hestia, of domestic life; and Deme′ter, the bountiful mother of harvests, — six gods and six goddesses.

24. Beside these, and in some cases equal in rank, were Hades, the god of the under-world; Helios and Hec′ate; Diony′sus, the patron of the vine, whose rites bore some resemblance to the drunken So′ma worship of the Hindus; the nine Muses, daughters of Zeus and Memory, who presided over music, literature, and all the arts; the Oceanids and the Nereids, daughters of Posidon; and multitudes more, whom to enumerate would require a volume, instead of a few pages.

25. The religion of the Greeks, properly so called, consisted in reverence toward a moral Ruler of the world, ever present and actively concerned in human affairs; and in obedience to him by truthfulness in thought, word, and deed. Zeus himself was believed to watch over the sacred performance of all oaths. Athena was the divine Wisdom, especially as exercised in civil affairs. Nem'esis was the divine Justice, as heard either in warnings of conscience within or the reproaches of the world without. The Erin'nyes, or as they were flatteringly called, Eumen'ides,* were the avengers of crime, older than all the Olympian divinities, and dreaded alike by gods and men. The cries of the injured aroused them from their dark abode in Tartarus; and to the guilty man they appeared as fierce, implacable furies, with flaming eyes and extended talons, who never slept, but walked or waited constantly by his side from the moment of his crime till its punishment; while to the innocent victim, whom they avenged, they wore the form of serene and stately goddesses, with faces beautiful though stern.

26. At a later period, new elements entered into the religious life of the Greeks, through their intercourse with other nations, especially with Egypt, Asia Minor, and Thrace. The most important of these was the idea of purification for sins, which was unknown to Homer and Hesiod, and was probably borrowed from the Lydians. The earliest sacrifices were merely expressions of gratitude, or means of obtaining the favor of the gods, and had nothing of the character of sin-offerings. In case of crime, it was impossible to turn aside the wrath of the Eumenides, either by prayers or sacrifices; the guilty person must suffer the extremest consequences of his guilt. But under the new system it was believed that the divine anger might be averted, and the stain of sin removed.

Persons guilty of homicide, whether intentional or accidental, were excluded from the society of man and the worship of the gods until certain rites had been performed. In earlier times, a chief or king might officiate in the ceremony of purification, but later it was intrusted to priests, or to persons supposed to be specially marked for the favor of heaven by holiness of life. In case of public calamity, such as plague, famine, or defeat in war, whole cities or states underwent the process of purification, with a view to appease the supposed wrath of the gods for some hidden or open crime.

27. Among other foreign observances were the ecstatic rites in honor of various divinities. Such were the Bacchanalian dances, celebrated at Thebes and Delphi, in honor of Dionysus, in which troops of women spent whole nights upon the mountains in a state of the wildest frenzy, shouting, leaping, clashing noisy instruments, tearing animals to pieces and devouring the raw flesh, and even cutting themselves with knives without feeling the wounds. Those who abandoned themselves freely to this excitement were

---

* The word Erinnyes meant *curses*, and hence the angry or persecuting goddesses. Fearing to call these terrible beings by their real name, the Greeks substituted the term Eumenides, which meant *soothed* or *benevolent*.

supposed to secure the favor of the god and escape future visitations, while those who resisted were punished with madness.

28. Among the most solemn rites were the Mysteries celebrated at Eleusis in honor of Demeter and Perseph'one. These could only be approached by a long and secret course of preparation, and it was a crime even to speak of them in the presence of the uninitiated. They commanded the deepest reverence of the Greeks, and the participants were regarded as more secure than others, both in temporal and spiritual perils. When exposed to shipwreck, passengers commonly asked each other, "Have you been initiated?"

The Eleusinian Mysteries, at least in their earlier form, are supposed to have been a remnant of the old Pelasgic worship, and thus "grounded on a view of nature less fanciful, more earnest, and better fitted to awaken both philosophical thought and religious feeling" than the Hellenic mythology.

29. Another custom adopted from abroad was the formation of secret societies, whose members bound themselves by ascetic vows, and the obligation to perform, at fixed seasons, certain solemnities. Such were the Orphic, and afterward the Pythagorean brotherhoods. Those who entered upon the "Orphic Life," as it was called, promised to abstain wholly from animal food, except the mystic sacrificial feast of raw flesh, and wore white linen garments like the Egyptian priests. Though worshipers of Dionysus, the Orphic brotherhood abstained from all wild and unseemly demonstrations, and aimed at the most severe simplicity and purity of life and manners. Their reputation for wisdom and holiness was abused by certain impostors, who used to visit the houses of the rich and offer to release them from the consequences both of their own sins and those of their forefathers, by sacrifices and expiatory songs prescribed in the Orphic books.

30. We have anticipated the five or six centuries which followed the Heroic Age, for the sake of giving a connected though brief account of the religious beliefs and customs of the Greeks, without which their history could not be understood. It only remains to mention those oracles through which, from the earliest times to the latest, and even long after the civil existence of Greece was ended, the gods were believed to make known their will to man.

31. The oldest of the oracles was that of Zeus at Dodona, where the message of the god was believed to be heard in the rustling of the sacred oaks and beeches, and interpreted by his chosen priests or prophetesses. At Olympia, in Elis, the will of Zeus was read in the appearance of victims sacrificed for the purpose. The oracles of Zeus were comparatively few. The office of revealing the divine will to man devolved usually upon Apollo, who had twenty-two oracles in European and Asiatic Greece.

32. Of these the most celebrated was at Delphi, in Phocis, where was a temple of Apollo containing his golden statue and an ever-burning fire of fir-wood. In the center of the temple was a crevice in the ground, whence arose a peculiarly intoxicating vapor. When the oracle was to be consulted, the Pythia, or priestess, took her seat upon the sacred tripod over this opening; and when bewildered or inspired by the vapor, which was supposed to be the breath of the god, she uttered a response in hexameter verses. It was often so obscure,* that it required more wit to discern the meaning of the oracle than to determine the best course of conduct without its aid. But so great was the reputation of the Delphic shrine, that not only Greeks, but Lydians, Phrygians, and Romans sent solemn embassies to consult it concerning their most important undertakings.

33. What Europe has been to the rest of the world, Greece was to Europe. The same peculiarities of coast and climate which made Europe the best adapted to civilization of all the continents, long made Greece its most highly civilized portion. But as Europe had her northern barbarians, always pressing upon the great mountain barrier of the Pyrenees, Alps, and Carpathians, sometimes bursting their limits and overrunning the more civilized but weaker nations to the southward, so Greece suffered, toward the close of the Heroic Age, from the incursions of the Illyrians on her north-western frontier. The time of this movement was fixed by Greek historians at sixty years after the fall of Troy, or, in our reckoning, B. C. 1124.

Though the Illyrians did not enter central or southern Greece, their southward movement produced a general change among the tribes of the peninsula. The Thessalians, who had previously been settled on the western coast of Epirus, now crossed the Pindus mountains, and cleared for themselves a place in the fertile basin of the Pene′us, hitherto occupied by the Bœotians. The Bœotians, thus dispossessed of their ancient seats, moved southward, across Mounts O′thrys and Œta, to the vale of the Cephissus, whence they drove the Cadmians and Minyæ. These tribes were scattered through Attica and the Peloponnesus. The Dorians, moving from the northward, occupied the narrow valley between Œta and Parnassus, which thus became *Doris;* while the Dryo′pians, earlier inhabitants of this region, took refuge in Eubœa and the islands of the Ægean.

34. B. C. 1104. Twenty years later, a still more important movement took place. The Dorians, cramped by the narrow mountain limits of their abode, united with their western neighbors, the Ætolians, to invade the Peloponnesus. It is said that they were conducted by Tem′enus, Cresphontes, and Ar′istode′mus, in pursuance of the claims of their great ancestor, Hercules, who had been expelled from the southern peninsula a

---

* For a specimen, see §§ 108-9, 114.

hundred years before. The Dorian migration is therefore often called the Return of the Heraclidæ. Aristodemus was killed by lightning when about to cross the Corinthian Gulf. His brothers were completely victorious over the king of the Achæans, then the most powerful monarch in the Peloponnesus, and proceeded to divide the peninsula between themselves and their allies. The Ætolians received Elis, on the western coast; the rest of the peninsula, except its northern border on the Corinthian Gulf, remained to the Dorians, who continued for five centuries to be the dominant race in Greece. The Heraclid princes then divided the various crowns by lot. That of Argos fell to Temenus; that of Messenia, to Cresphontes; and that of Sparta, to Eurysthenes and Procles, the twin sons of Aristodemus.

35. The conquered Achæans were forced either to emigrate to Asia and Italy, or to content themselves with the northern coast of their peninsula, from which they expelled its Ionian inhabitants, and gave it their own name, Achaia. The Ionians, after resting a few years in Attica, whose people were their kinsmen, sought more space in the Cyclades, in Chios and Samos, or on the neighboring coasts of Asia Minor. In the fertile region between the Hermus and Mæander, and on the islands, twelve Ionian cities* sprang up, and became rich and flourishing states. Though independent of each other in government, they were united in the worship of Posidon at one common temple, the Panio′nium, which crowned the headland of Mycale.

36. The Æolians had already been driven from their ancient home in central Greece, and had found refuge in Lesbos and the north-western coast of Asia Minor, between the Hermus and the Hellespont. They, also, formed twelve independent cities, but Mytile′ne, on the isle of Lesbos, was considered the metropolis.

37. The Dorians, extending their migrations beyond the conquered peninsula, took possession of the south-western coast of Asia Minor, with the islands of Cos and Rhodes. Their six cities—sometimes called the Doric Hexapolis—were Cni′dus and Halicarnassus, on the mainland; Ial′yssus, Cami′rus, and Lindus, on the isle of Rhodes; and Cos, on the island of its own name. Like the Ionians, they worshiped at a common sanctuary, the temple of the Triopian Apollo.

RECAPITULATION.

Greece was first occupied by the Pelasgi, but its ancient name is derived from the Hellenes, who early became the predominant race. Many arts were introduced by foreigners, among whom Cecrops and Danaus of Egypt, Pelops of Phrygia, and Cadmus of Phœnicia, are most famous in tradition. The Heroic

* My′us, Prie′ne, Eph′esus, Co′lophon, Leb′edos, Te′os, Er′ythræ, Clazom′enæ, Phocæ′a, Mile′tus, Chi′os, and Sa′mos.

Age was illustrated by the achievements of sons of the gods, the last and greatest of their works being a ten years' siege of Troy. Greece was governed at this period by many absolute monarchs: kings and nobles, as well as people, led simple and industrious lives. Not only tillage, weaving, and the manufacture of metals, but architecture, sculpture, music, and poetry were cultivated to a high degree. Greek religion was the most refined and beautiful form of Nature-worship. Six gods and six goddesses constituted the Supreme Council of Olympus, and a multitude of inferior divinities peopled the mountains, woods, and waters. Conscience was personified in Nemesis and the Erinnyes. Rites of atonement for sin, ecstatic celebrations, and ascetic brotherhoods were adopted by the Greeks from foreign nations. Of many oracles, the most celebrated was that of Apollo, at Delphi. The Heroic Age ended with a general migration of the tribes of Greece, which resulted in the settlement of the Dorians in the Peloponnesus, and the planting of many Ionian and Æolian colonies on the shores of Asia Minor.

Second Period. B. C. 1100–500.

38. The Heroic Age had ended with a general migration among the tribes of Greece, which for a time interrupted their improvement of manners. But Grecian liberty arose out of the ruins of the Heroic Age; and instead of absolute monarchies, various forms of free government were established in the several states. A state, indeed, was nothing more than a city with a small portion of land surrounding it. Except in Attica, no city at this time had control over any other town.

39. All the Greeks—though existing under a multitude of governments, and divided by rivalries and jealousies—considered themselves as children of one ancestor, Hellen, and gave the common name of *barbarians*, or *babblers*, to all other nations. The poems of Homer, which were chanted at the public festivals and repeated at every hearth-stone, described all the Greeks as united against a common foe, and made the feeling of brotherhood stronger than any occasional animosity. Beside the community of blood, language, and national history, the Greeks were strongly bound together by their equal interest in the oracles and the celebration of religious rites, and their participation in the great national festivals.

40. The Games. Of these the oldest and most celebrated were the Olympic Games. The date of their foundation is lost among the fables of the Heroic Age, but it is certain that these athletic contests were the favorite diversion of heroes in those primitive times. They were revived

B. C. 884. and invested with new importance in the time of Iph'itus, king of Elis, and Lycur'gus, regent of Sparta. In the next century their celebration, once in four years, began to afford the Greek measurement of time.

The first Olympiad was B. C. 776–772. The scene of the festival was upon the banks of the Alpheus, in Elis, near the ancient temple of the Olympian Zeus. During the month of the celebration wars were suspended throughout Greece. Deputies appeared from all the Hellenic states, who rivaled each other in the costliness of their offerings at the temple. The games were in honor of Zeus and Hercules. They were open to all Greeks, without distinction of wealth or birth; but barbarians, even of royal blood, were strictly excluded. They included running, jumping, wrestling, boxing, the throwing of quoits and javelins, and races of horses and chariots. The only reward of the victor was a crown of wild olive; but this was esteemed by every Greek as the highest honor he could attain. Its happy wearer was welcomed home with processions and songs of triumph; he entered the town through a breach made in the walls, to signify that a city possessed of such sons needed no other defense; he was thenceforth exempt from all taxes, as one who had conferred the highest obligation upon the state; he occupied the chief place in all public spectacles; if an Athenian, he ate at the table of the magistrates; if a Spartan, he had the privilege in battle of fighting near the person of the king.

41. Three other periodical festivals, which were at first confined to the states where they occurred, were at length thrown open to the whole Hellenic race. The Pythian Games, in honor of Apollo, were celebrated on the Cirrhæ′an plain, in Phocis, the third year of every Olympiad. They included competition in music and poetry as well as in athletic sports, and were, next to the Olympic, the most celebrated festival in Greece. The Ne′mean and Isthmian Games were celebrated once in two years; the former in the valley of Nemea, in Argolis, in honor of Zeus, and the latter on the Isthmus of Corinth, in honor of the sea-god, Posidon.

Thus every year was marked by at least one great national festival, and every second year by two, reminding the throngs which attended them of their common origin, and the distinction between themselves and barbarians. Beside keeping alive that athletic training which increased the strength of Grecian youth, these yearly assemblies served also the purposes of the modern European fairs, of the lecture hall, and, to a certain extent, of the printing-press; for booths were erected all around the sacred grove, in which the industries of all the Hellenic states and colonies found a ready market; while, in the intervals of athletic display, poets chanted to the eager throng their hymns and ballads; historians related the deeds of foreign and native heroes; and philosophers unfolded to all who were wise enough to listen, their theories of mind and matter, and the relation of gods to men.

42. Another bond of union among the Greeks was found in the Amphic′tyones, or voluntary associations of neighboring or kindred tribes, usually for the protection of some common temple or sanctuary. Such a one had its center at Delos, the religious metropolis of the Cyclades; and the three tribes of Dorians, Ionians, and Æolians in western Asia Minor had each its federal union on the same principle. But the most celebrated and lasting was the Amphictyonic league of twelve tribes, which had its semi-annual meetings, in the spring at Delphi, and in the autumn at Anthela, near Thermopylæ.

43. After the Dorian Conquest, Argos was for several centuries the leading power in Greece. In the earliest part of its history, the government was a monarchy, like those of the Heroic Age, the kings claiming descent from Hercules. But the spirit of freedom having been awakened in the people, they gradually took away power from their kings, and established a republic, though retaining the name of monarchy. About 780 B. C., one Phi′don came to the throne, who, having more talent than his predecessors, won back all the powers which they had lost, and made himself absolute with the now first-used name of "tyrant." He extended the dominion of Argos over the whole Peloponnese, and sent forth colonies which rendered the Argive name famous in Crete, Rhodes, Cos, Cnidus, and Halicarnassus. His intercourse with Asia led to the first use of coined money in Greece, and of a system of weights and measures which is supposed to be the same with the Babylonian. After the death of Phidon, Argive power rapidly declined. The subject and allied cities threw off the oppressive rule which he had exercised, and a new state was now gaining power in the Peloponnese which was destined to eclipse all the glories of Argos.

Sparta.

44. When the Dorians invaded Peloponnesus, the former inhabitants still retained their foothold in the country, and for three hundred years their fortress of Amy′clæ stood at only two miles distance from the Doric capital of Lacedæmon, defying assault. The Lacedæmonians consisted of three classes: 1. The Doric conquerors; 2. The subject Achæans of the country towns; and, 3. The enslaved Helots, who were bought and sold with the soil.

45. The government of Sparta was a double monarchy, its two kings being descended respectively from Procles and Eurysthenes, the twin sons of Aristodemus. They possessed little power in peace, but as generals, in these early times, they were absolute in war. They were held in great honor as the descendants of Hercules, and thus as connecting links between their people and the gods. The Spartan Senate consisted of thirty members, each of whom had passed the age of sixty, and had been a blameless servant of the state. The popular assembly was of little importance, though, as a matter of form, questions of peace or war and the election of certain officers were referred to it. At a later time, however, this assembly by a free vote chose five Ephors, who had absolute power even over the kings and senate, as well as over the people.

46. However subservient they might be to kings or senate, the people held themselves proudly above the industrious but dependent inhabitants of the towns. There was more difference of rank between Spartan and Achæan than between the meanest Spartan and his king. The Helots were marked for contempt by a garment of sheep-skin and a cap of dog-skin; and every year stripes were inflicted upon them for no fault, but that they might never forget that they were slaves.

47. About 850 B. C., arose Lycurgus, one of the most celebrated of ancient law-givers. He was of the royal family of Sparta; and upon the death of his brother, King Polydec'tes, he exercised supreme command in the name of his infant nephew, Charila'us. His administration was the most wise and just that the Spartans had known; but his enemies raised a report that he was seeking the crown for himself, and he resolved to withdraw from the country until his nephew should be of age.

The Spartans missed the firm and wise government of their regent. The young king came to the throne, but disorders were not checked, and a party of the better sort sent a message to Lycurgus urging his return. He first consulted the oracle at Delphi, and was hailed with the title, "Beloved of the gods, and rather a god than a man." To his prayer that he might be enabled to enact good laws, the priestess replied that Apollo had heard his request, and promised that the constitution he was about to establish should be the best in the world. Those who might envy the power and deny the authority of Lycurgus as a man, could not refuse obedience to his laws when thus enforced by the god. He effected a great revolution in Sparta, with the consent and coöperation of the king himself.

48. The laws of Lycurgus lessened the powers of the kings and increased those of the people, but their chief end was to secure the continuance of the state by making every Spartan a soldier. Modern nations believe that governments exist for the people; in Sparta, on the contrary, each person existed only for the state. His right to exist was decided upon the threshold of life by a council of old men, before whom each newly-born infant was presented. If it seemed to promise a vigorous and active life, it was accepted as a child of the state, and assigned a nine-thousandth part of the Spartan lands; but if weakly and deformed, it was cast into a ravine to perish.

At seven years of age every boy so allowed to live was taken from his home and subjected to a course of public training. The discipline of his body was considered of more importance than the improvement of his mind. He endured heat and cold, hunger and fatigue; and beside the gymnastic exercises, he was subjected to all the hardships of military service. His garment was the same summer and winter; the food given him was too little to sustain life, but he was expected to make up the deficiency by hunting or stealing. If caught in the latter act, he was severely punished; but it was not for the dishonesty, but for the awkwardness of allowing himself to be detected. It must be remembered, however, that where there was no property there could be no theft in any moral sense. Every thing in Sparta was ultimately the property of the state, and every interest was subordinate to the training of citizens to dexterity in war.

49. Another means of training the Spartan youth to fortitude, was a cruel scourging for no offense at the shrine of Artemis, which they endured without a sound, although the altar was sprinkled with their blood, and some even died under the lash. Those who were educated by such inhuman severities, were not likely to become either just or merciful toward others. The wretched Helots afforded a never-failing exercise for their skill in war. Under the institution called Crypti′a, they were frequently attacked and murdered by the select bands of young Spartans, who ranged the country by night in quest of military practice. When the Helots became more numerous than their masters, so as to be regarded with apprehension, these massacres became more frequent and general.

50. Spartan discipline did not end with youth. At thirty a man was permitted to marry, but he still lived at the barracks and ate at the common table. Public affairs were discussed at these tables with a freedom which partly repaid the suppression of speech in the assembly. The youth were permitted to attend in silence, and thus received their political education. The remaining hours of the day were divided by the men between gymnastic exercises and the instruction of youth. Not until his sixtieth year was a man released from this martial life.

51. Spartan girls were subjected to nearly as rigorous a training as their brothers. Their exercises consisted of running, wrestling, and boxing, and their characters became as warlike as those of men. Like other citizens, the Spartan women considered themselves and all that were most dear to them as the absolute property of the state.

52. That the minds of the Spartans might never be diverted from military pursuits, Lycurgus permitted no citizen to engage in agriculture, trade, or manufactures, all occupations which could be pursued for gain being left in the hands of the subject Achæans. To shut out foreign luxuries, he adopted a still more stringent measure. The possession of gold or silver was forbidden, and money was made of iron rendered worthless by being heated and plunged into vinegar. This bore so low a nominal value in proportion to its weight, that the amount of one hundred dollars was a load for a pair of oxen. So cumbrous a medium of exchange was despised by other nations; the ports of Sparta were unvisited by trading ships, and her villages by traveling minstrels or merchants; and as Spartans were forbidden to journey in other lands without the leave of their magistrates, while, with very rare exceptions, no foreigner was permitted to reside in their capital, the selfish exclusiveness of the nation seemed complete.

Love of country was limited to Laconia, and never included Hellas. Except when Sparta was threatened, they never united with the other Grecian states; and, in time of peace, bore more hatred to Athens than to Persia. The free, intellectual life of the Athenians was the object of their especial disgust; and the philosophy and eloquence which made the glory of Athens, were the scorn of the Spartans, who considered it a crime to use three words where two could be made to suffice.

53. Unlike other cities of Greece, Sparta was never protected by walls. The high mountains on the north and west were a safeguard against assaults by land, while the rock-bound coasts to the eastward prevented invasion by sea. The whole city was a camp, where each man knew his hourly duty, and endured more privation in time of peace than in war. The laws of Lycurgus were successful in making a race of soldiers, narrow-minded, prejudiced, and avaricious; destitute of those finer and sweeter traits which belonged to the higher order of Grecian character, but brave, hardy, self-sacrificing, and invincible.

54. Having completed his legislative work, Lycurgus secured its perpetuity by a sacrifice of himself. He declared that it was necessary to consult the oracle, and exacted an oath from kings, senators, and people that they would obey his laws until his return. He then went to Delphi, made offerings to Apollo, and received an assurance that Sparta should be the most glorious city in the world so long as she adhered to his laws. Having transmitted this message to his countrymen, Lycurgus resolved never to return. He is said to have starved himself to death. The time and place of his death are unknown. Cirrha, Elis, and the island of Crete claimed his tomb, while other accounts declare that his remains were brought to Sparta, and that a stroke of lightning gave the seal of divinity to his last resting-place.

55. Sparta kept her oath five hundred years, and during a great portion of that time maintained the first rank among Grecian states. Amyclæ was taken a few years after the departure of Lycurgus. From a mere garrison in a hostile country, Sparta now became mistress of Laconia, and began to make war with her northern neighbors, Argos and Arcadia. The chief object of her enmity was Messenia, another Doric kingdom to the westward, separated from Sparta by the ridge of Mount Taygetus.

56. First Messenian War. B. C. 743–724. The Messenians had adopted a more liberal policy toward their Achæan subjects than prevailed at Sparta, and the jealousy of the two nations had led to frequent mutual insults, when, at length, a slight occasion plunged them into open war. A distinguished Messenian, who had been crowned at the Olympic Games, pastured his cattle by agreement upon the lands of a certain Spartan. But the Spartan, seizing the opportunity for a fraud, sold both the cattle and the Messenian herdsmen who tended them, and crowned his iniquity by murdering the son of the owner, who came to demand the price. The unhappy father went to Sparta to demand justice from the kings, but his grief was disregarded and his claims unpaid. He then took revenge into his own hands, and murdered every Lacedæmonian who came in his way. The Spartans called upon the Messenians to surrender their countryman, but they refused to give him up, and war broke out.

57. For the first four years the Messenians made effectual resistance, B. C. 738. and their invaders gained nothing; but in the fifth a partial reverse compelled them to shut themselves up in the strong fortress of Itho'me. The Spartans took a solemn oath never to return to their families until they had subdued Messenia. In the thirteenth year, Theopompus, king of Sparta, marched against Ithome, and a great battle B. C. 730. was fought, in which the king of Messenia was slain. Aristodemus was chosen in his place, and the war went on. In the eighteenth year, Arcadia and Sicyon sent forces to aid the Messenians, while Corinth joined the Spartans. A third great battle was fought, in which the invaders were defeated and driven in disgrace to their own country. But at this time the oracles began to fàvor the Spartans, while B. C. 724. dreams and visions dismayed the soul of Aristodemus. He slew himself, and, with his life, success departed from the Messenians. Ithome was abandoned, the Spartans razed it to the ground, and the Messenians were reduced to slavery.

58. For thirty-nine years they endured a galling weight of oppression, but at the end of that time a hero of the royal line arose for their deliverance. The exploits of Aristom'enes form the chief history of the B. C. 685–668. Second Messenian War, though almost the entire Peloponnesus was engaged. The Corinthians, as before, fought for Sparta, while the Argives, Arcadians, Sicyonians, and Pisatans took part with the Messenians. After losing one battle, the Spartans sent to Delphi for advice, and received the unwelcome direction to apply to Athens for a leader. The Athenians, too, feared to disobey the oracle; but desiring to render no real assistance to their rivals, they sent a lame school-master, named Tyrtæ'us, to be their general. They found, as usual, that the Pythia was not to be outwitted. Tyrtæus reanimated the rude vigor of the Spartans by his martial songs, and it is to these that their final success is mainly attributed.

59. The Spartans were slow in regaining their former ascendency. In the battle of Stenycle'rus they were defeated with great loss, and pursued by Aristomenes to the very summit of the mountains. In the third year B. C. 683. the Messenians suffered a signal defeat through the treachery of an ally, and Aristomenes retired to the fortress of Ira. The Spartans encamped around the foot of the hill, and for fourteen years the war was actively prosecuted, the Messenian hero often issuing from his castle, and ravaging with fire and sword the lands held by the enemy. Three times he offered to Zeus Ithomates the sacrifice called Hecatomphonia, in token that he had slain a hundred enemies with his own hand.

60. But neither the valor nor the good fortune of the leader availed to save his country. Ira was taken by surprise. Aristomenes ended his days at Rhodes. His sons led a large number of the exiled Messenians into Italy, and settled near Rhegium. A few who remained were admitted to the condition of the subject Achæans; but, as before, the mass of the people were reduced to serfdom, and remained in that condition three hundred years. The conquest of Messenia was followed by a war against Arcadia which continued nearly a hundred years. The sole fruit to Sparta was the capture of the little city of Tegea.

B. C. 668.

61. From the earliest times Sparta had been the rival of Argos, which then ruled the whole eastern coast of the Peloponnesus. Soon after Lycurgus, the boundaries of Laconia were extended eastward to the sea, and northward beyond the city of Thyr'ea. About B. C. 547, the Argives went to war to recover this portion of their former territory. They were defeated and their power forever humbled.

62. Sparta was for a time the most powerful state in Greece. Her own territories covered the south of the Peloponnesus, and the neighboring states were so far subdued that they made no attempt to resist her authority. That authority had hitherto been exerted within the narrow limits of the Peloponnese, but about this time an embassy from Crœsus, king of Lydia, acknowledged her leadership in Greece, and invited her to join him in resisting the Persians. At this point began the foreign policy of Sparta. Her influence among the Grecian states was always in favor of either oligarchy or despotism — against such a government by the people as existed in Athens; and the aristocratic party in every city looked to Sparta as its natural champion and protector.

B. C. 547.

RECAPITULATION.

After the Dorian migrations, republics replaced most of the monarchies in Greece. Though divided into many rival states, the Hellenes were one race in origin, language, religion, and customs. The Olympic, Pythian, Nemean, and Isthmian Games promoted civilization by the free interchange of ideas. The Amphictyonic Council, at Delphi and Thermopylæ, united twelve Hellenic tribes for mutual defense. Phidon, king of Argos, founded many colonies, and first introduced weights, measures, and the coinage of money from the East.

The Spartan government consisted of a double line of Heraclid kings, a senate, and, in later times, five ephors. Lycurgus, as regent, reformed the laws by subjecting every person to military rule, forbidding lucrative employments, and discouraging all intercourse with foreign nations. By two long wars the Spartans enslaved their neighbors, the Messenians; and their power was always opposed to free institutions in the states of Greece, among which Lacedæmon held for some centuries the foremost rank.

Athens.

63. The history of Athens presents an infinitely greater variety of character and incident than that of Sparta. Unsurpassed by the Spartans in patriotism or valor, the Athenians differed from them in their love for rare sculpture, magnificent architecture, and the refined diversions of music, poetry, and the drama. The consequence is, that while the Spartans won the world's admiration only by their sacrifice of personal interests to those of the state, the Athenians were at once the models and the leaders of all civilized nations in the arts which give grace and loveliness to life. An Athenian visiting Sparta, and seeing the appointments of the public tables, said that he no longer wondered at Spartan bravery in battle, for life so nourished could not be worth preserving.

64. In the Heroic Age Athens was governed by kings. Theseus subdued the country towns of Attica, and made the city the capital of a centralized monarchy. Codrus, the last of the kings, fell in resisting the Dorian invaders, who had conquered the Peloponnesus and designed to subjugate Attica. The invasion was repelled, but the kingdom was not

B. C. 1050–752.

reëstablished. The eupatridæ, or nobles, secured the election of an archon for life, who was in a certain degree responsible to them for his actions. Though of the royal race of Codrus, he had neither the name nor the dignity of a king. This succession of archons continued about 300 years.

65. An important change was then made by limiting the term of office to ten years. At the expiration of his service, the archon could be tried and punished if his conduct was proved to have been unjust. At first the election was made, as before, from the descendants of Codrus; but one of these being deposed for his cruelty, the office was thrown open to all nobles. A third change appointed, instead of a single magistrate, a board

B. C. 684.

of nine, who were chosen yearly from among the eupatrids. Nobles alone had the right to vote, and for sixty years the government of Athens was a pure aristocracy.

66. But the people of Athens, afterward to fill so important a part in history, now made themselves heard in a demand for *written laws*, which should stand between them and the arbitrary will of their rulers. The

B. C. 621.

nobles acceded to the demand, but avenged their injured dignity by appointing Draco to prepare the code. This first Athenian law-giver made a collection of statutes so severe that they were said to be indeed the work of a dragon, and to be written not with ink, but with blood. The smallest theft, not less than murder and sacrilege, was punished by death, and the life of every citizen was left absolutely at the mercy of the ruling order.

67. Great dissatisfaction arose among the Athenians in consequence of

these laws, and Cylon, an aspiring young noble, aided by his father-in-law, the tyrant of Megara, took advantage of the disturbance to seize the Acropolis, with a view to making himself tyrant B. C. 620.
of Athens. The archons quelled this rash rebellion, but in so doing they themselves incurred the guilt of sacrilege, for the criminals were put to death at the very altar of the Eumenides.* While the people were thrown into a tumult of superstitious fear, a plague broke out, which was believed to be a judgment of the gods. The Delphic oracle being invoked, commanded that Athens should be purified by priestly rites. Epimen'ides, a sage and seer, who was reputed to have great insight into the healing powers of Nature, was brought from Crete, and by B. C. 596.
his sacrifices and intercessions the plague was believed to be arrested. The archons, however, saw a cause of their recent danger, deeper than the transient outbreak, and they appointed Solon, the wisest of their number, to frame a new code of laws.

68. The condition of Attica demanded immediate remedies. The three factions, consisting of the wealthy nobles of the Athenian *Plain*, the merchants of the *Shore*, and the poor peasantry of the Attic *Mountains*, were opposed to each other by the most bitter enmities. Some of the latter in their need had been compelled to borrow money, at exorbitant interest, from the nobles, and being unable to pay, had become the slaves of their creditors.

69. Solon, though a noble, had been forced by the ruin of his fortune to engage in commerce, choosing this means of support, however, with a view to the improvement of his mind by observation of foreign lands. While he was exchanging his Attic oil and honey for Egyptian millet, at Naucratis, he had not failed to study the laws of the Pharaohs, or to observe their effects upon the interests and character of the people. His wisdom and integrity commanded the confidence of all B. C. 594.
classes of his fellow-citizens, and he was made sole archon for life, with unlimited power to alter the existing state of things.

70. His first object was to improve the condition of the poor debtors, not merely by alleviating present distress, but by removing its causes. To this end he enacted a bankrupt law, canceling all contracts in which the land or person of a debtor had been given as security; and to avoid such evils in the future, he abolished slavery for debt. The rate of interest was abated, and the value of the currency lowered, so that the debtor gained about one-fourth by paying in a depreciated medium. Above all, provision was made against a recurrence of the same distress, by requiring every father to teach his son some mechanical art. If this was neglected, the son was freed from all responsibility for supporting his father in old age.

---

* See § 25.

Foreigners were not allowed to settle in the country, unless skilled in some form of industry which they engaged to carry on.

71. The chief design of the new constitution was to set up a free and moderate government, instead of the oppressive tyranny of the nobles. Solon divided the people into four classes, according to their possessions. The poorest were permitted to vote, but not to hold office. The upper three classes alone were subject to direct taxation, which fell with greatest weight upon the wealthiest. The code of Draco was repealed. Instead of severe punishments, Solon introduced the fear of shame and the hope of honor as preventives of crime. Among the rewards for faithful citizenship were crowns presented by senate or people; public banquets in the hall of state; statues in the Agora or the streets; places of honor in the theater or popular assembly. As persons distinguished by these various honors were constantly seen by the youth of Athens, their ambition was kindled to deserve similar rewards.

72. A new legislative Council of Four Hundred was formed, consisting of one hundred members from each tribe, to be chosen yearly by a free vote in the popular assembly. The source of power was in the assembly of all the people, which elected the archons and councilors, accepted or rejected the laws proposed by the latter, and judged the former at the end of their term of office. Popular courts of law were also instituted, to which a criminal might appeal when condemned by another tribunal. The Council of the Areopagus continued to be the highest court in the state, and was especially charged with the maintenance of religion and morals. Originally it included all the nobles, but Solon restricted it to those who had worthily discharged the duties of the archonship.

73. There were no professional lawyers in Athens, for the knowledge and enforcement of the laws were held to be the duty of every citizen. In case of popular sedition, every man was to be dishonored and disfranchised who took no part on either side. This rule was designed to stimulate public spirit, and to supply the want of a regular police or military force by the active interference of the citizens. Already a large body of wealthy and respectable men kept themselves aloof from public affairs, which fell thus into the hands of unscrupulous and ambitious plotters.

74. Solon is reckoned the greatest of the Seven Wise Men * of Greece, and some of his sayings have been the maxims of the best legislators of all ages. When asked how injustice could be banished from a republic, he replied, "By making *all* men feel the injustice done to *each*." His new constitution failed, however, to satisfy all classes of his fellow-citizens. The nobles blamed him for having gone too far; the common people, for

---

*Of the Seven Wise Men, six were rulers and statesmen. The seven were Solon of Athens, Periander of Corinth, Cleobulus of Lindus, Bias of Prie'ne, Pittacus of Mytilene, Thales of Miletus, and Chilo of Sparta.

having withheld too much. He himself admitted that his laws were not the best possible, but the best that the people would receive. He obtained, however, from the government and people, an oath to maintain the constitution ten years; and then, to rid himself of perpetual questions and complaints, he departed into foreign lands. B. C. 570.

75. On returning to Athens, Solon found that the flames of faction had broken out with more fury than ever. The *Plain* had for its leader Lycurgus; the *Shore*, Megacles; and the *Mountain*, Pisis′tratus, a kinsman of Solon. The latter was idolized by the people for his personal beauty, his military fame, his persuasive eloquence, and his unbounded generosity. But beneath many real virtues he concealed an insatiable ambition, which could not rest short of supremacy in the state. When his plans were ready for execution, he appeared one day in the market-place bleeding with self-inflicted wounds, which he assured the people he had received in defense of their rights, from the hands of his and their enemies, the factious nobles. The people, in their grief and indignation, voted him a guard of fifty clubmen. Solon saw the danger that lurked in this measure, but his earnest remonstrances were unheeded. B. C. 560.

Pisistratus did not limit himself to the fifty men allotted him, but raised a much larger force, with which he seized the Acropolis and made himself master of the city. Notwithstanding his resistance to the usurpation, Solon was treated with great deference by his cousin, who constantly asked his counsel in the administration of affairs. But the aged lawgiver did not long survive the freedom of Athens. After his death his ashes were scattered, as he had directed, around the island of Salamis, which in his youth he had won for the Athenians.

76. The First Tyranny of Pisistratus was not of long duration. For six years he had maintained the laws of Solon, when the two factions of the Plain and the Shore combined against him, and he was driven from the city. An incident which occurred during his first reign had an important bearing on the later history of Greece. A noble named Milti′ades, of the highest birth in Athens, was sitting one day before his door, when he saw strangers passing whom he knew to be foreigners by their spears and peculiar garments. With true Athenian hospitality, he invited them to enjoy the comforts of his house, and was rewarded by a singular disclosure. B. C. 560-554.

They were natives of the Thracian Chersonesus — that narrow tongue of land which lies along the north shore of the Hellespont — and had been to consult the oracle at Delphi concerning the war in which their countrymen were now engaged. The priestess had directed them to ask the first man who should offer them hospitality after leaving the temple, to found a colony in the Chersonesus. They had passed through Phocis and Bœotia without receiving an invitation, and they now hailed their host as the person described by the oracle, and entreated him to come to their assistance. Miltiades and his family were regarded with especial enmity by Pisistratus, and were discontented under his rule. He accepted the invitation of his guests, collected a party of the similarly affected among his fellow-citizens, and with them planted an independent principality on the Hellespont. It was his nephew who commanded at Marathon.*

77. SECOND TYRANNY. Within six years from the expulsion of Pisistratus, his rivals quarreled between themselves, and Megacles, the leader of the Shore, invited him to return and resume the sovereignty. But Athens could not yet remain at peace. In a short time Pisistratus offended Megacles, who had brought him back, and who again united with Lycurgus to expel him. This time the tyrant was ten years in exile, but he was constantly engaged in raising men and money in the different states of Greece. He landed at length with a powerful army at Marathon, and, joined by many friends, advanced toward the city. He had pitched his tent near the temple of Athena before his enemies had mustered any force to oppose him, and their hastily gathered troops were then signally defeated. The people willingly changed masters, and Pisistratus became for the third time supreme ruler of Athens.

B. C. 548, 547.

B. C. 537.

78. THIRD TYRANNY. He now established his government upon firmer foundations, and the people forgot its arbitrary character in the liberality and justice which marked his administration. He maintained all the laws of Solon, and in his own person set the example of strict and constant obedience. He took care to fill the highest offices with his own kinsmen, but the wealth which he accumulated was at the service of all who needed assistance. His library, the earliest in Greece, and his beautiful gardens on the Ilissus, were thrown freely open to the public. He first caused the poems of Homer to be collected and arranged, that they might be chanted by the rhapsodists at the greater Panathenæ'a,† or twelve days' festival in honor of Athena. He ministered at once to the taste and the necessities of the people, by employing many poor men in the construction of magnificent public buildings with which he adorned the city. The opinion of Solon was justified, that he was the best of tyrants, and possessed no vice save that of ambition.

B. C. 537-527.

---

* See Book II, §§ 37, 39; Book III, §§ 99-102.

† The Panathenaic festival was celebrated every year from the time of Theseus, in honor of Athena Polias, the guardian of the city. It included torch races, musical and gymnastic contests, horse, foot, and chariot races, and costly sacrifices. The greater Panathenæa took place in the third year of every Olympiad. It was distinguished by a sacred procession, bearing to her temple in the Erechtheum a crocus-colored garment embroidered with representations of the victories of the goddess.

79. After a reign of seventeen years in all, Pisistratus died at an advanced age, and his eldest son, Hippias, succeeded to his power, his brother Hippar'chus being so closely associated with him that they were frequently mentioned as the Two Tyrants. Their united government was carried on in the same mild and liberal spirit that had distinguished their father, and their reign was considered a sort of Golden Age in Athens. They reduced the tax on produce from a tenth to a twentieth, and yet, by a prudent management of resources, continued to add embellishments to the city.

B. C. 527.

Fourteen years had thus passed in peace and prosperity, when Hipparchus gave serious offense to a citizen named Harmo'dius, who thereupon united with his friend Aristogi'ton in a plot to murder the two tyrants. Hipparchus was slain. Hippias saved himself by promptness and presence of mind; but from that day his character was changed. His most intimate friends had been accused by the conspirators as concerned in the plot, and executed. Though the charge was false and made only for revenge, the suspicions of Hippias never again slept. The property and lives of the citizens were alike sacrificed to his cruel and miserly passions.

B. C. 527–514.

80. The faction of the Alcmæon'ids, who had been exiled under their leader, Megacles, now gained strength for an active demonstration. They bribed the Delphic priestess to reiterate in the ears of the Spartans that "Athens must be delivered." These brave but superstitious people had a friendship of long standing with the Pisistrat'idæ, but they dared not disobey the oracle. An army was sent to invade Attica: it was defeated and its leader slain. A second attempt was more successful: the Thessalian cavalry which had aided the tyrant was now defeated, and Hippias shut himself up in the citadel. His children fell into the hands of the Spartans, who released them only on condition that he and all his kin should withdraw from Attica within five days. A perpetual decree of banishment was passed against the family, and a monument recording their offenses was set up in the Acropolis.

B. C. 510.

81. Clisthenes, the head of the Alcmæonidæ, now rose into power. Though among the highest nobles, he attached himself to the popular party, and his measures gave still greater power to the people than the laws of Solon had done. Instead of the four tribes, he ordained ten, and subdivided each into demes, or districts, each of which had its own magistrate and popular assembly. The Senate, or Great Council, was increased from 400 to 500 members, fifty from each tribe, and all the free inhabitants of Attica were admitted to the privileges of citizens.

To guard against the assumption of power by one man, as in the case of Pisistratus, Clisthenes introduced the singular custom of *ostracism*, by which any citizen could be banished without accusation, trial, or defense.

If the Senate and Assembly decided that this extreme measure was required for the safety of the state, each citizen wrote upon a tile or oyster-shell the name of the person whom he wished to banish. If the name of any one person was found upon six thousand ballots, he was required to withdraw from the city within ten days. The term of his exile was at first ten years, but it was afterward reduced to five.

82. Isag′oras, leader of the nobles, disgusted by the rise of his rival, called again upon the Spartans to interfere in Athenian affairs. Cleom′-enes, king of Sparta, advanced upon Athens, and demanded the expulsion of Clisthenes and all his family, as accursed for the sacrilege committed, nearly a hundred years before, in the murder of Cylon. Clisthenes retired, and Cleomenes proceeded with his friend Isagoras to expel seven hundred families, dissolve the Senate, and revolutionize the city. But the people rose against this usurpation, besieged Isagoras and his Spartans in the citadel, and only accepted their surrender on condition of their withdrawing from Attica. Clisthenes was recalled and his institutions restored.

83. Cleomenes had been stirring up Greece to aid his vengeance against Athens. He advanced with a considerable army and seized the city of Eleusis, while the Bœotians ravaged the western, and the Chalcidians from Eubœa the eastern borders of Attica. Undismayed by this threefold invasion, the Athenians marched first against Cleomenes; but the irrational conduct of the Spartan had disgusted his allies and defeated his designs before a battle could take place. The Athenians turned upon the Bœotians and defeated them with great slaughter; then pressed on without delay, crossed the channel which divided them from Eubœa, and gained an equally decisive victory over the Chalcidians.

B. C. 507.

Hippias now covered his old age with infamy, by going over to the king of Persia and exerting all his eloquence in directing the power of the empire against his native city. The Athenians sent to Artaphernes, begging him not to place confidence in one who had been banished only for his crimes. "If you wish for peace, recall Hippias," was the peremptory reply.

Grecian Colonies.

84. The history of the other continental states is more or less involved in that of Sparta and Athens; but before entering upon the Persian wars, we will take a rapid survey of those foreign settlements which afforded an outlet for the enterprise and the crowded population of the Hellenic peninsula. In very early times, colonies were led forth from Greece by leaders who were afterward worshiped as heroes in the states they founded. Fire, the emblem of civilization, was carried from the *prytaneum* of the mother city, and placed upon the new hearth-stone of the colony. The Agora, the

Acropolis, the temples, and the peculiar worship of the older city were imitated in the new. The colonists bore part in the religious festivals of the metropolis by delegates and offerings, and it was considered sacrilege to bear arms against the parent state.

85. There was, however, a great difference in the relations of the several colonies with the states from which they sprang. The Æolian, Ionian, and Dorian settlements in Asia, and the Achæan in Italy, were independent states. Commerce, literature, and the arts flourished at an earlier period on the eastern side of the Ægean than in the cities of Greece. Homer, the father of Greek poetry, was an Ionian. Alcæ′us and Sappho, the greatest of Greek poetesses, were natives of Lesbos. Ana′creon was an Ionian of Teos; and four of the Seven Wise Men of Greece lived in the Asiatic colonies.

Coin of Ephesus, enlarged one-half.

86. *Miletus* was for two centuries not only the chief of the Asiatic colonies, but the first commercial city in all Hellas. Her sailors penetrated to the most distant corners of the Mediterranean and its inlets, and eighty colonies were founded to protect and enlarge her commerce. *Ephesus* succeeded Miletus as chief of the Ionian cities. Its commerce was rather by land than sea; and instead of planting distant colonies, it extended its territory on the land at the expense of its Lydian neighbors. *Phocæa*, the most northerly of the Ionic cities, possessed a powerful navy, and its ships were known on the distant coasts of Gaul and Spain. The beautiful city of Massilia (now Marseilles) owed to them its origin.

87. The first Greek colony in Italy was at *Cumæ*, near the modern Naples, which sprang from it. It is said to have been founded about 1050 B. C., and continued five centuries the most flourishing city in Campania. *Syb′aris* and *Croto′na* were Achæan colonies upon the Gulf of Taren′tum. Several native tribes became their subjects, and their dominions extended from sea to sea across the peninsula of Calabria. The Crotonians were early celebrated for the skill of their physicians, and for the number of their athletes who won prizes at the Olympic Games. The Sybarites were noted for their wealth, luxury, and effeminacy. In public festivals they mustered 5,000 horsemen fully equipped, while Athens could only show 1,200 even for the grand Panathenæa.

The fall of Sybaris, B. C. 510, was occasioned by war with the sister but now rival city Crotona. The popular party had supplanted an oligarchy in Sybaris, and the exiled citizens had taken refuge in Crotona. The Sybarites demanded their rendition. The Crotonians trembled, for they had to choose between two great perils: they must incur either the wrath of the gods by betraying suppliants, or the vengeance of the Sybarites, whose army was supposed to number 300,000 men. Pythagoras urged them to adopt the more generous alternative, and his disciple, Milo, the most celebrated athlete of his time, became their general. In a battle on the Trais the Crotonians were victorious. They became masters of Sybaris, and determined to destroy it so thoroughly that it should never again be inhabited. For this purpose they turned the course of the river Crathis, so that it overflowed the city and buried its ruins in mud and sand. To this day a wall can be seen in the bed of the river when the water is low, the only monument of the ancient grandeur of Sybaris.

88. The people of *Locri* were the first of the Greeks who possessed a body of written laws. The ordinances of Zaleucus, a shepherd whom they made their legislator by the command of the Delphic oracle, were forty years earlier than those of Draco, which they resembled in the severity of their penalties. The Locrians, however, held them in so high esteem, that if any man wished to propose a new law or repeal an old one, he appeared in the public assembly with a rope around his neck, which was immediately tightened if he failed to convince his fellow-citizens of the wisdom of his suggestions.

89. *Rhegium,* on the Straits of Messina, was founded by the Chalcidians of Eubœa, but greatly increased by fugitives from the Spartans during the first and second Messenian wars. The straits and the opposite town in Sicily, formerly called Zan′cle, received a new name from these exiled people. *Taren′tum* was a Spartan colony founded about 708 B. C. Its harbor was the best and safest in the Tarentine Gulf, and after the fall of Sybaris it became the most flourishing city in Magna Græcia. Though its soil was less fertile than that of other colonies, its pastures afforded the finest wool in all Italy. Tarentine horses were in great favor among the Greeks; and its shores supplied such a profusion of the shell-fish used for coloring, that "Tarentine purple" was second only to the Tyrian. So extensive were the manufactories of this dye, that great mounds may even yet be seen near the ancient harbor, composed wholly of broken shells of the *murex.*

90. The prosperity of Magna Græcia declined after the close of the sixth century B. C., when the warlike Samnites and Lucanians began to press southward from their homes in central Italy. The Greek colonies gradually lost their inland possessions, and became limited to mere trading settlements on the coast.

91. *Massilia,* in Gaul, has already been mentioned as a colony of the

Ionic Phocians. It exerted a controlling influence upon the Celtic tribes by which it was surrounded, and who derived from it the benefits of Greek letters and civilization. A Massiliot mariner, Pytheas, navigated the Atlantic and explored the western coasts of Europe, as far, at least, as Great Britain. Five colonies on the Spanish coast were founded by Massilia.

92. The fertile island of Sicily early attracted the attention of the Greeks. The Carthaginians already occupied the western side of the island, but for two and a half centuries the commercial settlements of either people flourished side by side without collision. Twelve flourishing Greek cities sprang up within 150 years, among which *Syracuse*, on the eastern, and *Agrigentum*, on the southern coast, were the most important. Syracuse, the earliest, except Naxos, of the Sicilian colonies, was founded by Corinthians, B. C. 734. Its position made it the door to the whole island, and in Roman times it was the capital of the province. In its greatest prosperity it contained half a million of inhabitants, and its walls were twenty-two miles in extent. Agrigentum, though of later origin (B. C. 582), grew so fast that it outstripped its older neighbors. The poet Pindar called it the fairest of mortal cities, and its public buildings were among the most magnificent in the ancient world.

93. AFRICAN COLONIES. Greek colonization was at first confined to the northern shores of the Mediterranean, Egypt and Carthage dividing between them the southern. But the policy of Psammetichus, and, after him, of Amasis, favored the Greeks, who were thenceforth permitted to settle at Naucratis, and enjoy there a monopoly of the Mediterranean commerce of Egypt. Twenty years after the first establishment at Naucratis, *Cyrene* was founded by the people of Thera, a Spartan colony on the Ægean. Unlike most Greek colonies, Cyrene was governed by kings during the first two centuries of its existence.

94. The peninsula of Chalcid′ice, in Macedonia, was covered with the settlements of colonists from Chalcis and Eretria, from the former of which it derived its name. *Potidæ′a*, on the same coast, was planted by Corinthians. *Byzantium* was founded by Megarians, on the strait which connects the Propontis with the Euxine. Few cities could boast so splendid a position; but the power of the Megarian colony bore little proportion to what it was afterward to attain as the capital of Constantine and the mistress of the world. The most northerly Grecian settlement was *Istria*, founded by Milesians near the mouth of the Danube.

RECAPITULATION.

Codrus, the last king of Athens, was succeeded during three centuries by archons for life, chosen from his family. Seven archons afterward reigned successively ten years each, and the government was then intrusted to a commission of nine, annually elected. The people demanding written laws, Draco prepared a code of inhuman severity. A more moderate constitution was framed by Solon, one of the Seven Wise Men of Greece; but the contention of the three rival factions of the *Plain*, the *Shore*, and the *Mountain* soon resulted in the subjection of Athens to the tyranny of Pisistratus. Twice expelled, Pisistratus twice re-established his power, and by his justice and liberal encouragement of all the arts, consoled the people for his unwarranted seizure of the government. His son Hippias was expelled by the Alcmæonidæ, with the aid of the Spartans. Clisthenes completed the liberal reforms of Solon, and introduced the singular custom of ostracism. In three attempts to overthrow the free constitution of Athens, the Spartans and their allies were signally defeated.

THIRD PERIOD. B. C. 500–338.

95. The details of the Ionian Revolt (B. C. 499–494) have been found in the History of Persia.* Reserving his vengeance for the European Greeks who had interfered in the quarrel, Darius sought to console the conquered Ionians for the loss of their political independence by greater personal freedom. Just laws, equal taxes, peace and good order began to restore their prosperity; and when Mardonius, the son-in-law of Darius, succeeded Artaphernes in the satrapy, he signalized his reign by removing all tyrants and restoring to the cities a republican form of government. All this was done to secure their friendship or neutrality in his approaching expedition against Greece. That expedition (B. C. 492) failed, as we have seen, in its principal object.

96. The next year messengers were sent by Darius to each of the states

B. C. 491.

of Greece, demanding earth and water, the customary symbols of obedience. None of the island states and few on the continent dared refuse. The people of Athens and Sparta returned an answer which could not be mistaken. The latter threw the envoys into a well, and the former into a pit where the vilest criminals were punished, telling them to get earth and water for themselves.

97. The youth and ill success of Mardonius led Darius to recall him, and place the command of his new expedition against the Greeks in the hands of Datis, a Mede, and Artaphernes, his own nephew. In the spring of 490 B. C., the great host was drawn up off the coast of Cilicia — a fleet of 600 triremes, carrying not less than 100,000 men. They sailed westward and ravaged the isle of Naxos, but spared Delos, the reputed birth-place of Apollo and Artemis, because the Median Datis recognized them as identical with his own national divinities, the sun and moon. The fleet then advanced to Eubœa, Eretria being the first object of vengeance. Carystus, refusing to join the armament against her neighbors, was taken and destroyed. Eretria withstood a siege of six days; but the unhappy city was a prey to the same dissensions which constituted the fatal weakness of Greece.†

---

* See Book II, § 34.

† Almost every Grecian state was divided between two parties, which preferred respectively *democracy* and *oligarchy*; *i. e.*, government by many and by few.

Two traitors of the oligarchical party opened the gates to the barbarians. The place was given up to plunder, the temples burnt, and the people enslaved.

98. A swift-footed messenger was now dispatched from Athens to Sparta imploring aid. The distance was ninety miles, and he reached his destination the day after his departure. The Spartans did not refuse their assistance, but they declared that religion forbade their marching before the full moon, and it was now only the ninth day. The Persians were already landed on the coast of Attica, and, guided by Hippias, advanced to the plain of Marathon. The Athenian army, posted upon the heights, had to consider whether to await their tardy allies or meet these overwhelming numbers alone. At the last moment there arrived an unexpected reinforcement, which, though small in numbers, raised the spirits of the Athenians by the friendliness it expressed. It was the entire fighting population of the little town of Platæa, a thousand men in all, who came to testify their gratitude for a former service rendered by the Athenians.

99. All the other generals, who were to have commanded in turn, gave up their days to Miltiades, whose genius and experience alike won their confidence; but he, fearful of arousing envy, waited until his own turn came, and then gave orders for battle. The sacrifices and prayers were offered, the trumpets sounded, and, chanting a battle-hymn, the eleven thousand Greeks rushed down from the heights where they had been encamped. Instead of the usual slow march of the phalanx, they traversed the mile or more of level ground which separated them from the Persians at a full run, bearing their level spears in a straight, unwavering line.*

The front rank of Asiatics fell instantly before this unusual assault; but the resistance was not less determined. Rushing upon the spears of the Greeks, in the attempt to make an opening in the phalanx where their short swords and daggers might serve them, the Persians freely sacrificed their lives. It was the belief of many on the field that the gigantic shade of Theseus, the great Attic hero, might be seen in the ranks. Night approached before the desperate conflict was decided. But the Greeks, though wearied with the long action, never wavered, and at length the shattered remains of the Asiatic host turned and fled.†

100. The Persians had brought with them a mass of white marble, with which they meant to erect upon the field of Marathon a monument of their victory. It was carved by Phid′ias into a gigantic statue of

* "The first Greeks," says Herodotus, "who ever ran to meet a foe; the first, too, who beheld without dismay the garb and armor of the Medes, for hitherto in Greece the very name of Mede had excited terror."

† Read the movements of Datis after the battle, p. 86.

Nemesis, the impersonation of divine vengeance. From the brazen spoils of the Persians was cast that colossal statue of Athena Promachos, whose glittering spear and helmet, from the summit of the Athenian citadel, could be seen far off at sea beyond the point of Sunium. The armed goddess, "First in the Fight," seemed to be keeping a perpetual guard over her beloved city.

Coin of Athens, enlarged three-fourths.

101. For a time after the victory at Marathon, Miltiades was the best beloved of the Athenians. Even while prince in the Chersonesus, he had won their gratitude by annexing Lemnos and Imbros to their dominions. To this claim on their regard he now added that of having delivered them from their greatest peril, and there was no limit to their confidence. When, therefore, he promised them a still more lucrative though less glorious enterprise than the recent one against the Persians, they were not slow to consent, though the conditions were a fleet of seventy ships and a large supply of men and money for his use, of which he was to render no account until his return. They were granted, and Miltiades set sail for the isle of Paros, which had furnished a trireme to
B. C. 489. the Persians during the recent invasion. The chief city was besieged and on the point of being taken, when suddenly, for no sufficient cause, Miltiades burnt his fortifications, drew off his fleet, and returned to Athens, having no treasures and only disgrace and loss to report as the result of his expedition.

102. The glory of Miltiades was now departed. He was accused by Xanthip′pus, a leader of the aristocracy, of having accepted a bribe from the Persians to withdraw from Paros. Severely wounded, Miltiades was brought into the court upon a couch; and although his brother Tisag′oras undertook his defense, the only plea he cared to make was in the two words, "Lemnos" and "Marathon." The offense, if proved, was capital; but the people refused to sentence their deliverer to death. They commuted his punishment to a fine of fifty talents; but before it was paid he expired from his wound.

103. The greatest citizen of Athens, after the death of Miltiades, was Aristides, called "the Just." He was of noble birth and belonged to the Alcmæonid party, but he was ardently devoted to the interests of the people. Stern toward crime, whether in friends or foes, he was yet mild toward all persons; and so proverbial were his truth and impartiality, that when he held the office of archon the courts of law were deserted, all suitors preferring to submit their causes to his arbitration.

104. His chief rival was Themis′tocles, a young man of great talents, and, perhaps, still greater ambition. At length his opposition rose to the pitch of proposing the ostracism, and Aristides was banished. It is said that, during the voting, the great archon was requested by a man who could not write, to inscribe the name of Aristides on an oyster-shell for him. "Has he ever injured you?" Aristides asked. "No," said the man, "nor do I even know him by sight; but it vexes me to hear him always called the Just." Aristides wrote his name on the shell, which was cast into the heap. As he left his native city he said, with his usual generosity, "May the Athenian people never know a day which shall force them to remember Aristides!"

105. Themistocles was now without a rival in Athens. His acute mind perceived what his countrymen too willingly ignored, that the Persian invasions were only checked, not ended. Proud of the victory of Marathon, the Athenians believed that the Persians would never again dare to attack them. But Ægina was yet powerful, and a fierce enmity had long existed between the two states. Their merchants regarded each other as rivals in trade, while the free people of Athens hated the oligarchy of Ægina. Themistocles resolved to turn this enmity to account, in arming Athens against the greater though more distant danger. He persuaded the citizens to construct a fleet which should surpass that of Ægina, and to apply to that purpose the revenues from the silver mines of Laurium, near the extremity of the Attic peninsula.

Two hundred triremes were built and equipped, and a decree was passed which required twenty to be added every year. Hitherto Attica had been more an agricultural than a maritime state; but Themistocles clearly saw that, with so small and sterile a territory, her only lasting power must be upon the sea. So strenuous were his exertions, that in the ten years that intervened between the first and the second Persian wars, the Athenians had trained a large number of seamen, organized their naval power, and were ready to be as victorious at Salamis as they had been at Marathon.

106. In 481 B. C., a Hellenic Congress was held at Corinth. The command of the Greek forces, both by land and sea, was assigned to Sparta. An appeal for coöperation was sent to the distant colonies in Sicily, as well as to Corcyra and Crete. Emissaries were also sent into Asia to watch the movements of the Persian army. They were seized at Sardis, and would have been put to death, had not Xerxes believed that their reports would do more to terrify and weaken than to assist their countrymen. He caused them to be led through his innumerable hosts, and to mark their splendid equipments, then to be dismissed in safety.

107. The most difficult duty of the Congress was to silence the quarrels of the several states. Athens, by the entreaties of Themistocles, consented to peace and friendship with Ægina, and all the delegates formally bound their states to act together as one body. Still many elements of disunion remained. Bœotia, with the honorable exceptions of Thespiæ and Platæa, sent earth and water to the Persian king. Argos was at once weakened and enraged against Sparta by the massacre of 6,000 of her citizens, who had been burned, by order of Cleomenes, in a temple where they had taken refuge. Unwilling to refuse her aid in the common danger, she consented to join the league only upon terms which Sparta refused to accept.

108. Even the gods seemed to waver, and the timid answers of the Pythia prevented some states from engaging in the war. The Athenian messengers at Delphi received an oracle that would have appalled less steadfast minds. "Unhappy men!" cried the Pythia, "leave your houses and the ramparts of the city, and fly to the uttermost parts of the earth. Fire and keen Ares, compelling the Syrian chariot, shall destroy; towers shall be overthrown, and temples destroyed by fire. Lo, now, even now, they stand dropping sweat, and their house-tops black with blood, and shaking with prophetic awe. Depart, and prepare for ill!"

109. The Athenians put on the mourning garb of suppliants, and entreated Apollo for a more favorable answer, declaring that they would not depart without it, but remain at his altar until they died. The second response was still more obscure, but possibly more hopeful. "Athena is unable to appease the Olympian Zeus. Again, therefore, I speak, and my words are as adamant. All else within the bounds of Cecropia and the bosom of the divine Cithæron shall fall and fail you. The wooden wall alone Zeus grants to Pallas, a refuge to your children and yourselves. Wait not for horse and foot; tarry not the march of the mighty army; retreat even though they close upon you. O divine Salamis! thou shalt lose the sons of women, whether Demeter scatter or hoard her harvest!" Themistocles, who had, perhaps, dictated the response, now furnished an apt solution. The "walls of wood," he said, meant the fleet, in which the citizens and their children should take refuge. The last sentence threatened woe not to the Athenians, but to their foes, else why was Salamis called "divine"?

110. Arriving with his vast army at the head of the Malian Gulf,

B. C. 480. Xerxes sent a spy to ascertain the force sent against him. The messenger saw only the Spartan three hundred. They were engaged either in gymnastic exercises or in dressing their long hair as if for a festival. Demaratus, an exiled king of Sparta, was with the Persian army, and he was questioned by the great king as to the meaning of this behavior in the face of overwhelming danger. Demaratus replied, "It is manifestly their intention, sire, to dispute the pass, for it is the custom of the Spartans to adorn themselves on the eve of battle. You are about to attack the flower of Grecian valor." Xerxes could not yet believe that such a handful of men meant serious resistance. He waited four days to give them time to retreat, but sent a messenger in the interval to Leonidas, demanding his arms. "Come and take them!" replied the Spartan.

111. BATTLE OF THERMOPYLÆ. On the fifth day the patience of the great king was exhausted. He sent a detachment of Medes and Cissians into the pass, with orders to bring its defenders alive into his presence. The assailants were repulsed with loss. The Immortal Band were then sent forward, but with no better success. The next day the contest was renewed, with great loss to the Persians and no signs of yielding on the part of the Greeks. But treachery now accomplished what force had failed to do.* A council of war was held among the defenders of the pass, and it was resolved to retreat, since defeat was certain. Leonidas did not oppose, but rather favored the decision on the part of the other generals; he only remarked that it was not permitted to Spartans to fly from any foe. He knew, too, that the Delphic oracle had declared that either Sparta must fall or a king of the blood of Hercules be sacrificed. He believed that he should save at least his hereditary kingdom, if not the whole of Greece, by the voluntary devotion of his life.

The Thespians insisted upon sharing the fate of the Spartan three hundred. The four hundred Thebans, whose loyalty had been suspected from the first, were held as hostages. The remainder of the Greeks hastily withdrew before the arrival of the Persians. Thus left alone, the Spartans and Thespians went forth to meet the immense army, which was now in motion to attack them. The Orientals, when their courage failed, were driven into battle by the lash, and thousands were doomed to perish before the desperate valor of the Greeks. At length Hydar'nes, with his Immortal Band, appeared from behind, and the Spartans drew back to the narrowest part of the pass, where they fought to the last breath, and were crushed at last by the numbers, rather than slain by the swords of the Persians.

112. The memory of Leonidas was honored by games celebrated around his tomb in Sparta, in which none but his countrymen were allowed to have part. A lion of stone was placed, by order of the Amphictyonic Council, on the spot where he fell; and other monuments at the same place preserved the memory of his brave companions. That of the Three Hundred bore these words: "Go, stranger, and tell the Spartans that we obeyed the laws, and lie here!"

113. Learning the fate of Leonidas and his men, the fleet retired southward for the protection of the coast. The Spartans acted with their

---

* See p. 90, § 51.

accustomed selfishness, by leaving Athens and the rest of Greece to their fate, while they employed their land forces in fortifying the isthmus, to bar the entrance of their own peninsula. It was with difficulty that Themistocles even persuaded his maritime allies to remain at anchor off Salamis, long enough to allow some measures to be taken for the safety of the Athenian people.

114. Abandonment of Athens. Nor was it easy to persuade the Athenians themselves to leave their beloved city to the revengeful hands of barbarians. But as no other means remained for averting total destruction, Themistocles had recourse, as usual, to a stratagem. The serpent sacred to Athena suddenly disappeared from the Acropolis, the cakes of honey were left untasted, and the priests announced that the goddess herself had abandoned the city, and was ready to conduct her chosen warriors to the sea. The people now consented to depart. Women, children, and old men were hastily removed to places of greater security, while all who could fight betook themselves to the fleet. Only a few Athenians, either too poor to meet the expense of removal, or still convinced that the "wooden walls" of the oracle meant the citadel, remained and perished, after a brave but useless resistance, by the swords of the Persians. Beautiful Athens was reduced to a heap of ashes, in revenge for the destruction of Sardis, twenty years before.

115. The commanders of the fleet now resolved to withdraw from Salamis, and station themselves near the isthmus to coöperate with the Peloponnesian land forces. The Athenians strongly opposed this retreat, which would leave the refuges of their wives and children at the mercy of the barbarians. It was midnight, and the council had broken up, when Themistocles again sought the ship of Eurybi'ades, and convincing him at length of the greater wisdom of his own plan, persuaded him to reassemble the council. The leaders were recalled from their ships and a violent discussion ensued. The Corinthian, Adimantus, opposed Themistocles not only with argument, but with insult. Alluding to the recent destruction of Athens, he maintained that one who had no longer a city to represent should have no voice in the deliberation.

Themistocles kept his temper and replied with dignity and firmness. He showed that the naval advantages of the Greeks in the present war had always been in the narrow seas, where the immense numbers of the Persians gave them no superiority, while their better discipline and acquaintance with the currents and soundings were all in favor of the Greeks. He argued that by transferring the war to the Peloponnesus they would only attract thither the armies and ships of the Persians; while, by defeating them before they could arrive at the isthmus, they would preserve southern Greece from invasion. He ended by declaring that, if Salamis were abandoned, the Athenians would abandon Greece, and taking their wives and children on board their fleet, sail to the coasts of Italy, where the oracle had commanded them to found a new city.

116. Lest even this argument should not be sufficient, Themistocles had recourse to another of his wiles. He retired a moment from the council and dispatched a trusty messenger to the Persian fleet, assuring its commander that the Greeks, struck with consternation, were preparing to flee, and urging him to seize the opportunity, while they were divided among themselves, to gain a decisive victory. The Persian admiral knew too well the frequent dissensions of the Greeks to doubt the truth of the message. He immediately moved his squadrons to cut them off from the possibility of retreat.

In the meantime Themistocles was again called from the council by the arrival of a messenger. It was his ancient rival, the brave and upright Aristides, still in exile through the influence of Themistocles, but watchful as ever for the interests of his country. He had crossed from Ægina in an open boat to inform the Greeks that they were surrounded by the Persians. "At any time," said the just Athenian, "it would become us to forget our private dissensions, and at this time especially, in contending only who should most serve his country." Themistocles led him at once to the council. His intelligence was soon confirmed by a Tenian deserter, and the leaders were now forced to unite in preparation for immediate battle.

117. BATTLE OF SALAMIS. When the sun arose upon the straits of Salamis, the Attic shores were seen lined with the glittering ranks of the Persian army, drawn up by order of Xerxes to intercept fugitives from the Grecian fleet. The king himself, on a throne of precious metals, sat to watch the coming contest. His ships were fully three times the number of the Greeks, and no serious disaster had yet stayed his progress. The Greeks advanced, singing that battle-song which the great poet Æschylus, who himself fought on this memorable day, has preserved for us: "On, sons of the Greeks! Strike for the freedom of your country! strike for the freedom of your children and your wives — for the shrines of your fathers' gods, and for the sepulchers of your sires! All, all are now staked upon your strife!"

B. C. 480.

Themistocles held them back until a wind began to blow, which usually arose in the morning, causing a heavy swell in the channel. This seriously incommoded the cumbrous vessels of the Persians, while the light and compact Greek craft easily drove their brazen beaks into the sides of the enemy. The Athenians, on the right, soon broke the Phœnician line which was opposed to them; and the Spartans, on the left, gained victories over the Ionian allies of the Persians. The sea was strewn with dead bodies, entangled in the masts and cordage of the ships. Aristides, who had been waiting with his command on the coast of Salamis, now crossed to the little island of Psyt'tali'a, and put the Persian garrison to the sword. Xerxes, from his throne on Mount Ægaleos, helplessly watched the confusion and slaughter of his men. The contest lasted until evening, when the straits of Salamis were abandoned by the barbarians.

118. When morning came, the Greeks were ready to renew the battle. The Persians had still a large fleet and a numerous army; and, in the night, the Phœnician transports had been joined so as to make a bridge between Salamis and the mainland. But this was only a feint to cover the real movement. The fleet was already under orders to sail to the Hellespont, and the army retired in a few days to Bœotia. Leaving 300,000 men with Mardonius to renew the war in the following year, Xerxes hastened into Asia. His army was reduced on the way by famine and pestilence, and it was but a fragment of the great host which had crossed the Hellespont in the spring of 480, that returned in the autumn.

119. As spring opened, Mardonius prepared to renew the war; but first he sought to accomplish by diplomacy what he had hitherto failed to do by force. Deeply impressed with the valor of the Athenians, he was sure that if he could withdraw them from the confederacy, the rest of Greece would be an easy prey. To this end he sent Alexander I., king of Macedon, his ally, but a former friend of the Athenians, to flatter them with promises of favor and solicit their alliance. The Athenians refused him an audience until they had time to summon delegates from Sparta. When the Spartans had arrived, Alexander delivered his message. The great king offered to the Athenians forgiveness of the injuries they had done him, the restoration of their country and its extension over neighboring territories, the free enjoyment of their own laws, and the means of rebuilding all their temples. He urged the Athenians to embrace so favorable an offer, for to them alone of all the Greeks was forgiveness extended.

B. C. 479.

120. The Athenians replied: "We are not ignorant of the power of the Mede, but for the sake of freedom we will resist that power as we can. Bear back to Mardonius this our answer: So long as yonder sun continues his course, so long we forswear all friendship with Xerxes; so long, confiding in the aid of our gods and heroes, whose shrines and altars he has burnt, we will struggle against him for revenge. As for you, Spartans, knowing our spirit, you should be ashamed to fear our alliance with the barbarian. Send your forces into the field without delay. The enemy will be upon us when he knows our answer. Let us meet him in Bœotia before he proceed to Attica."

121. The Athenians had rightly judged the immediateness of the danger. Scarcely was their answer received when the Persian general was in motion, and advanced by rapid marches to the borders of Attica. He was re-enforced at every halt by northern Greeks, moved either by terror of his power or by long-standing jealousies against the members of the League. The Attic territory was utterly desolate and Athens a second time deserted. Taking possession of that city, Mardonius dispatched a Greek messenger to Salamis, repeating his former propositions, which were as instantly rejected as before.

The Athenians were a second time homeless, and, for the moment, standing alone against the enemies of Greece. The Spartans were engaged in some long-continued solemnities — perhaps the funeral of their regent, Cleom′brotus — and allowed the Athenian messengers to wait ten days for an answer. Not until the indignant envoys had threatened to make terms with Mardonius and leave Sparta to her fate, did the ephors bestir themselves, but then it was with true Spartan energy and dispatch. Five thousand Spartans and 35,000 slaves were sent, under the command of Pausanias, the new regent, to whom the ephors added a guard of 5,000 heavy-armed Laconians.

122. Hearing of the advance of the Spartans, the Persian thought best to retreat. He again set fire to Athens, leveled to the ground whatever remained of its walls and temples, and retired into Bœotia. Here he arranged his camp on a branch of the Asopus, not far from the city of Platæa. The Spartans followed, having been joined at the isthmus by the Peloponnesian allies, and, at Eleusis, by the Athenians. The Greek forces occupied the lower slopes of Mount Cithæron, with the river before them, separating them from the Persians.

123. Battle of Erythræ. The battle was opened by the Persian cavalry, commanded by Masis′tius, the most illustrious general in the army, except Mardonius. His magnificent person, clad in complete scale-armor of gold and burnished brass, was conspicuous upon the battle-field; and his horsemen, then the most famous in the world for their skill and bravery, severely harassed the Megarians, who were posted on the open plain. Olym′piodo′rus with a select body of Athenians went to their assistance, and Masistius spurred his Nisæan steed across the field to meet him. In the sharp combat which followed, the Persian was unhorsed, and as he lay along the ground was assailed by a swarm of enemies. The heavy armor, which prevented his rising, protected him from their weapons, until, at length, an opening in his visor allowed a lance to reach his brain. His death decided the fate of the battle.

124. After this victory the Greek army moved nearer to Platæa, where was a more abundant supply of water and a more convenient ground. It was the strongest force which the Persians had yet encountered in Greece, numbering, with allies and attendants, 110,000 men. For ten days they lay facing each other with no important action. The Persians, however, intercepted convoys of provisions, and succeeded in choking up the spring which supplied the Greeks with water, while, by their arrows and javelins, they prevented their approach to the river. Pausanias then resolved to fall back to a level and well-watered meadow still nearer to Platæa.

125. BATTLE OF PLATÆA. The Spartans were attacked while on the march, and sent immediately to the Athenians for aid. The latter marched to their assistance, but were intercepted by the Ionian allies of the Persians, and cut off from the intended rescue. Pausanias, thus compelled to engage with a small portion of his army, ordered a solemn sacrifice, and his men stood awaiting the result, unflinching, though exposed to a storm of Persian arrows. The omens were unfavorable, and the sacrifices were again and again renewed. At length Pausanias, lifting his eyes streaming with tears toward the temple of Hera, besought the goddess that if fate forbade the Greeks to conquer, they might, at least, die like men. At this moment the sacrifices assumed a more favorable aspect, and the order for battle was given.

B. C. 479.

The Spartan phalanx in one dense mass moved slowly but steadily against the Persians. The latter acted with wonderful resolution, seizing the pikes of the Spartans or snatching away their shields, while they wrestled with them hand to hand. Mardonius himself, at the head of his chosen guards, fought in the foremost ranks, and animated the courage of his men both by word and example. But he received a mortal wound, and his followers, dismayed by his fall, fled in confusion to their camp. Here they again made a stand against the Lacedæmonians, who were unskilled in attacking fortified places, until the Athenians, who had meanwhile conquered their Ionian opponents, came up and completed the victory. They scaled the ramparts and effected a breach, through which the remainder of the Greeks poured into the camp. The Persians now yielded to the general rout. They fled in all directions, but were so fiercely pursued, that, except the 40,000 of Artaba′zus, who had already secured their retreat, scarcely 3,000 escaped. The victory was complete, and immense treasures of gold and silver, besides horses, camels, and rich raiment, remained in the hands of the Greeks.

126. Mounds were raised over the brave and illustrious dead. Only to Aristodemus, the Spartan, who had incurred disgrace by returning alive from Thermopylæ, no honors were decreed. The soil of Platæa became a second "Holy Land." Thither every year embassies from the states of Greece came to offer sacrifices to Zeus, the deliverer, and every fifth year games were celebrated in honor of liberty. The Platæans themselves, exempt henceforth from military service, became the guardians of the sacred ground, and to attack them was decreed to be sacrilege.

127. On the day of the victory of Platæa, a no less important advantage was gained by the Greeks at Mycale, in Ionia. Here a large land force, under Tigra'nes, had been stationed by Xerxes for the protection of the coast, and hither the Persian fleet retired before the advance of the Greeks. The Persians drew their ships to land, and protected them by intrenchments and strong earth-works. The Greeks, finding the sea deserted, approached near enough to make the voice of a herald heard, who exhorted the Ionians in the army of Tigranes to remember that they, too, had a share in the liberties of Greece. The Persians, not understanding the language of the herald, began to distrust their allies. They deprived the Samians of their arms, and placed the Milesians at a distance from the front to guard the path to the heights of Mycale. The Greeks, having landed, drove the Persians from the shore to their intrenchments, and the Athenians first became engaged in storming the barricades. The native Persians fought fiercely, even after their general was slain, and fell at last within their camp. All the islands which had given assistance to the Medes were now received into the Hellenic League, with solemn pledges never again to desert it.

RECAPITULATION.

Athens incurred the vengeance of the Persian king by aiding a revolt of the Asiatic Greeks. The first invasion of Greece, by Mardonius, failed; a second and larger force, under Datis and Artaphernes, ravaged Naxos and part of Eubœa, but was defeated by Miltiades and 11,000 Greeks, at Marathon. An unsuccessful attempt upon Paros destroyed the fame of Miltiades, and he died under a charge of having received bribes from the Persians. Aristides succeeded him in popular favor, but was at length exiled through the influence of Themistocles. The latter urged the naval preparations of his countrymen, and Athens then first became a great maritime power. A congress at Corinth, B. C. 481, united the Greek forces under Spartan command. The Delphic oracle promising safety to the Athenians only within walls of wood, they abandoned their city and took refuge on the fleet. A few hundreds of Spartans and Thespians withstood the Persian host at Thermopylæ, until betrayed by a Malian guide. The invaders were totally defeated in a naval combat at Salamis, and Xerxes retired to Persia. Mardonius, failing to end the war by diplomacy, was finally overthrown in the battles of Erythræ and Platæa; and the land and naval forces of the Persians were at the same time destroyed at Mycale, in Asia Minor.

GROWTH OF ATHENS.

128. Though their immediate danger was past, the Greeks did not suffer their enemies to rest. A fleet of fifty vessels was prepared, with the intention to rescue every Greek city in Europe or Asia which still felt the power of the Persian. Though Athens, as before, furnished more ships than all the other states, Pausanias commanded. He first wrested Cyprus from the Persians, and then proceeded to Byzantium, which he also liberated and occupied as a residence for seven years.

129. Siege of Sestus. The Athenians resolved to win back the colony founded by Miltiades in the Chersonesus. The whole remaining force of the Persians made a last stand at Sestus, and endured a siege so obstinate that they even consumed the leather of their harness and bedding for want of food. They yielded at last, and the natives gladly welcomed back the Greeks. Laden with treasures and secure of a well-earned peace, the Athenians returned home in triumph. Among their relics, the broken fragments and cables of the Hellespontine bridge of Xerxes were long to be seen in the temples of Athens.

B. C. 478.

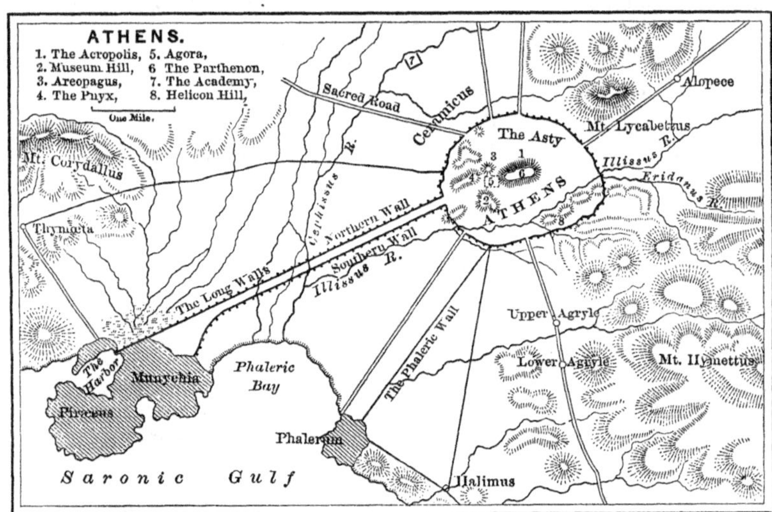

130. Notwithstanding her losses, Athens came forth from the Persian wars stronger, and with a higher rank among the Grecian states, than she had entered them. Her efforts and sacrifices had called forth a power which she was scarcely conscious of possessing, and with the consent of Sparta, whose constitution illy fitted her for distant enterprises, Athens was now recognized as the leader of the Greeks in foreign affairs. In the meantime important changes had occurred in her internal policy. The power of the great families was broken, and the common people, who had borne the brunt of hardship and peril in the war, were recognized as an important element in the state. Aristides, though the leader of the aristocratic party, proposed and carried an amendment by which all the people, without distinction of rank or property, obtained a share in the government, the only requisites being intelligence and moral character. The archonship, which had hitherto been confined to the eupatrids, was now thrown open to all classes.

Themistocles was the popular leader. His first care was the rebuilding of the walls of Athens, and he provided means by levying contributions upon those islands which had given aid to the Persians. The jealous opposition of the Spartans was overcome by gold and management. To accommodate the greatly increased navy, he improved the port of Piræus and protected it by strong walls. He hoped, by building up the naval power of Athens, to place her at the head of a great maritime empire, comprising the islands and Asiatic coasts of the Ægean, thus eclipsing the Spartan supremacy on the Grecian mainland.

131. Pausanias, now commanding at Byzantium, had lost all his Spartan virtue in the pride of conquest and the luxury of wealth. After the victory at Platæa, he had engraven on the golden tripod dedicated to Apollo by all the Greeks, an inscription in which he claimed for himself the exclusive glory. His government, justly offended, caused this inscription to be replaced by another, naming only the confederate cities, and omitting all mention of Pausanias. Both the pride and the talents of the Spartan commander were too great for the private station into which he must soon descend; for though so long generalissimo of the Greeks, he was not a king in Sparta, but only regent for the son of Leonidas. The conversation of his Persian captives, some of whom were relatives of the great king, opened brilliant views to the ambition and avarice of Pausanias. His own relative, Demara′tus, had exchanged the austere life of a Spartan for all the luxury of an Oriental palace, with the government of three Æolian cities. The greater talents of Pausanias would entitle him to yet higher dignities and honors.

In view of these glittering bribes, the victor of Platæa was willing to become the betrayer of his country. He released his noble prisoners with messages to Xerxes, in which he offered to subject Sparta and the rest of Greece to the Persian dominion, on condition of receiving the king's daughter in marriage, with wealth and power suitable to his rank. Xerxes welcomed these overtures with delight, and immediately sent commissioners to continue the negotiation. Exalted by his new hopes, the pride of Pausanias became unbearable. He assumed the dress of a Persian satrap, and journeyed into Thrace in true Oriental pomp, with a guard of Persians and Egyptians. He insulted the Greek officers and subjected the common soldiers to the lash. Even Aristides was rudely repulsed when he sought to know the reason of this extraordinary conduct.

Reports reached the Spartan government, and Pausanias was recalled. He was tried and convicted for various personal and minor offenses, but the proof of his treason was thought insufficient to convict him. He returned to Byzantium without the permission of his government, but was expelled by the allies for his shameful conduct. Again recalled to Sparta, he was tried and imprisoned, only to escape and renew his intrigues both with the Persians and with the Helots at home, to whom he promised freedom and the rights of citizenship if they would aid him to overthrow the government and make himself tyrant.

He was caught, at length, in his own snares. A man named Argilius, whom he had intrusted with a letter to Artabazus, remembered that none of those whom he had seen dispatched on similar errands, had returned. He broke the seal and found, together with much treasonable matter,

B. C. 471.

directions for his own death as soon as he should arrive at the satrap's court. The letter was laid before the ephors, and the treason being now fully proved, preparations were made to arrest Pausanias. He was warned and took refuge in the temple of Athena Chalciœ′cus. Here he suffered the penalty of his crimes. The roof was removed, and his own mother brought the first stone to block up the entrance to the temple. When he was known to be nearly exhausted by hunger and exposure, he was brought out to die in the open air, lest his death should pollute the shrine of the goddess.

132. On the first recall of Pausanias, B. C. 477, the allies had unanimously placed Aristides at their head. This was the turning-point of a peaceful revolution which made Athens, instead of Sparta, the leading state in Greece. Cautious still of awakening jealousy, Aristides named, not Athens, but the sacred isle of Delos, as the seat of the Hellenic League. Here the Congress met, and here was the common treasury, filled by the contributions of all the Grecian states, for the defense of the Ægean coasts and the furtherance of active operations against the Persians. In the assessment of these taxes, Aristides acted with so much wisdom and justice, that, though all the treasures of Greece were in his power, no word of accusation or complaint was uttered by any of the allies.

133. Having thus laid the foundation of Athenian supremacy by his

B. C. 476.

moderation, Aristides retired from command, and was succeeded by Cimon, the son of Miltiades. This young noble was distinguished by his frank and generous manners, as well as by his bravery in war, which had already been proved against the Persians. The recovery of his father's estates in the Chersonesus gave him immense wealth, which he used in the most liberal manner. He kept open table for men of all ranks, and was followed in the streets by a train of servants laden with cloaks, which they gave to any needy person whom they met. At the same time he administered to the wants of the more sensitive by charities delicately and secretly offered. Though doubtless injurious to the spirit of the Athenian people, this liberality was gladly accepted, and resulted in unbounded popularity to Cimon. His brave and sincere character commended him to the Spartans, and of all the Athenians he was probably the most acceptable leader to the allies.

134. His first expedition was against the Thracian town Ei′on, now held by a Persian garrison. The town was reduced by famine, when its governor, fearing the displeasure of Xerxes more than death, placed himself, his family, and his treasures upon a funeral pile, and perished by fire. The place surrendered, and its defenders were sold as slaves. Cimon then proceeded to Scyrus, whose people had incurred the vengeance of the League by their piratical practices. The pirates were expelled, and the place occupied by an Attic colony. As the fear of Asiatic invasion subsided, the bond between the allies and their chief relaxed. Carystus refused to pay tribute, and Naxos, the most important of the Cyclades, openly revolted. Cimon was on the alert. Carystus was subdued, and a powerful fleet was led against Naxos. The siege was long and obstinate, but it resulted in favor of Athens. The island was reduced from an ally to a subject.

135. BATTLE OF THE EURYMEDON. The victorious fleet of Cimon now advanced along the southern shores of Asia Minor, and all the Greek cities, either encouraged by his presence or overawed by his power, seized the opportunity to throw off the yoke of the Persians. His force was increased by their accession when he came to the river Eurymedon, in Pamphylia, and found a Persian fleet moored near its entrance, and a powerful army drawn up upon the banks. Already more numerous than the Greeks, they were expecting reinforcements from Cyprus; but Cimon, preferring to attack them without delay, sailed up the river and engaged their fleet. The Persians fought but feebly, and as they were driven to the narrow and shallow portion of the river, they forsook their ships and joined the army on the land. Cimon increased his own fleet by two hundred of the deserted triremes, beside destroying many.

B. C. 466.

Thus victorious on the water, the men demanded to be led on shore, where the Persian army stood in close array. Fatigued with the sea fight, it was hazardous to land in the face of a superior enemy still fresh and unworn, but the zeal of the Greeks surmounted all objections. The second battle was more closely contested than the first; many noble Athenians fell, but victory came at last; the field and the spoils remained to the Greeks. To make his victory complete, Cimon proceeded to Cyprus, where the Phœnician reinforcements were still detained. These were wholly captured or destroyed, and the immense treasure which fell into the hands of the victors increased the splendor of Athens. The tide of war had now rolled back so powerfully upon Persia, that the coasts of Asiatic Greece were free from all danger. No Persian troops came within a day's journey on horseback of the Grecian seas, whose waters were swept clear of Persian sails.

136. Aristides was now dead, and Themistocles in exile, having been ostracised in 471 B. C. Cimon was therefore both the greatest and richest of the Athenians; and while his wealth was freely used for the adornment of Athens and the pleasure of her citizens, it continually added to his power. He planted the market-place with Oriental plane-trees; laid out in walks and adorned with groves and fountains the Acade′mia, afterward made celebrated by the teachings of Plato; he erected beautiful colonnades of marble, where the Athenians long loved to assemble for social intercourse; and he caused the dramatic entertainments to be celebrated with greater elegance and brilliancy. With this increase of wealth, the tastes of the citizens became luxurious, and Athens rose from her poverty and secondary rank to be not only the most powerful, but the most magnificent of Grecian cities.

137. Though of the opposite political party to Themistocles, Cimon carried forward that statesman's great design of exalting by all means the naval power of Athens. To this end he yielded to the request of the allies, who desired to commute their quotas of ships or men for the general defense into a money payment. Other admirals had been less accommodating, but Cimon masked a profound policy under his apparent good-nature. The forces of the other states became enfeebled by want of discipline, while the Athenians were not only enriched by their tribute, but strengthened in the hardy drill of the soldier and sailor, which Cimon never suffered them to relax.

138. The fall of Themistocles was indirectly brought about by that of Pausanias. The great Athenian, living in exile, but watchful as ever in all that concerned the interests of Greece, had entered so far into the intrigues of Pausanias as to become possessed of all his plans. The Spartan ephors, finding his letters among the papers of Pausanias, and glad of such a pretext against their old enemy, sent them to Athens, accusing him of a share in the conspiracy. The party led by Cimon and friendly to Sparta was now predominant in Athens, and the people listened too readily to these suspicions. A combined force of Spartan and Athenian troops was sent forth, with orders to seize Themistocles wherever he could be found.

B. C. 466.

The exile, after many adventures, took refuge at the court of Persia, that power which, more than any man living, he had contributed to destroy, but which was ever personally generous toward its foes. The three cities, Myus, Lamp′sacus, and Magnesia, were assigned him for his support. In the latter city he passed his remaining days in affluence and honor. Two accounts have been given of his death. The more probable one is, that when Egypt revolted and was aided by Athens (B. C. 449), the Persian king called upon Themistocles to make good his promises and begin operations against Greece. But the Athenian had only wished to escape from his ungrateful countrymen, not to injure them, and he could not help to destroy that supremacy of Athens which he had spent the best years of his life in building up. Falsehood to the great king seemed to him a less heinous crime than treason against his country. He made a solemn sacrifice to the gods, took leave of his friends, and ended his days by poison.

139. The Thasians, meanwhile, had a contest with Athens for some gold mines in Thrace. Cimon conducted a fleet to Thasos, gained a naval victory, and began a three years' siege of the principal town. B. C. 465. The Thasians sent to Sparta for help, and that state was preparing to render it with great alacrity, when her attention was suddenly absorbed at home by unforeseen calamities. An earthquake of unprecedented violence first destroyed the city. Great rocks from Mount Taygetus rolled into the streets, and multitudes of B. C. 464. persons were engulfed or buried beneath the ruins of their houses. The shocks were long-continued, and terror of the supposed wrath of Heaven was added to the anguish of poverty and bereavement. The dreaded vengeace soon appeared in human form; for the persecuted Helots, hearing the signal of their deliverance in the stroke of doom to Sparta, flocked together from the fields and villages, and mingled their revenge with the commotions of Nature.

It was a terrible moment for Sparta; but her king, Archidamus, was true to the stern valor of his race. The shocks of the earthquake had hardly ceased, when he ordered the trumpets to sound to arms. Even at that fearful moment Spartan discipline prevailed. Every man who survived hastened to the king, and when the disorderly, servile crowd approached, they found a disciplined force ready to resist them. Sparta was saved for the moment; the insurgents fled and scattered themselves over the country, calling to their standard all who were oppressed. The Messenians rose in a mass, seized Ithome, where their never-forgotten hero, Aristomenes, had so long withstood the Lacedæmonian arms, fortified it anew, and formally declared war against Sparta. The ten years' conflict which followed is known as the Third Messenian War (B. C. 464–455).

In her extremity, Sparta sent to Athens for aid, and the appeal produced a violent controversy between the two parties into which that city was divided. Cimon favored the Spartans; he had always held up their brave and hardy character as a model to his countrymen, and had even sacrificed much of his popularity by naming his son Lacedæmonius. When others urged that it was well the pride of Sparta should be humbled, and her power for mischief curtailed, Cimon exhorted his countrymen not to suffer Greece to be maimed by the loss of one of her two great powers, thus depriving Athens of her companion. His generous counsel prevailed, and Cimon led a strong force against the insurgents, who were now driven from the open country and compelled to shut themselves up in the castle of Ithome.

140. The influence of Cimon had greatly declined at Athens. The democratic party had recovered from its loss in Themistocles, for a new leader was arising whose popularity and services to the state were destined to eclipse even the great men who had preceded him. This was Per′icles, the son of that Xanthippus who had impeached Miltiades. His mother was niece of Clisthenes, who is called the second founder of the Athenian constitution. Born of an illustrious family, and educated in all the opportunities of Athenian camps and schools, Pericles was said to have nothing to contend against except his advantages. His beautiful face, winning manners, and musical voice reminded the oldest citizens of Pisistratus; and the vigilance with which the Athenians guarded their liberties, turned the admiration of some into jealousy. Pericles, however, made no haste to enter on his public career, but prepared himself by long and diligent study for the influence he hoped to attain. He sought the wisest teachers, and became skilled in the science of government, while he cultivated his gifts in oratory by training in all the arts of expression.

Anaxag′oras, the first Greek philosopher who believed in one supreme Intelligence, creating and governing the universe, was the especial friend and instructor of Pericles, and to his sublime doctrines men attributed the elevation and purity of the young statesman's eloquence. Instead of relying solely upon the wisdom of his counsels, like Themistocles, or upon his natural gifts, like Pisistratus, Pericles chose every word with care, and was the first who committed his orations to writing, that he might subject every sentence to the highest polish of which it was capable. The Athenian people, the most sensitive, perhaps, to beauty of style of any that ever existed, enjoyed with keen delight the clear reasoning and brilliant language which characterized the discourses of Pericles. Nor was his perfection of detail gained by any sacrifice of energy. His public speaking was compared to thunder and lightning, and he was said to carry the weapons of Zeus upon his tongue. Above all, the sweetness of his temper, and the command which philosophy had enabled him to gain over his passions, gave him advantage over less disciplined orators. The fiercest debate or the most insulting interruptions never disturbed for a moment the cheerful and dignified composure of his manner.

141. Thasos surrendered B. C. 463; its walls were leveled, its shipping transferred to the Athenians, and all its claims upon the Thracian gold mines were given up. The people were compelled to pay all their arrears of tribute to the Delian treasury, beside engaging to meet their dues punctually in future.

142. A second time the Spartans asked the aid of Athens in their servile

B. C. 461. war, and Cimon again led an army to their relief. But the superiority of the Athenians in siege operations aroused the envy of the Lacedæmonians, even when employed in their defense; and the

WEST VIEW OF THE ACROPOLIS.

Pelasgian Walls. *Erechtheum.* *Athena Promachos.* *Parthenon.* *Walls of Cimon.*
Cave of Pan. *Propylæa.* *Temple of Nike Apteros.*

long siege of Ithome afforded time for the rivalries of the two nations to break out into open feuds. The Spartans declared that they had no further need of the Athenians, and dismissed their troops. Other allies were retained, including Ægina, the ancient rival of Athens. The latter, considering herself insulted, made an alliance with the Argives and the Aleuads of Thessaly against Sparta. The Hellenic treasury was removed from Delos to Athens, for safe keeping, it was said, against the needy and rapacious hands of the Spartans.

The popular resentment naturally extended itself to Cimon. The favor with which he was regarded in Sparta was now his greatest crime. The Athenians had indeed some reason to fear, for the Spartan nobles always maintained a party in their city who were supposed to be secretly plotting against its free government. However honestly Cimon supported aristocratic principles, the people, with equal honesty and greater wisdom, opposed him. He was subjected to the ostracism and banished for ten years.

RECAPITULATION.

The power of Athens was increased by the Persian war; and her home government, which had been confined to the nobles, was thrown open to the people. Themistocles rebuilt the walls and improved the harbor. Pausanias, becoming a traitor, died of starvation in the temple of Athena, at Sparta. Athens became the chief of the Hellenic League, whose seat and treasury were at Delos. Cimon, son of Miltiades, in command of the allied forces, captured Eion, cleared Scyros of pirates, subdued rebellions in Carystus and Naxos, and conquered the Persians, both on sea and land, in the battle of the Eurymedon. He beautified Athens by a liberal use of his enormous wealth, and improved the military and naval discipline of his fellow-citizens, at the expense of their allies. Themistocles, exiled through suspicion, took refuge in the Persian dominion, where he died. Sparta suffered a double calamity, in an earthquake and a servile rebellion, known as the Third Messenian War. Her insulting treatment of her Athenian aids destroyed the popularity of Cimon; and Pericles, the most accomplished of the Athenians, rose into power.

SUPREMACY OF ATHENS.

143. Athens, under the lead of Pericles, now entered upon the most brilliant period of her history. A dispute between Megara and Corinth involved Athens on the former and Sparta on the latter side, and thus led to the First Peloponnesian War (B. C. 460-457). At the same time, a more distant enterprise tempted the Athenians. Egypt had now cast off the last semblance of obedience to Persia, and hailed a deliverer and sovereign in the person of Inarus. In looking about him for allies, Inarus naturally sought the aid of those who, at Marathon, had first broken the power of the Persians. The Athenians engaged gladly in the war, and sent a fleet of two hundred triremes to the Nile. The events of the campaign have been recorded in the History of Persia.*

---

* See p. 93.

144. The war in Greece went on with great vigor. The Athenians were defeated at Halæ, but soon after won a naval battle at Cec′ryphali′a,* which more than retrieved their reputation. Ægina now joined in the war, and the Athenians landed upon the island and besieged the city. A Peloponnesian army came to the aid of Ægina, while the Corinthians seized the opportunity to invade Megaris. With all her forces employed either in Egypt or Ægina, they hoped that Athens would be overcome by this new attack. But Myron′ides mustered an army of boys and old men exempt from service, and marched at once to the assistance of Megara. In the battle which ensued, neither party acknowledged itself defeated, but the Corinthians withdrew to their capital, while the Athenians held the field and erected a trophy. Unable to bear the reproaches of their government, the Corinthian army returned after twelve days and raised a monument upon the field, claiming that the victory had been theirs. But the Athenians now attacked them anew, and inflicted a decisive and disgraceful defeat.

B. C. 457.

145. In the midst of these enterprises abroad, great public works were going on in Athens. Cimon had already planned a line of fortifications to unite the city with its ports, and the spoils of the Persians, taken at the Eurymedon and at Cyprus, had been assigned for the expense. Under the direction of Pericles, the building began in earnest. One wall was extended to Phalerum, and another to Piræus; but as it was found difficult to defend so large an inclosed space, a second wall to Piræus was added, at a distance of 550 feet from the first. Between these Long Walls a continuous line of dwellings bordered the carriage-road, nearly five miles in length, which extended from Athens to its principal harbor.

146. The Spartans were still too much absorbed in the siege of Ithome to interfere with the great and sudden advancement of Athenian power; but a disaster which befell their little ancestral land of Doris, in war with the Phocians, withdrew their attention even from their own troubles. An army of 1,500 heavy-armed Spartans and 10,000 auxiliaries, sent to the relief of the Dorians, drove the Phocians from the town they had taken, and secured their future good behavior by a treaty. The retreat of the Spartans was now cut off by the Athenian fleet in the Gulf of Corinth and the garrison in the Megarid. Their commander, Nicome′des, had, however, reasons beyond the necessity of the case for remaining a while in Bœotia. He was plotting with the aristocratic party in Athens for the return of Cimon, and he also desired to increase the power of Thebes, as a near and dangerous rival to the former city.

The conspiracy becoming known, the Athenians were roused to revenge. They raised an army of 14,000 men and marched against Nicomedes, at

* A small island in the Saronic Gulf, between Ægina and the coast of Argolis.

Tan′agra. Both sides fought with equal bravery and skill, and the victory was undecided until the Thessalian cavalry deserted to the Spartans. The Athenians and their allies still held out for some hours, but when the contest ended with the daylight, the victory remained with their adversaries. Nicomedes reaped no other fruit from his victory than a safe return home, but Thebes gained from it an increase of power over the cities of Bœotia.

B. C. 457.

147. Battle of Œno′phyta. The Athenians were only spurred to fresh exertions. The brave Myronides entered Bœotia two months after the battle of Tanagra, and gained at Œnophyta one of the most decisive victories ever achieved by Greeks. The walls of Tanagra were leveled with the ground. Phocis, Locris, and all Bœotia, except Thebes, were brought into alliance with Athens. These alliances were rendered effective by the establishment of free governments in all the towns, which, for self-preservation, must always range themselves on the side of Athens; so that Myronides could boast that he had not only subdued enemies, but filled central Greece with garrisons of friends.

B. C. 456.

148. Soon after the completion of the Long Walls, in 456, the island of Ægina submitted at last to Athens. Her shipping was surrendered, her walls destroyed, and the life-long rival became a tributary and subject. A fleet of fifty Athenian vessels, commanded by Tol′mides, cruised around the Peloponnesus; burned Gyth′ium, a port of Sparta; captured Chalcis, in Ætolia, which belonged to Corinth, and defeated the Sicyonians on their own coast. Returning through the Corinthian Gulf, they captured Naupac′tus, in western Locris, and all the cities of Cephallenia.

B. C. 455.

In the same year, the tenth of its siege, Ithome surrendered to the Spartans. So long and brave a defense won the respect even of bitter enemies. The Helots were reduced again to slavery, but the Messenians were permitted to depart in safety to Naupactus, which Tolmides presented them from the fruits of his victories.

149. In Egypt, the resistance of the Athenians to the Persians ended the same year, but not until after long and desperate adventures. When the citadel of Memphis was relieved by a Persian force, the Greeks withdrew to Prosopi′tis, an island in the Nile around which their ships lay anchored. The Persians following, drained the channel, and thus left the ships on dry land. The Egyptian allies yielded, on this loss of their most effective force; but the Athenians, after burning the stranded vessels, retired into the town of Byblus, resolved to hold out to the last. The siege continued eighteen months. At last the Persians marched across the dry bed of the channel and took the place by assault. Most of the Athenians fell; a few crossed the Libyan desert to Cyrene, and thus returned home.

A fleet of fifty vessels, which had been sent to their relief, came too late, and was defeated by the Persians and Phœnicians.

150. Other enterprises of the Athenians at this time were scarcely more successful, and Cimon, who had now been recalled from exile, used all his influence in favor of peace. A five years' truce was made with Sparta in 451 B. C. The Isle of Cyprus was the next object of Athenian ambition. Divided into nine petty states, it seemed to offer an easy conquest; and as the Persian king still claimed the sovereignty, the enterprise was but a renewal of ancient hostilities. Cimon sailed from Athens with a fleet of two hundred vessels; and in spite of the Persian force of three hundred ships which guarded the coast of Cyprus, he landed and gained possession of many of its towns. While besieging Citium the great commander died. By his orders his death was concealed from his men, until they had gained another signal victory, both by land and sea, in his name. The naval battle occurred off the Cyprian Salamis—a name of good omen to the Athenians.

B. C. 449.

151. A slight incident about this time brought on renewed hostilities with Sparta. The city of Delphi, though on Phocian soil, claimed independence in the management of the temple and its treasures. The inhabitants were of Dorian descent, and were, therefore, closely united with the Spartans. Where the interests of Greece were divided, the great influence of the oracle was always on the side of the Doric as opposed to the Ionic race. The Athenians did not therefore object when their allies, the Phocians, seized the Delphian territory and assumed the care of the temple. The Spartans instantly undertook what they called a holy war, by which they expelled the Phocians and reinstated the Delphians in their former privileges. Delphi now declared itself a sovereign state; and to reward the Spartans for their intervention, conferred upon them the first privilege in consulting the oracle. This decree was inscribed upon a brazen wolf erected in the city. The Athenians could not willingly resign their share in a power which, through the superstition of the people, was often able to bestow victory in war and prosperity in peace. No sooner had the Spartans left the sacred city, than Pericles marched in and restored the temple to the Phocians. The brazen wolf was now made to tell another tale, and award precedence to the Athenians.

B. C. 448.

152. At this signal of war, the exiles from various Bœotian cities, who had been driven out by the establishment of democratic governments, joined for a concerted movement. They seized Chærone′a, Orchom′enus, and other towns, and restored the oligarchic governments which the Athenians had overthrown. These changes caused great excitement in Athens. The people clamored for immediate war; Pericles strongly opposed it: the season was unfavorable, and he considered that the honor of Athens was not immediately at stake. But the counsel of Tolmides prevailed, and with a thousand young Athenian volunteers, assisted by an army of allies, he marched into Bœotia. Chæronea was soon subdued and garrisoned with Athenians.

Flushed with its speedy victory, the army was returning home, when, in the vicinity of Coronæa, it fell into an ambush and suffered a most signal and memorable defeat. Tolmides himself, with the flower and pride of the Athenian soldiery, was left dead upon the field. A large number of prisoners were taken, and to recover these the government had to enter into a treaty with the new oligarchies, and withdraw its forces from Bœotia. Locris and Phocis lost their free institutions and became allies of Sparta. The island of Eubœa threw off the Athenian yoke, and other subject islands showed signs of disaffection. At the same time, the five years' truce with Sparta expired, and that state prepared with new zeal to avenge its humiliation at Delphi.

B. C. 447.

B. C. 445.

153. Pericles, whose remembered warnings against the Bœotian war only heightened the respect and confidence of the people, now acted with energy and promptness. He landed in Eubœa with a sufficient force to reduce that island, but had scarcely crossed the channel when he learned that the Megarians were in revolt. Aided by allies from Sicyon, Epidaurus, and Corinth, they had put all the Athenian garrisons to the sword, except a few in the fortress of Nisæa, and all the Peloponnesian states had combined to send an army into Attica. To meet this greater danger, Pericles returned home. The Peloponnesian army soon appeared, under the young Spartan king, Plisto′anax; but instead of the decisive operations that were expected, it only plundered the western borders of Attica, and retired without striking a blow. Plistoanax and his guardian were accused, on their return, of having accepted bribes from the Athenians; and as both fled the country, rather than meet the prosecution, we may presume that the charge was just. Returning to Eubœa, Pericles reduced the island to complete subjection, and established a colony at Histiæa.

154. All parties now desired peace. A thirty years' truce was concluded between Athens and Sparta, in which the former submitted to the loss of her empire on land. The foothold in Trœzene, the right to levy troops in Achaia, the possession of the Megarid, the protectorate of free governments in central Greece, all were given up. But the losses of the war had fallen most heavily on the party which began it, while Pericles stood higher than ever in the esteem of his fellow-citizens. Thucyd′ides,* a kinsman of Cimon, and his successor as leader of the aristocracy, was summoned to the ostracism, and when he rose to make his defense he had not a word to say. He was banished, and retired to Sparta, B. C. 444.

B. C. 445.

* This exiled politician must not be confounded with Thucydides the great historian, who was living at the same time.

155. Pericles now united all parties, and for the rest of his life held supreme control of affairs. The nobles respected him as one of their own order; the merchants and alien settlers were enriched by his protection of trade; the shippers and sailors, by his attention to maritime affairs; artisans and artists, by the public works he was incessantly carrying on; while the ears of all classes were charmed by his eloquence, and their eyes by the magnificent buildings with which he adorned the city. At this time was erected the Parthenon, or temple of Athena the Virgin, adorned by Phidias with the most beautiful sculptures, especially with the colossal statue of the goddess in ivory and gold, forty-seven feet in height. The Erechtheum, or ancient sanctuary of Athena Polias, was rebuilt; the Propylæ′a, of Pentelic marble, erected; and the Acropolis now began to be called the "city of the gods."

156. Only three islands in the neighboring seas now maintained their independence, and of these the most important was Samos. The Milesians, who had some cause of complaint against the Samians, appealed to the arbitration of Athens, and were joined by a party in Samos itself which was opposed to the oligarchy. The Athenians readily assumed the judgment of the case, and as Samos refused their arbitration, resolved to conquer the island. Pericles with a fleet proceeded to Samos, revolutionized the government, and brought away hostages from the most powerful families. But no sooner was he departed than some of the deposed party returned by night, overpowered the Athenian garrison, and restored the oligarchy. They gained possession of their hostages, who had been deposited on the Isle of Lemnos, and being joined by Byzantium, declared open war against Athens.

B. C. 440.

157. When the news of this event reached Athens, a fleet of sixty vessels was immediately sent forth, Pericles being one of the ten commanders. Several battles were fought by sea, and the Samians were at length driven within the walls of their capital, where they endured a nine months' siege. When at last they were forced to yield, they were compelled to destroy their fortifications, surrender their fleet, give hostages for their future conduct, and pay the expenses of the war. The Byzantines submitted at the same time. Athens was completely triumphant; but the terror she had inspired was mixed with jealousy. During the revolt, the rival states had seriously discussed the question of aiding the rebels; and it was decided in the negative mainly by the influence of Corinth, which, though no friend to Athens, feared that the precedent might be remembered in case of a revolt of her own colonies.

158. Corcyra, a colony of Corinth, had itself founded, on the Illyrian coast, the city of Epidamnus. This city, attacked by the Illyrians, led by some of her own exiled nobles, sent to Corcyra for aid, but was refused, as the exiles belonged to the party in

B. C. 435.

power in the mother city. The Epidamnians now resorted to Corinth, which undertook their defense with great energy. Corcyra, alarmed in turn, applied to Athens for assistance. Opinions were divided in the assembly, but that of Pericles prevailed, who urged that war could not in any case be long delayed, and that it was more prudent to make it in alliance with Corcyra, whose fleet was, next to that of Athens, the most powerful in Greece, than to be driven at last to fight at a disadvantage.

Considering, however, that Corinth, as an ally of Sparta, was included in the thirty years' truce, it was resolved to make only a defensive alliance with Corcyra; *i. e.*, to render assistance in case its territories should be invaded, but not to take part in any aggressive action. A naval battle soon occurred off the coast of Epirus, in which the Corinthians were the victors, and prepared to effect a landing in Corcyra. Ten Athenian vessels were present, under the command of Lacedæmonius, son of Cimon, and they were now, by the letter of their agreement, free to engage. But suddenly, after the signal of battle had been given, the Corinthians drew back and stood away for the coast of Epirus. Twenty Athenian ships had appeared in the distance, which they imagined to be the vanguard of a large fleet. Though this was a mistake, it had the effect of preventing further hostilities, and the Corinthians returned home with their prisoners.

159. Incensed at the interference of Athens, the Corinthians sought revenge by uniting with Prince Perdic′cas of Macedonia, to stir up revolts among the Athenian tributaries in the Chalcidic peninsulas. A battle ensued at Olynthus, in which the Athenians were victorious over the Corinthian general, and blockaded him in Potidæa, where he had taken refuge.

B. C. 432.

A congress of the Peloponnesian states was held at Sparta, and complaints from many quarters were uttered against Athens. The Æginetans deplored the loss of their independence; the Megarians, the crippling of their trade; the Corinthians, that they were overshadowed by the towering ambition of their powerful neighbor. At the same time, the Corinthians contrasted the restless activity of Athens with the selfish inertness of Sparta, and threatened that if the latter still delayed to do her duty by the League, they would seek a more efficient ally.

The envoys having departed, Sparta decided to undertake the war. Before proceeding to actual hostilities, it was thought best to send messengers to Athens, demanding, among other things, that she should "expel the accursed" from her presence — referring to Pericles, whose race they chose to consider as still tainted with sacrilege. But Pericles replied that the Spartans themselves had heavy accounts to settle on the score of sacrilege, not only for starving Pausanias in the sanctuary of Athena, but for dragging away and murdering the Helots who had taken refuge, during the late revolt, in the temple of Posidon. The other demands were rejected, though with more hesitation. They concerned the independence of Megara and Ægina, and, generally, the abdication by Athens of her position as head of the League. The Athenians declared that they would refrain from commencing hostilities, and would make just satisfaction for any infringement on their part of the thirty years' truce; but that they were ready to meet force with force.

160. WAR IN BŒOTIA. While both parties hesitated to begin the war, the Thebans precipitated matters by a treacherous attack upon the city of Platæa. This city, instead of joining the Bœotian League, had been in friendly alliance with Athens, and was hence regarded with great jealousy by the Thebans. A small oligarchical party in Platæa favored the Thebans, and it was Naucli′des, the head of this party, who, at dead of night, admitted three hundred of them into the town. The Platæans were roused from sleep to find their enemies encamped in their market-place; but though scattered and betrayed, they did not yield. They secretly communicated with each other by breaking through the walls of their houses; and having thus formed a plan for defense, fell upon the enemy a little before daybreak.

B. C. 431.

The Thebans were exhausted by marching all night in the rain; they were entangled in the narrow, crooked streets of the town; and even women and children fought against them by hurling tiles from the roofs. The reinforcement which they expected was delayed, and before it arrived the three hundred were either slain or captured. The Thebans without the walls now seized whatever persons and property they could lay their hands on, as security for the release of the prisoners. The Platæans sent a herald to declare that the captives would be immediately put to death, unless the ravages should cease; but that, if the Thebans would retire, they should be given up. The marauders withdrew, but the Platæans, instead of keeping their word, gathered their movable property into the town, and then put all their prisoners to death. Fleet-footed messengers had already been sent to Athens with the news. They returned with orders to the Platæans to do nothing of importance without the advice of the Athenians. It was too late, however, to save the lives of the prisoners or the honor of their captors.

RECAPITULATION.

In the First Peloponnesian War (B. C. 460-457), Athens was allied with Megara; Sparta and Ægina, with Corinth. At the same time, the Athenians aided a revolt of Egypt against Persia, and built long walls to connect their city with its ports. Sparta, interfering in a war between Phocis and Doris, defeated the Athenians at Tanagra; but the latter gained a more decisive victory at Œnophyta, which brought Phocis, Locris, and all Bœotia, except Thebes, into their alliance. Ægina was conquered and made tributary to Athens. Ithome surrendered to Sparta; the Helots were re-enslaved and the Messenians exiled. In a new war, occasioned by the interference of Sparta at Delphi, the Athenians, under Tolmides, gained some advantages, but were disastrously defeated at Coronæa, with great loss of influence in central Greece. Assailed at once by rebellions in Eubœa and Megaris, and by a Spartan invasion, Pericles defeated the latter by bribes and the former by arms. The peace which followed was concluded on terms unfavorable to Athens. Being called to aid a popular revolution in Samos, the Athenians captured its chief city and re-established their own influence. Epidamnus, in war with her mother city, was aided by Corinth; while Athens, taking the part of Corcyra, defeated the Corinthians at Olynthus, and besieged them two years in Potidæa. A more general war was hastened by the mutual treachery of the Thebans and Platæans.

THE PELOPONNESIAN WAR.

161. All Greece now prepared for war—a war of twenty-seven years, which was to be marked by more calamities and horrors than Hellas had ever yet endured. On the side of Sparta fought all Peloponnesus, except Argos and Achaia, together with Megara, Bœotia, Phocis, Opuntian Locris, Ambracia, Leucadia, and Anactoria. Athens had for allies, on the mainland, Thessaly and Acarnania, with the cities of Naupactus and Platæa. There were also her tributaries on the coast of Thrace and Asia Minor, and on the Cyclades, beside her island allies, Chios, Lesbos, Corcyra, Zacynthus, and, later, Cephallenia.

B. C. 431-404.

162. Archidamus, king of Sparta, having collected his allies at the isthmus, marched into the Attic territory about the middle of June. The inhabitants quitted their fields, and with all the property they could remove, took refuge within Athens and the Piræus. Every corner and recess of the city walls became a dwelling. In the market-place, the public squares, and the precincts of the temples, temporary habitations arose, and the poorer sort found shelter in tents, huts, and even casks, placed against the Long Walls. Among this crowded population, violent debates arose concerning the conduct of the war. Great indignation was felt against Pericles for the inaction of the army, while Archidamus was ravaging the fields almost under their eyes.

B. C. 431.

But the leader had resolved to carry the war out of Attica. For this purpose a combined fleet of Athenians and Corcyræans sailed around the Peloponnesus, disembarking troops at various points to ravage the country. Two Corinthian settlements in Acarnania were captured, and the island of Cephallenia transferred its allegiance from Sparta to Athens. The Æginetans were expelled, and their island occupied by Athenian settlers. Archidamus, after five or six weeks, marched out of Attica and disbanded his army. The Athenians then put their forces in motion to punish the Megarians, whom they considered as revolted subjects. They laid waste the whole territory to the gates of the capital, and the devastations were renewed every year while the war continued.

163. The next spring, with a new Spartan invasion, brought a still greater calamity to the Athenians. The plague, originating in Ethiopia, had traveled along the Asiatic coasts of the Mediterranean until it reached their city, where the crowded condition of the people made it spread with frightful rapidity. A terror seized the populace, some of whom believed that their enemies had poisoned the wells, while a greater number ascribed the pestilence to the wrath of Apollo, who was the especial protector of the Dorian race.

B C. 430.

164. In their passion of despair the Athenians turned against Pericles, whose cautious policy they considered as the cause of their misfortunes. Though still refusing battle, which, with the reduced numbers and exhausted spirit of the army, would have been almost certain defeat, he actively pushed his operations against the Peloponnesus. To relieve the crowded city of its mischievous elements, he fitted out a fleet and led it in person to ravage the enemy's coasts. On his return he found the opposition stronger than ever, and an embassy had even been sent to Sparta to sue for peace. The suit had been contemptuously rejected, and the rage of the Athenians was only increased. Pericles persuaded them to persevere in the war, but his eloquence was unavailing to silence the fury of his personal enemies. By the influence of Cleon, his chief opponent, he was even accused of embezzling the public funds, and was fined to a large amount.

165. But the life and adversities of the great statesman were alike near their end. The plague had robbed him of his nearest relatives. A lingering fever, following an attack of the pestilence, terminated his life. As he lay, seemingly unconscious, the friends surrounding his death-bed were rehearsing his great deeds, when the dying man interrupted them, saying, "All that you are praising was either the result of good fortune, or, in any case, common to me with many other leaders. What I chiefly pride myself upon is, that no Athenian has ever mourned on my account."

B. C. 429.

166. The second Lacedæmonian foray was more destructive than the first, for the ravages extended over all Attica, even to the silver mines of Laurium. The fleet of the Peloponnesians destroyed the fisheries and commerce of Athens, and devastated the island of Zacynthus. During the following winter Potidæa surrendered, after a blockade of two years, and was occupied by a thousand Athenian colonists.

B. C. 430.

The third campaign of the Spartans was directed against Platæa. On the approach of Archidamus, the Platæans sent a solemn remonstrance, reminding him of the oath which Pausanias had sworn on the evening of their great battle, making Platæa forever sacred from invasion. The king replied that the Platæans, too, were bound by

B. C. 429.

oath to labor for the independence of every Grecian state. He reminded them of their heinous crime in the slaughter of the Theban prisoners, but promised that, if they would abandon the cause of Athens and remain neutral during the war, their privileges should be respected. The Platæans refused to forsake their ancient ally, and the siege of their city began.

167. The garrison which thus defied the whole Peloponnesian army, consisted of only 480 men, but they made up in energy what they lacked in numbers. Archidamus began by shutting up every outlet of the town with a palisade of wood, then erected against this a mound of earth and stone, forming an inclined plane, up which his troops could march. The Platæans undermined the mound, which fell in, and thus defeated seventy days' work of the whole besieging army. They also built a new wall within the old one, so that, if this were taken, the Spartans would still be no nearer the possession of the city.

B. C. 429–427.

Seeing that the will of the Platæans could only be subdued by famine, the allies now turned the siege into a blockade. They surrounded the city with a double wall, and roofed the intervening space, so as to afford shelter to the soldiers on duty. The Platæans thus endured a complete separation from the outer world for two years. Provisions began to fail; and, in the second year, nearly half the garrison made their escape, by climbing over the barracks and fortifications of their besiegers in the rain and darkness of a December night. The Platæans, though thus reduced in numbers, came at length to absolute starvation. A herald now appeared from the Spartan commander, requiring their submission, but promising that only the guilty should be punished. They yielded. When brought before the five Spartan judges, every man was found guilty and led to execution. The town and territory of Platæa were made over to the Thebans, who destroyed all private dwellings, and with the materials erected a huge barrack, to afford shelter to visitors, and dwellings to the serfs who cultivated the land. The city of Platæa was blotted out from the map of Greece.

168. The Athenians, with their ally Sital′ces, a Thracian chief, were warring in the north with little success. Sitalces, with an irregular but powerful host of 150,000 Thracians, invaded Macedonia with the intention of dethroning Perdiccas. The Macedonians, unable to meet him in the open field, withdrew into their fortresses, and Sitalces, who had no means for conducting sieges, retired after thirty days. Phor′mio, an Athenian captain, gained two victories, meanwhile, in the Corinthian Gulf, over a vastly superior number of Spartans. In the first engagement he had but twenty ships, to the Spartan forty-seven; in the second, without reinforcements, he met a fresh Spartan fleet of seventy-seven sail.

B. C. 429.

The fourth year of the war was marked by the revolt of Mytilene,
B. C. 428. capital of Lesbos. Envoys were sent to Sparta to implore assistance, which was willingly granted, and the Mytilenians were received into the Peloponnesian League.

169. In the spring of 427, the Spartan fleet advanced to Mytilene, but it arrived only to find the town in the possession of the Athenians. Nearly reduced by famine, the governor, by the advice of a Spartan envoy, had armed all the men of the lower classes for a last desperate sortie. The result was contrary to his expectations. The mass of the Mytilenian people preferred the Athenian supremacy to that of their own oligarchic government. Emboldened by their arms, they declared that they would treat directly with the Athenians, unless all their demands were granted. The governor had no choice but to open negotiations himself. The city was surrendered, and the fate of its inhabitants was left to be decided by the popular assembly in Athens, whither the ring-leaders of the revolt were sent.

170. A thousand Athenians assembled in the Agora to decide the fate of their prisoners. Salæ′thus, the Spartan envoy, was instantly put to death. With regard to the rest, a spirited debate ensued. Cleon the tanner, the former opponent of Pericles, took a prominent part; and in spite of more humane and moderate counsels, actually succeeded in carrying his brutal proposition, to put to the sword all the men of Mytilene, and sell the women and children into slavery. Iniquitous as such an order would be in any case, it was the more so in this, because the greater number of the Mytilenians were friendly to Athens, while the revolt had been the act of the oligarchy, who were enemies of the people. So strong had been the opposition, that Cleon feared a reversal of the sentence, and therefore had a galley instantly dispatched to Lesbos, with orders for its immediate execution.

His apprehensions were well founded. A single night's reflection filled the better sort of Athenians with horror at the inhuman decision into which they had been hurried. They demanded a new assembly to reconsider the question; and though this was contrary to law, the *strategi* consented and convened the citizens. In the second day's debate the atrocious decree was rescinded. Every nerve was now strained to enable the mercy-bearing barque to overtake the messengers of death, who were a whole day's journey in advance. The strongest oarsmen were selected, and urged to their greatest exertion by the promise of large rewards if they should arrive in time. Their food was given them while they plied the oar, and sleep was allowed them only in short intervals, and by turns. The weather proved favorable, and they arrived just as Paches, who had received the first dispatch, was preparing for its execution. The Mytilenians were saved, but the walls of their city were leveled, and its fleet surrendered to the Athenians. The island of Lesbos, with the exception of Methym′na, which had refused all share in the revolt, was divided into 3,000 parts, of which 300 were devoted to the gods, and the rest assigned by lot to Athenian settlers. The prisoners at Athens were tried for their share in the conspiracy, and put to death.

171. The Corcyrean prisoners who had been carried to Corinth in 432, were now sent home, in the hope that their account of the generous treatment they had received would induce their countrymen to withdraw from the Athenian alliance. They joined with the oligarchical faction to effect a revolution in Corcyra, killed the chiefs of the popular party, gained possession of the harbor, the arsenal, and the market-place, and thus, by overawing the people, obtained a vote in the assembly to maintain in future a strict neutrality. The people, however, fortified themselves in the higher parts of the town, and called to their aid the serfs from the interior of the island, to whom they promised freedom.

B. C. 427.

The oligarchists set fire to the town, but while it was burning a small Athenian squadron arrived from Naupactus, and its commander attempted, with great wisdom, to make peace between the contending parties. He had to all appearance effected this design, when a Peloponnesian fleet, more than four times as numerous as his own, appeared, under the command of Alci′das. The Athenians withdrew without loss, and Alcidas had Corcyra for the moment in his power; but with his usual want of promptness, he spent a day in ravaging the island, and, at night, beacon fires on Leucas announced the approach of an Athenian fleet outnumbering his own. Alcidas drew off before daybreak, leaving the oligarchists in the city to their fate. The next seven days were a reign of terror in Corcyra. The popular party, protected by the presence of the Athenians, abandoned itself to revenge. Civil hatred was stronger than natural affection. A father slew his own son; brothers had no pity for brothers. The aristocratic party was nearly exterminated; but five hundred escaped, and fortified themselves on Mount Isto′ne, near the capital.

172. The sixth year of the war opened with floods and earthquakes, which seemed an echo in nature of the moral convulsions of Greece. The plague was raging again at Athens. To appease the wrath of Apollo, a solemn purification of the isle of Delos, his birth-place, was performed in the autumn. All bodies that had been buried there were removed to a neighboring island, and the Delian festival was revived with increased magnificence. The usual Spartan invasion of Attica had been prevented this year, either by awe of the supposed wrath of the gods, or by fear of the plague; but in the seventh year of the war (B. C. 425), their king, Agis, again crossed the borders and ravaged the country. He was recalled, after fifteen days, by the news that

B. C. 426.

the Athenians had established a military station on the coast of Messenia.

173. A fleet bound for Sicily, under Eurymedon and Sophocles, had been delayed for a time by a storm, near the harbor of Pylos. The commanders selected this place for a settlement of Messenians from Naupactus, who would thus be able to communicate with their Helot kinsmen, and harass the Spartans. Demosthenes was left with five ships and two hundred soldiers, who were increased, by a reinforcement of Messenians, to a thousand men. The wrath of the Spartans was only equaled by their alarm at this infringement of their territory. Their fleet was instantly ordered from Corcyra, while Agis, with his army, marched from Attica. The long and narrow island of Sphacte′ria, which covered the entrance to the Bay of Pylos, was occupied by Thrasymel′idas, the Spartan, while his ships were sheltered in the basin which it inclosed. Demosthenes, while awaiting reinforcements, had to meet a vastly superior number with his handful of men. The attack from the sea was led by Bras′idas, one of the greatest captains whom Sparta ever produced. He fought on the prow of the foremost vessel, urging his men forward by looks and words; but he was severely wounded, and the battle ended with no advantage to the Spartans. It was renewed the second day with no better success, and the Athenians erected a trophy, which they ornamented with the shield of Brasidas.

B. C. 425.

The arrival of the Athenian fleet was followed by a severe and still more decisive battle. The victorious Athenians proceeded to blockade Sphacteria, which contained the choicest Peloponnesian troops. So serious was the crisis, that the ephors saw no escape except to sue for peace. An armistice was agreed upon, and the better spirits on both sides began to hope for a termination of the war. But the foolish vanity of Cleon and his party demanded the most extravagant terms, and the voice of reason was drowned. Hostilities re-commenced, with equal vexation to both parties. Demosthenes, fearing that the storms of winter would interrupt his blockade, resolved to make an attack upon the island, and sent to Athens explaining his position and demanding reinforcements. The report was disheartening to the Assembly, which now began to accuse Cleon for having persuaded it to let slip the occasion for an honorable peace. Cleon retorted by accusing the officers of cowardice and incapacity, and declared that, if *he* were general, he would take Sphacteria at once! At this boast of the tanner, the whole assembly broke out into laughter, and cries, "Why do n't you go, then?" were heard on all sides. The lively spirits of the Athenians recovered with a bound from their unusual depression, and the mere joke soon grew into a purpose. Cleon tried to draw back, but the Assembly insisted. At last he engaged, with a certain number of auxiliaries added to the troops already at Pylos, to take the island in twenty days, and either kill all the Spartans upon it, or bring them in chains to Athens.

174. Singular as were the circumstances of Cleon's commission, his success was equally remarkable. Demosthenes had made all ready for the attack; and to his prudence, aided by the accidental burning of the woods on Sphacteria, rather than to the generalship of Cleon, the victory was due. The Athenians, landing before daybreak, overpowered the guard at the southern end of the island, and then drew up in order of battle, sending out parties of skirmishers to provoke the enemy to a combat. The Spartan general, blinded by the light ashes raised by the march of his men, advanced, with some difficulty, over the half-burnt stumps of the trees. He was greatly outnumbered by his assailants, who harassed him from a distance with arrows, and forced him at length to retire to the extremity of the island. Here the Spartans fought again with their accustomed bravery; but a party of Messenians, who had clambered over some crags usually deemed inaccessible, appeared upon the heights above, and decided the fate of the battle. All the surviving Spartans surrendered, and Cleon and Demosthenes, setting out immediately after the battle, arrived at Athens with their prisoners within the twenty days. This victory was one of the most important that the Athenians had gained. The harbor of Pylos was strongly fortified and garrisoned with Messenian troops, for a base of operations against Laconia.

175. At the beginning of the eighth year the Athenians were everywhere triumphant, and the Spartans, humbled and distressed, had repeatedly asked for peace. Nicias, in the early part of the year, conquered the island of Cythera, and placed garrisons in its two chief towns, which were a continual defiance of the Lacedæmonians. He then ravaged the coasts of Laconia, and captured, among other places, the town of Thyr'ea, where the Æginetans, after their expulsion from their own island, had been permitted to settle. Those of the original exiles who survived were carried to Athens and put to death. The brutalizing influences of war were more apparent every year, and these cold-blooded massacres had become almost of common occurrence.

B. C. 424.

The Spartans, about the same time, alarmed by the nearness of the Messenian garrisons of Pylos and Cythera, gave notice that those Helots who had distinguished themselves by their faithful services during the war, should be set at liberty. A large number of the bravest and ablest appeared to claim the promise. Two thousand of these were selected as worthy of emancipation, crowned with garlands, and dignified with high religious honors. But in a few days they had all disappeared, by means known only to the Spartan ephors—men unmoved, either by honor or pity, from their narrow regard to the supposed interest of the state.

176. The success of the Athenians did not entirely desert them in their

Megarian expedition, but their attempt upon Bœotia resulted only in disaster. The chief movement was executed by Hippoc′rates, who led an army of more than 32,000 soldiers across the Bœotian frontier to Delium, a place strongly situated near Tanagra, among the cliffs of the eastern coast. Here he fortified the temple of Apollo, and placing a garrison in the works, set out for home. The Bœotians had collected a large army at

B. C. 424. Tanagra, which now moved to intercept the Athenians upon the heights of Delium. The battle commenced late in the day. The Athenian right was at first successful, but their left was borne down by the Theban phalanx. In their ranks were Socrates, the philosopher, and his pupils, Alcibi′ades and Xenophon, all destined to the highest fame in Grecian history. At length the Bœotian cavalry appeared, and decided the fortunes of the day. The Athenians fled in all directions, and only the fall of night prevented their complete destruction. Delium was taken by siege after seventeen days.

177. Soon after these disasters, the Athenians lost all their dominion in Thrace. Brasidas had led a small but well chosen army to the aid of Perdiccas and the Chalcidian towns. The bravery and integrity of this great general led many of the allies of Athens to forsake her party, and when he suddenly appeared before Amphipolis, that city surrendered with scarcely an attempt at resistance. Thucydides,* the historian, was general in that region. The Athenian party in Amphipolis sent to him for aid, but he arrived too late. For this failure, whether proceeding from necessity or carelessness, the general was sentenced to banishment, and spent his next twenty years in exile, during which he contributed more by his literary work to the glory of Greece, than he would probably have done in military command. Brasidas proceeded to the easternmost of the three Chalcidian peninsulas, and received the submission of nearly all the towns.

The Athenians were now so disheartened by their losses, that they, in turn, began to propose peace; and the Spartans, anxious for the return of their noble youths who were prisoners in Athens, were equally desirous of a treaty. To this end a year's truce was agreed upon, in 423, to afford time for permanent negotiations. Unhappily, two days after the beginning of the truce, Scio′ne revolted from the Athenians, who demanded its restitution. The Spartans refused, and the whole year was suffered to pass away without any further efforts toward peace. At its expiration, Cleon advanced into Thrace with a fleet and army. He took the towns of Toro′ne and Galepsus, and was proceeding against Amphipolis, when a battle ensued which ended at once his life and his assumption of power. Brasidas, too, was mortally wounded, but he lived long enough to know that he was victorious.

* See note. p. 157,

178. Peace of Nicias. The two great obstacles to peace were now removed, and, in the spring of 421, a treaty for fifty years, commonly called the "Peace of Nicias," was concluded between Athens and Sparta. Some allies of the latter complained that Sparta had sacrificed their interests to her own, and formed a new league, with Argos for their head. Athens made a new alliance for a hundred years with Argos, Elis, and Mantine′a, B. C. 420.

RECAPITULATION.

In the greater Peloponnesian war (B. C. 431–404), nearly all central and southern Greece were allied with Sparta; most of the maritime states, with Athens. Within the latter city were crowded most of the people of Attica, in terror of the Spartan invasions. Great numbers died of the plague; its most illustrious victim was Pericles. A two years' blockade of Platæa, by the Spartans, ended with the annihilation of the city. The revolt of Lesbos was subdued by Athens, and the Mytilenians were condemned to death, but the revengeful sentence was reversed. A revolution in Corcyra resulted in a seven days' massacre of the aristocratic party. A solemn purification of Delos was performed, to mitigate the plague at Athens. The Athenians established a colony at Pylos, to harass Laconia, and were victors in several naval battles. Cleon, the tanner, with Demosthenes, the general, conquered the Spartans at Sphacteria. Nicias captured Cythera, and garrisoned its towns. The brutal character of the war was shown in the massacre of exiled Æginetans at Athens, and of two thousand Helots at Sparta. The disastrous battle of Delium ended the invasion of Bœotia by the Athenians, who lost, at the same time, all their possessions in Thrace. The Peace of Nicias was concluded B. C. 421, and Athens made a new league with some former allies of Sparta.

The Sicilian Expedition.

179. From two previous celebrations of the Olympic Games the Athenians had been excluded, but, in the summer of this year, the Elean heralds appeared again to invite their attendance. B. C. 420. Those who looked to see Athens poverty-stricken, from her many losses, were surprised at the magnificence of her delegates, who made the most costly display in all the processions. Alcibiades entered on the lists seven four-horse chariots, and received two olive crowns in the races. This young man was among the ablest citizens that Athens ever possessed. His genius, bravery, and quickness in emergencies might have made him her greatest benefactor; but, through his unregulated ambition and utter lack of conscience, he became the cause of her greatest calamities.

180. War soon broke out between the Spartans and the Argives, in which the Spartan king, Agis, won the important battle of Mantinea, B. C. 418. The oligarchical party, gaining power at Argos, cast off the alliance with Athens, and made a treaty with Sparta. But the nobles abused their power in brutal outrages upon the people, who effected another revolution and obtained possession of the city. By their request, Alcibiades came to their aid with a fleet and army. Though the Spartans and Athenians were nominally at peace, the garrison of Pylos was still committing depredations in Laconia, and Spartan privateers were seriously injuring Athenian commerce.

181. About this time, an embassy from Sicily besought the aid of the Athenians for the city of Egesta. It was involved in a contest with its neighbor, Selinus, which had obtained help from Syracuse. The "war of races" had, indeed, broken out twelve years before in Sicily, and the Athenians had more than once sent aid to the Ionian cities, Leonti′ni and Camari′na, against their Dorian neighbors, who had joined the Peloponnesian League. Alcibiades threw his whole influence into the cause of Egesta, hoping at once to improve his wasted fortunes with Sicilian spoils, and gratify his ambition with the glory of conquest. He even hoped, beside making Athens supreme over all the Hellenic colonies, to conquer the empire of Carthage, in the western Mediterranean.

Nicias and all the moderate party opposed the enterprise. They only prevailed in having an embassy sent to Egesta, to ascertain if its people were really able to fulfill their promise of furnishing funds for the war. The envoys were completely outwitted. In the temple of Aphrodite they saw a magnificent display of vessels which appeared to be solid gold, but were really silver-gilt. They were feasted at the houses of citizens, and were surprised by the profusion of gold and silver plate which adorned their sideboards, not suspecting that the same articles were passing from house to house, and doing repeated service in their entertainment. Sixty talents of silver were paid as a first installment, and the commissioners went home with glowing accounts of Egestan wealth.

182. All doubt disappeared from most minds in Athens, and Nicias, Alcibiades, and Lamachus were appointed to lead an expedition to Sicily. The zeal of the Athenians knew no bounds. Young and old, rich and poor, alike demanded a share in the great expedition. The generals had difficulty in selecting from the throng of volunteers. The fleet was on the point of sailing, when a mysterious event threw the excited multitude into consternation. The *Hermæ*, which stood before every door in Athens, before every temple or gymnasium, and in every public square, were found one morning reduced to shapeless masses of stone. Not one escaped. The people, in an agony of superstitious horror, demanded the detection and punishment of the criminal. Suspicion fell upon Alcibiades, because he was known to have burlesqued the Eleusinian mysteries in a drunken frolic, and was supposed to be capable of any sacrilege. He indignantly denied his guilt, and demanded an immediate examination. But his enemies contrived to have it postponed until his return, thus sending him out under the burden of an unproved charge, which might be revived for his condemnation in case of disaster.

B. C. 415.

183. On the day appointed for the sailing of the armament, nearly the whole population of Athens accompanied the soldiers on their march at day-break to Piræus. When all were on board, the trumpet commanded silence, and the voice of the herald, in unison with that of the people, was heard in prayer. The pæan was then sung, while the officer at the prow of each vessel poured a libation from a golden goblet into the sea. At a given signal, the entire fleet slipped its cables and started at the utmost speed, each crew striving to be first at Ægina.

184. The whole armament of Athenians and allies mustered at Corcyra in July, 415. It numbered 136 vessels of war and 500 transports, carrying 6,300 soldiers, beside artisans and a large provision of food and arms. When the fleet approached the coast of Italy, three fast-sailing triremes were sent to notify the Egestæans of its arrival, and to learn their present condition. These rejoined the fleet at Rhegium, with the unwelcome report that the wealth of Egesta was wholly fictitious, and that thirty talents more were the extent of the aid to be expected. The three admirals were now divided in opinion. Nicias was for sailing at once to Selinus, making the best terms possible, and then returning home. Alcibiades proposed to seek new allies among the Greek cities, and with their aid to attack both Selinus and Syracuse. Lamachus urged an immediate attack upon the latter city, the greatest and wealthiest on the island. This counsel was at once the boldest and the safest, for the Syracusans were unprepared for defense, and their surrender would have decided the fate of the island; but, unhappily, Lamachus was neither rich nor influential. His plan was disregarded, and that of Alcibiades adopted.

185. The fleet, sailing southward, reconnoitered the defenses of Syracuse, and took possession of Catana, which became its headquarters. At this point, Alcibiades received from Athens a decree of the Assembly, requiring his return for trial. A judicial inquiry had acquitted him of the mutilation of the Hermæ, but he was still charged with profaning the Eleusinian Mysteries, by representing them at his own house for the entertainment of his friends. This was an unpardonable crime, and those noble families which had derived from their heroic or divine ancestors an especial right to officiate in the ceremonies, felt themselves grossly insulted. The public trireme which brought the summons to Alcibiades, was under special orders not to arrest him, but to suffer him to return in his own vessel. The wily general availed himself of this courtesy to effect his escape. Landing at Thurii, he eluded his pursuers, and the messengers returned to Athens without him. Here in his absence he was condemned to death, his property confiscated, and the Eumolpidæ solemnly pronounced him "accursed."

186. The Athenians had spent three months in Sicily with so little effect, that the Syracusans began to regard them with contempt. Nicias, thus shamed into attempting something, spread a report that the Catanæans were inclined to expel the Athenians from their city, and thus drew a large army from Syracuse to their aid. During its absence from home, the whole Athenian fleet sailed into the Great Harbor of Syracuse, and landed a force which intrenched itself near the mouth of the Anapus. A battle followed on the return of the Syracusans, and Nicias was successful. Instead of following up this advantage, he retired into winter-quarters at Catana, and afterward at Naxos, while he sent to Athens for a supply of money, and to his Sicilian allies for a re-enforcement of men.

The Syracusans spent the winter in active preparation. They built a new wall across the peninsula, between the Bay of Thapsus and the Great Port, covering their city on the west and north-west. They sent, at the same time, to Corinth and Sparta for help, and found in the latter city an unexpected ally. Alcibiades had crossed from Italy to Greece, and had received a special invitation to Sparta. Here he indulged his spite against his countrymen by revealing all their plans, and urging the Spartans to send an army into Sicily to disconcert their movements.

187. With the opening of spring, Nicias commenced the siege by fortifying the heights of Epipolæ, which commanded the city. He built, also, a fort at Sy′ke, and dislodged the Syracusans from the counter-walls which they were constructing. The Athenian fleet was stationed in the Great Harbor, and the Syracusans, despairing of effectual resistance, sent messengers to arrange terms of surrender. But the brave Lamachus had been slain, and Nicias, now sole commander, was too inactive to seize the victory just within his grasp.

B. C. 414.

188. At this point, Gylip′pus, the Spartan, arrived with only four ships on the Italian coast, and supposing that Syracuse and all Sicily were irrecoverably lost, sought only to preserve the cities on the peninsula. To his delight, he learned that the Athenians had not even completed their northern line of works around Syracuse. He hastened through the Straits of Messina, which he found unguarded, and, landing at Him′era, began to raise an army from the Dorian cities of Sicily. With these he marched to Syracuse directly over the heights of Epipolæ, which Nicias had neglected to hold. Entering the city, he sent orders to the Athenian general to leave the island within five days. Nicias disregarded the message, but the acts which followed proved that the Spartan was master of the situation. He captured the Athenian fort at Labalum, built another upon the heights of Epipolæ, and connected it with the city by a strong wall.

The Sicilian towns which had hesitated now joined the winning side. Re-enforcements arrived from Corinth, Leucas, and Ambracia; and Nicias, unable to continue the siege with his present force, withdrew to the headland of Plemmyr′ium, south of the Great Port. His ships were out of repair, his men disheartened and inclined to desert, and his own health declining. He wrote to Athens, begging that the army might be instantly re-enforced and he himself recalled. Athens was in a state of siege, for the Spartan king, Agis, was encamped at Decele´a, fourteen miles north of the city, in a position to command the whole Athenian plain. The public funds were nearly exhausted, hunger began to be felt, and the diminished number of citizens were worn out with the labor of defending the walls day and night. It was resolved, however, to re-enforce Nicias, and, at the same time, harass Sparta on her own territory. For this purpose, Char´icles was sent to plant a military station on the south coast of Laconia, similar to that of Pylos in Messenia; while Demosthenes and Eurymedon conducted a fleet and army to Sicily. The first enterprise was successful; the second was too late.

B. C. 413.

189. The Syracusans had been defeated in one naval battle, but in a second, lasting two days, they were completely victorious, and the Athenian ships were locked up in the extremity of the harbor. Demosthenes' arrival with his fresh forces had some effect in checking the enemy and raising the spirits of his countrymen. Perceiving at once that Epipolæ was the vital point, he directed all his efforts to its re-capture, but without success. Seeing, now, that the siege was hopeless, he urged Nicias to return home and drive the Spartans out of Attica. But, remembering the lively hopes and the magnificent ceremonies with which the armament had set forth, Nicias could not consent to return to Athens covered with the disgrace of failure. Neither would he withdraw to Thapsus or Catana, where Demosthenes urged the advantages of an open sea and constant supplies of provisions. But, large re-enforcements arriving for Syracuse, this retreat became necessary, and the plans were so well laid that it might easily have been effected without the knowledge of the enemy.

Unhappily, an eclipse of the moon occurred on the very eve of the intended movement. The imperfect astronomy of those days had not foretold the event, and the soothsayers could only conclude that Artemis, the especial guardian of Syracuse, was showing her anger against its assailants. They declared that the army must remain three times nine days in its present position. During this delay, the disconcerted plan became known to the Syracusans, who resolved to strike a blow while the enemy was within their reach. A battle by land and sea was the result. In the former, the Athenians beat off their assailants; but, in the latter, their fleet was utterly defeated and Eurymedon slain.

Aug. 27, 413.

190. The Syracusans now resolved upon the total destruction of their enemy. They blocked up the Great Harbor by a line of vessels moored across its entrance. The only hope for the Athenians, perhaps for Athens itself, was to break this line, and to this end Nicias again prepared for battle. The amphitheater of hills which surround the harbor was crowded with spectators of either party, watching with anxious eyes the conflict upon which their fates depended. The water was covered with the yachts of wealthy Syracusans, ready to offer their services whenever they might be demanded. The first attack of the Athenians was upon the barrier of ships at the entrance of the harbor. It failed, and the Syracusan fleet of 76 triremes then engaged the 110 of the Athenians. The crash of the iron prows, the shouts of the combatants, and the answering groans or cheers of their friends upon the shore, filled the air with a perpetual clamor. For a long time the issue was doubtful, but, at last, the fleet of Nicias began to retreat toward the shore. A cry of despair arose from the Athenian army, answered by shouts of triumph from the pursuing vessels and the citizens on the walls.

The Athenian fleet was now reduced to sixty vessels, and the Syracusan to fifty. Nicias and Demosthenes besought their men to renew the effort to force their way out of the harbor, but their spirits were so far broken that they refused any further combat by sea. The army still numbered 40,000 men, and it was resolved to retreat by land to some friendly city, where they could defend themselves until transports should arrive. If this design had been instantly put in execution, it might have been successful; for the Syracusans had given themselves up to drunken revelries, occasioned equally by the rejoicings over their victory and by the festival of Hercules, and had no thoughts to spare for their fugitive foe. But Hermoc′rates, the most prudent of their number, resolved to prevent what he foresaw would be the Athenian movement. He sent messengers to the wall, who pretended to come from spies of Nicias within the city, and warned the generals not to move that night, as all the roads were strongly guarded. Nicias fell into the snare, and sacrificed his last hope of escape.

191. On the second day after the battle, the army began its march toward the interior, leaving the deserted fleet in the harbor, the dead unburied, and the wounded to the vengeance of the foe. On the third day of the march, the road lay over a steep cliff, which was guarded by a Syracusan force. Two days' assaults upon this position were unsuccessful, and the generals took counsel during the night to turn toward the sea. Nicias, with the van, succeeded in reaching the coast; but Demosthenes lost his way, was overtaken by the enemy, and surrounded in a narrow pass, where he surrendered the shattered remnants of his army, numbering six thousand men. Nicias was now pursued, and overtaken at the river Asina′rus. Multitudes perished in the attempt to cross. Pressed closely by the army of Gylippus, the rear rushed forward upon the spears of their comrades, or were hurled down the steep banks and carried away by the current. All order was lost, and Nicias surrendered at discretion. The generals were condemned to death. The common soldiers, imprisoned in the stone-quarries, without food or shelter, suffered greater miseries than all that had preceded. A few who survived were sold as slaves, and their talents and accomplishments won, in some instances, the friendship of their masters.

RECAPITULATION.

Alcibiades sustained the credit of Athens in the Olympic Games, carried aid to the Argives against the Spartans, and zealously promoted the Sicilian expedition of his countrymen. On the eve of departure he was accused of sacrilege, and after his arrival in Sicily he was sentenced to death, and pronounced accursed. The siege of Syracuse, notwithstanding the great efforts of the Athenians, resulted in failure and disaster, while Athens itself was besieged by the king of Sparta. Reinforcements, led forth by Demosthenes, only completed the exhaustion of the city. The Syracusans gained a naval battle in their harbor, and captured the two Athenian armies in their retreat.

Decline of Athens.

192. In the midst of private grief and national dismay, the Athenians learned that their allies were deserting them. Alcibiades was stirring up revolts in Chios, which, with Lesbos and Eubœa, implored the aid of Sparta to free them from their dependence. The two satraps of Asia Minor sent envoys to the same power, inviting her coöperation in overthrowing the Athenian empire in Asia, and pledging Persian gold for the entire expense. To the lasting shame of Sparta, she concluded a treaty at Miletus, engaging to unite with Persia in a war against Athens, and to restore to the Persian dominion all the cities and territories which it had formerly embraced. This clause was explained, in a subsequent treaty, to include not only all the islands of the Ægean, but Thessaly and Bœotia, thus yielding to the Persians the field of Platæa, and fixing their frontier on the very border of Attica. Miletus itself was immediately surrendered to Tissaphernes.

B. C. 412.

193. In this general defection Samos remained faithful, and afforded a most important station for the Athenian fleet during the remaining years of the war. The Samians, warned by the example of Chios, overthrew their oligarchical government, and the democracy thus established was acknowledged by Athens as an equal and independent ally. Great preparations were now made in Athens. The reserve fund of a thousand talents, which had lain untouched since the time of Pericles, was applied to fitting out a fleet against Chios. Once more the Athenians were successful, both by sea and land. Lesbos and Clazomenæ were reconquered, the Chians defeated, and, in a battle near Miletus, the Spartans themselves were overcome. That city remained in the hands of the Persians and Lacedæmonians, but the relations between these widely contrasted allies were no longer cordial. The Spartans were ashamed of their dealings with the great enemy of Greece, and Tissaphernes was under the influence of Alcibiades. This deeply plotting Athenian persuaded the satrap that it was not the interest of Persia to allow any party in Greece to become powerful, but, rather, to let them wear each other out by mutual hostilities, and then appropriate the domains of both. This advice tended most against the Spartans, who were now so strongly reinforced that they might soon have put an end to the war. Tissaphernes, accordingly, held the Spartan fleet inactive, waiting for the Phœnicians, who were never to appear; and when this pretext would no longer avail, he applied his golden arguments to its commanders with the same effect.

194. Alcibiades now sought to bring the satrap into alliance with Athens; and failing in this, he tried at least to convince his countrymen at Samos that he had power to effect such an alliance, for his sole desire was to be recalled to his native city. Hating and fearing the Athenian democracy, he made one condition, however, to his intercession with the Persian, which was, that a revolution should be effected, and an oligarchical government established. The generals at Samos acceded to this plan, and Pisander was sent to Athens to organize the political clubs in favor of the revolution.

When he presented the scheme of Alcibiades in the Assembly, a great tumult arose. The people clamored against the surrender of their rights; the Eumolpidæ protested against the return of a wretch who had profaned the Mysteries. Pisander could only plead the exhaustion and the misery of the Republic; but this argument, though distasteful, was unanswerable. The people reluctantly consented to the change in the constitution, and Pisander, with ten colleagues, was sent to treat with Alcibiades. The exile well knew that he had promised more than he could perform. To save his credit, he received the eleven ambassadors in the presence of Tissaphernes, and made such extravagant demands in his name, that they themselves angrily broke up the conference and withdrew.

195. Though convinced that they had been cheated by Alcibiades, they had now gone too far to recede from the proposed revolution. Pisander, with five of his colleagues, returned to Athens, while the rest went about among the allies to establish oligarchies. At Athens the old offices were abolished, and a Council of Four Hundred, chiefly self-elected, held power for four months. By the aid of the army at Samos, a counter-revolution was effected, and the leaders of the oligarchy were accused of treason for their dealings with the Spartans. Most of them fled; but two, Ar′cheptol′emus and Antiphon, were tried and executed.

B. C. 411.

196. The remainder of the Peloponnesian war was wholly maritime, and its scene of operations was on the coast of Asia Minor. The Spartans, by long practice and close collision with their great rivals, had become nearly equal to the Athenians in naval skill. Their attention to this arm of the service was shown by the yearly appointment of the *navarchus*, an officer whose power, while it lasted, was even greater than that of the kings, for he was above the control of the ephors.

197. Min′darus, the Spartan commander at Miletus, becoming disgusted with the fickle policy of Tissaphernes, set sail for the Hellespont, hoping to find the other satrap more constant to the Spartan alliance. He was followed by an Athenian fleet, under Thrasyl′lus, which, though less numerous than his own, inflicted upon him a severe defeat in the strait between Sestus and Abydus. Mindarus now sent for the allied fleet at Eubœa, but in passing Mount Athos it was overtaken by a violent storm, and wholly destroyed. The Athenians followed up their advantage by the capture of Cyz′icus, which had revolted from them; and, a few weeks later, gained another great battle near Abydus, by the timely aid of Alcibiades. B. C. 411.

198. In the spring of 410, Mindarus was besieging Cyzicus, and the Athenians determined to relieve it. They passed up the Hellespont in the night, and assembled at Proconnesus. Alcibiades moved toward Cyzicus with his division of the fleet, and succeeded in enticing Mindarus to a distance from the harbor, while the other two divisions stole between him and the city, and thus cut off his retreat. A battle ensued, in which Mindarus was slain, the Spartans and their Persian allies routed, and the entire Peloponnesian fleet captured, except the Syracusan ships, which Hermocrates caused to be burnt.

199. This victory restored to the Athenians the control of the Propontis and the trade of the Euxine. Ships laden with corn now entered Piræus, bearing relief to the hungry poor, and discouragement to King Agis, who still held the heights of Decelea, in the vain hope of starving the city into surrender.

Pharnabazus, meanwhile, was aiding the Spartans by every means in his power. He fed and clothed, armed and paid their seamen, allowed them to cut timber in the forests of Mount Ida, and build their ships at his docks of Antandros. Through his assistance, Chalcedon, on the Bosphorus, was enabled to hold out two years against Alcibiades. It surrendered at last, in 408. Selym′bria and Byzantium were taken about the same time.

200. These repeated successes restored the credit of Alcibiades, and, in the spring of 407, he was welcomed back to his native city. All the people met him at Piræus, with as much joy and enthusiasm as they had escorted him thither, eight years before, when sailing for the fatal expedition to Sicily. He protested his innocence before the Senate and Assembly. His sentence was reversed by acclamation, his property restored, the curse revoked, and he was made general, with unlimited powers. Before his departure, with the large fleet and army which were now at his disposal, he resolved to atone to Demeter for whatever slight had been thrown upon her by his alleged sacrilege. The sacred procession from Athens to Eleusis had been intermitted these seven years, owing to the nearness of the Spartan troops. Alcibiades now delayed his departure, in order to escort and protect the participants.

201. The arrival of two new officers upon the Asiatic field of war turned the scale against Athens. The one was Cyrus, a son of the Persian king; the other was Lysander, the new Spartan *navarchus*, who took command of the Peloponnesian fleet at Ephesus. These two made common cause, and together took measures for severe and unrelenting war against the Athenians. The gold which the Persian prince lavished without stint, the Spartan applied to increasing the wages of his seamen. By this well-timed liberality, he drew over great numbers of men from the opposing fleet, and rendered even those who did not desert, discontented and mutinous.

B. C. 407.

202. Alcibiades arrived with his fleet to find the situation less favorable than he had hoped. The Spartan troops were better paid and equipped than his own, and to raise funds he resorted to levying forced contributions on friendly states. During his absence on one of these forays, the fleet became engaged in battle with the Spartans, and was defeated with considerable loss. The Athenians began to perceive that eight years' exile and two or three years' good behavior, had not altered the character of the man, but that he was as dissolute, fickle, and unscrupulous as ever. They dismissed him from his command, and appointed ten generals, with Conon at their head.

203. At the same time that Conon arrived to take command of the Athenians, Cal′licrat′idas succeeded Lysander as *navarchus*. He found an empty treasury and a cold reception, alike from his own countrymen and the Persians, whom Lysander had purposely prejudiced against him. Cyrus refused to see or aid him. Callicratidas now took bolder counsel. He sailed to Miletus, and urged its citizens to throw off the Persian alliance. Many rich men came forward with generous contributions of money, with which he equipped fifty new triremes, and sailed to Lesbos with a fleet twice as numerous as that of the Athenians.

B. C. 406.

204. He had a battle with Conon in the harbor of Mytilene, in which the Athenians lost nearly half their ships, and only saved the rest by drawing them ashore under the walls of the town. Callicratidas then blockaded the city by sea and land; and Cyrus, perceiving his success, assisted him with supplies of money. Great efforts were made at Athens, as soon as the condition of Conon was known. A large fleet was sent out in a few days, and being reinforced by the allies at Samos, arrived at the south-eastern extremity of Lesbos, numbering 150 vessels. Callicratidas left fifty ships to continue the blockade, and sailed to meet his enemy.

BATTLE OF ARGINUSÆ. A long and obstinate combat followed; but Callicratidas was at length thrown overboard and drowned, and victory declared for the Athenians. The Spartans had lost seventy-seven vessels, and their fleet at Mytilene hastily withdrew, leaving the harbor open for the escape of Conon.

205. At the beginning of the next year, Lysander was again placed in command of the Spartan fleet. His numbers being still inferior, he avoided an engagement, but he crossed the Ægean to the coast of Attica, for a personal consultation with Agis, and thence proceeded to the Hellespont, where he commenced the siege of Lampsacus. The Athenian fleet followed, but arrived too late to save the town. Conon stationed himself, however, at Ægos-Potami (Goat's River), on the northern side of the channel, with the intention of bringing the Spartan to an engagement. The Athenians were upon a barren plain; while the Spartans, better situated and abundantly supplied with provisions, were in no haste to begin the battle. Alcibiades, who was living near in his own castle, saw the danger of his countrymen, and advised their generals to remove to Sestus, but his counsels were resented as impertinence; and attributing the Spartan delay to cowardice, the Athenians became every day more neglectful of discipline.

B. C. 405.

206. BATTLE OF ÆGOS-POTAMI. At length Lysander, seizing a moment when the Athenian seamen were scattered over the country, crossed the strait with his entire force. Only a dozen vessels, in Conon's personal command, were in condition for battle; and the whole fleet, with the exception of the flag-ship, the sacred Par′alus, and eight or ten others, fell into the Spartan possession without a blow. Three or four thousand prisoners, including officers and men, were massacred, in retaliation for recent cruelties of the Athenians in the treatment of their captives. The defeat at Ægos-Potami was the death-blow of the Athenian empire. Chalcedon, Byzantium, and Mytilene soon surrendered; and all the Athenian towns, except that of Samos, fell without resistance into the hands of the Spartans. Popular governments were every-where overthrown, and a new form of oligarchy was established, consisting of ten citizens, with a Spartan officer, called a *harmost*, at their head.

B. C. 405, Sept.

207. The news of the great calamity arrived in the night at Piræus. A cry of sorrow and despair spread instantly from the port to the city, as each man passed the terrible tidings to his neighbor. "That night no man slept;"* and in the morning the Assembly was called, to consider how the existence of the city might be prolonged. The situation was desperate. Even though no hostile force should approach Athens, Lysander, by holding the Euxine, could effectually reduce it to starvation.

* The words of Xenophon, who was present in Athens.

The number of citizens was so diminished, that even criminals could not be spared from public service. All prisoners were released, except a few murderers and desperate villains; private offenses were forgotten in the common danger, and all Athenians united in a solemn oath of mutual forgiveness.

208. Two months after the defeat, Lysander appeared at Ægina with
B. C. 405, Nov. an overwhelming naval force; and, at the same time, the Peloponnesian army encamped in the groves of Academia, near the gates of Athens. Yet, though some of the people were already dying of hunger, their spirit was not broken; and when the Spartan ephors proposed peace on condition of the destruction of the Long Walls, a senator was imprisoned for merely discussing the acceptance of these terms. When, at last, the Athenians sent offers of capitulation, three months were wasted in vain debate before the terms could be settled. The Thebans and Corinthians insisted that no conditions should be granted, but that the very name of Athens should be blotted out, her site become a desert, and her people be sold into slavery. The Spartans, with more generosity, refused to "put out one of the eyes of Greece," or to enslave a people which had rendered such services to the whole Hellenic race in the great crisis of the Persian wars.

It was finally agreed that the Long Walls and the fortifications of Piræus should be destroyed, the ships of war surrendered, all exiles restored to their rights of citizenship, and all the foreign possessions of Athens relinquished. These hard conditions were executed with needless insolence. Lysander himself presided at the demolition of the walls; and the work, which was rendered very difficult by the solidity of their construction, was turned into a sort of festal celebration. A chorus of flute-players and dancers, wreathed with flowers, animated the workmen at their toil; and as the massive walls of Pericles fell, stone by stone, shouts of triumph arose from the army of destroyers that this day witnessed the dawn of the liberties of Greece.

209. The Athenian supremacy had lasted seventy-three years from the
B. C. 477-404. confederation at Delos. The power which had been intrusted to the imperial city for the common defense, had, in some cases, been made to bear heavily on the subject allies, and her later history is stained by many acts of cruelty. But the true empire of Athens has never been overthrown; for, through poetry, art, and philosophy, she still rules the minds of men with a power which has never been surpassed.

RECAPITULATION.

The rivals, subjects, and enemies of Athens united to hasten her fall; and to this end Sparta promised to the Persians Thessaly, Bœotia, the islands of the Ægean, and the coast of Asia Minor. Alcibiades partly neutralized the Spartan influence with the satraps, and secured an oligarchical revolution in Athens as the price of his efforts in her favor. Through his aid the Athenians gained several great naval victories in the northern Ægean, which restored to them the corn-trade of the Euxine, and relieved the famine in their besieged city. The gold of Cyrus the Younger, and the skill of Lysander, again turned the tide against the Athenians, who were twice defeated; and, though afterward triumphant near the Arginusæ, received a final and disastrous overthrow at Ægos-Potami, which ended their supremacy in Greece. The subject towns fell into the power of the Spartans; and, the following spring, Athens itself was surrendered to Lysander, and its Long Walls destroyed.

SPARTAN SUPREMACY.

210. Sparta, in alliance with Persia, now became the leading state in Greece; and all the cities yielded to her influence, by abolishing their free governments and setting up oligarchies in their stead. Athens herself received a thoroughly Spartan constitution. A provisional committee of five, called ephors, invited Lysander from Samos to preside over the reorganization of Athens. Under his direction, thirty officers were appointed for the government of the city, who have always been known in history as the "Thirty Tyrants."

211. Critias was their chief. Having been banished formerly by a vote of the people, he now wreaked his vengeance with unsparing cruelty on the best and noblest citizens. Blood flowed daily and fines, imprisonments, and confiscations were the events of every hour. By the advice of Theram'enes, who was the head of the more moderate party, three thousand citizens were chosen from the adherents of the Thirty, whose sanction was required for important proceedings. But all, except this enfranchised number, were placed beyond the protection of the law, and might be put to death, at the word of the tyrants, without even a show of trial. A list was made of those who were destined to death, and any of the ruling party might add to it such names as either avarice or hatred suggested to him. The wealthiest citizens were, of course, the first victims, for the estate of the murdered man went to his accuser. Theramenes, in his turn, was offered a wealthy alien to destroy and plunder, but he indignantly rejected the proposal. This implied protest against the reign of terror cost him his life. He was denounced as a public enemy, his name stricken from the roll of the Thirty, and from that of the Three Thousand, and he was ordered to instant execution. He sprang to the altar in the senate-house; but fear of divine vengeance had disappeared, together with humanity and justice, from the rulers of Athens. He was dragged away to prison, and condemned to drink the hemlock.

B. C. 404.

212. The tide was already turning, both in the ill-fated city and throughout Greece. Athens, in her humiliation, no longer excited the fear or jealousy of her former allies; while Sparta, instead of making good her assumed title of "Liberator of the Greeks," was setting up a new empire more oppressive than that of her rival. Even in Sparta itself, the pride and harshness of Lysander excited disgust, and the Thirty Tyrants at Athens were universally regarded as the tools of his scheming ambition.

The Athenian exiles, who had been biding their time, now issued from Thebes, under the lead of Thrasybu'lus, and seized the fortress of Phy'le, in the mountain barrier of Attica, on the road to the capital. The tyrants, with the Spartan garrison of the Acropolis and the Three Thousand, marched out to attack them, but were repulsed with spirit, and a timely snow-storm broke up their attempt to besiege the fortress, and drove them back to the city. Foreseeing their expulsion, the Thirty now provided for themselves a place of refuge by another horrid outrage. They caused all the inhabitants of Salamis and Eleusis, who were capable of bearing arms, to be brought as prisoners to Athens, and the towns to be occupied by garrisons in their own interest. Then filling the Odeon with Spartan soldiers and their three thousand adherents, they extorted from this assembly a vote for the immediate massacre of the prisoners.

213. Thrasybulus, supported by the indignation of the people, now marched with a thousand men to Piræus, seized the port without opposition, and fortified himself upon its castle-hill, Munych'ia. The whole Lacedæmonian party in Athens marched against him, and was defeated with considerable loss, in which must be reckoned the death of Critias. The more moderate party now gained ascendancy; the Thirty were deposed after a reign of eight months, and ten less atrocious rulers were elected in their place. The more violent members of the Thirty retired to Eleusis, and both parties sent envoys to Sparta asking aid. Lysander again entered Athens with an army, while his brother blockaded Piræus with a fleet.

B. C. 403.

At this point, however, Lysander was superseded, and the Spartan king, Pausanias, after being first repulsed, but afterward victorious over Thrasybulus, entered upon negotiations for peace. Amnesty was decreed for all past offenses, except those of the Thirty, the Eleven,* and the Ten. The exiles were restored, and Thrasybulus with his comrades now marched in solemn procession from Piræus, to present their thank-offerings to Athena on the Acropolis. In a subsequent assembly of the people, all the acts of the Thirty Tyrants were annulled, the archons, judges, and Senate of Five Hundred were restored, and a revised code of the laws of Draco and Solon was ordered. Thrasybulus and his party were rewarded with wreaths of olive for their rescue of the city.

214. Death of Socrates. Though humbled and reduced from their former greatness, the Athenians now rejoiced in the restoration of their ancient laws. Their city, their temples, and all their old customs and beliefs became doubly dear and sacred, from the

B. C. 399.

* The executioners who had put in effect the bloody sentences of the tyrants.

perils through which they had passed. The worst effect of this conservative reaction was the condemnation and death of Socrates. This great philosopher belonged to no political party, and had opposed the extreme measures of both; but he had fought on many battle-fields, and had always used his power as a citizen in favor of justice and mercy. Critias had been his pupil, but when in power had hated and persecuted his former instructor. His impeachment now came from the opposite party. He was accused of despising the gods of Athens, of introducing a new worship, and of corrupting the Athenian youth. The dissoluteness of Alcibiades may have given some color to this charge, though it is certain that his youthful impieties and subsequent misconduct were in spite of his master's instructions, not on account of them.

Being called upon for his defense, Socrates replied that, so far from violating the state religion, he had constantly admonished his disciples not to depart from the established customs. He refused to be released on terms which required him to desist from teaching. To develop wisdom and virtue in the young had been the passion of his life. He claimed no wisdom of his own, but sought to draw out the thoughts of others to just conclusions. And if he could persuade any that the care of becoming every day wiser and better must take precedence of all other cares, he was sure that he had conferred the greatest possible benefit. The high tone of his defense only irritated his judges, and he was condemned to death by poison.

The Paralus had now gone on its sacred yearly mission to the isle of Delos, and no execution could take place until its return. The thirty days thus spent by Socrates in prison were filled with inspiring converse with his friends. He spoke cheerfully of the past and the future, and expressed his immovable conviction of the immortality of the soul. His last request was that a cock should be sacrificed in his name to Æscula'pius,* an offering which persons were accustomed to make on their recovery from illness—by this common symbol testifying to all the people that he considered death as a joyful release from a state of imperfection and disease. When the appointed moment arrived, he drank the hemlock and calmly expired.

215. INVASION OF ELIS. The Eleans were among the first to feel the unchecked power of Sparta. As guardians of the sacred grove at Olympia, they had excluded the Spartans from the games at the time when the Athenians appeared, with such magnificence, under the direction of Alcibiades, and they had borne arms against them, in alliance with the Argives and Mantineans (B. C. 420–416). They had crowned their insults by ejecting King Agis from their temple, when he had come with sacrifices to consult the oracle. Agis now demanded satisfaction, which the Eleans

* The god of healing, a son of Apollo.

refused to give, and he crossed their borders with a considerable force. B. C. 402. An earthquake alarmed his superstition, and he retired without any active hostility. But the next year renewed his courage. With a large number of allies, among whom even the B. C. 401. Athenians appeared, he overran and plundered the sacred land, and performed by force the sacrifice which he had been prevented from offering peaceably. Thus victorious in his first expedition, the Spartan turned his vengeance upon the Messenians, who had been settled in his territory or upon the neighboring islands, and expelled or enslaved them all.

216. A year later King Agis died, and his brother Agesila′us received B. C. 398. his crown. Agesilaus was brave, honest, and energetic, and the circumstances of his reign called for a constant exercise of these Spartan virtues. The aid rendered by the Lacedæmonians, in the revolt of Cyrus, had not escaped the notice of the Persian king; and Tissaphernes, who now possessed the satrapy of the rebellious prince, was instructed to drive them from all their cities on the Asiatic coasts. The first efforts of the Spartans, under inferior commanders, had but indifferent success, and Agesilaus himself prepared to assume the command in Asia.

217. The headquarters of the Grecian forces were at Ephesus, where the army arrived B. C. 396. The winter was spent in busy preparations, which gave this wealthy city the appearance of one immense arsenal. In the spring of 395 he advanced upon Sardis, and put the Persian cavalry to flight. The plunder of their camp enriched the Spartans, who now ravaged the country almost under the eyes of Tissaphernes. But about this time the satrap fell into the power of Parysatis, the queen mother, who caused him to be beheaded for his former opposition to Cyrus. His successor, Tithraus′tes, proposed terms of peace, the Greek cities to remain independent, with the exception of a yearly tribute, the same that they had paid to Darius Hystaspes.

218. Meanwhile war had broken out in Greece between Thebes and Sparta, and the former had called in Athens, her ancient enemy and rival, with a promise to aid in restoring her lost supremacy. Lysander, who B. C. 395. commanded the Spartan forces in Bœotia, was defeated and slain at Haliar′tus. Pausanias, arriving too late for his assistance, dared not return to Sparta with the army, but took refuge in the temple of Athena at Tegea; and being sentenced to death by his countrymen, passed the remainder of his days in the sanctuary. His son, Agesip′olis, succeeded to his throne.

219. THE CORINTHIAN WAR. Athens, Corinth, Argos, and Thebes B. C. 394–387. now formed a close alliance against Sparta, which was soon strengthened by the addition of Eubœa, Acarnania, western Locris, Ambracia, Leucadia, and Chalcidice in Thrace. The allies assembled a large army at Corinth in the spring of 394, and it was proposed to march directly upon Sparta, and "burn the wasps in their nests before they could come forth to sting." The Lacedæmonians, however, had advanced to Sicyon by the time the allies reached Nemea, and the latter were obliged to fall back for the protection of Corinth. The Spartans attacked them near the city and gained a victory, July, 394.

220. Agesilaus had been unwillingly recalled from his war against Persia, and now appeared in the north with a powerful army, in which were numbered Xenophon* and many of the Ten Thousand. On hearing of the victory of Corinth, the king exclaimed, "Alas for Greece! she has killed enough of her sons to have conquered all the barbarians." Agesilaus advanced to Coronæa, where another battle was soon fought. B. C. 394.
The Thebans were at first successful, and, having routed the Orchomenians, pressed through to their camp in the rear. But while they were plundering this, Agesilaus had been victorious along the rest of the line, and had driven the allies to take refuge upon the slope of Mount Helicon. The Thebans, thus surrounded, had to sustain the whole weight of the Spartan attack, and no severer combat had ever been known in Grecian annals. They succeeded at last in rejoining their comrades, but the victory remained with Agesilaus.

221. Battle of Cnidus. Their two successful battles of Corinth and Coronæa were far from compensating the Spartans for the disastrous defeat which befell them the same season at Cnidus. Conon, who had spent the seven years since his disgrace at Ægos-Potami, with Evagoras of Cyprus, now reappeared, in alliance with the ancient foe of Greece, against the bitter enemy and rival of Athens. Artaxerxes, perceiving the hatred which began to be felt against the growing power of Sparta, had sent envoys to the principal cities of Greece, to unite them in a league for resistance, while he dispatched a large sum of money to Conon, to equip a fleet among the Greeks and Phœnicians of the sea-board. In command of this fleet, Conon was blockaded at Caunus by the Spartan, Pharax; but a reinforcement arriving for the Persians, the blockading squadron withdrew to Rhodes. The people of that island had unwillingly endured so long the rule of the Spartans. They rose against Pharax, compelled him to depart, and placed themselves under the protection of Conon. This admiral immediately sailed to Rhodes and took possession of the island;

---

* Though an Athenian, Xenophon was an exile, and preferred the institutions of Sparta to those of his native city. Among the principal works of this historian are the *Anabasis*, an account of the rebellion of Cyrus the Younger, and the retreat of the Ten Thousand; the *Hellenica*, a history of the Greeks from the close of the period described by Thucydides to the battle of Mantinea, B. C. 362; the *Cyropædia*, an historical romance in praise of Cyrus the Great; and the *Memorabilia*, a defense of the memory of Socrates from the charge of irreligion.

then repaired to Babylon, where he obtained a still more liberal grant of money from Artaxerxes, for the active prosecution of the war.

With the aid of Pharnabazus, who was joined with him in command, he equipped a powerful fleet and offered battle to Pisan′der, the Spartan admiral, off Cnidus, in Caria. The Persian force, consisting of Greeks and Phœnicians, was superior from the first, and especially when Pisander was deserted, in the course of the battle, by his Asiatic allies. He fought, however, with the bravery of a Spartan, until his death put an end to the contest. More than half the Spartan fleet was either captured or destroyed. As a result of this defeat, the Spartan empire fell even more rapidly than it had risen eight years before. Conon and Pharnabazus sailed from port to port, and were received as deliverers by all the Asiatic Greeks. The Spartan *harmosts* every-where fled before their arrival. Abydus and the Thracian Chersonesus alone withstood the power of Athens and Persia.

222. The following spring, the fleet of Conon and Pharnabazus crossed the Ægean, laid waste the eastern borders of Laconia, and established an Athenian garrison on the island of Cythera. The Persian, by gold and promises, assured the allies, whom he met at Corinth, of his unfailing support against Sparta; and he employed the seamen of the fleet in rebuilding the Long Walls of Athens and the fortifications of the Piræus. The recent services of Conon more than erased the memory of his former disasters, and he was hailed by his countrymen as a second founder of Athens and restorer of her greatness.

B. C. 393.

223. The war was henceforth carried on in the Corinthian territory, and the main object of the allies was to guard the three passes in the mountains which extend across the southern part of the isthmus. The most westerly of these was defended by the long walls which ran from Corinth to Lechæ′um; the other two, by strong garrisons of the allied troops. The Spartans were at Sicyon, whence they could easily ravage the fertile plain, and plunder the country-seats of the wealthy Corinthians. The aristocratic party in Corinth began to complain, and to sigh for their ancient alliance with Sparta. The ruling faction, on the other hand, invited a company of Argives into the city, and massacred a large number of their opponents. The aristocrats avenged themselves by admitting Praxi′tas, the Spartan leader, within their long walls, and a battle was fought within this confined space, in which the Corinthians were defeated. The Spartans destroyed a large portion of the walls, and, marching across the isthmus, captured two places on the Saronic Gulf.

The Athenians, alarmed by the door being thus thrown open for the invasion of their own territory, marched with a force of carpenters and masons to the isthmus, and aided the Corinthians to rebuild the walls. They were building, however, for their enemies; for the next summer, Agesilaus, with the Spartan fleet, gained

B. C. 392.

possession not only of the walls, but the port of Lechæum. Several other towns on the Corinthian Gulf, with much booty and many captives, also fell into his possession. The Lacedæmonians now surrounded Corinth on all sides, and the Thebans, despairing of success for the allies, sent envoys demanding peace.

224. While they were still in the presence of Agesilaus, he received news of an unprecedented and mortifying disaster. Iphicrates, the Athenian, had been for two years drilling a troop of mercenaries in a new system of tactics, which was intended to combine the advantages of both heavy and light-armed troops. He had proved their efficiency in several trials, and was now ready to test them upon the Spartan battalion, which was considered almost invincible. The Spartans were returning to the camp at Lechæum—having escorted their Amyclæan comrades some distance on their way homeward to celebrate a religious festival—when they were attacked, in flank and rear, with arrows and javelins. Burdened with their heavy armor, they were unable to cope with their agile antagonists, while their long pikes were of little use against the short swords of the *peltasts.* They broke at length in confusion, and many were driven into the sea, followed by their assailants, who wrestled with and slew them in the water.

225. The war in Asia went on with varying success. Thimbron, the Spartan, was defeated and slain by the Persian, Struthas, with the total loss of his army of 8,000 men. About the same time an Athenian squadron, which was going to assist Evagoras against Persia, was captured by a Spartan fleet. Thrasybulus was then sent with a larger naval force, with which he re-established Athenian power in the Propontis, and re-imposed the toll anciently collected by Athens on all vessels passing out of the Euxine. In the midst of this expedition Thrasybulus was slain. The Spartans, by renewed exertions, again became for a time masters of the straits; but Iphicrates, with his peltasts, surprised their leader among the passes of Mount Ida, and gained a decisive victory, which restored the Athenian supremacy in that region.

B. C. 390.

226. PEACE OF ANTALCIDAS. The Spartans now made an effort toward peace by sending Antalcidas to the Persian court. The king accepted their propositions, and furnished means to enforce them. A large fleet, commanded by Antalcidas and Tiribazus, visited the Hellespont, and by cutting off the supplies of corn from the Euxine, threatened Athens with famine. All the states were now ready to listen to terms, and in a congress of deputies Tiri′bazus presented the following propositions: "King Artaxerxes thinks it just that the cities in Asia, and the islands of Clazomenæ and Cyprus should belong to him. He thinks it just to leave all the other Grecian cities, both small and great, independent, except Lemnos, Imbros, and Scyros, which are to belong to Athens, as of

B. C. 387.

old." The Thebans at first objected, but being threatened with war by the Spartans, at length took the oath. The terms which thus prostrated Greece at the feet of Persia, were engraven on tablets of stone and set up in every temple.

RECAPITULATION.

The second period of Spartan supremacy was signalized by the abolition of free governments throughout Greece. Athens, under the Thirty Tyrants, suffered for eight months a reign of terror. Thrasybulus, with the Athenian exiles, effected the expulsion of the tyrants, the restoration of free government, and a conservative reaction which occasioned, among other results, the execution of Socrates. The Spartans plundered the sacred land of Elis, and expelled or enslaved all the Messenians who remained upon their soil. Agesilaus, succeeding his brother as king of Sparta, became involved in war with Persia. In the contest with Thebes, Lysander was killed, and the king Pausanias disgraced. During the Corinthian War which followed, Sparta was victorious at Corinth and Coronæa, but suffered a disastrous overthrow from the Persian fleet under Conon, in the battle of Cnidus, which resulted in the sudden downfall of her supremacy. The Long Walls of Athens and the fortifications of the Piræus were rebuilt, under the superintendence of Conon. The Peace of Antalcidas gave to the Persian king a controlling voice in Grecian affairs, with the sovereignty of Asiatic Greece, and of the islands of Cyprus and Clazomenæ.

SUPREMACY OF THEBES.

227. The Spartan hatred of Thebes was not allayed by the return of peace. To annoy the latter city, Platæa* was rebuilt, and as many as possible of its former citizens brought back. An expedition against Olynthus gave occasion for a more decided act of hostility. Phœ'bidas, on his march through Bœotia, happened to approach Thebes on a festal day, when the citadel was occupied only by women. Aided by some citizens who were in secret alliance with Sparta, he seized the Cadmea, had the chief of the patriotic party put to death on a false charge, and effected a revolution in the government which made Thebes only a subservient ally of Sparta. The Lacedæmonians pretended to join in the general indignation of Greece at this outrage; but though they dismissed Phœbidas, they kept the Cadmea.

B. C. 386.

228. OLYNTHIAN WAR. The war in Macedonia was now prosecuted with the aid of Thebes. Olynthus, in the Chalcidian peninsula, had become the head of a powerful confederacy of Grecian cities; but Acan'thus and Apollo'nia refused to join it, and applied to Sparta for help. Amyn'tas, king of Macedonia, took their part, and joined his troops with those of Eudamidas. Olynthus, by means of its excellent cavalry, held out bravely for four years; but at last it fell, and the league was dissolved. The Macedonian ports returned into subjection to Amyntas, while the Greek cities joined the Spartan alliance.

B. C. 382.

* See p. 163.

Sparta was now leagued on all sides with the enemies of Greece: with the Persians, with Dionysius of Syracuse, and with Macedon. By the destruction of the Olynthian League, she had removed the chief obstacle to the Macedonian power, which was soon to overthrow the freedom of the Greeks.

229. Thebes remained three years in the control of the Lacedæmonian party. But the citizens were discontented, and a company of exiles at Athens were awaiting an opportunity of vengeance. Among them was Pelop′idas, a noble and wealthy youth, who had already distinguished himself by his patriotism. He was the ardent friend of Epam′inon′das, a Theban of greater age and still more exalted virtue than himself. A plan was now formed among the exiles for the deliverance of Thebes. Pelopidas was its leader; but Epaminondas at first held back, because the execution of the plot required deceit, and the possible shedding of innocent blood. He was a strict Pythagorean; and so pure were his principles, that he was never known to trifle with the truth even in jest, or to sacrifice it for any interest.

B. C. 379.

230. Phyl′lidas, secretary of the Theban government, was in the plot, and took a leading part in its execution. He invited to supper the two polemarchs, Ar′chias and Philip′pus, with the principal Spartan leaders; and when they were sufficiently stupefied with eating and drinking, he proposed to introduce some Theban ladies. Before these entered, a messenger brought a letter to Archias, and begged his attention, as it contained a matter of serious importance. But the polemarch only thrust the letter under the cushions of his couch, saying, "Serious matters tomorrow!"

Pelopidas and his friends, who had arrived in the city disguised as hunters, now entered the banquet-room in the long white veils and festive garb of women. They were loudly welcomed by the half-drunken guests, and dispersed themselves with apparent carelessness among the company; but as one of the Spartan lords attempted to lift the veil of the person who was addressing him, he received a mortal wound. It was the signal for a general attack. Swords were drawn from beneath the silken garments, and no Spartan left the room alive. The prisons were now opened, and five hundred Thebans, who had been immured there for their love of freedom, were added to the armed force of the revolutionists. As day dawned, all citizens who valued liberty were summoned to the market-place. A joyful assembly was held, the first since the Spartan usurpation. The Lacedæmonians in the citadel were besieged, and their expected reinforcements being cut off, they speedily surrendered.

231. It was now the depth of winter, but when the news arrived at Sparta, instant preparations were made for war. Cleombrotus led an army into Bœotia, and Athens was called to account for having sheltered the exiles. Unable to enter upon war with Sparta, the Athenians consented to sacrifice their two generals who had rendered the most efficient aid to the Thebans. One was executed, and the other, having fled, was sentenced to banishment. The Thebans feared that they should be left to fight single-handed against Sparta. In order to compel Athens to take part in the war, they bribed Spho′drias, the Spartan general, to invade her territory. He entered Attica in the night and committed various ravages, but retired the next day. The Spartan government disclaimed all knowledge of the affair, and brought Sphodrias to trial for it; but, through the influence of Agesilaus, he was acquitted. Athens immediately made an active alliance with Thebes, and a declaration of war against her ancient rival.

232. A new confederacy was now formed on the plan of that of Delos,
B. C. 378. including, in its most prosperous period, seventy cities. Athens was the head, but the independence of the members was carefully guarded. A congress at Athens regulated the share of each in the general expenses. The fortifications of Piræus were completed, new ships of war were built, and all the allies hastened forward their contingents of troops. In Thebes, the Sacred Band was formed—a heavy-armed battalion, consisting of three hundred chosen citizens of the noblest families, bound to each other by ties of the closest friendship. Though Pelopidas was bœotarch, Epaminondas had the most prominent share in the drill and discipline of the troops.

During two summers the army of Agesilaus invaded the country, and
B. C. 378–376. carried its depredations to the very gates of Thebes. The third year the Thebans held the passes of Mount Cithæron, and kept out the invaders. The Spartans were no longer successful at sea. They were thoroughly defeated off Naxos by the Athenians, who thus regained their maritime empire in the East; while, in the western seas, Corcyra, Cephallenia, and the neighboring tribes on the mainland
B. C. 375. joined the Athenian alliance. The Thebans were no less victorious on land. During the two years that they were free from Spartan invasion, most of the Bœotian cities submitted to their control. In 374 B. C., all Spartans were expelled, free governments were restored to every city, except Orchomenus and Chæronea, and the Bœotian League was revived. The Phocians, who had, twenty years before, invited the Spartans into central Greece, were now the objects of vengeance, and not the less because the treasures of Delphi would be the prize of the victor. But Cleombrotus came to the aid of the Phocians, and the aggression was checked.

233. The Athenians had now various reasons for enmity against Thebes, and messengers were sent to Sparta with proposals of peace. They were eagerly accepted; but the inopportune restoration of the Zacynthian exiles by Timo'theus, son of Conon, at this crisis, broke off the negotiations, and war was renewed. It was carried on in the western sea, with great expense and no gain to either party; the main object of the Spartans being the conquest of Corcyra, and, of the Athenians, the protection of its independence. At length all parties were weary of war, and a general congress was appointed at Sparta in the spring of 371. B. C. 374.

234. PEACE OF CAL'LIAS.* It was agreed that the Spartan garrisons should be withdrawn from every city, and independence secured to all. Athens and her allies signed the treaty separately, but Sparta took the oaths for the whole Lacedæmonian Confederacy. When the Thebans were called upon, Epaminondas refused to sign except for the whole Bœotian League, claiming that Thebes was as rightfully the sovereign city of Bœotia, as Sparta of Laconia. He defended his view in a speech of great eloquence; but Agesilaus was violently incensed. Peace was concluded between the other states, but Thebes and Sparta continued at war.

235. The courage of the Thebans seemed to the rest of the Greeks like madness, and it was believed that a very few weeks would see them crushed by the overwhelming power of Sparta. But Thebes now possessed the greatest general whom Greece ever produced. Knowing his own power, and the value of those new tactics which were destined to supersede the Spartan system, he revived the drooping confidence of his countrymen, reasoned down their evil omens or invented good ones, and by his own greatness of soul sustained the spirit of a whole nation.

236. BATTLE OF LEUC'TRA. Cleombrotus, the Spartan, was already in Phocis with a considerable army. He began with energy by seizing Creusis, on the Crissæan Gulf, with twelve Theban vessels which lay in the harbor, thus providing at once a base of supplies and a line of retreat. He then marched along the Gulf of Corinth into Bœotia, and encamped upon the plains of Leuctra. Three of the seven bœotarchs were so much alarmed as to propose retreating upon Thebes, and sending their wives and children for safety to Athens; but their plan was overruled. Epaminondas and Pelopidas were alert and cheerful. Though outnumbered by the Spartans, they so arranged their forces as to be always superior at the actual point of contact, instead of engaging all at once, which had been the uniform method in Grecian warfare. The Theban left was a dense column, fifty deep, led by the Sacred Band. This was hurled upon the Lacedæmonian right, which contained their choicest troops, led by Cleombrotus himself; while the Theban center and right, facing the Spartan allies, were kept out of action. The onset of B. C. 371.

*So called from one of the Athenian envoys, who, being hereditary *proxenus* of Sparta (a term nearly corresponding to our modern *consul*), had a leading part in the negotiation. His personal character was worthless, and his influence slight.

the Thebans was irresistible. Never had more furious fighting been seen on any Grecian battle-field. The Spartans maintained their ancient virtue; but Cleombrotus was mortally wounded, his whole division were driven to their camp, and the victory of the Thebans was complete. The allies of the Spartans, many of whom were present more through fear than choice, scarcely regretted the result of the battle.

At Sparta the fatal news was not permitted to interrupt the festival then in progress. All signs of mourning were forbidden, except on the part of those whose relatives had survived the defeat. The disaster was, nevertheless, the greatest that had ever befallen Sparta. Her influence was destroyed, even over the Peloponnesian cities. Her dependencies north of the Corinthian Gulf were divided between the Thebans and Jason, tyrant of Pheræ, in Thessaly, a man of singular talent and unbounded ambition, who aimed at the sovereignty of all Greece. The Thebans had courted his alliance, but they began to be alarmed by the extent of his projects, and all Greece was relieved when he was assassinated in 370. The Spartan sovereignty, which had lasted thirty-four years since the battle of Ægos-Potami, now gave way to the THEBAN SUPREMACY (B. C. 371–362).

237. The Mantineans seized the occasion to revenge their former wrongs, and besought the aid of Epaminondas. He entered Arcadia with an army near the end of the year 370, and was joined by Argives and Eleans, who increased his number to 70,000 men. By the entreaties of his allies, he marched into Laconia, and advanced upon Sparta itself. During all the centuries that the fame of Spartan valor had held Greece and Asia in awe, the Spartan women had never seen an enemy in arms, and the unwalled city was now filled with terror. But the energy of old King Agesilaus was equal to its defense. He repulsed the cavalry of Epaminondas, who retired down the valley of the Eurotas, burning and plundering as he went, and then returned to Arcadia.

238. The main objects of his expedition were yet to be fulfilled. A union of Arcadian towns had already been formed, which Epaminondas wished to organize and strengthen. Lest jealousy should be excited by the choice of any existing place as capital of the league, a new city, called Megalop′olis, was built, and peopled by colonists from forty towns. Here a congress of deputies, called the "Ten Thousand," was to be regularly convened; and a standing army of deputies from the various cities was also raised.

239. A still more cherished plan was the restoration of the Messenians. For three hundred years this noble race had been fugitive and exiled, while its lands were in the possession of the Lacedæmonians. The exiles were now recalled, by the letters of Epaminondas, from the shores of Italy, Sicily, Africa, and Asia, and eagerly sprang to arms for the recovery of their ancient seats. The citadel of Ithome was fortified anew, and the town of Messe'ne, which arose upon the western slope of the mountain, was protected by strong walls. The Messenian territories extended southward to the gulf which bore their name, and northward to Elis and Arcadia.

240. Common jealousy of Thebes now led to a closer alliance between Athens and Sparta. Their forces were united in guarding the mountain-passes of the isthmus, in order to prevent another invasion of the Peloponnesus. Epaminondas, however, broke their line by defeating a Spartan division, and Sicyon deserted the Spartan for the Theban alliance. The Thebans were, in their turn, defeated in an attack upon Corinth, and their enemies were strengthened by a squadron which arrived at Lechæum, from Dionysius of Syracuse, bearing two thousand auxiliaries from Gaul and Spain.

B. C. 369.

241. THE TEARLESS BATTLE. The Arcadians, meanwhile, rejoicing in their newly acquired power, became ambitious to share the sovereignty with Thebes, as Athens did with Sparta. Under their leader, Lycome'des, who had first proposed the league, they gained several advantages in the west, and completed the overthrow of the Spartan power in the Messenian part of the peninsula. In a later enterprise, they were routed, however, with great slaughter by the Spartans, who lost not a man in the engagement, and gave it, therefore, the name of the "Tearless Battle." The Thebans did not mourn this defeat of their allies, which had the effect of curbing their pride, and showing their need of protection from the sovereign state.

B. C. 368.

The same year the Thebans, under Pelopidas, organized a league among the cities of Thessaly, and formed an alliance with Macedonia. Among the hostages sent from the Macedonian court was the young prince, Philip, son of Amyntas, now fifteen years of age, who was destined to act an important part in the later history of Greece.

242. In the years 367 and 366, the Thebans obtained from the Persian king that sanction of their power which the peace of Antalcidas had rendered necessary, or, at least, customary in Greece. Artaxerxes recognized the Hellenic supremacy of Thebes, and the independence of Messene and Amphip'olis; decided a dispute between the Arcadians and Eleans in favor of the latter, and commanded Athens to reduce her navy to a peace footing. This royal rescript naturally provoked a violent opposition among the states of Greece; and when Pelopidas visited Thessaly to obtain compliance with its terms, he was seized and imprisoned by Alexander of Pheræ. The Thebans instantly sent a force to recover or avenge their ambassador. But, unhappily, Epaminondas was now degraded from command; the army was defeated, and barely escaped total destruction. The great general was serving as a private in the ranks; he was called by his comrades to be their leader, and conducted them safely home. He then received the command of a second expedition, which secured the release of Pelopidas.

Two years later, Pelopidas himself conducted an army against Alexander, and gained a great victory over him at Cyn'oceph'alæ.

B. C. 363.

Rage at the sight of his old enemy overcame his prudence, and he fell furiously fighting in the midst of Alexander's guards. The Thebans felt more grief at his death than joy in the victory, but they did not fail to follow it up with a fresh army, which stripped Alexander of all his possessions except the city of Pheræ, and established Theban supremacy throughout northern Greece.

243. The war in the Peloponnesus was now varied by an act of sacrilege. The Arcadians seized the Sacred Grove at Olympia during the year of the festival, expelled the Eleans from their supervision of the games, and installed the Pisatans in their place. A large army of the Arcadians and their allies was present to enforce this irregular proceeding. The Eleans came up in the midst of the games, supported by their allies, the Achæans, and a battle was fought on the sacred ground. The very temple of Olympic Zeus became a fortress, and the gold and ivory statue by Phidias looked down upon a scene of unprecedented strife. The treasury of the shrine was despoiled by the invaders. Arcadia itself was divided by this impious act. The Mantineans refused all share in the spoils, and were on that account proclaimed traitors to the league. Peace was at length made with Elis, but two parties remained in Arcadia: the Mantineans, in alliance with Sparta; and the Tegeans, with the other towns which favored Thebes. Hostilities were frequent, and envoys were sent to Epaminondas demanding his intervention.

244. In the summer of 362 B. C., the great general invaded Peloponnesus for the fourth and last time. At Tegea he was joined by his allies, while Agesilaus moved with a Spartan force toward Mantinea. Placed thus between the king and his capital, Epaminondas seized the occasion to make a sudden attack upon Sparta. Agesilaus heard of it in time to return, and though a battle was fought in the very streets of the capital, the invader was compelled to retire. With his usual swiftness, Epaminondas moved back to surprise Mantinea while the Spartan army was withdrawn. The citizens with their slaves were dispersed in the fields, for it was the time of harvest; but a troop of Athenian cavalry had just arrived, and, though tired and hungry, they succeeded in repulsing the Thebans.

245. BATTLE OF MANTINEA. It was now evident that a great battle must take place, and the elevated plain between Tegea and Mantinea, inclosed on every side by mountains, was the destined field. The Thebans, on arriving, laid down their arms, as if preparing to encamp; and the Spartans, inferring that they did not mean to fight, dispersed themselves in some confusion. Some were tending their horses, some unbuckling their breastplates, when they were surprised by the charge of the deep and heavy column of Bœotian troops, which Epaminondas had swiftly put in order for attack. The Spartans fought bravely, but under the disadvantage which disorder always occasions, they were unable to recover themselves at once. Epaminondas seized the moment to lead a band of chosen troops directly upon the enemy's center. The Mantineans and Spartans turned and fled; but at this moment the Theban general fell, pierced with a mortal wound. His followers stood paralyzed with dismay, unable to pursue and reap the advantage he had prepared for them. The Spartans acknowledged themselves defeated, by requesting permission to bury their dead, but both armies erected trophies of victory.

246. Epaminondas, with the spear-head in his breast, was carried off the field. He first assured himself that the battle was won, then tried to make a disposition of his command; but the two generals whom he would have chosen were already slain. "Then make peace," was his last public command. The spear-head was now removed, and with the rush of blood which followed it, his life passed away. No Greek ever more truly merited, by character and talent, the title "Great." Many of the worthiest who succeeded him took him for their model; and even the Christian ages have seen none who better fulfilled the description of a brave knight, "without fear and without reproach." The greatness of Thebes began and ended with his public career. After the fatal result of the battle of Mantinea, she fell to her former position.

247. Peace was made, leaving all parties in the same position as before the war. Agesilaus, untamed by his eighty years, sought a field of glory beyond the sea. Tachos, king of Egypt, had asked the aid of Sparta in his revolt against Persia. Agesilaus went to his assistance, at the head of a thousand heavy-armed troops. The appearance of the little, lame old man, utterly destitute of the retinue or splendor of a king, excited the ridicule of the Egyptians; but when he transferred his aid from Tachos to Nectan′abis, who had risen against him, the importance of the little Spartan was felt, for Nectanabis obtained the throne. Agesilaus did not live to bear back to Sparta his honors and rewards. He died on the road to Cyrene, and his body, embalmed in wax, was conveyed with great pomp to his native city. An ancient oracle had foretold that Sparta would lose her power under a lame sovereign. It was now fulfilled, but through no fault of the king. Agesilaus had all the virtues of his countrymen, without their common faults of avarice and deceit; and he added a warmth and tenderness in friendship which Spartans rarely possessed. He has been called "Sparta's most perfect citizen and most consummate general, in many ways, perhaps, her greatest man." B. C. 361.

248. THE SOCIAL WAR. Athens still maintained her wars in the north;

by sea against Alexander of Pheræ, and by land against Macedonia and the Thracian princes. The second period of Athenian greatness reached its height in the year 358, when Eubœa, the Chersonesus, and Amphipolis were again subdued. In that year a serious revolt, called the Social War, was begun by Rhodes, Cos, Chios, and Byzantium. Sestus and other towns on the Hellespont joined in the quarrel, and Mauso'lus, king of Caria, sent aid to the insurgents. The war was inglorious and exhaustive to Athens. To obtain means of paying their sailors, the commanders aided Artabazus in his revolt against Persia, and thereby incurred the vengeance of the great king. Athens had to consent to the independence of the four rebel states, in order to avoid still greater losses and calamities. During the four years that her attention had been thus absorbed, Philip of Macedon had been able to grasp all her dependencies on the Thermaic Gulf, and thus to extend his power as far as the Peneus.

249. THE SACRED WAR. During the progress of the Social War, another fatal quarrel began in central Greece, through the enmity of Thebes and Phocis. Driven to fight for their existence, the Phocians seized the sacred treasures at Delphi, which enabled them to raise and maintain a large army of mercenaries, and even to bribe some of the neighboring states either to aid them or remain neutral. Their first general, Philome'lus, was defeated and slain at Titho'rea. His brother, Onomar'chus, who succeeded to his command, used the Delphian treasures with still less scruple, beside confiscating the property of all who opposed him. By these means he conquered Locris and Doris, invaded Bœotia, and captured Orchomenus.

B. C. 357.

250. Lyc'ophron, tyrant of Pheræ, now sought his aid against Philip of Macedon, whose increasing power pressed heavily upon Thessaly. Phaÿl'lus, who first led a force to the aid of Lycophron, was defeated; but Onomarchus himself marched into Thessaly, worsted the king in two pitched battles, and drove him from the country. He then returned into Bœotia, where he captured Coronæa, but was recalled into Thessaly by another invasion of Philip. This time his fortune changed; he was defeated, and, with many other fugitives, plunged into the sea, hoping to reach the Athenian ships which were lying off shore to watch the battle. He perished, and his body, falling into the hands of Philip, was crucified as a punishment of his sacrilege.

B. C. 352.

251. This battle secured the ascendency of Philip in Thessaly. He established a more popular government in Pheræ, took and garrisoned Magnesia, and then advanced upon Thermopylæ. The Athenians anticipated the danger, and guarded the pass with a strong force. But the liberty of Greece was destined to be sacrificed to her internal dissensions. The Sacred War had continued eleven years, when the Thebans called in the aid of Philip to complete the destruction of Phocis. The Athenians now remained neutral, and Philip passed Thermopylæ without opposition. In a short campaign he crushed Phocis, and was admitted as a member of the Amphictyonic Council, in the place of the conquered state.

252. Athens was now the only power in Greece capable of opposing the Macedonian king, and Athens was no longer possessed of a Miltiades, a Conon, or a Themistocles. A great orator, however, had arisen, and when Olynthus sent envoys to implore aid against the invader, who was now attacking the Chalcidian cities, the eloquence of Demosthenes aroused some faint show of their former spirit. The attempted rescue was defeated, however, by treachery within the walls; and, in 347, Olynthus fell. The threefold peninsula was now in the power of Philip, and he was able to push his interests throughout Greece rather by intrigue than force. Even in Athens a powerful party, sustained by his bribes, labored to undermine the efforts of the true patriots, of whom Demosthenes was chief. Æs'chines was the mouth-piece of the Macedonian party, an orator second only to Demosthenes himself, and won to Philip's side, probably, more by flatteries than gifts. He constantly urged peace with the king, while Demosthenes, as soon as he perceived the extent of Philip's designs, opposed them with all the unsparing vehemence of his nature. His *Philippics* are the most forcible examples in any language of bold and eloquent opposition to an unjust usurpation of power.

B. C. 349.

253. In 340, war was declared on account of the aggressions of Philip on the Bosphorus; and the Second Sacred War, which broke out in the following year, gave him a reason for again passing Thermopylæ. He was now appointed general-in-chief of the Amphictyonic forces, and thus gained a position in the very heart of Greece, which he did not fail to use for his own advantage.

B. C. 339.

254. The Thebans, in alarm, applied to Athens for aid, which was not refused. The armies met in battle at Chæronea, and the victory of Philip gave the death-blow to Grecian independence. All the states except Sparta acknowledged his sovereignty, and he was made generalissimo of the Hellenic forces in the war now projected against Persia. To overawe the hostility of Sparta, he marched through the Peloponnesus to the southern extremity, and returned by the western coast, meeting no serious opposition.

Aug. 7, B. C. 338.

Philip's death by assassination interrupted the movement against the Persians, and for a moment revived the hopes of the patriots; but the Macedonian party prevailed under the youthful Alexander, who surpassed his father both as general and as king.

RECAPITULATION.

Sparta destroyed the Olynthian confederacy, and seized upon Thebes, which was rescued after three years by Pelopidas and his fellow exiles. Athens regained her dominion both in the eastern and western seas, while Thebes became the head of the new Bœotian League. The treaty of Callias secured peace among all the states, except Thebes and Sparta. The victory of Epaminondas over the Spartans at Leuctra established the Theban supremacy, which was recognized and supported by the Persians during the remaining years of his life. He four times invaded Peloponnesus; organized an Arcadian confederacy, with the new city, Megalopolis, at its head; restored the exiled Messenians to the lands of their ancestors; twice attacked Sparta itself; and, finally, triumphed and fell at Mantinea. Agesilaus died on his return from Egypt, where his aid had secured the throne to Nectanabis. Athens declined from her second period of greatness in consequence of the Social War, B. C. 357-355. The Phocians, with the Delphic treasures which they confiscated, gained ascendency in central Greece, but lost it in war with Philip of Macedon. This king ended the Sacred War (B. C. 357-346) by the destruction of Phocis, assumed her place in the Amphictyonic Council, conquered the Chalcidian peninsulas, led the allied forces in the Second Sacred War, and by his victory at Chæronea established his supremacy over Greece. His son Alexander inherited his civil and military command.

QUESTIONS FOR REVIEW.

Book III.

1. By what names has Greece been known? . . . . § 8.
2. What tribes were included among the Hellenes? . . . . . . 9.
3. What foreigners aided to civilize Greece? . . . . 10.
4. Describe three of the Greek heroes. . . . . 11-13.
5. What can be said of the siege of Troy? . . . . 14.
6. What was the state of the country and people in the Heroic Age? 11, 17-20.
7. Describe the kings. . . . . 15, 16.
8. What connections between Greek and Asiatic religions? . . . . 21.
9. Name the twelve Olympian deities. . . . . 23.
10. What bearing had Greek belief upon human conduct? . . . . . 25.
11. What foreign ceremonies were borrowed by the Greeks? . . . 26, 27, 29.
12. What is known of the Mysteries? . . . . 28.
13. Describe the oracles. . . . . 30-32.
14. What migrations in Greece, B. C. 1124-1100? . . . . 33, 34.
15. Describe the Asiatic settlements. . . . . 35-37, 85, 86.
16. What political changes at the close of the Heroic Age? . . . . 38.
17. What were the bonds of union among the Greeks? . . . . . . 39, 42.
18. Describe the games and the rewards of victors. . . . . . . 40, 41.
19. Recount the history of Argos. . . . . 43.
20. What were the condition and government of Sparta, B. C. 900? . . 44-46.
21. Describe the discipline of Lycurgus. . . . . 47-53.
22. The wars of Sparta during the Second Period. . . . . . 55-61.
23. What was the character of Spartan influence in Greece? . . . . 62.
24. What difference of character between Athenians and Spartans? . . 63.
25. What changes in Athenian government within 400 years? . . . 64, 65.
26. Describe the laws of Draco and their results. . . . . 66, 67.
27. What political parties in Attica? . . . . 68.
28. What were the character and history of Solon? . . . . . . 69, 70, 74.
29. What was the spirit of his laws? . . . . 71-73.
30. Describe the rise of Pisistratus. . . . . 75.

31. What occurred during his first tyranny? . . . . § 76.
32. What occasioned his second expulsion? . . . . 77.
33. Describe his third reign. . . . . 78.
34. The reign and expulsion of Hippias. . . . . 79, 80.
35. What changes were introduced by Clisthenes? . . . . 81.
36. Who opposed him? . . . . 82.
37. What dangers threatened Athens at this time? . . . . 83.
38. What ceremonies attended the founding of Greek colonies? . . . 84.
39. Describe the colonies in Italy. . . . . 87–89.
40. In Gaul, Sicily, Africa, Thrace. . . . . . . 91–94.
41. Describe the movements of Darius against Greece. . . . . . . 95–97.
42. The battle of Marathon. . . . . 98, 99.
43. The fall of Miltiades. . . . . 101, 102.
44. The character and history of Aristides. . . 103, 104, 116, 117, 130, 132.
45. The character and career of Themistocles. 104–109, 113–117, 130, 136, 138.
46. The battle of Thermopylæ. . . . . 111, 112.
47. The battle of Salamis. . . . . 117.
48. The retreat of Xerxes. . . . . 118.
49. The embassy of Alexander. . . . . 119, 120.
50. The condition of Athens. . . . . 121.
51. Describe the campaign in Bœotia. . . . . 122–126.
52. The subsequent operations of the Greeks. . . . . . . 128, 129.
53. What changes in the rank and politics of Athens? . . . . . . 130.
54. Tell the story of Pausanias. . . . . 131.
55. Describe the rise of the Delian Confederacy. . . . . 132.
56. The career of Cimon. . . . . 133–137, 139–142, 150.
57. The causes and events of the Third Messenian War. . . 139, 142, 148.
58. The history of Pericles. . . . . 140, 143, 145, 152–157, 159, 161–165.
59. Tell the story of the First Peloponnesian War. . . . . 143–147.
60. What occurred at Delphi, B. C. 448? . . . . 151.
61. Describe the battle of Coronæa, and its consequences to Athens. . . 152–154.
62. The Samian revolt. . . . . 156, 157.
63. The war between Corinth and Corcyra. . . . . 158.
64. The Theban attack upon Platæa. . . . . 160.
65. How was Greece divided in the Peloponnesian War? . . . . . 161.
66. What was the condition of Athens during the first two years? . 162–164, 166.
67. Describe the siege of Platæa. . . . . 167.
68. The revolt of Mytilene. . . . . 168–170.
69. The revolution in Corcyra. . . . . 171.
70. The condition of Greece in the sixth year of the war. . . . 172.
71. Describe the campaign at Pylos and Sphacteria. . . . . 173, 174.
72. What massacres occurred in the eighth year? . . . . 175.
73. Describe the invasion of Bœotia. . . . . 176.
74. The campaign of Brasidas. . . . . 177.
75. How long did the Peace of Nicias continue? . . . . 178, 180, 188.
76. Describe the career of Alcibiades. . . . . . 179–186, 192–194, 198–200, 202.
77. The Sicilian expedition. . . . . 179–191.
78. What occasioned a revolution in Athens? . . . . 194, 195.
79. Describe the maritime movements of 411, 410 B. C. . . . . . . 197–199.
80. What part was taken by Persia in the Peloponnesian War? 192–194, 198, 201, 204.
81. What occurred at Ægos-Potami? . . . . 205, 206.
82. What were the results to Athens? . . . . 207–209.
83. Describe the reign of the Thirty Tyrants. . . . . 210, 211.
84. The reaction under Thrasybulus. . . . . 212, 213.
85. The trial and death of Socrates. . . . . 214.

86. Describe the war of Sparta against Elis. . . . . § 215.
87. Agesilaus, and his Asiatic campaign. . . . . . . 216, 217.
88. The death of Lysander, and retirement of Pausanias. . 218.
89. The three great battles of 394 B. C. . . . . 219-221.
90. Who restored the walls of Athens? . . . . 222.
91. Describe the last two years of the Corinthian War. . . . . 223.
92. What were the terms of the Peace of Antalcidas? . . . . . . 226.
93. What occurred at Thebes, from 382 to 379 B. C.? . . . . . 227, 229, 230.
94. Describe the war in Bœotia and the western seas. . . . . . . 232.
95. The treaty of Callias. . . . . 233, 234.
96. The character and tactics of Epaminondas. . 229, 235-240, 244-246.
97. The consequences to Sparta of the battle of Leuctra. . . 236.
98. The restoration of the Messenians. . . . . 239.
99. The ambition of the Arcadians. . . . . 241.
100. The intervention of the Persians. . . . . 242.
101. The plunder of Olympia. . . . . 243.
102. The last campaign of Agesilaus. . . . . 247.
103. The second period of Athenian greatness, and Social War. 248.
104. The Sacred War. . . . . 249.
105. The advance of Philip of Macedon. . . . . 250, 251.
106. Demosthenes and his *Philippics*. . . . . 252.
107. The results of the battle of Chæronea. . . . . . . 254.
108. Who succeeded Philip as head of the Grecian armies? . . . . . 254.
109. How long was Athens the leading state of Greece?
110. What two periods of Spartan supremacy?
111. Length of the Theban supremacy?
112. What was an Olympiad? . . . . 40.

BOOK IV.

History of the Macedonian Empire and the Kingdoms formed from it, until their Conquest by the Romans.

First Period. *From the Rise of the Monarchy to the Death of Alexander the Great, about B. C.* 700–323.

1. The Kingdom of Macedon, lying north of Thessaly and east of Illyr′icum, was of little importance before the reign of Philip II., whose aggressions ended the independent history of Greece. (See Book III, §§ 248–254.) In 507 B. C., Amyntas I. submitted to Darius Hystaspes; and fifteen years later, in the first expedition of Mardonius, the country became a mere province of the Persian empire, the native kings governing as tributaries. After Xerxes' retreat, B. C. 480, Macedonia became free again, and began to push eastward along the northern coast of the Ægean. Here it met two rivals: the new Thracian kingdom of Sitalces upon its eastern frontier, and the Athenian power in the Greek cities of the Chalcidian peninsulas.

2. When Athens was prostrated by her Sicilian disasters, the short but brilliant reign of Ar′chela′us I. (B. C. 413–399) laid the foundation of Macedonian greatness. He improved his country by roads, strengthened it by forts, and introduced a better discipline into the army. His death was followed by forty years of great tumult, a continued scene of plots and assassinations, to recount which would only confuse without profiting the student. When Perdiccas III. died in battle, he left an infant son, Amyntas, under the regency of his brother Philip. At least five other princes claimed the crown; the victorious Illyrians occupied the western provinces, and Thrace and Pæo′nia were ready to absorb the eastern.

3. Philip overcame all these perils with admirable spirit and ability. He made himself king instead of his nephew, defeated the Illyrians, and took advantage of the Social War to seize Amphipolis, Pydna, and Potidæa. He pushed the Macedonian boundary eastward as far as the Nestus, and built the town of Philip′pi for the protection of the gold mines. These had fallen into neglect during the wars of Athens, but under his improved management they soon yielded a yearly revenue of a thousand talents ($1,250,000).

4. Philip, in his youth, had spent three years in Thebes, where he had studied the tactics of Epaminondas, as well as the language, character, and politics of the Greeks. On coming to power, he devoted unwearied attention to the drilling of his army, until it far surpassed that of any Hellenic state. No less skilled in diplomacy than in military science, he knew how to take advantage of the rivalries in Greece, and the corruptibility of all parties, to play off one against the other, and so render himself supreme. His rapid movements made him seem to be in many places at the same moment, and no circumstance which either threatened or favored his interests escaped his eye.

5. The Olynthian War ended with the capture of thirty-two cities in Chalcidice; the Sacred War made Philip master of Phocis and head of the Amphictyonic League. In eastern Thrace, the Athenians found aid in the Persians, who were already alarmed by the rapid rise of the Macedonian power, and Perin′thus and Byzantium were thus saved for a time. Philip was victorious (B. C. 339) against a Scythian prince of what is now Bulga′ria; and though he was defeated and wounded on his return, in a battle with the Triballi, his plots went on with uninterrupted success. The Second Sacred War gave him supremacy in central Greece, and the victory at Chæronea prostrated all remaining opposition. The Congress at Corinth (B. C. 337) acknowledged his headship, and appointed him to lead the Greek forces against Persia. The advanced guard of the Macedonian army was already in Asia, when Philip was assassinated, during the festivities attending the marriage of his daughter, B. C. 336.

6. In the midst of Philip's early victories, he had heard of the birth of his son Alexander at Pella. He wrote immediately to his friend Ar′istot′le,* expressing his joy that the young prince was born during the life of the philosopher to whom he could most gladly commit his education. On the same day that Alexander was born, the temple of Artemis at Ephesus was burnt to the ground. The priests and soothsayers, regarding the fire as an evil omen, ran about the city beating their breasts and crying

* Aristotle was a native of Stagi′ra, a Chalcidian sea-port. His father had been physician to Amyntas II., the father of Philip; and the prince and the philosopher in their boyhood formed a friendship, which outlasted the life of the former and was inherited by his son. The enlarged political views of Alexander, his fondness for discovery and physical science, his lively interest in literature, especially the poems of Homer, and his love of the noble and great in character, were largely due to his teacher's influence. When he became the conqueror of Asia, he caused rare collections of plants and animals, from all his provinces, to be sent to Aristotle, who found in them the materials for valuable works on Natural History.

aloud, "This day has brought forth the scourge and destroyer of Asia." B. C. 356.

7. At the age of sixteen, Alexander was left regent of the kingdom during his father's campaign against Byzantium. At Chæronea, two years later, he led a corps of Macedonian youth against the Sacred Band of Thebes, and the victory was mainly due to his courage and impetuosity. Upon the death of his father, Alexander, at twenty years of age, ascended a throne beset with many dangers. He expelled or killed his nearest rivals, marched into Greece and convened at Corinth a new congress, which conferred upon him the same dignities and powers previously granted to his father; then instantly returning to Macedon, he signally defeated his enemies on the west and north, some of whom he pursued even beyond the Danube. During these campaigns a false report of his death reached Greece, and Thebes seized the occasion to revolt. But Alexander appeared suddenly before her gates, stormed and took the city, which, by way of warning to others, he completely destroyed—saving only the house of Pindar, the poet—and either enslaved or massacred the inhabitants.

Coin of Alexander, enlarged one-half.

8. Greece was now awed into submission, and Alexander prepared to execute his father's and his own schemes of Asiatic conquest. In the spring of 334 B. C., he crossed the Hellespont with 35,000 men. The Persians awaiting him at the Granicus were defeated, and Alexander, with his usual celerity, overran Asia Minor, which submitted with little opposition. Memnon, a Rhodian Greek in the service of Darius, and his greatest general, desired to carry the war into Macedonia, by means of the overwhelming fleet of the Persians. His movements detained Alexander some months near the Ægean coast; but his death, in the spring of 333 B. C., left the invader free to march toward the heart of the empire. Darius led a vast army to the plain of the Orontes, where he might have had the advantage over his assailant; but Alexander lingered in the Cilician mountain passes, until the Persian king was impatient and came to meet him. The battle of Issus (B. C. 333, Nov.) resulted in the defeat of the Persians with great slaughter.

9. Instead of following Darius, Alexander proceeded to conquer the sea-coast of the Mediterranean as far as Egypt, thus providing for the security of Macedon and Greece. Most of the Phœnician cities submitted as he approached, but Tyre withstood him seven months. When it was taken (B. C. 332, July), 8,000 of its people were massacred and 30,000 sold into slavery. Ga′za was captured after a siege of two months. According to Josephus, the conqueror then marched upon Jerusalem. The high priest, Jad′dua, came forth to meet him, wearing the breastplate of precious stones and the miter inscribed with the Holy Name. Alexander prostrated himself with profound reverence before the priest, and explained to his followers that in a vision, before leaving Europe, he had seen such a figure, which had invited him to the conquest of Asia. The high priest pointed out to him the prophecies of Daniel concerning his career; and Alexander, in adding the Jews to his empire, exempted them from tribute every seventh year, when, according to their law, they could neither sow nor reap.

10. In Egypt the Macedonian king was gladly welcomed, for the people hated the Persians for having insulted their gods and profaned their temples. At the western mouth of the Nile he founded a new capital, which he designed as the commercial exchange of the eastern and western worlds. Alexandria, with its great advantages of position, soon became a rich and magnificent city. A less judicious proceeding of the conqueror was a toilsome march across the desert to the temple of Amun. He was rewarded, however, in being saluted by the priests as the son of the god, a distinction which Alexander greatly valued.

11. Turning to the north and east, Alexander now sought the grand contest which was to transfer to him the dominions of Cyrus. He had purposely given Darius time to collect the entire force of his empire, so that one battle might decide its fate. The battle of Arbela (B. C. 331, Oct.) has been described in Book II. As its result the three capitals, Susa, Persep′olis, and Babylon, surrendered almost without resistance; and Alexander might, without further effort, have assumed the pomp and ease of an Oriental monarch. But his restless spirit carried him on to the conquest of the eastern provinces and India. He first marched into Media, where Darius had rallied the remnants of his forces to oppose him, but on his approach the dethroned king fled through the Caspian Gates to Bactria. Before Alexander could overtake him, he was murdered by his rebellious satrap, Bessus, who assumed the title of king of Persia.

12. The Greek mercenaries of Darius, who had formed his most effective force, were now added to the army of the conqueror. From province to province Alexander marched, receiving submission and organizing governments. Bessus fled into Sogdiana, but was taken, and suffered a cruel death for his treason and usurpation. A new city of Alexandria was founded on the Jaxartes; and having chastised the Scythians to the northward, the conqueror returned to Bactria, where he spent the winter of 329 B. C.

13. The genius of Alexander began to be disgraced by the pride and unscrupulous cruelty of an Eastern king. He adopted the Persian dress and ceremonial, and required his courtiers to prostrate themselves before him, as to a divinity rather than a mortal. He had already put to death his friend Philo′tas, on an unproved charge of plotting against his life; and the aged Parme′nio, father of Philotas, was subjected without trial to a similar fate. At Bactria, in a drunken revel, Alexander murdered his friend Clitus with his own hand.

14. During his two years' war against Sogdiana, Alexander captured a mountain fortress, where Oxyar′tes, a Bactrian prince, had deposited his family. Roxa′na, one of the princesses, became the wife of the conqueror. In the spring of 327 B. C., the Macedonian army crossed the Indus and invaded the Punjab. No resistance was encountered until it reached the Hydas′pes, where Porus, an Indian king, was drawn up with his elephants and a formidable body of men. An obstinate battle resulted in the defeat and capture of Porus; but his brave spirit so commanded the respect of his conqueror, that he was permitted to retain his kingdom.

Alexander founded two cities near the Hydaspes, one named Buceph′ala, in honor of his favorite horse, which died there, and the other, Nicæ′a, in commemoration of his victories. He gave orders for the building of a fleet from the Indian forests, while he advanced with his army still farther to the eastward. All the tribes as far as the Hypha′sis (Sutlej) were conquered, one by one. On arriving at that river, the Macedonians refused to go farther. They declared that they had more than fulfilled the terms of their enlistment, and that they were worn out by the hardships of eight unprecedented campaigns.

15. Alexander was compelled to turn back. His fleet was now ready, and he descended the Hydaspes to the Indus, in the autumn and winter of 327 B. C. His army marched in two columns along the banks, the entire valley submitting with little resistance. Two more cities were founded, and left with Greek garrisons and governors. Arriving at the Indian Ocean, Near′chus was sent with the fleet to the Persian Gulf, while Alexander returned by land. His march through Gedro′sia was the most severe of all his operations, the army suffering for the want of food and water. At Pura he obtained supplies, and proceeded through Kerman to Pasargadæ, and thence to Persepolis. Arriving at Susa in the spring of 325 B. C., he allowed his army some months of needed rest, while he began to organize the vast empire which he had so rapidly built up.

16. Desiring to unite his eastern and western dominions by every bond of sympathy and common interest, he assigned to eighty of his officers Asiatic wives with rich dowries. He had himself set the example by taking for his second wife Barsi′ne, daughter of Darius III.; and when ten thousand of the soldiery married Asiatic women, he gave presents to them all. Twenty thousand Persians were received into the army, and drilled in Macedonian tactics; while Persian satraps were placed over several provinces, and the court was equally composed of Asiatics and Europeans. Some of Alexander's veterans, seeing the conquered nations placed on a level with themselves, broke into open mutiny. He silenced their complaints with great address, and then sent 10,000 of them home.

17. Unlike most conquerors, Alexander improved the countries which he had won by arms. Rivers were cleared from obstructions, commerce revived, and western enterprise took the place of Asiatic indolence and poverty. The Greek language and literature were planted every-where: every new exploration added to the treasures of science and the enlightenment of the human race. On his march from Ecbatana to Babylon, Alexander was met by embassadors from almost every part of the known world, who came to offer either submission or friendship.

18. He designed to conquer first Arabia, then Italy, Carthage, and the West, extending his empire from the Indus to the Pillars of Hercules. Babylon was to be his capital; and Alexander descended the river, to inspect in person the improvement of the canals which distributed water over the plain. But his magnificent schemes were cut short from their accomplishment by his early death. On his return from visiting the canals, he found the Arabian expedition nearly ready to sail, and he celebrated the occasion by a banquet to Nearchus and the chief officers. In the midst of the subsequent preparations, the king was attacked by a fever, occasioned by his exertions among the marshes, and aggravated, perhaps, by the wine he had taken at the festival. After an illness of eleven days he died, at the age of thirty-two, having reigned twelve years and eight months.

RECAPITULATION.

Macedonia rose to greatness under Archelaus (B. C. 413–399); was greatly increased by Philip II. (B. C. 359–336), who became master of Greece. Alexander, trained in his youth to war and diplomacy, began his reign at twenty; led a Greek army into Asia; defeated the Persians at the Granicus and at Issus; conquered Phœnicia, Syria, and Egypt; founded Alexandria on the Nile; gained a decisive victory over Darius at Arbela, B. C. 331; subdued the eastern and northern provinces of the empire; founded cities in western India; explored its rivers and coasts in the interest of science; planned the amalgamation of Europe and Asia, and the extension of his empire westward to the Atlantic; died B. C. 323.

SECOND PERIOD. *From the Death of Alexander to the Battle of Ipsus,* B. C. 323–301.

19. Alexander named no successor, but shortly before his death he gave his ring to Perdiccas. This general, as prime minister, kept the empire united for two years in the royal family. An infant prince, Alexander IV., born after his father's death, was associated on the throne with

Philip Arrhidæ'us, half-brother of the great Alexander. Four regents or guardians of the empire were appointed — two in Europe and two in Asia. One of these was murdered by Perdiccas, who thus acquired for himself the sole administration of Asia, Antipater and Crat'erus ruling west of the Bosphorus.

The provinces not already bestowed by the conqueror were divided among ten of his generals, who were expected to govern in the name and for the benefit of the two kings. Finding it impossible, however, either by management or force, to keep these lieutenants in subjection to the mere name of royalty, Perdiccas formed a plan to seize the sovereignty for himself. Eu'menes was on his side, while his colleagues in the regency, and the two great provincial governors, Ptol'emy and Antig'onus, were his most powerful opponents. In a campaign against Ptolemy, in Egypt, Perdiccas was slain by his own mutinous soldiers. Craterus fell in a battle with Eumenes, in Cappadocia, and the sole regency devolved upon Antip'ater. This general defeated the schemes of Euryd'ice — niece of Alexander the Great, and wife of the imbecile king, Philip Arrhidæus — who even harangued the army at Tripar'adi'sus, in Syria, demanding to be admitted to a share in the government. A fresh division and assignment of the provinces was now made. Antigonus was charged with the prosecution of the war against Eumenes, in which he made himself master of the greater part of Asia Minor.

20. Antipater died in Macedon, B. C. 319, leaving the regency, not to his son Cassan'der, but to his friend Polysper'chon. Cassander, in disgust, fled to Antigonus; and in the war which followed, these two, with Ptolemy, sought the disruption of the empire, while Eumenes and Polysperchon fought for its unity. Eumenes collected a force in Cilicia, with which he meant to conquer Syria and Phœnicia, and thus gain command of the sea. Antigonus first defeated a royal fleet near Byzantium, and then marched across the country to the borders of Syria, and pursued Eumenes inland beyond the Tigris. A number of the eastern satraps here joined Eumenes, but after two indecisive battles he was seized by his own troops and given up to Antigonus, who put him to death, B. C. 316.

21. In Macedonia, the mock king, Philip Arrhidæus, and his wife were executed, by order of Olympias, the mother of Alexander the Great. But this imperious princess was captured, in her turn, at Pydna; and, in violation of the terms of her surrender, was murdered by her enemies. Cassander became master of Macedonia and Greece. He married Thes'-saloni'ca, half-sister of the Conqueror, and founded in her honor the city which bears her name, B. C. 316.

22. The ambition of Antigonus now began to alarm his colleagues, for he was evidently not to be satisfied with less than the entire dominion of Alexander. He gave away the eastern satrapies according to his pleasure.

From Babylonia he drove Seleu′cus, who took refuge with Ptolemy in Egypt, and formed a league with Cassander, Lysim′achus, and Asander. A war of four years followed (B. C. 315–311), which resulted in the re-establishment of Seleucus in Babylon and the East, while Antigonus gained power in Greece, Syria, and Asia Minor. The peace of B. C. 311 provided for the independence of the Greek cities, but allowed each general to keep what he had gained, and left Cassander regent of Macedonia until Alexander IV. should be of age. It was probably understood between the contracting parties that this last event was never to occur. The young king and his mother were murdered, by order of Cassander.

23. At the end of a year, Ptolemy broke the peace, on the pretense that Antigonus had not liberated the Greek cities of Asia Minor. He was opposed in Cilicia by Deme′trius, son of Antigonus, who gained in this war the title of *Po′liorce′tes,* the Besieger. Ptolemy, entering Greece, seized Sicyon and Corinth, and aimed to marry Cleopatra, the last survivor of the royal house of Macedon; but the princess was assassinated, by order of Cassander, B. C. 308. Demetrius now arriving with a fleet to the relief of Athens, Ptolemy withdrew to Cyprus, and gained possession of the island. A great battle followed off Salamis, one of the most severe in the world's history. Ptolemy was defeated, with the loss of all but eight of his ships, leaving 17,000 prisoners in the hands of the enemy.

24. The five principal generals now assumed the kingly title. Demetrius spent a year in the siege of Rhodes, which, by its brave and memorable defense, secured the privileges of a neutral in the remaining years of the war. Returning to Greece, he assembled a congress at Corinth, which conferred upon him the titles formerly bestowed on Philip and Alexander, and then marched northward against the regent, or, rather, king of Macedon. Alarmed at his endangered position, Cassander stirred up his allies to invade Asia Minor.

25. The decisive battle took place, B. C. 301, at Ipsus, in Phrygia. Demetrius had arrived from Europe to the assistance of his father; but Seleucus, with the forces of the East, including 480 Indian elephants, increased the army of Lysimachus. Antigonus, in his eighty-first year, was slain; Demetrius, completely defeated, took refuge in Greece, but was not permitted to enter Athens. The two conquerors, Seleucus and Lysimachus, divided the dominions of Alexander, with due regard to their own interests Seleucus received the Euphrates Valley, Upper Syria, Cappadocia, and part of Phrygia. Lysimachus added the rest of Asia Minor to his Thracian dominion, which extended along the western shores of the Euxine as far as the mouths of the Danube; Ptolemy retained Egypt, and Cassander continued to reign in Macedonia until his death.

26. The results of the twenty years' war were disastrous to Greece and Macedonia, not only by the exhausting expenditure of blood and treasure, but by the introduction of Oriental habits of luxury and unmanly servility, in place of the free and simple manners of former times. Though the minds of the Greeks were enlarged by a knowledge of the history and philosophy of the Eastern nations, and by observation of the natural world and its productions in new climates and circumstances, yet most of the influences which had kept alive the free spirit of the people had ceased to work. Patriotism was dead; learning took the place of genius; and imitation, the place of art.

27. At the same time, Asia had gained many splendid cities, her commerce had vastly increased, and the Greek military discipline and forms of civil government gave new strength to her armies and states. From the Indus to the Adriatic, and from the Crimea to the southern bounds of Egypt, the Greek language prevailed, at least among the educated and ruling classes. In Asia Minor, Syria, and Egypt, the influence of Hellenic thought continued a thousand years in full force, until Mahomet and his successors set up their new Semitic empire. The wide diffusion of the Greek language in western Asia was among the most important preparations for the spread of Christianity. If Alexander had lived to complete his great scheme of interfusing the eastern and western races, Asia would have gained and Europe lost in still greater measure.

RECAPITULATION.

Perdiccas became vizier, Philip Arrhidæus and Alexander IV being nominally kings. Wars of the generals for the division of the empire, B. C. 321-316; 315-311; 310-301. Murder of the two kings, 316, 311. Battle of Salamis in Cyprus, 306. The decisive combat at Ipsus gave Syria and the East to Seleucus; Egypt, to Ptolemy; Thrace, to Lysimachus; Macedonia, to Cassander.

THIRD PERIOD. *History of the Several Kingdoms into which Alexander's Empire was divided.*

I. THE SYRIAN KINGDOM OF THE SELEU′CIDÆ. B. C. 312–65.

28. After the restoration of Seleucus to the government of Babylonia (see § 22), he extended his power over all the provinces between the Euphrates and the Indus. He even made war against an Indian kingdom upon the western headwaters of the Ganges, gaining thereby a great extension of commerce, and the addition of five hundred elephants to his army. The battle of Ipsus added to his dominions the country as far west as the Mediterranean and the center of Phrygia, making his kingdom by far the greatest that had been formed from the fragments of Alexander's empire.

This vast dominion was organized by Seleucus with great skill and energy. In each of the seventy-two provinces new cities sprang up, as monuments of his power and centers of Greek civilization. Sixteen of these were named Antioch, in honor of his father; five Laodice'a, for his mother, Laod'ice; seven for himself, Sel'euci'a; and several for his two wives, Apame'a and Stratoni'ce. To watch more effectually the movements of his rivals, Ptolemy and Lysimachus, he removed the seat of government from the Euphrates to his new capital, Antioch, on the Orontes, which continued nearly a thousand years to be one of the richest and most populous cities in the world.

29. In 293 B. C., Seleucus divided his empire with his son Anti'ochus, giving the younger prince all the provinces east of the Euphrates. Demetrius Poliorcetes, after gaining and then losing Macedonia, sought to make for himself a new kingdom in Asia, out of the possessions of Lysimachus and Seleucus. He was defeated by the latter, and remained a prisoner the rest of his life.

Coin of Antioch, twice the size of the original.

30. Lysimachus, king of Thrace, under the influence of his Egyptian wife and her brother, Ptolemy Cerau'nus, had alienated the hearts of his subjects by the murder of his son. The widow of the murdered prince fled for protection to the court of Seleucus, who undertook her cause and invaded the territories of Lysimachus. The two aged kings were now the only survivors of the companions and generals of Alexander. In the battle of Corupe'dion, B. C. 281, Lysimachus was slain, and all his Asiatic dominions were transferred to Seleucus. The empire of Alexander seemed about to be united in the hands of one man. Before crossing the Hellespont to seize the European provinces, the Syrian king committed the government of his present dominion to his son, Antiochus. Then passing the strait, he advanced to Lys'imachi'a, the capital of his late enemy; but here he was killed by the hand of Ptolemy Ceraunus, B. C. 280. Thrace and Macedonia became the prize of the murderer.

31. Antiochus I, (Soter) inherited the Asiatic dominions of his father, and made war in Asia Minor against the native kings of Bithynia. One of these, Nicomedes, called to his assistance the Gauls, who were ravaging eastern Europe, and rewarded their services with a large territory in northern Phrygia, which was thence called Gala'tia. North-western

Lydia was also wrested from Antiochus, and formed the kingdom of Per′-gamus. From his only important victory over the Gauls, B. C. 275, the Syrian king derived his title *Soter* (the Deliverer); but his operations were usually unsuccessful, and his kingdom was much reduced both in wealth and power during his reign. He was defeated and slain near Ephesus, in a battle with the Gauls, B. C. 261.

32. Antiochus II. bore the blasphemous title of *Theos* (the God), but he showed himself less than a man by the weakness and licentiousness of his reign. He abandoned all affairs to worthless favorites, who were neither feared nor respected in the distant provinces, and two independent kingdoms sprang up unchecked in Parthia and Bactria, B. C. 255. The influence of his wife, Laodice, involved him in a war with Egypt. It was ended by the divorce of Laodice, and the marriage of Antiochus with Ber′eni′ce, daughter of Ptolemy Philadelphus (B. C. 260–252). On the death of Philadelphus, Antiochus sent away Berenice and took back Laodice; but she, doubting his constancy, murdered him to secure the kingdom for her son, Seleucus. Berenice and her infant son were also put to death.

33. Seleucus II. (Callini′cus) was first engaged in war with the king of Egypt, Ptolemy Euer′getes, who came to avenge the deaths of his sister and nephew. With the exception of part of Lydia and Phrygia, all Asia west of the Tigris, and even Susiana, Media, and Persia, submitted to the invader; but the severity of his exactions excited discontent, and a revolt in Egypt called him home, whereupon Callinicus regained his territories. Antiochus Hi′erax (the Hawk), a younger brother of the king, revolted at fourteen years of age, with the assistance of his uncle and a troop of Gauls. At the same time, Arsa′ces II., the Parthian king, gained great advantages in Upper Asia, and signally defeated Callinicus (B. C. 237), who led an expedition in person against him. The war between the brothers ended, B. C. 229, in the defeat of the rebellious prince. Seleucus died by a fall from his horse, B. C. 226.

Seleucus III. (Ceraunus) reigned only three years. In the midst of an expedition against Attalus, king of Pergamus, he was killed in a mutiny by some of his own officers.

34. Antiochus III., the Great, had an eventful reign of thirty-six years. Molo, his general, first revolted, and made himself master, one by one, of the countries east of the Euphrates, destroying all the armies sent against him. Antiochus at length defeated him, B. C. 220, and then made war upon Egypt for the recovery of Syria and Palestine, which had hitherto been held by Ptolemy. He was successful at first, but his defeat at Raph′ia robbed him of all his conquests, except Seleucia in Syria. Achæ′us, his cousin, and hitherto a faithful servant of Antiochus and his father, had meanwhile been driven into revolt by the false accusations of Hermi′as, the prime minister. He subjected to his control all the countries west of the Taurus. As soon as peace had been made with Egypt, the king of Syria marched against him, deprived him of all his possessions in one campaign, besieged him two years in Sardis, and finally captured and put him to death.

35. The Parthian king, Arsaces III., had taken up arms against Media. Antiochus led an army across the desert to Hecatom′pylos, the Parthian capital, which he captured; but the battle which followed was indecisive, and Arsaces remained independent, with the possession of Parthia and Hyrcania. The war against the Bactrian monarch had a similar result, Euthyde′mus retaining Bactria and Sogdiana. Antiochus penetrated India, and renewed the old alliance of Seleucus Nicator with the king of the upper Ganges. Wintering in Kerma′nia, the Syrian king made a naval expedition, the next year, against the piratical Arabs of the western shores of the Persian Gulf. On his return from his seven years' absence in the East, Antiochus received the title of "Great," by which he is known in history.

36. The same year, B. C. 205, Ptolemy Epiph′anes, a child of five years, succeeded his father in Egypt. Tempted by the unprotected state of the kingdom, Antiochus made a treaty with Philip of Macedon to divide the dominions of Ptolemy between them. Philip's designs were interrupted by a war with Rome, the now powerful republic of the West. Antiochus carried on the contest with great energy, but with varying success, in Cœle-Syria and Palestine. By the decisive battle of Pa′neas, B. C. 198, he gained complete possession of those provinces; but desiring to prosecute his wars in another direction, he married his daughter Cleopatra to the young king of Egypt, and promised the conquered country as her dower.

37. He then overran Asia Minor, and crossing the Hellespont, seized the Thracian Chersonesus. The Romans, who had conquered Philip and were guardians of Ptolemy, now sent an embassy to Antiochus, requiring him to surrender all his conquests of territory belonging to either prince, B. C. 196. Antiochus indignantly rejected their interference, and prepared for war, with the aid of their great enemy, Hannibal, who had taken refuge at his court. In 192 B. C., he crossed into Greece and captured Chalcis; but he was signally defeated soon after by the Romans, at Thermopylæ, and compelled to withdraw from Europe. They followed him across the sea, and by two naval victories gained the western coast of Asia Minor. The two Scip′ios crossed the Hellespont and defeated Antiochus a fourth time, near Magnesia, in Lydia. He obtained peace only by surrendering all Asia Minor except Cilicia, with his navy and all his elephants, and by paying an enormous war indemnity. Twenty hostages were given for the payment, among whom was Antiochus Epiphanes, the king's son. The king of Pergamus received the ceded provinces, and became a most formidable rival to Syria. To meet his engagements with the Romans, Antiochus plundered the temples of Asia, and in a commotion excited by this means in Elyma′is, he lost his life.

38. Seleucus IV. (Philop′ator) had a reign of eleven years, unmarked by important events. The kingdom was exhausted, and the Romans were ready to seize any exposed province at the least hostile movement of the Syrians. Heliodo′rus, the treasurer, at length murdered his master and assumed the crown; but his usurpation was cut short by the arrival of Antiochus Epiphanes, brother of the late king, who with the aid of Eumenes, king of Pergamus, established himself upon the throne.

39. Antiochus IV. had been thirteen years a hostage at Rome, and surprised his people by the Roman customs which he introduced. He made a four years' war against Egypt, and had nearly conquered the country when the Romans interfered, and commanded him to give up all his conquests. He was forced to obey, but he vented his rage upon the Jews, whose temple he plundered and desecrated. They sprang to arms, under the leadership of Mat′tathi′as, the priest, and his brave son, Judas Maccabæ′us, and defeated the army sent to subdue them. Antiochus, who was now in the East, set forth in person to avenge this insult to his authority. On his way, he attempted to plunder the temple at Elymais, and was seized with a furious insanity, in which he died. Both Jews and Greeks believed his madness to be a judgment for his sacrilege.

40. Antiochus V. (Eu′pator), a boy of twelve years, came to the throne under the control of Lys′ias, the regent. But his father, when dying, had appointed him another guardian in the person of Philip, who returned to Antioch bearing the royal signet, while the young king and his minister were absent in Judæa. Lysias, on hearing this, hastened to make peace with Judas Maccabæus, and turned back to fight with Philip, whom he defeated and put to death. The Parthians, meanwhile, were overrunning the kingdom on the east; and the Romans, on the west, were harshly enforcing the terms of the treaty made by Antiochus the Great. Demetrius, the son of Seleucus Philopator, now escaped from Rome, and gained possession of the kingdom, after ordering the execution of both Eupator and his guardian.

41. Demetrius I. spent some years in vain attempts to put down the Jewish rebellion. His armies were defeated by Judas Maccabæus, and the Romans entered into alliance with Judæa, which they now declared an independent kingdom. The Syrian king was no more successful in Cappadocia; and in Babylon, the satrap whom he had deposed set up an impostor, Alexander Balas, who claimed to be a son of Antiochus Epiphanes. Aided by the forces of Rome, Pergamus, Cappadocia, Egypt, and Judæa, this man conquered Demetrius and kept the kingdom five years.

42. Alexander Balas proved unworthy of a crown, by leaving public affairs in the weak and incompetent hands of his favorite, Ammo′nius, while he abandoned himself to indolence and luxury. Demetrius Nica′tor, eldest son of the former king, encouraged by the contempt of the Syrians for the licentiousness of Alexander, landed in Cilicia and made war for the recovery of his kingdom. Ptolemy of Egypt, who had entered Syria with an army for the aid of his son-in-law, Alexander, became disgusted by his ingratitude and came over to the side of Demetrius. A battle near Antioch was decided in favor of the allies. Alexander fled into Arabia, where he was assassinated by some of his own officers.

43. Demetrius II. (Nicator) ruled with such wanton cruelty as to alienate his subjects. One of them, Diod′otus Tryphon, set up a rival king in the person of Antiochus VI., a child two years of age, the son of Alexander Balas. After three or four years he removed this infant monarch and made himself king, with the aid of Judas Maccabæus. Demetrius, after fighting ineffectually seven years against his rivals in the west, left the regency of Syria to his wife, Cleopatra, while he turned against the Parthians, who had nearly conquered his eastern provinces. He was defeated and made prisoner by Arsaces VI., and remained ten years a captive, though he was treated with all the honors of royalty, and received a Parthian princess for his second wife.

44. Cleopatra, unable to wage war alone against Tryphon, called in Antiochus Side′tes, her husband's brother, who conquered the usurper and seated himself on the vacant throne. He made war against the Jews, and captured Jerusalem by a siege of nearly a year. He afterward turned against the Parthians and gained some advantages, but he was finally defeated and lost his life after a reign of nine years. Demetrius Nicator had been released by the Parthian king, and now re-established himself in Syria. But Ptolemy Phys′con, of Egypt, raised up a new pretender, Zabi′nas, who defeated Demetrius at Damascus. Attempting to enter Tyre, the Syrian king was captured and put to death.

45. Seleucus V., his eldest son, assumed the crown without the permission of his mother, who thereupon caused him to be executed, and associated with herself her second son, Antiochus VIII. (Grypus). Zabinas, the pretender, reigned at the same time in part of Syria, until he was defeated by Antiochus, and put to death by poison, B. C. 122. The same year Cleopatra was detected in a plot against the life of her son, and was herself executed.

46. Exhausted by long wars, and greatly reduced both in power and extent, Syria now enjoyed eight years of peace. Judæa and the provinces east of the Euphrates were wholly independent. The few Syrians who possessed wealth were enfeebled by luxury, while the mass of the people were crushed by want. In 114 B. C., Antiochus Cyzice′nus, a half-brother of the king, revolted against him, and involved the country in another bloody war of three years. The territory was then divided between them; but war broke out afresh in 105 B. C., and continued nine years, resulting in no gain to either party, but great loss and misery to the nation. Tyre, Sidon, Seleucia, and the whole province of Cilicia became independent. The Arabs on one side, and the Egyptians on the other, ravaged the country at pleasure. At length the reign of Antiochus VIII. was ended with his life, by Hera′cleon, an officer of his court, B. C. 96.

47. The murderer did not receive the reward of his crime, for Seleucus VI. (Epiphanes), the eldest son of Grypus, gained possession of the kingdom. In two years he conquered Cyzicenus, who committed suicide to avoid capture; but the claims of the rival house were still maintained by Antiochus X. (Eu′sebes), his eldest son. Seleucus was now driven into Cilicia. Here he came to a miserable end, for he was burnt alive by the people of a town from which he had demanded a subsidy. Philip, the brother of Seleucus, and second son of Antiochus Grypus, became king, and with the aid of his younger brothers continued the war against Eusebes. This prince was defeated and driven to take refuge in Parthia: But no peace came to the country, for Philip and his brothers, Antiochus XI., Demetrius, and Antiochus XII., made war with each other, until the unhappy Syrians called upon Tigra′nes, king of Armenia, to end their miseries.

48. Tigranes governed, wisely and well, fourteen years (B. C. 83–69); but having at length incurred the vengeance of the Romans, by rendering aid to his father-in-law, Mithridates of Pontus, he was forced to give up all except his hereditary kingdom. Four years longer (B. C. 69–65), Syria continued its separate existence, under Antiochus XIII. (Asiaticus), the son of Eusebes. At the end of that time the kingdom was subdued by Pompey the Great, and became a Roman province.

RECAPITULATION.

Seleucus I. (B. C. 312–281) extended his empire beyond the Indus, built many cities, gained all Asia Minor by the defeat of Lysimachus. Antiochus I. (B. C. 280–261) lost the territories of Pergamus and Galatia; Antiochus II. (261-246), those of Parthia and Bactria. Under Seleucus II. (246–226), the greater part of the empire was conquered by Ptolemy, but soon recovered. Seleucus III. reigned three years (B. C. 226-223). Antiochus III. (B. C. 223–187) quelled the revolts of Molo and Achæus; had wars with the kings of Parthia and Bactria; penetrated India as far as the Ganges; punished the pirates of the Persian Gulf; wrested from Egypt the provinces of Syria and Palestine; overran Asia Minor, and invaded Greece. He was defeated by the Romans, twice by sea and twice by land. Seleucus IV. (B. C. 187-176) was murdered by his treasurer, Heliodorus. Antiochus IV. (B. C. 176-164) was prevented by the Romans from conquering Egypt; excited by his persecutions a revolt in Judæa, which became independent under the Maccabees. The short reign of Antiochus V. (B. C. 164-162) was filled with wars of the regents.

His uncle, Demetrius I. (B. C. 162-151), had unsuccessful wars with the Jews and Cappadocians; was conquered by Alexander Balas, who reigned B. C. 151-146. Demetrius II. had a disputed reign (B. C. 146-140); a ten years' imprisonment in Parthia (B. C. 140-130), while his wife and his brother, Antiochus VII., ruled Syria; and a second contest with a pretender, B. C. 129-126. Antiochus VIII. (B. C. 126-96) reigned five years jointly with his mother, seven years alone, and eighteen years side by side with his brother, Antiochus IX. (Cyzicenus), who ruled Cœle-Syria and Phœnicia, B, C. 111-96. Seleucus V. (B. C. 96, 95) conquered Cyzicenus, but carried on the same war with his son, Eusebes, until his own violent death. His younger brothers fought first Eusebes, and then each other, until Tigranes, king of Armenia, conquered the country and ruled it fourteen years (B. C. 83-69). Antiochus XIII. the last of the Seleucidæ, reigned B. C. 69-65.

II. Egypt under the Ptolemies. B. C. 323–30.

49. The Macedonian Kingdom in Egypt presented a marked and brilliant contrast to the native empires and the Egyptian satrapy. By removing the capital to Alexandria, the conqueror had provided for free intercourse with foreign countries, and the old exclusiveness of the Egyptians was forever broken down. While Palestine was attached to this kingdom, especial favor was shown to the Jews; and in the Greek conquerors, the native Egyptians, and the Jewish merchants, the three families of Shem, Ham, and Japhet were reunited as they had never been since the dispersion at Babel. The Egyptians, who had abhorred the Persian dominion, hailed the Macedonians as deliverers; the common people engaged with zeal in the new industries that promised wealth as the reward of enterprise, and the learned class found their delight in the intellectual society, as well as the rare treasures of literature and art, that filled the court of the Ptolemies.

50. Ptolemy I. (Soter *) received the Egyptian province immediately upon the death of Alexander, and proceeded to organize it with great energy and wisdom. Desiring to make Egypt a maritime power, he sought at once to conquer Palestine, Phœnicia, and Cyprus, whose forests were as needful to him for ship-building as their sea-faring people for sailors. The two countries on the mainland were occupied by Ptolemy in 320 B. C., and remained six years in his possession. They were lost in the war with Antigonus, and only fully regained after the battle of Ipsus, B. C. 301. Cyprus was the scene of many conflicts, of which the great naval battle off Salamis, B. C. 306, was the most severe and decisive. It was then lost to Egypt, but in B. C. 294 or 293 it was regained, and continued her most valuable foreign possession as long as the kingdom existed. Cyrene and all the Libyan tribes between it and Egypt were also annexed by Ptolemy.

51. Few changes were made in the internal government of Egypt. The country, as before, was divided into nomes, each having its own ruler,

---

* He is frequently called Ptolemy Lagi, from the name of his father, Lagus.

who was usually a native Egyptian. The old laws and worship prevailed. The Ptolemies rebuilt the temples, paid especial honors to the Apis, and made the most of all points of resemblance between the Greek and Egyptian religions. A magnificent temple to Sera′pis was erected at Alexandria. The priests retained their privileges and honors, being exempt from all taxation. The army was chiefly, and its officers wholly, Greek or Macedonian, and all civil dignities of any importance were also filled by the conquering people. The Greek inhabitants of the cities alone possessed entire freedom in the management of their affairs.

52. Ptolemy followed the liberal policy of Alexander toward men of genius and learning. He collected a vast and precious library, which he placed in a building connected with the palace; and he founded the "Museum," which drew students and professors from all parts of the world. No spot ever witnessed more literary and intellectual activity than Alexandria, the University of the East. There Euclid first unfolded the "Elements of Geometry"; Eratos′thenes discoursed of Geography; Hipparchus, of Astronomy; Aristoph′anes and Aristar′chus, of Criticism; Man′etho, of History; while Apel′les and Antiph′ilus added their paintings, and Phile′tas, Callim′achus, and Apollonius their poems, for the delight of a court whose monarch was himself an author, and in which talent constituted rank. Alexandria during this reign was adorned with many costly and magnificent works. The royal palace; the Museum; the great light-house on the island of Pharos, which has given its name to many similar constructions in modern times; the mole or causeway which connected this island with the mainland; the Hip′podrome, and the Mausole′um, containing the tomb of Alexander, were among the chief. Ptolemy Soter was distinguished by his truth and magnanimity from most of the princes and generals of his age. His unlimited power never led him to cruelty or self-indulgence. He died at the age of eighty-four, B. C. 283.

53. Ptolemy II. (Philadelphus), through the influence of his mother, had been raised to the throne two years before his father's death, instead of his elder brother, Ceraunus. He had been carefully educated by several of the learned men whom the patronage of his father had drawn to the court; and he continued, on a still more liberal scale, that encouragement of science and literature which had already made Alexandria a successful rival of Athens. He so greatly increased the Alexandrian Library that he is often mentioned as its founder. Agents were appointed to search Europe and Asia for every literary work of value, and to secure it at any cost. An embassy was sent to the high priest at Jerusalem to bring a copy of the Holy Scriptures, together with a company of learned men who could translate them into Greek. The translators were entertained by the king with the greatest honor. The first five books were completed in the reign of Philadelphus, the rest were translated by order of the later Ptolemies; and the entire version—still an invaluable treasure to Biblical scholars—is known as the Sep′tuagint, either from the seventy translators, or because it was authorized by the San′hedrim of Alexandria, which consisted of the same number.

54. Ptolemy II. was engaged in various wars; first for the furtherance of the Achæan League, and the protection of the Greeks against Macedonian aggressions; afterward against his half-brother, Magas, king of Cyrene, and the kings of Syria, with whom Magas was allied. He gained possession of the whole coast of Asia Minor, with many of the Cyclades. By the wisdom of his internal policy, Egypt was meanwhile raised to her highest pitch of wealth and prosperity. He re-opened the canal made by Rameses the Great (see Book I, §§ 153, 154), and built the port of Arsinoë, on the site of the modern Suez. To avoid the dangers of Red Sea navigation, he founded two cities, named Berenice, farther to the southward, and connected one of them by a highway with Coptos on the Nile. Egypt thus reaped the full commercial advantage of her position midway between the East and the West. For centuries the rich productions of India, Arabia, and Ethiopia were conveyed along these various highways to Alexandria, whence they were distributed to Syria, Greece, and Rome. The revenues of Egypt were equal to those which Darius had derived from the vast empire of Persia.

55. The personal character of Philadelphus was less admirable than that of his father. He killed two of his brothers, banished a most faithful counselor, and by marrying his own sister, Arsinoë, introduced a custom which caused untold misery and mischief in the kingdom. He died B. C. 247, having reigned thirty-eight years, or thirty-six from the death of his father.

56. Ptolemy III. (Euergetes) was the most enterprising monarch of his race, and pushed the boundaries of his kingdom to their greatest extent. He gained the Cyr′ena′ica by marriage with the daughter of Magas, and annexed portions of Ethiopia and Arabia. In his war against Syria to avenge his sister Berenice (see §§ 32, 33), he even passed the Euphrates and conquered all the country to the borders of Bactria; but he lost all this by his sudden recall to Egypt. His conquests on the sea-board, which could be defended by his fleet, remained permanently in his possession. All the shores of the Mediterranean, from Cyrene to the Hellespont, with many important islands, and even a portion of Europe, including Lysimachia in Thrace, belonged to his dominion.

He continued the patronage of art and letters, and enriched the Alexandrian libraries with many rare manuscripts. The Egyptians were still more gratified by the recovery of some ancient images of their gods, which had been carried away to Assyria by Sargon or Esarhaddon, and were brought back by Ptolemy from his eastern campaign. Euergetes died B. C. 222, after a prosperous reign of twenty-five years; and with him ended the glory of the Macedonian monarchy in Egypt. "Historians reckon nine Ptolemies after Euergetes. Except Philome′tor, who was mild and humane; Lath′yrus, who was amiable but weak; and Ptolemy XII., who was merely young and incompetent, they were all, almost equally, detestable."

57. Ptolemy IV. was suspected of having murdered his father, and therefore took the surname Philopator to allay suspicion. He began his reign, however, by murdering his mother, his brother, and his uncle, and marrying his sister Arsinoë. A few years later she, too, was put to death, at the instigation of a worthless favorite of the king. The control of affairs was left to Sosib′ius, a minister who was equally wicked and incompetent. Through his neglect, the army became weakened by lack of discipline, and the Syrians seized the opportunity to recover their lost possessions. They were defeated, however, at Raph′ia, and gained only their port of Seleucia. A revolt of the native Egyptians occupied many years of this reign.

58. Ptolemy V. (Epiphanes) was only five years old at his father's death. The kings of Syria and Macedon plotted to divide his dominions between them, and the only resource of the incompetent ministers was to call the Romans to their aid. All the foreign dependencies, except Cyprus and the Cyrenaica, were lost; but by the good management of M. Lep′idus, Egypt was saved to the little Ptolemy. Aristom′enes, an Acarnanian, succeeded Lepidus as regent, and his energy and justice restored for a time the prosperity of the kingdom. At the age of fourteen, Epiphanes was declared of age, and the government was thenceforth in his name. Few events of his reign are known. He married Cleopatra of Syria, and soon after poisoned his late guardian, Aristomenes. His plans for a war with Syria were prevented by his own assassination, B. C. 181.

59. Ptolemy VI. (Philometor) became king at the age of seven, under the vigorous regency of his mother, Cleopatra. She died B. C. 173, and the power passed into the hands of two weak and corrupt ministers, who involved the kingdom in war, and almost in ruin, by their rash invasion of Syria. Antiochus IV. defeated them at Pelusium, and advancing to Memphis, gained possession of the young king, whom he used as a tool for the reduction of the whole country. The Alexandrians crowned Ptolemy Physcon, a younger brother of the king, and successfully withstood the besieging army of Antiochus. The Romans now interposing, he was obliged to retreat.

The two brothers agreed to reign together, and prepared for war with Antiochus. He captured Cyprus, invaded Egypt a second time, and would doubtless have added the entire dominion of the Ptolemies to his own, if the Romans, who claimed the protectorate of Egypt, had not again interfered and commanded him to withdraw. The Syrian king reluctantly obeyed, and the brothers reigned four years in peace. They then quarreled, and Philometor went to plead his cause before the Roman Senate. The Romans re-instated him in the possession of Egypt, giving to his brother Physcon Libya and the Cyrenaica. Dissatisfied with his portion, Physcon went to Rome and obtained a further grant of Cyprus; but Philometor refused to give it up, and the brothers were preparing for war, when a revolt in Cyrene engaged the attention of its king. After nine years he renewed his claim, and obtained from Rome a small squadron to aid in the capture of the island. He was defeated and made prisoner by his brother; but his life was spared, and he was restored to his kingdom of Cyrene. Philometor fell, B. C. 146, in a battle near Antioch, with Alexander Balas, whom he had himself encouraged to assume the crown of Syria. (See § 42.)

60. Ptolemy VII. (Eupator) had reigned but a few days when he was murdered by his uncle, Ptolemy Physcon, who, aided by the Romans, united in himself the two kingdoms, Egypt and Cyrene. This monster created such terror by his inhuman cruelties, and such disgust by his excesses, that his capital became half depopulated, and the citizens who remained were almost constantly in revolt. At last he was forced to take refuge in Cyprus, the crown remaining to his sister, Cleopatra. To wound the queen most deeply, he murdered her son, and sent her the head and hands of the victim. The Alexandrians were so enraged by this atrocity, that they fought bravely for Cleopatra; but when she applied for aid to the king of Syria, they became alarmed and recalled Physcon, after an exile of three years. Warned by his punishment, Physcon now desisted from his cruelties, and devoted himself to literary pursuits, even gaining some reputation as an author.

61. Ptolemy VIII. (Lath′yrus) succeeded his father in Egypt, while his brother Alexander reigned in Cyprus, and A′pion, another son of Physcon, received the Cyrenaica. Cleopatra, the queen mother, had the real power. After ten years, Lathyrus offended his mother by pursuing a policy of his own, and was compelled to change places with Alexander, who reigned eighteen years in Egypt, with the title of Ptolemy IX. Cleopatra was then put to death, Alexander expelled, and Ptolemy Lathyrus recalled. He reigned eight years as sole monarch, defeated Alexander, who attempted to regain Cyprus, and punished a revolt in Thebes by a siege of three years, ending with the destruction of the city, B. C. 89–86.

62. Berenice, the only legitimate child of Lathyrus, reigned six months alone, and was then married and associated upon the throne with her cousin, Ptolemy X., a son of Alexander, whose claims were supported by the Romans. Within three weeks he put his wife to death, and the Alexandrians, revolting, slew him in the gymnasium, B. C. 80. Fifteen years of great confusion followed, during which the succession was disputed by at least five claimants, and Cyprus became a separate kingdom.

63. Ptolemy XI. (Aule´tes, or the Flute-Player) then obtained the crown, and dated his reign from the death of his half-sister, Berenice. In 59 B. C., he was acknowledged by the Romans; but by that time his oppressive and profligate government had so disgusted the people, that they drove him from the kingdom. He took refuge four years in Rome, while his two daughters nominally governed Egypt, first jointly, and then the younger alone, after her sister's death. In 55 B. C. Auletes returned, supported by a Roman army, put to death his daughter, who had opposed his restoration, and reigned under Roman protection three and a half years. He died, B. C. 51, leaving four children: the famous Cleopatra, aged seventeen; Ptolemy XII.; another Ptolemy, and a daughter Arsinoë, still younger.

64. The princess Cleopatra received the crown under Roman patronage, in conjunction with the elder Ptolemy. The brother and sister quarreled, and Cleopatra was driven into Syria. Here she met Julius Cæsar, and by her talents and accomplishments gained great ascendency over his mind. By his aid Ptolemy was conquered and slain, and Cleopatra established in the kingdom. She removed her younger brother by poison, and had thenceforth no rival. With consummate ability, mixed with the unscrupulous cruelty of her race, she reigned seventeen years in great prosperity. Cæsar was her protector while he lived, and Antony then became her slave, sacrificing all his interests, and his honor as a Roman and a general, to her slightest caprices. In the civil wars of Rome, Antony was at length defeated at Actium; Cleopatra committed suicide, and her kingdom became a Roman province, B. C. 30.

Coin of Antony and Cleopatra, twice the size.

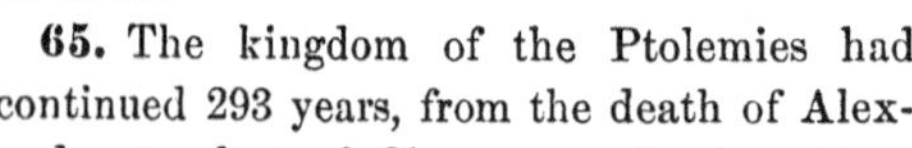

65. The kingdom of the Ptolemies had continued 293 years, from the death of Alexander to that of Cleopatra. During 101 years, under the first three kings, it was the most flourishing, well organized, and prosperous of the Macedonian monarchies; the nearly two centuries which remained were among the most degraded periods in the history of the human race.

RECAPITULATION.

Prosperity of Egypt under the Ptolemies. Concourse of races at Alexandria. Ptolemy I. (B. C. 323–283) conquered Palestine, Phœnicia, Cyprus, and the African coast as far as Cyrene. Old laws and worship retained. Alexandrian Library and Museum, professors and public works. Ptolemy Philadelphus (B. C. 283–247) ordered a Greek version of the Hebrew Scriptures; constructed cities, roads, and canals for purposes of commerce. Acquisitions of Ptolemy III. (B. C. 247–222). Rapid conquests in Asia, speedily lost. Collection of manuscripts and recovery of images. Decline of the Ptolemaic kingdom. Crimes of Ptolemy IV. (B. C. 222–205). Victory at Raphia, B. C. 217. Roman interference during the minority of Ptolemy V. (B. C. 205–181). Ptolemy VI. (B. C. 181–146) taken by Antiochus IV., of Syria. His brother Physcon crowned. Rome protected Egyptian dependencies against Syria, and divided them between the brothers. Ptolemy VII. was murdered by his uncle, Ptolemy Physcon, who reigned B. C. 146–117. He was exiled for his crimes, but recalled in three years. Ptolemy VIII. and his brother Alexander reigned alternately in Egypt and Cyprus while their mother lived (B. C. 117–89). After her death, the former was sole monarch until B. C. 81. Berenice reigned six months (B. C. 81, 80), and was then murdered by her husband, Ptolemy X. He was slain by the Alexandrians. Ptolemy XI. (B. C. 80–51) made good his claim after fifteen years' anarchy; was acknowledged by the Romans, but expelled (B. C. 59–55) by his subjects; returned to reign under Roman protection. Cleopatra poisoned her two brothers, and by favor of Cæsar and Antony kept her kingdom twenty-one years, B. C. 51–30.

III. Macedonia and Greece.

66. Upon the death of Alexander, the greater part of Greece revolted against Macedon, Athens, as of old, being the leader. Antipater, the Macedonian regent, was defeated near Thermopylæ, and besieged in Lamia, in Thessaly. The confederates were afterward worsted at Cranon, and the good management of Antipater dissolved the league by treating with its members separately, and offering the most lenient terms to all except the leaders. Athens suffered the punishment she had often inflicted. Twelve thousand of her citizens were forcibly removed to Thrace, Illyria, Italy, and Africa, only nine thousand of the wealthier sort being left, who willingly submitted to the Macedonian supremacy. Demosthenes, with the principal members of his party, were executed, and the last remains of Athenian independence destroyed.

67. The wars of the generals and the intrigues of the Macedonian princesses belong to Period II. (See §§ 19–25.) Three years after the battle of Ipsus, Cassander died, B. C. 298, leaving the crown to his son, Philip IV. The young king reigned less than a year, and his mother, Thessalonica, then divided Macedonia between her two remaining sons, Antipater and Alexander. The former, being dissatisfied with his portion, murdered his mother and called in his father-in-law, Lysimachus, to aid him in gaining the whole. His brother, at the same time, asked aid of Demetrius, who reigned in Greece, and of Pyrrhus, king of Epirus. With their help he drove Antipater out of Macedonia; but he gained nothing by the victory, for Demetrius had undertaken the war solely with the view of placing himself upon the throne, which he accomplished by the murder of Alexander. Antipater II. was put to death the same year by Lysimachus, B. C. 294.

68. The kingdom now included Thessaly, Attica, and the greater part of the Peloponnesus, Pyrrhus having received several countries on the western coast of Greece. Demetrius, however, sacrificed all his dominions to his unbounded ambition and conceit. He failed in an attack on Pyrrhus, and being invaded both from the east and west, was compelled to abandon Macedonia, B. C. 287. In a later expedition into Asia, he became the prisoner of Seleucus, and died in the third year of his captivity. (See § 29.)

69. Pyrrhus remained king of the greater part of Macedonia nearly a year, but was then driven back to his hereditary kingdom by Lysimachus, who thus extended his own dominions from the Halys to Mount Pindus, B. C. 286. The capital of this consolidated kingdom was Lysimachia, in the Chersonese, and Macedonia for five years was merely a province. The nobles, becoming discontented, called in Seleucus, who defeated and killed Lysimachus, B. C. 281.

70. For a few weeks the aged Seleucus governed nearly all the dominions of Alexander, except Egypt. He was then assassinated by Ptolemy Ceraunus,* who became king in his stead. The Egyptian prince was soon overwhelmed by a new peril in the invasion of the Gauls. This restless people had been pouring for nearly a century into northern Italy, where they had driven out the Etruscans from the plain of the Po, and given their own name to Gallia Cisalpina. Now turning eastward, they occupied the plain of the Danube, and pressed southward as far as Illyricum, whence they proceeded in three divisions, one falling upon the Thracians, another upon the Pæonians, and a third upon the Macedonians. The last army encountered Ptolemy Ceraunus, who was defeated and slain in battle. For two years they ravaged Macedonia, while Melea′ger, a brother of Ceraunus, and Antipater, a nephew of Cassander, successively occupied the throne, B. C. 279–277.

71. Brennus, a Gallic leader, with more than 200,000 men, marched through Thessaly, laying all waste with fire and sword. A furious battle took place at Thermopylæ, and the Gauls, at last, only gained the rear of the Greek army by the same mountain path which had admitted the troops of Xerxes two hundred years before. Brennus pushed on to

---

* Brother of Philadelphus. (See § 55.)

plunder Delphi, but an army of 4,000, well posted upon the heights of Parnassus, withstood him with success; and a violent wintry storm, which confused and benumbed the assailants, convinced devout Greeks that Apollo was once more defending his sanctuary. The Gallic leader was severely wounded, and unwilling to survive his disgrace, put an end to his own life. His army broke up into a multitude of marauding bands, without order or discipline, and the greater part perished from cold, hunger, or battle. Their countrymen, however, established a kingdom in Thrace; and another band, invited into Asia Minor by Nicomedes, became possessed of a large tract of country, which received their name as Gala′tia.

72. During the disorders in Macedonia, Sosthenes, an officer of noble birth, had been placed at the head of affairs, instead of Antipater, who was deposed for his incapacity. After the Gauls had retired, Antipater regained the throne. But Antigonus Gonatas, who had maintained himself as an independent prince in central and southern Greece, ever since the captivity of his father, Demetrius, now appeared with an army composed mainly of Gallic mercenaries, defeated Antipater, and gained possession of Macedonia. Antiochus Soter made war against him, but was opposed with so much energy that he acknowledged Antigonus as king, and gave him his sister Phila in marriage. But Antigonus was never acceptable to either Greeks or Macedonians, and when Pyrrhus, the most popular prince of his age, returned from Italy, the whole Macedonian army was ready to desert to his side. Antigonus was defeated, and for a year or more was a fugitive, B. C. 273–271.

73. Pyrrhus was the greatest warrior and one of the best princes of his time — a time from which truth and fidelity seemed almost to have disappeared. He might have become the most powerful monarch in the world, if his perseverance had been equal to his talents and ambition. But instead of organizing the territory he possessed, he was ever thirsting for new conquests. In a war upon southern Greece he was repulsed from Sparta, and in attempting to seize Argos by night, he was killed by a tile thrown by a woman from a house-top.

74. Antigonus Gonatas now returned and reigned thirty-two years. He extended his power over most of the Peloponnesus, and waged war five years against the Athenians, who were aided by Sparta and Egypt. In the meantime, Antigonus was recalled by the incursion of Alexander, son of Pyrrhus, who was carrying all before him, and had been acknowledged king of Macedon. Demetrius, son of Antigonus, chased him out of Macedonia, and even out of Epirus; and though he was soon restored to his paternal dominion, he remained thenceforth at peace with his neighbors. Athens fell in 263 B. C. Nineteen years later, Antigonus gained possession of Corinth; but this was the last of his successes.

75. The Achæan League, which had been suppressed by the immediate successors of Alexander, had soon revived, and extended itself beyond the limits of Achaia, receiving cities from all the Peloponnesus. In 243 B. C., Ara′tus, its head, by a sudden and well-concerted movement captured Corinth, which immediately joined the League. Several important cities followed the example; and Antigonus, who had grown old and cautious, was unable to oppose them, except by stirring up Ætolia to attack the Achæans. He died B. C. 239, having lived eighty and reigned thirty-seven years.

76. Demetrius II. allied himself with Epirus, and broke friendship with the Ætolians, who were enemies of that kingdom. The consequence was, that the Ætolians made a junction with the Achæan League to oppose him. He was able to defeat them in Thessaly and Bœotia, but south of the isthmus the ascendency of Macedon was at an end. The Romans now for the first time interfered in Grecian affairs, by requiring the Ætolian confederacy to abstain from aggressions upon Acarnania. Corcyra, Apollonia, and Epidamnus fell into their hands, B. C. 228, a year after the death of Demetrius II.

77. Philip V. was but eight years old when he inherited his father's dominions, under the guardianship of his kinsman, Antigonus Doson. During this regency great changes took place in Sparta, which led to a brief return of her old energy. The laws of Lycurgus had continued in force more than five centuries, but the time of their fitness and usefulness had passed away. The rigid separation which they made between the different classes, now limited the number of true Spartans to 700, while the property tests were so severe, that only 100 enjoyed the full rights of citizens. The wealth of the community was concentrated in the hands of a few, who violated the old law by living in great luxury. In this condition, Sparta was unable even to defend herself against Illyrian pirates or Ætolian marauders, still less to exert any influence, as of old, in the general affairs of Greece.

The reforms proposed B. C. 230, by Agis IV., and carried, four years later, by Cleomenes, added 3,800 *periœ′ci* to the number of citizens, and re-divided the lands of the state between these and 15,000 selected Laconians. Debts were abolished, and the old simple and frugal customs of Lycurgus restored. Sparta was now able to defeat the forces of the Achæan League, and to draw from it, into her own alliance, most of the Peloponnesian towns out of Achaia. But Aratus, the head of the League, violated all its principles by calling in Antigonus, the Macedonian regent, and putting him in possession of Acro-Corinthus. In the battle of Sella′sia, B. C. 221, Cleomenes was defeated, and forced to take refuge at the court of Ptolemy Philopator. The League which had been created to defend the liberties of Greece, had betrayed them; and there was no longer any hope either of restoring the glories of Sparta, or of checking the overwhelming power of Macedon and Rome.

78. Antigonus died B. C. 220, and Philip, now seventeen years of age, assumed the government. The great advantages gained during the regency were soon lost by his rashness. He hastily allied himself with Hannibal against Rome, and then with Antiochus of Syria against Egypt. (See §§ 37, 59.) His first war, however, was against Ætolia, which had sprung to arms immediately upon his accession, hoping at once to overbalance its rival, Achaia, and to increase its own territories at the expense of Macedon. As early as the time of Alexander the Great, the Ætolian tribes had formed themselves into a federal republic, which occupied a similar position in central Greece to that of the Achæan League in the Peloponnesus. By the subjection or annexation of several states, it was now extended from the Ionian to the Ægean Sea. Philip overran Ætolia with great energy, captured its seat of government, and by his brilliant successes showed a military talent worthy of the early days of Macedonian conquest. But the news of a great victory gained by Hannibal at Lake Thrasyme′ne, recalled his attention to the object of his chief ambition, a war with Rome.

79. The first movement in the new war was the siege of Apollonia, a Roman colony in Illyricum. Philip hoped to drive the Romans from the western coast of Greece, and thus prepare the way for an invasion of Italy. His camp was surprised at night by Vale′rius, and he was forced to burn his ships and retreat in all haste. The Ætolians and all their allies — Sparta, Elis, and the kings of Illyricum and Pergamus — took sides with Rome, and carried the war into Macedonia; forcing Philip to ask the aid of Carthage. The Romans captured Zacynthus, Ne′sos and Œniadæ, Antic′yra in Locris, and the island of Ægina, and presented all to the Ætolians.

At this crisis, Philopœ′men, the greatest Greek of his time, became commander of the Achæan cavalry, and, two years later, the head of the League. He improved the drill and tactics of the army, and infused new spirit into the whole nation. His invasion of Elis, in concert with Philip, was unsuccessful, and the king was defeated by Sulpic′ius Galba; but, in 207 B. C., the great victory of Mantinea placed the Macedonians and Achæans on a more equal footing with the Romans. Peace was made on terms honorable to all parties.

80. Philip, spoiled by ambition, had become unscrupulous and reckless. Instead of securing what he already possessed, he continually grasped after new conquests; and disregarding the storm that was sure to burst upon him sooner or later from the west, he now turned to the east and south. He made a treaty with Antiochus the Great for a partition of the Egyptian dependencies, by which he was to receive Thrace and the western part of

Asia Minor. This led at once to war with At'talus of Pergamus, an ally of Rome, as well as with Rhodes, which took the part of Egypt. His fleet was signally defeated off Chios, B. C. 201; and though he afterward gained a victory at Lade, his losses were not retrieved. He captured, however, the important islands of Samos, Thasos, and Chios, with the province of Caria, and several places in Ionia.

81. The great disaster of the war was the rupture of the treaty with Rome. That power interfered in behalf of her allies, Egypt, Rhodes, and Pergamus; and when Philip rejected all reasonable demands, she declared the peace at an end. In the second war with Rome, Greece was at first divided into three parties, some states remaining neutral, some siding with Rome, and some with Macedon. But when the consul, Fla'mini'nus, proclaimed liberty to all the Greeks, and declared himself their champion against the long detested power of Macedon, nearly every state went over to the Roman side. On the land, Macedonia was attacked by Sulpicius Galba, aided by the Illyrians and Dardanians; while by sea, a Roman fleet, increased by Rhodian and Pergamene vessels, threatened the coast. Several important towns in Eubœa were taken, but the great decisive battle was fought (B. C. 197) at Cynocephalæ, where Philip was defeated and his power utterly prostrated. He was compelled to abandon all the Greek cities which he held, either in Europe or Asia, to surrender his entire navy, and to pay a war indemnity of one thousand talents ($1,250,000).

82. In settling the affairs of Greece, the Romans subdivided the states into still smaller sections than of old, and guaranteed perfect independence to each. The two leagues of Achaia and Ætolia were, however, left to balance each other. The states were generally satisfied with the arrangement, but the Ætolians stirred up a new war in the very year of Flamininus's departure, and called in Antiochus from Asia to their aid. He was defeated at Thermopylæ by the Romans, B. C. 191, and the great battle of Magnesia, in the following year, ended all hope of resistance to the power of Rome. The Achæan League, sustained by the wise and able management of Philopœmen, gained in power by the weakening of its rival, and now included the whole Peloponnesus, with Megaris and some other territories beyond the peninsula.

83. Philip had aided the Romans in the recent war, and had been permitted to extend his dominions over part of Thrace, and southward into Thessaly. But when peace was secured, he was required to give up all except his hereditary kingdom. Demetrius, the second son of Philip, had long been a hostage at Rome, and acted now as his father's embassador. The Roman Senate conceded many points, for the sake of the warm friendship which it professed for this young prince; but its favor only aroused the suspicions of his father and the jealousy of his elder brother, Per'seus. The latter forged letters to convince his father of the treason of Demetrius, and the innocent youth was put to death by order of the king. But the grief and remorse of Philip exceeded all bounds, when he learned the deception that had been practiced. He believed that he was haunted by the spirit of Demetrius, and it was agony of mind, rather than bodily illness, that soon occasioned his death.

An ancient historian remarked that there were few monarchs of whom more good or more evil could justly be said, than of Philip V. If the promise of his youth had been fulfilled, and the opportunities of his reign improved, he would have done great things for Macedonia and Greece. But his talents became obscured by drunkenness and profligacy, his natural generosity was spoiled by the habit of supreme command, and he became in later years a gloomy, unscrupulous, and suspicious tyrant.

84. Philip had designed to punish the crime of Perseus by leaving the throne to a distant relative, Antigonus; but the sudden death of the father, while Antigonus was absent from court, enabled the son to make himself king without opposition. He pursued with much diligence the policy of Philip, in preparing Macedonia for a second struggle with Rome. The revenues were increased by a careful working of the mines; the population, wasted by so many wars, was recruited by colonies of Thracians and others; and close alliances were made with the kings of Asia, and with the hardy barbarians of the north, Gauls, Illyrians, and Germans, whose aid might be invaluable when the decisive moment should arrive. But Perseus failed to unite the states of Greece, in which a large party already preferred his supremacy to that of Rome; and instead of using his treasures to satisfy and confirm his allies, he hoarded them penuriously, only to enrich his enemies at the end of the war.

85. In the spring of 171 B. C., the Romans landed in Epirus, and spent some months in winning the Greek states to their side by money and influence. In the autumn they met Perseus in Thessaly, with nearly equal forces, and were defeated. The Macedonian made no use, however, of his victory, and nothing of importance was done for two years. In 168 B. C., L. Æmil'ius Paulus assumed the command, and forced Perseus to a battle near Pydna. Here the fate of Macedon was finally decided. Perseus was defeated and fled to Samothrace, where he was soon captured with all his treasures. He was taken to Rome, and compelled to walk in chains in the splendid triumph of Æmilius. After several years, the last of the Macedonian kings died in imprisonment at Alba.

Macedonia was not immediately made a Roman province, but was divided into four distinct states, which were forbidden all intercourse with each other. The people were consoled by a great reduction in the taxes, the Romans demanding only half the amount which they had been accustomed to pay their native kings.

86. In Greece, all confederacies, except the Achæan League, were dissolved. Achaia had been the constant friend of Rome during the war; but to insure its submission, one thousand of the principal citizens were accused of having secretly aided Perseus, and were carried to Italy for trial. They were imprisoned seventeen years without a hearing; and then, when all but three hundred had died, these were sent back, in the certainty that their resentment against Rome would lead them to some rash act of hostility.

All happened as the Romans had foreseen. The three of the exiles who were most embittered by this unprovoked outrage came into power, and their enmity gave to their foes what they most desired, a pretext for an armed invasion of the territories of the League. In 146 B. C., war was declared. One of the Achæan leaders was disastrously defeated and slain near Thermopylæ; another, with the remnant of the army, made a last stand at Corinth, but he was defeated and the city was taken, plundered, and destroyed. Within a few years Greece was placed under proconsular government, like other provinces of Rome. It remained nearly sixteen centuries a part of that great empire, which, though driven from Italy, maintained its existence in the East, until it was overthrown by the Turks, A. D. 1453.

RECAPITULATION.

Lamian War ended in the subjection of Greece to Macedonia. Cassander reigned B. C. 316-297. Death of all his sons within three years, left the crown to Demetrius, son of Antigonus, (B. C. 294-287,) who lost it by rash enterprises, and died a prisoner in Asia. Pyrrhus, the Epirote, reigned a year. Macedonia was then annexed to Thrace (B. C. 286-281). On the death of Lysimachus, it fell to Seleucus, who was murdered in turn by Ptolemy Ceraunus. In the reign of Ptolemy (B. C. 281-279), Meleager, Antipater II., and Sosthenes (B. C. 279-277), the Gauls ravaged Macedonia and Greece, gained Thermopylæ, but were defeated at Delphi. Antigonus, son of Demetrius (B. C. 277-273), was expelled by Pyrrhus, whose second reign lasted B. C. 273-271, but who was killed at Argos, and Antigonus restored (B. C. 271-239). He captured Athens and Corinth; the latter was retaken by the Achæan League. Demetrius II. (B. C. 239-229) allied himself with Epirus against the Achæan and Ætolian Leagues. First interference of Rome in Grecian affairs, B. C. 238. Regency of Antigonus Doson, B. C. 229-220. Reform and renewed energy in Sparta. Macedonians, in alliance with the Achæan League, defeated the Spartans at Sellasia, B. C. 221. Independent reign of Philip V., B. C. 220-179. His wars against Ætolia, Rome, Egypt. Romans, in a second war, proclaimed liberty to the Greeks; overthrew Philip at Cynocephalæ, B. C. 197; subdivided and reorganized the Grecian states. The Ætolians provoked another war, their ally, Antiochus, was defeated at Thermopylæ and Magnesia. Death of Prince Demetrius and his father. Efforts of Perseus, the last king of Macedon (B. C. 179-168). His war with Rome; defeat at Pydna; capture and death. Division of Macedonia. Reduction of tribute. Treachery of the Romans toward the Achæan League. Last war with Rome. Battle of Leucopetra, near Corinth, B. C. 146.

IV. Thrace.

87. The Thracian kingdom of Lysimachus has no history that need detain us. Unlike Egypt or Syria under Macedonian rule, it contributed nothing to literature, science, or general civilization. The several tribes were powerful by reason of their numbers, their hardy contempt of danger and exposure, and their untamable love of freedom; but their strength was too often wasted in fighting against each other, and thus they were reduced either to subjects or humble allies of the more civilized nations to the southward. At the same time, their position on the Danube rendered them the most exposed of all the ancient kingdoms, to the incursions of the northern barbarians; and the history of Thrace under the Romans is only a record of wars and devastations.

V. Kingdom of Pergamus.

88. Beside the four great monarchies already described, a number of smaller kingdoms arose from the ruins of Alexander's empire. A few of these will be briefly mentioned. Pergamus, on the Ca′icus in Mysia, possessed a strong fortress, which was used by Lysimachus as a place of safe keeping for his treasures, under the charge of Philetæ′rus, of Tium, an officer in whom he reposed the greatest confidence. This person, provoked by ill-treatment from the Thracian queen, made himself independent, and by means of the ample treasures of Lysimachus, maintained his principality undisturbed for twenty years, B. C. 283–263. (See §§ 30, 31.)

His nephew, Eumenes, who succeeded him, increased his territories by a victory over Antiochus I., near Sardis. After reigning twenty-two years (B. C., 263–241), he was succeeded by his cousin, Attalus I., who gained a great victory over the Gauls, and, first of his family, took the title of king. Ten years later, he defeated Antiochus Hierax (see § 33), and included in his own dominions all the countries west of the Halys and north of the Taurus. In wars with the kings of Syria, he lost these conquests, and was limited for seven years to his own principality of Pergamus; but by the aid of Gallic mercenaries and his own good management, he won back most of the territories. He earned the favor of Rome by joining that Republic against Philip V. of Macedon. The country was ravaged by Philip in the interval of his Roman wars (see § 80); but the great victory off Chios compensated Attalus for his losses, and the treasures he amassed made his name proverbial for wealth. His exertions in behalf of his allies, during the second war of Rome and Macedon, ended his life at an advanced age, B. C. 197.

89. Eumenes II., his eldest son and successor, aided the Roman operations against the kings of Syria and Macedonia, with so much energy and talent, that he was rewarded with an increase of territory on both sides of the Hellespont, and his kingdom was for a time one of the greatest in Asia. He continued his father's liberal policy in the encouragement of art and literature, founded the great Library of Pergamus, which was second only to that of Alexandria, and beautified his capital with many magnificent buildings. At his death his crown was assumed by his brother, Attalus II. (Philadelphus), as the son of Eumenes was still a child. More than half the twenty-one years of Philadelphus's reign were occupied by wars, especially against Pru′sias II., king of Bithynia. By aiding the revolt of Nicomedes, who gained that kingdom instead of his father, Attalus secured some years of peace, which he employed in building cities and increasing his library. Chief of the cities were Eumeni′a, in Phrygia; Philadelphia, in Lydia; and Attali′a, in Pamphylia.

90. Philadelphus died B. C. 138, leaving the kingdom to his nephew, Attalus III. (Philometor), the son of Eumenes II. This king crowded into the short period of five years more crimes and atrocities than can be found in all the other reigns of his dynasty put together. He murdered all the old friends of his father and uncle, with their families; all who still held any office of trust in the kingdom; and, finally, his own nearest relatives, including his mother, for whom he had professed the warmest affection by the surname he adopted. At last he retired from this atrocious career of misgovernment, to the more innocent pursuits of painting, sculpture, and gardening. He died of a fever, leaving his kingdom a legacy to the Roman people. Aristoni′cus, a half-brother of Attalus III., successfully resisted the Roman claims for three years, even defeating and capturing Licin′ius Crassus, who was sent to take possession; but he was in turn made prisoner, and Pergamus was added to the territories of Rome, B. C. 130.

VI. Bithynia.

91. This tributary province of Persia regained its independence upon the overthrow of that empire, and resisted all the efforts of Alexander's generals to reduce it. Among its kings were Nicomedes I., who founded Nicomedia on the Propontis; Zeilas, who gained his crown by the aid of the Gauls; and Prusias, his son, who extended his kingdom by constant wars, and would have raised it to great importance but for the offense he gave the Romans, by making war against Pergamus and by sheltering Hannibal. He was forced to surrender to Eumenes some important territories.

Prusias II. suffered still greater disasters, owing to his own contemptible wickedness. He sent his son Nicomedes to Rome, with secret orders for his assassination. But the plot failed; and Nicomedes II., whose popularity had excited his father's jealousy, now returned with the support of the

Romans and the Pergamene king, and gained possession of the throne. He reigned fifty-eight years with the title Epiphanes (Illustrious). His son, Nicomedes III., in alliance with the Romans, made war seven years with Mithridates, king of Pontus, their most able and resolute opponent. He was twice expelled from his dominions; but after the close of the first Mithridatic War, he reigned peacefully ten years, and, having no children, left his kingdom to the Romans, B. C. 74.

VII. Pontus.

92. Cappadocia under the Persians had been a satrapy, governed by the descendants of that Ota′nes who conspired with Darius I. against the false Smerdis. (See Book II.) In 363 B. C., a son of the satrap Mithridates revolted, and made himself king of that portion of Cappadocia which lay next the sea, and was thence called Pontus by the Greeks. This kingdom was for a short time subject to the Macedonian power; but Mithridates I., in 318 B. C., became again independent. The annals of the next two reigns are of no great importance. Mithridates III. (B. C. 245–190) enlarged and strengthened his dominion by alliances with the Asiatic monarchs, as well as by wars. His son Phar′naces conquered Sinope from the Greeks, and made it his capital. The next king, Mithridates IV. (B. C. 160–120), aided Rome against Carthage and Pergamus, and was rewarded by the addition of the Greater Phrygia to his dominions.

93. Mithridates V., the Great, came to the throne at the age of eleven years, his father having been murdered by some officers of the court. The young prince, distrusting his guardians, began in his earliest years to accustom himself to antidotes against poison, and to spend much of his time in hunting, which enabled him to take refuge in the most rough and inaccessible portions of his kingdom. He had, however, received a Greek education at Sinope; and when, at the age of twenty, he assumed the government, he possessed not only a soul and body inured to every sort of peril and hardship, but a mind furnished with all the knowledge needful to a king. He spoke twenty-five languages, and could transact business with every tribe of his dominions, in its own peculiar dialect.

The Romans had already seized his province of Phrygia, and he clearly saw the conflict which must soon take place with the all-absorbing Republic. He determined, therefore, to extend his kingdom to the eastward and northward, thus increasing its power and wealth, so as to make it more nearly a match for its great western antagonist. In seven years he added to his dominions half the shores of the Black Sea, including the Cimme′rian peninsula — now the Crimea — and extending westward to the Dniester. He made alliances with the wild and powerful tribes upon the Danube, and with the kings of Armenia, Cappadocia, and Bithynia. From the last two countries he afterward drove out their hereditary kings, placing his own son on the throne of Cappadocia, and Socrates, a younger brother of Nicomedes III., on that of Bithynia.

94. The Roman Senate now interfered, and with their favor Nicomedes invaded Pontus. Mithridates marched into Cappadocia and drove out its newly reinstated king; then into Bithynia, where he routed the army of Nicomedes and defeated the Romans. He speedily made himself master of all Asia Minor, except a few towns in the extreme south and west; and from his headquarters at Pergamus, gave orders for a general massacre of all Romans and Italians in Asia. Eighty thousand persons fell in consequence of this atrocious act, but from that moment the tide turned against Mithridates. Two large armies which he sent into Greece, were defeated by Sulla at Chæronea. A great battle in Bithynia was lost by the Pontic generals. Pontus itself was invaded, and its king became a fugitive.

Peace was at length made, on terms most humiliating to Mithridates. He surrendered all his conquests, and a fleet of seventy vessels; agreed to pay 2,000 talents; and recognized the kings of Cappadocia and Bithynia, whom he had formerly expelled. The reverses of Mithridates naturally led the subject nations on the Euxine to throw off his yoke. He was preparing to march against them, when a second Roman war was kindled by a sudden and unprovoked aggression of Murena, the general of the Republic in the East. The Romans were defeated on the Halys, and peace was restored, B. C. 82.

95. In the seven years' breathing-space which followed, Mithridates subdued all his revolted subjects, and recruited his forces with the utmost energy. His army, drawn largely from the barbarous nations on the Danube and Euxine, was drilled and equipped according to the Roman system, and his navy was increased to four hundred vessels. Both the Pontic king and the Romans would willingly have remained some years longer at peace, but, in 74 B. C., the legacy of Bithynia to the latter power, by Nicomedes III., brought them into unavoidable collision. Mithridates first seized the country, and gained a double victory over Cotta, by sea and land. But he failed in the sieges of Chalcedon and Cyzicus, and in the second year he was repeatedly worsted by Lucul'lus. His fleet was first defeated off Tenedos, and then wrecked by a storm. In the third year Mithridates was driven out of his own dominions, and those of his son-in-law, Tigranes. For three years the war was carried on in Armenia, where the two kings were twice defeated by Lucullus.

In 68 B. C., Mithridates returned to his kingdom, and defeated the Romans twice within a few months. But in 66 B. C., Pompey assumed the command, and Mithridates, after the loss of nearly his whole army, abandoned Pontus, and retired into the barbarous regions north of the Euxine, where the Romans did not care to pursue him. With a spirit untamed either by years or misfortunes, he plotted the bold design of gathering to his standard the wild tribes along the Danube, and marching upon Italy from the north. But his officers did not share his enthusiasm. A conspiracy against him was headed by his own son; and the old king, deserted by all whom he would have trusted, attempted to end his life by poison. His constitution had been for many years so guarded by antidotes, that the drugs had no effect, and he was finally dispatched by one of his Gallic soldiers. Pontus became a Roman province, only a small portion of its territory continuing, a century or more, under princes of the ancient dynasty.

VIII. Cappadocia.

96. The southern part of Cappadocia remained loyal to the Persian kings until their downfall at Arbela. It was conquered by Perdiccas after the death of Alexander, but within six years became independent, and continued under native kings until it was absorbed into the Roman dominions, A. D. 17. The history of these monarchs is of little importance, except so far as it is included in that of the neighboring nations. The fifth king, Ariara′thes IV., made, in his later years, a close and friendly alliance with the Romans, which continued unbroken under his successors.

Coin of Ariarathes V., twice the size of original.

Ariarathes V. (B. C. 131–96) presents the sole example of a "blameless prince" in the three centuries following Alexander. No act of deceit or cruelty is recorded against him. Cappadocia, under his reign, became a celebrated abode of philosophy, under the patronage and example of the king. With Ariarathes VIII., the royal Persian line became extinct, and the Cappadocians chose a new sovereign in Ariobarza′nes I. (B. C. 93–64). This king was three times driven out of his dominions by the sovereigns of Armenia and Pontus, and three times reinstated by the Romans. The last king, Archelaus (B. C. 36–A. D. 17), was summoned by Tibe′rius to Rome, where he died, and his kingdom became a Roman province.

IX. Armenia.

97. Armenia was included in the kingdom of the Seleucidæ, from the battle of Ipsus to that of Magnesia, B. C. 190. Two generals of Antiochus

III. then revolted against him, and set up the kingdoms of Armenia Major on the east, and Armenia Minor on the west of the Euphrates. The greatest king of Armenia Major was Tigranes I. (B. C. 96–55), who not only gained important victories from the Parthian monarch, but conquered all Syria, and held it fourteen years. He incurred the vengeance of Rome in various ways, but chiefly by sustaining his father-in-law, Mithridates, in his wars against the Republic. He suffered several calamitous defeats, with the loss of his capital, Tigran′ocer′ta.

In 67 B. C., the disaffection of the Roman troops gave the two kings the opportunity to recover much of what they had lost. The appearance of the great Pompey upon the scene again turned the tide. The young Tigranes rebelled against his father, with the aid of Parthia and Rome. The king surrendered all his conquests, retaining only his hereditary kingdom of the Greater Armenia. His son, Artavas′des I. (B. C. 55–34), aided the expedition of Crassus against the Parthians; but having afterward offended Antony, he was taken prisoner and put to death by order of Cleopatra. Artaxias, his son, ordered a massacre of all the Romans in Armenia. In 19 B. C., he was himself murdered by his own relations. The remaining kings were sovereigns only in name, being set up or displaced alternately by the Romans and Parthians, until Armenia was absorbed by the former, A. D. 114. Armenia Minor was usually a dependency of some neighboring kingdom, from the time of Mithridates to that of Vespa′sian (A. D. 69–79), when it, too, became a Roman province.

X. Bactria.

98. Bactria was a part of the Syrian empire from 305 to 255 B. C. Diodotus, the satrap, then made himself independent, and established a new Greek kingdom, the most easterly of all the scattered fragments of Alexander's conquests. Euthydemus, the third king, was a native of Magnesia, and a usurper (B. C. 222–200). His son Demetrius made many victorious campaigns, extending over Afghanistan and into India (B. C. 200–180). He lost a part of his native dominions to a rebel, Eucrat′ides, who reigned north of the Pa′ropam′isus range during the life of Demetrius, and after his death, over the whole country. He, too, carried on Indian wars with great energy and success. Under his son, Heli′ocles (B. C. 160–150), the Bactrian kingdom rapidly declined, being invaded by the Parthian kings on the west, and the Tartar tribes from the north.

XI. Parthian Empire of the Arsacidæ.

99. The Parthians established their independence about B. C. 250, under the lead of the Scythian Arsaces. The people were of the same race with the modern Turks—treacherous in war, indolent and unaspiring in peace, rude in arts and barbarous in manners. Their warlike hardihood, however, gave the Romans a more troublesome resistance than they encountered in any other portion of Alexander's former empire; and the dominion of the Arsacidæ lasted nearly 500 years, until it was overthrown by the new Persian kingdom, A. D. 226. The greatness of the Parthian empire dates from Mithridates, who is also called Arsaces VI., B. C. 174–136. The neighboring kingdom of Bactria, with its Greek monarchs and its higher civilization, had hitherto maintained the ascendency; but while these kings were absorbed in their Indian conquests, Mithridates seized upon several of their provinces, and eventually absorbed their whole dominion.

Coin of Arsaces III., twice the size of original.

The Parthian empire, at its greatest extent, comprised all the countries between the Euphrates and the Indus; from the Araxes and the Caspian on the north, to the Persian Gulf and Indian Ocean on the south. Its numerous parts were not consolidated into one government, as were the satrapies of Persia or the provinces of Rome; but each nation, with its own laws and usages, retained its native king, who was tributary to the lord-paramount in the Arsacid family. Hence the Parthian coins, like the Assyrian monuments, commonly bear the title "King of Kings." The wars of Mithridates made the Euphrates the boundary-line between the Parthian and Roman empires. The wealth and power of the Oriental monarchy provoked at once the avarice and the jealousy of the western Republic, and a collision could not long be delayed. The details of the Parthian wars of Rome will be found in Book V.

RECAPITULATION.

Bravery and barbarism of the Thracians. Rise of Pergamus, B. C. 283. Reigns of Philotærus, Eumenes, Attalus I. Success and enlightened policy of Eumenes II. Wars of Attalus Philadelphus. His new cities. Crimes of Attalus III. Bequest of his kingdom to Rome. Short reign of Aristonicus. Bithynia ruled by Nicomedes I., Zeilas, Prusias I. and II., Nicomedes II. and III., B. C. 278–74. Rise of the kingdom of Pontus, B. C. 363. Independent of Macedon, B. C. 318; enlarged by Mithridates III. and Pharnaces, B. C. 245–160. Education of Mithridates V., his conquests and alliances; first collision with the Romans, B. C. 88; massacre of 80,000 Italians; disasters and humiliating peace. Second Roman War, B. C. 83, 82. Seven years' drill of Pontic forces in Roman tactics. Third Roman War, B. C. 74–65; Mithridates driven into Armenia, B. C. 71; recovered his kingdom, B. C. 68;

defeated by Pompey, B. C. 66; took refuge in the northern wilds, and ended his life by violence, B. C. 63. Pontus became a Roman province. Cappadocia in alliance with Rome, B. C. 188. Just and peaceful reign of Ariarathes V. End of the dynasty in Ariarathes VIII. Exiles and returns of Ariobarzanes I. The country absorbed into the Roman dominion, A. D. 17. Armenia a part of the Syrian empire, B. C. 301-190. "Greater" and "Lesser" kingdoms then formed on the east and west of the Euphrates. Conquest of Syria by Tigranes I., B. C. 83. His wars with Rome, B. C. 69-66. Losses. Fate of Artavasdes. Massacre of the Romans by Artaxias. Alternate dependence upon Rome and Parthia, B. C. 19-A. D. 114. Bactria dependent upon Syria, B. C. 305-255. Diodotus reigned, B. C. 255-237. The third king a Lydian, B. C. 222-200. Indian campaigns of Demetrius and Eucratidas, B. C. 200-160. Decline and fall of the kingdom under attacks of surrounding barbarians, B. C. 160-80. Parthian empire powerful, but uncivilized. Absorption of Bactrian provinces, B. C. 174-136. A group of kingdoms, rather than a nation, side by side with Rome.

XII. JUDÆA.

100. Judæa, with the rest of Syria, had been assigned to Laom′edon upon the partition of Alexander's conquests; but it was soon annexed by Ptolemy Soter, and continued 117 years a part of the Egyptian empire. Its history in this Book will be considered in three periods:

I. From the Fall of the Persian Empire to the Rise of an Independent Jewish Kingdom, B. C. 323-168.

II. The Time of the Maccabees, B. C. 168-37.

III. The Time of the Herods, B. C. 37-A. D. 44.

FIRST PERIOD. Under the first three Ptolemies, the Jews were peaceful and prosperous. The high priest was at the head of the state, and in local matters ruled with little interference from Egypt. Ptolemy Philopator, however, a wicked and foolish prince, attempted to profane the temple, and the Jews, in alarm, sought protection from Antiochus the Great. That monarch, with their aid, gained possession of all the coast between Upper Syria and the Desert of Sinai; and though often disputed, and once recovered by the Egyptians, this district remained a part of the Syrian kingdom.

101. For thirty years the privileges of the Jews were respected by their new sovereigns; but toward the close of his reign, Seleucus IV. resolved to appropriate the sacred treasures of the temple to his own pressing needs, and sent Heliodorus, his treasurer, for this purpose to Jerusalem. According to the Jewish tradition,* three angels appeared for the defense of the holy place. One of them was seated on a terrible horse, which trampled Heliodorus under its feet, while the others scourged him until he fell lifeless to the ground. He was only restored by the prayers of the high priest, and the treasury remained unmolested.

---

* Read, in the Apocrypha, 2 Maccabees iii: 4-40.

Antiochus Epiphanes, the brother and successor of Seleucus, was guilty of still more impious outrages. He put up the high priesthood at auction, and twice awarded it to the highest bidder, on condition of his introducing Greek rites and customs into Jerusalem. One of these mercenary pontiffs stole the sacred vessels of the temple and sold them at Tyre. An insurrection arose at Jerusalem, but it was punished by Antiochus in person, who seized the city, set up an altar to Zeus Olympius, with daily sacrifices of swine's flesh in the sacred inclosure of the temple, and put to death a great number of the people. Two years later, B. C. 168, he ordered a general massacre of the Jews, and by a frightful persecution sought to exterminate the last remnant of the ancient religion. The Asmonæ'an family now arose, and by their brave fidelity made themselves at last sovereigns of Judæa.

102. Second Period. Mattathias, a priest, living between Jerusalem and Joppa, killed with his own hand the king's officer who was sent to enforce the heathen sacrifices, together with the first renegade Jew who consented to offer. He then took refuge in the mountains with his five sons, and was reinforced daily by fugitives from various parts of Judæa. As their numbers increased, this band issued frequently from their fastnesses, cut off detachments of the Syrian army, destroyed heathen altars, and in many places restored the Jewish worship in the synagogues. The aged Mattathias died in the first year of the war, and was succeeded in command of the forces by his third son, Judas, who obtained the name of *Maccabæus* from his many victories.

During the disputes for the Syrian regency, which followed the death of Antiochus Epiphanes (see §§ 40, 41), Judas Maccabæus gained possession of all Jerusalem, except the citadel on Mount Zion, and held it three years. He purified the temple, restored the incense, lights, and sacrifices, and drove out Syrians near Hellenizing Jews from every part of Judæa. The Syrian general, Nicanor, was twice defeated with great loss. In the second battle, near Beth-horon, Nicanor fell, and his whole army was cut to pieces. The Romans made alliance with the Maccabees; but before their aid could arrive, Judas had fallen in battle, B. C. 160. Jerusalem was lost, and for fourteen years Jonathan Maccabæus could only carry on a guerrilla warfare from his fastness in the Desert of Teko'ah. The disputes for the Syrian throne, between Demetrius and Alexander Balas, which were continued under their sons (see §§ 42–46), gave a respite to the Jews, and even made their alliance an object of desire to both parties. Jonathan was thenceforth recognized as prince and high priest, with full possession of the Holy City.

103. His brother Simon succeeded him in both dignities, and under his prosperous administration Judæa recovered, in great measure, from the long-continued ravages of war. The life of Simon was ended by treachery. His son-in-law, Ptolemy, the governor of Jericho, desiring to seize the government for himself, murdered the high priest and two of his sons at a banquet. But the other son, John Hyrcanus, escaped and succeeded his father. At the beginning of his reign, Jerusalem endured a long and painful siege by Antiochus Sidetes, B. C. 135–133. Its walls, which had been restored, were leveled with the ground; and a tribute was again demanded, which lasted, however, no longer than the life of Sidetes. Hyrcanus captured Samaria, and destroyed the temple on Mount Gerizim (see Book II, § 64). He conquered Id′ume′a, rendering Judæa fully equal in power to Syria, which was now reduced from a great empire to a petty and exhausted kingdom.

104. Aristobu′lus, son of Hyrcanus, was the first of the family who assumed the title of king. He reigned but a year, and was succeeded by his brother, Alexander Jannæ′us (B. C. 105–78). This prince was a Sadducee, and the opposite sect of the Pharisees stirred up a mob to attack him, while officiating as high priest in the Feast of Tabernacles. The riot was put down with a slaughter of 6,000 insurgents. Alexander gained victories over the Moabites and the Arabs of Gilead; but in a subsequent war with the latter he suffered a great defeat, and the malcontents at home seized the occasion for a new outbreak. The civil war now raged six years. For a time Alexander was driven to the mountains, but at length he regained the ascendency, and revenged himself upon the rebels with frightful cruelty. He left the crown to his widow, Alexandra, who joined the Pharisees, and was maintained in power by their influence.

105. After her death, her two sons, Hyrcanus and Aristobulus, quarreled seven years for the sovereignty. Pompey the Great, who was then at Damascus, interfered and captured Jerusalem, carried off Aristobulus to Rome, and established the elder brother in the government. He reigned six years in peace, B. C. 63–57. In the latter year Aristobulus escaped, and being joined by many of his partisans, renewed the war. He was besieged and taken in Machæ′rus by the Roman proconsul, who also deposed Hyrcanus, and set up a sort of oligarchy in Jerusalem. Pompey, in taking the city, had left its sacred treasures untouched, but during this period, Crassus, on his way to Parthia, seized and plundered the temple. After ten years (B. C. 57–47), Hyrcanus was restored to the high priesthood, while his friend Antipater, the Idumæan, was appointed procurator, or civil governor, of Judæa.

In B. C. 40, Antigonus, son of Aristobulus, with the aid of a Parthian force, captured Jerusalem and reigned three years, the last of the Asmonæan princes. Antipater had been poisoned; his son Herod repaired to Rome, and received from the Senate the title of King of Judæa. Returning speedily, he conquered Galilee and advanced to the siege of Jerusalem. This was protracted several years, for the Jews were firmly attached to

Antigonus, and resented equally the interference of Rome and the reign of an Edomite. After hard fighting the walls were taken, and the king was executed like a common criminal.

106. THIRD PERIOD, B. C. 37–A. D. 44. Herod was justly surnamed "the Great," for his talents and the grandeur of his enterprises, though his character was stained by the worst faults of a tyrant, cruelty and reckless caprice. At the age of fifteen he had been made governor of Galilee by Julius Cæsar, and had ruled with great energy and success, suppressing the banditti who infested the country, and putting their leaders to death. He began his reign in Judæa by a massacre of all who had been opposed to him, especially those whose wealth would best enable him to reward his Roman benefactors. The Temple, which, being used as a fortress, had been nearly destroyed in the repeated sieges, was rebuilt, by his orders, with a magnificence which rivaled the glories of Solomon. His liberality was equally shown during a famine which visited Judæa and the surrounding countries. He bought immense quantities of corn in Egypt, and fed the entire people at his own expense, beside supplying several provinces with seed for the next harvest.

Herod affected Roman tastes: he built a circus and amphitheater in a suburb of Jerusalem, where games and combats of wild beasts were celebrated in honor of the emperor Augustus. To show his impartiality, he restored the Samaritan temple on Mount Gerizim, while he adorned his new and magnificent city of Cæsare'a with imposing shrines of the Roman gods. This universal tolerance was most unpleasing to the Jews, and their disposition to revolt was only kept down by the vigilance of innumerable spies, and the construction of a chain of fortresses around Jerusalem.

107. The last two members of the Asmonæan family were Mariam'ne and Aristobulus, grandchildren of Hyrcanus II. Herod married the former, and bestowed upon the latter the office of high priest; but the great popularity of the young prince alarmed his jealousy, and he caused him to be secretly assassinated. Though devotedly attached to Mariamne, Herod twice ordered her put to death in case of his own decease, during perilous expeditions for which he was leaving the capital. These atrocious orders coming to the knowledge of the queen, naturally increased the aversion for Herod which had been inspired by the murder of her grandfather and her brother.

Her high spirit scorned concealment; she was brought to trial, and her bitter enemies persuaded Herod to consent to her execution. But the violence of his grief and remorse kept him a long time on the verge of insanity, and a raging fever nearly ended his life. His temper, which had been generous though hasty, now became so ferocious that his best friends were often ordered to death on the slightest suspicion. Three of his sons were executed on charges of conspiracy. From his

TEMPLE AT JERUSALEM, AS REBUILT BY HEROD.

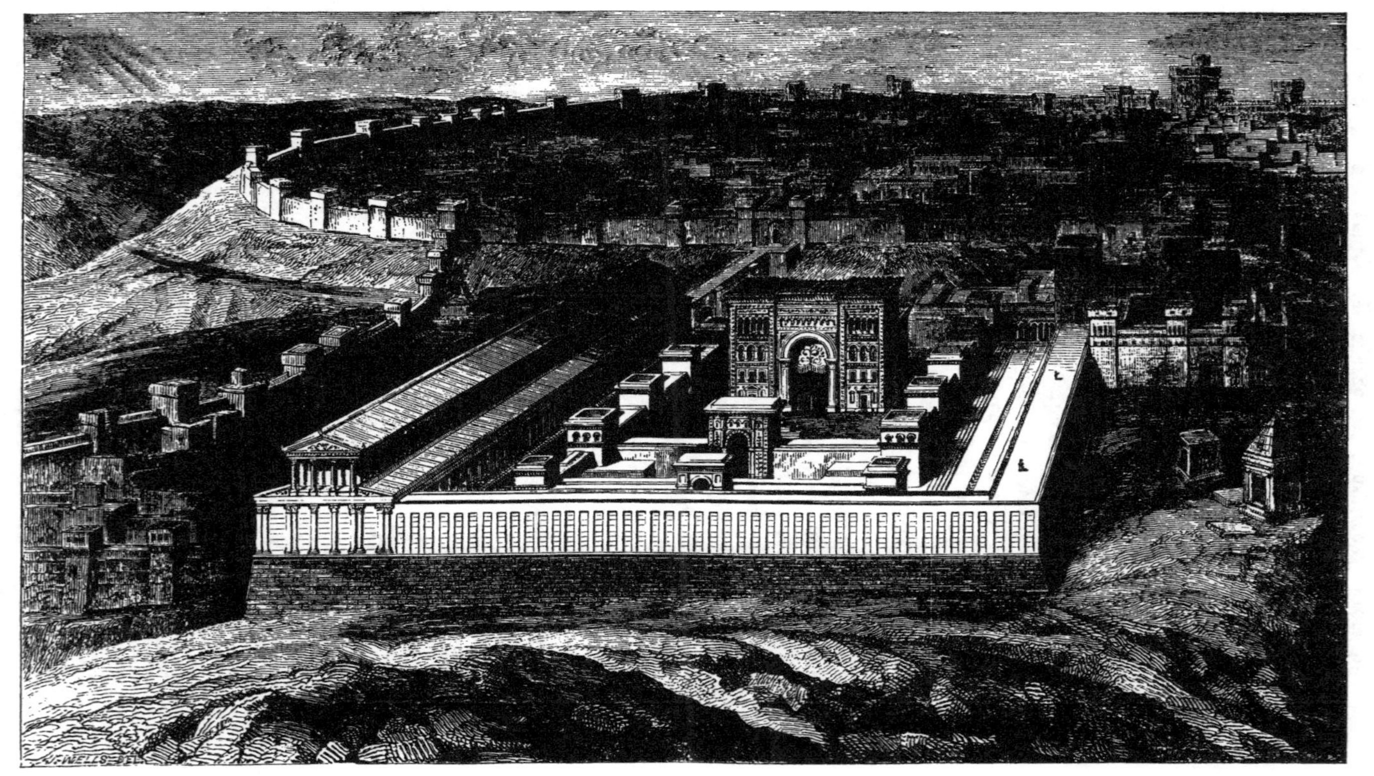

Herod's Porch. *Solomon's Porch.* *Castle of Antonia.*

death-bed he ordered a massacre of the infants in Bethlehem, because wise men from the East had informed him that in that little village the Messiah was born. About the same time, he had set up a golden eagle over the gate of the Temple. A sedition immediately arose, and its leaders were punished with atrocious cruelty, by the command of the dying king. Herod died in the same year with the birth of our Lord, which the common chronology places, by an error, B. C. 4.

108. His dominions, except Abilene in Syria, were divided among his three sons, Archelaus, Antipas, and Philip, the eldest receiving Judæa and Samaria. He reigned so oppressively that he was removed by the Romans, A. D. 8; and until A. D. 36, the province was managed by procurators, or governors, subject to the præfects of Syria. Under the fifth of these, Pontius Pilate, Christ was crucified by Roman authority, through the accusations of the chief officers of the Jews. Herod Antipas was meanwhile ruling in Galilee (B. C. 4–A. D. 39; see Luke xxiii: 6–12), and Philip in Trachoni′tis (B. C. 4–A. D. 37; see Mark vi: 17, 18). When these provinces became vacant, they were bestowed by the Emperor Calig′ula upon his favorite, Herod Agrip′pa I., grandson of Herod the Great and Mariamne. A. D. 41, Samaria and Judæa were also added to his dominions, which for three years covered the entire territory of Herod the Great.

109. Agrippa began to persecute the Christians in the year 44, and the Romans again placed Judæa under the government of procurators. Gessius Florus, the sixth of the new series, was a cruel and crafty tyrant, who plundered his province without pity or shame. He shared the spoils of highway robbers, whom he permitted and even encouraged. Twice he stirred up riots in Jerusalem, sacrificing the lives of thousands of people, only that he might avail himself of the confusion to pillage the Temple.

His atrocities at length drove the Jews to open revolt. A Roman army of 100,000 men, commanded by Titus, the son of the emperor Vespasian, besieged the Holy City five months. The three walls, the fortress of Mount Zion, and the Temple had each to be taken by separate assault; and never was a siege more memorable for the obstinacy of the resistance. The Temple was surrendered Sept. 8, 70. All the people who had not perished by the hardships of the siege, were made slaves and divided among the victors as prizes. Large colonies were transported into the heart of Germany or to Italy, where the golden vessels of the Temple adorned the triumphal procession of Titus at Rome. No ancient city of any fame was ever so completely ruined as Jerusalem. Mount Zion was plowed as a field and sown with salt, and the buildings of the Temple were leveled to the ground.

RECAPITULATION.

Judæa subject to Egypt, B. C. 320-203; to Syria, B. C. 203-168. Persecution by Antiochus Epiphanes, and revolt of Mattathias, B. C. 168. Victories of Judas Maccabæus, B. C. 166-160. Jonathan prince and high priest, B. C. 160-143. Prosperous reign of Simon, B. C. 143–135. Siege and capture of Jerusalem by Antiochus Sidetes, B. C. 135–133. Conquests of John Hyrcanus, B. C. 135–106. Aristobulus I. takes the royal title. Civil wars of Pharisees and Sadducees, under Alexander Jannæus, B. C. 105–78. Reign of Alexandra, B. C. 78–69. Hyrcanus II., B. C. 69, 68. Aristobulus II., B. C. 68–63. Jerusalem taken by Pompey, who awards the sovereignty to Hyrcanus. After six years, Hyrcanus deposed and an oligarchy set up, B. C. 57–47. Jerusalem plundered by Crassus, B. C. 54. Antipater, the Idumæan, governor, B. C. 47–40, while Hyrcanus is again high priest. Antigonus prince and priest, B. C. 40–37. Herod, son of Antipater, invested at Rome with the royalty of Judæa, conquers Galilee, and by a long siege takes Jerusalem, B. C. 37. His greatness and tyranny. His public works. Execution of Queen Mariamne, B. C. 29. "Murder of the Innocents," and death of Herod, B. C. 4. Division of his kingdom into tetrarchies. Archelaus succeeded in his government by Roman governors, A. D. 8–36. The Crucifixion, A. D. 29 or 30. Four provinces united under Herod Agrippa, A. D. 41. Procurators restored, A. D. 44. Gessius Florus, A. D. 65, 66. Siege and capture of Jerusalem by Titus, A. D. 70.

QUESTIONS FOR REVIEW.

Book IV.

1. Describe the rise of Macedonia. . . . . §§ 1, 2.
2. The successive steps of the ascendency of Philip. . . . 2–5.
3. The youth, education, and character of Alexander. . . . 6, 7.
4. His conquests and Asiatic policy. . . . . 8–12, 14–17.
5. His projects and death. . . . . 18.
6. The war of the regents. . . . . 19.
7. What was done by Antipater? . . . . 19, 20, 66, 67.
8. By Antigonus and his son? . . . . 20, 22–25, 29, 68.
9. What became of the near relatives of Alexander? . . . . . . 21–23.
10. What were the results of the battle of Ipsus? . . . . 25.
11. Effects upon Europe and Asia of Alexander's conquests? . . . . 26, 27.
12. Describe the extent and organization of the kingdom of Seleucus. . . 28–30.
13. Name the Seleucidæ, and relate one incident of each. . . . . . 28–48.
14. Describe in detail the reign of Antiochus the Great. . . . . 34–37, 100.
15. The last but one of the kings of Syria. . . . . . . 48, 97.
16. The incursions of the Gauls. . . . . 31, 70, 71.
17. The condition of Egypt under the Ptolemies. . . . 49, 51, 54.
18. Alexandria and its schools. . . . . 52, 53.
19. The conquests of the first three Ptolemies. . . . . 50, 54, 56.
20. The character of their successors. . . . . . 56, 57, 60, 62–65.
21. What was the result to Athens of the Lamian War? . . . . . . 66.
22. What became of the sons of Cassander? . . . . 67.
23. How many kings of Thrace and Macedonia B. C. 281? . . . . . 69, 70.
24. Describe the two reigns of Antigonus Gonatas. . . . . 72, 74.
25. The character of Pyrrhus. . . . . 72, 73.
26. Tell the history of the Achæan League. . . . . 75–79, 82, 86.
27. What occurred in Sparta during the Macedonian regency of Antigonus Doson? . . . . 77.

28. Describe the character and reign of Philip V. . . . . . . §§ 78–81, 83.
29. The successive interventions of the Romans in affairs of Macedonia and Greece. . . . . 76, 79, 81–83, 85, 86.
30. The last of the Antigonidæ. . . . . 84.
31. How many kings of other families or nations reigned in Macedonia during the Third Period?
32. Describe the Thracians. . . . . 87.
33. The origin and history of Pergamus. . . . . 88–90.
34. Of Bithynia. . . . . 91.
35. The early history of Pontus. . . . . 92.
36. Tell the story of Mithridates V. . . . . 93–95.
37. Describe Cappadocia. . . . . 96.
38. Tell in brief the history of Armenia, B. C. 301–A. D. 114. . . . . . 97.
39. Describe the most easterly of the Greek kingdoms in Asia. . . . 98.
40. The character and history of the Parthians. . . . . . . 99.
41. How was Judæa governed, B. C. 323–168? . . . . 100, 101.
42. Describe its condition under the Syrian kings. . . . . 101.
43. The rise and reign of the Maccabees. . . . . 102–105.
44. The character of Herod, and the great events of his reign. . 106, 107.
45. How were his dominions distributed B. C. 4–A. D. 44? . . . . . . 108.
46. Describe the last twenty-six years of Jewish history. . . . . . . 109.
47. How many battles have been described at Bethhoron?
48. How many at Thermopylæ?
49. How many at Mantinea?
50. How many at Salamis in Cyprus?
51. How many at Chæronea?

BOOK V.

History of Rome, from the Earliest Times to the Fall of the Western Empire, A. D. 476.

GEOGRAPHICAL SKETCH OF ITALY.

1. Italy, bounded by the Alps, and the Adriatic, Ionian, and Tyrrhe′nian seas, is the smallest of the three peninsulas of southern Europe. It is inferior to Greece in the number of its harbors and littoral islands, but excels it in the richness and extent of its plains and fertile mountain-sides, being thus better fitted for agriculture and the rearing of cattle than for maritime interests. Still, from its long and narrow shape, Italy has an extended coast-line; the slopes of the Apennines abounded, in ancient times, with forests of oak suitable for ship-timber; and the people, especially of Etru′ria, were early attracted to the sea.

2. The Alps, which separate Italy from the rest of Europe, have had an important effect upon her history. At present they are traversed securely only by five or six roads, which are among the wonders of modern engineering. In early times they formed a usually effectual barrier against the barbarous nations on the north and west. The Apennines leave the Alpine range near the present boundary between Italy and France, and extend in a south-easterly and southerly direction to the end of the peninsula, throwing off lateral ridges on both sides to the sea, and forming that great variety of surface and climate which is the peculiar charm of the country. A multitude of rivers contribute vastly to the fertility of the soil, though, from their short and rapid course, they are of little value for navigation. Varro preferred the climate of Italy to that of Greece, as producing in perfection every thing good for the use of man. No barley could be compared with the Campa′nian, no wheat with the Apu′lian, no rye with the Faler′nian, no oil with the Vena′fran.

3. Northern Italy lies between the Swiss Alps and the Upper Apennines, and is almost covered by the great plain of the Po, which is one of the most fertile regions of Europe. It comprised, in the most

ancient times, the three countries of Ligu′ria, Upper Etruria, and Vene′tia. The second of these divisions, together with some portions of the Ligurian and Venetian territories, was conquered, in the sixth century before Christ, by a Celtic population from the north and west, and was thenceforth known as Cisalpine Gaul. The region north of the Apennines does not belong to Roman or even Italian history until about the time of the Christian Era, when it became incorporated in the territories of Rome.

4. The peninsula proper is divided into the two regions of central and southern Italy, by a line drawn from the mouth of the Tifer′nus, on the Adriatic, to that of the Sil′arus, on the western coast. CENTRAL ITALY comprised six countries, of which three, Etruria, La′tium, and Campania, were on the Tyrrhenian Sea, and three others, Um′bria, Pice′num, and the Sabine country, on the Adriatic. *Etruria* was, in the earliest times, the most important division of Italy proper. It was separated from Liguria by the river Macra; from Cisalpine Gaul, by the Apennines; and from Umbria, the Sabine territory, and Latium, by the Tiber.

Latium, lying south of Etruria, was chiefly a low plain; but its surface was varied by spurs of the Apennines on the north, and by the Vol′scian and Alban ranges of volcanic origin in the center and south. It included the Roman Campagna, now a solitary and almost treeless expanse, considered uninhabitable from the noxious exhalations of the soil, but during and before the flourishing period of Rome, the site of many populous cities. Several foreign tribes occupied portions of the Latin territory, among whom the Volsci, on the mountains which bear their name, and the Æqui, north of Prænes′te, were best worthy of mention. In the view of history, a cluster of low hills — seven east and three west of the Tiber — which constitute in later ages the site of Rome, is not only the most important part of Latium, but that which gives its significance to all the rest.

5. *Campania* was a fertile and delightful region, extending from the Liris to the Silarus, and from the Apennines to the sea. Greek and Roman writers never wearied of celebrating the excellence of its harbors, the beauty of its landscape, the exuberant richness of its soil, and the enchanting softness of its air. The coast is varied by the isolated cone of Vesu′vius and a range of volcanic hills, including the now extinct crater of Solfata′ra. *Umbria* was a mountainous country east of Etruria. Before the coming of the Gauls, it extended northward to the Ru′bicon and eastward to the Adriatic; but its coast was wholly conquered by that people, who drove the Umbrians beyond the mountains.

Picenum consisted of a flat, fertile plain along the Adriatic, and a hilly region, consisting of twisted spurs of the Apennines, in the interior. Poets praised the apples of Picenum, and its olives were among the choicest in Italy. The *Sabine* territory, at its greatest extension, was 200 miles in length, and reached nearly from sea to sea. It was inhabited by many tribes, probably of common origin. Beside the Sabines proper, were the Sam′nites, the Frenta′ni, and the Marsi, Mar′ruci′ni, Pelig′ni, and Ves-ti′ni, who formed the League of the Four Cantons. The Sabine country, though rough, was fertile, and its wine and oil chiefly supplied the common people of Rome.

6. SOUTHERN ITALY included four countries: Luca′nia and Brut′tium on the west, Apulia and Cala′bria on the east. *Lucania* is a picturesque and fertile country, watered by many rivers. *Bruttium* is of similar character, and was especially valued in old times for its pine forests, which, from their timber and pitch, yielded an important revenue to the Roman government. Both countries attracted multitudes of Greek colonists, whose cities early rose to a high degree of wealth and civilization. (See Book III, §§ 87, 90.) *Apulia,* unlike any other division of central or southern Italy, consists chiefly of a rich, unbroken plain, from twenty to forty miles in width, gently sloping from the mountains to the sea. In ancient times it maintained great numbers of horses and sheep, the latter of which were famed for the fineness of their wool. When the plain became parched by summer heats, the flocks were driven to the neighboring mountains of Samnium; while, in winter, the Samnite flocks forsook their bleak and snowy heights to find pasturage in the rich meadows of Apulia. The northern portion of Apulia is mountainous, being traversed by two strong spurs of the Apennines, one of which projects into the sea and forms the rocky headland of Mount Garga′nus.

*Calabria,** called by the Greeks Iapyg′ia or Messa′pia, occupied the long peninsula which is commonly called the heel of Italy. Its soft limestone soil quickly absorbs moisture, rendering the country arid, and the heats of summer intense. The products of the soil were, however, in ancient times, abundant and of great value. Its oil, wine, and honey were widely celebrated, the wool afforded by its flocks was of the finest quality, and the horses which recruited the Tarentine cavalry were among the most excellent in the world.

7. Italy possessed three islands of great importance: Sicily, noted for its excellent harbors and inexhaustible soil; Sardin′ia, for its silver mines and harvests of grain; and Cor′sica, for its dense forests of pine and fir. The position as well as the valuable productions of these islands, early tempted the enterprise of both Greeks and Carthaginians; and rivalry in their possession first drew these nations into hostility with each other, and with the ultimately victorious power of Rome.

---

* It should be noticed that the name Calabria is now applied to the other peninsula of southern Italy, that which included the ancient Bruttium. The name was changed about the eleventh century of the Christian Era.

HISTORY OF ROME.

8. Our history in this Book falls naturally into three divisions:

I. THE ROMAN KINGDOM, ... B. C. 753–510.
II. THE ROMAN REPUBLIC, ... " 510–30.
III. THE ROMAN EMPIRE, ... " 30–A. D. 476.

The records of the First Period, so far as they relate to persons, are largely mixed with fable, and it is impossible to separate the fanciful from the real. The student is recommended to read the stories of the kings, in their earliest and most attractive form, in Dr. Arnold's History of Rome. Under their beautiful mythical guise, these legends present, doubtless, a considerable amount of truth. Our limits only admit a statement of the popular ancient belief concerning the rise of Rome, among the other and older nations which inhabited Italy.

9. Central and southern Italy were occupied, from the earliest known times, by three races, the Etrus′cans, Italians, and Iapygians. The latter were nearly related to the Greeks, as has been proved by their language and the identity of their objects of worship. They therefore mingled readily with the Hellenic settlers (see § 6), and Greek civilization quickly took root and flourished throughout southern Italy. The Italians proper—so called because, when united, they became the ruling race in Italy—arrived later in the peninsula than the Iapygians. They came from the north, and crowded into closer quarters the half-Hellenic inhabitants of the south. They consisted of four principal races: the Umbrians, Sabines, Oscans, and Latins. Of these the first three were closely connected, while the Latins were distinct. The latter formed a confederacy of thirty cities, or cantons, and met every year on the Alban Mount to offer a united sacrifice to Jupiter Latia′ris, the protecting deity of the Latin race. During this festival wars were suspended, as in Elis during the Olympic Games.

10. The Etruscans, or Tuscans, were wholly different in language, appearance, and character from the other nations of Italy. Their origin is wrapped in mystery. Some suppose them to have been Turanian, and thus allied to the Lapps, Finns, and Estho′nians of northern Europe, and the Basques of Spain; others, and the greater number, believe the mass of the people to have been Pelasgi—that race which overspread Greece and Italy at a remoter period than history can reach—but to have been absorbed and enslaved by a more powerful people from the north, who called themselves *Ras′ena*, while they were named by others Etruscans. History first finds these invaders in Rhæ′tia, the country about the head-waters of the Ad′ige, the Danube, and the Rhine; then traces them to the plain of the Po, where, at a very early period, they formed a league of twelve cities; and thence south of the Apennines into Tus′cany, which, reduced in limits, still bears their name.

Here they formed a similar but quite distinct confederacy of the same number of cities. For a time their dominion extended across the peninsula, and their fleets commanded both the "Upper" and the "Lower Sea," the latter of which derived from them its ancient name, Tyrrhenian. They conquered Campania, and built there a third cluster of twelve cities, of which Cap′ua was the chief; but they lost this portion of their territory in wars with the Samnites. Many relics of Etruscan art exist, in the massive walls of their cities, their castings in bronze, figures in terra-cotta, and golden chains, bracelets, and other ornaments, which prove them to have been a luxurious and wealthy people. Their religion was of a gloomy and superstitious character. They sought to know the will of their gods by auguries drawn from thunder and lightning, from the flight of birds, or from the entrails of slain beasts; and to avert their wrath by sacrifices prescribed and regulated by an elaborate ritual. To learn these rites formed a large part of the education of a young Tuscan noble.

11. The Romans, who were destined to be for nearly twelve centuries the dominant race of Italy and the world, belonged to the Latin branch of the Italian family. A Greek tradition celebrated by Virgil, and believed by most Romans in the days of the empire, traced their origin to a company of Trojan emigrants, led to the shores of Italy by Æne′as, son of Priam, after the fall of Troy. (See Book III, § 14.) But the Latin coast was at that time densely populated, and the new comers, if any such there were, must soon have been absorbed and lost among the older inhabitants.

12. The common legends assigned the building of Rome to Rom′ulus, grandson of Nu′mitor, an Alban prince. Numitor had been deprived of his crown by his brother Amu′lius, who also killed the son of the deposed king, and compelled his daughter Silvia to become a vestal. Beloved of Mars, she became, however, the mother of Romulus and Remus, whereupon her uncle caused her to be thrown, with her twin sons, into the Anio, a tributary of the Tiber. The rivers had overflowed their banks; when they subsided, the cradle containing the infant princes was overturned at the foot of the Palatine Mount. Nourished by a wolf, and fed by a woodpecker sacred to Mars, they grew to be hardy young shepherds, and distinguished themselves in combats with wild beasts and robbers.

At the age of twenty they became aware of their royal birth, and having conquered Amulius, restored their grandfather to his throne. But they still loved the home of their youth, and resolved to build a new city on the banks of the Tiber. The brothers, differing in their choice of a site, consulted the auspices. After watching all night, Remus, at dawn, saw six vultures; but Romulus, at sunrise, saw twelve. The majority of the shepherds voted the decision to Romulus, and it was ever after believed that the twelve vultures denoted twelve centuries, during which the dominion of the city should endure.

13. His shepherd comrades being too few to satisfy his ambition, Romulus offered asylum on the Cap′itoline to homicides and runaway slaves, thus enrolling among his subjects the refuse of the neighboring tribes. To obtain wives for these adventurers, he invited the Latins and Sabines to witness games in honor of Neptune; and when not only men, but women and children were assembled, the runners and wrestlers rushed into the crowd and carried away whom they would. War followed, in which the Latins were thrice defeated. The Sabine king, Titus Tatius, marched with a powerful army upon Rome, obtained possession of the Capitoline fortress through the treachery of the maiden Tarpe′ia, the daughter of its commander, and nearly defeated the forces of Romulus in a long and obstinate battle.

The Sabine women, however, now reconciled to their fate, came between their fathers and husbands, beseeching them with tears to be reconciled, since, whoever should be conquered, the grief and loss must be their own. A lasting peace was made, and the two kings agreed to reign jointly over the united nations, Romulus holding his court on the Palatine, and Titus Tatius on the Capitoline and Quirinal hills. After the death of Tatius, Romulus ruled alone. At the end of a prosperous reign of thirty-seven years, he was reviewing his troops one day in the Field of Mars, when the sun became suddenly darkened, a tempest agitated earth and air, and Romulus disappeared. The people mourned him as dead, but they were comforted by his appearing in a glorified form to one of their number, assuring him that the Romans should become lords of the world, and that he himself, under the name of Quiri′nus, would be their guardian.

14. After a year's interregnum, Numa, a Sabine of wise and peaceful character, was chosen king. He was revered in after ages as the religious founder of Rome, no less than Romulus as the author of its civil and military institutions. The wisdom and piety of his laws were attributed to the nymph Ege′ria, who met him by a fountain in a grove, and dictated to him the principles of good government. The few records of this king and his predecessor belong rather to mythology than to history.

15. Tullus Hostil′ius, the third king of Rome, is the first of whose deeds we have any trustworthy account. He conquered Alba Longa, and transferred its citizens to the Cæ′lian Hill in Rome. This new city then became the protectress of the Latin League, with the right of presiding at the annual festival, though it was never, like Alba, a member of the League, but a distinct power in alliance with it. The federal army was commanded alternately by a Roman and a Latin general; and the lands acquired in the wars of the League were equally divided between the two contracting parties, thus giving to Rome, it is evident, a far greater share than to any other city.

16. The citizens of consolidated Rome now constituted three tribes: the *Ram'nes*, or original Romans, on the Palatine; the *Tit'ies*, or Sabines, on the Capitoline and Quirinal; and the *Lu'ceres*, on the Cælian. Each tribe consisted of ten *cu'riæ*, or wards, and each *curia* of ten *houses*, or clans (*gentes*). The patrician, or noble, houses, which alone enjoyed the rights of citizenship, thus numbered three hundred. The heads of all the houses constituted the Senate, while the *Comit'ia Curia'ta*, or public assembly, included all citizens of full age.

Rome, at this period, contained only two classes beside the Patricians. These were the *clients* and *slaves*. The former were the poorer people who belonged to no *gens*, and therefore, though free, had no civil rights. They were permitted to choose a patron in the person of some noble, who was bound to protect their interests, if need were, in courts of law. The client, on the other hand, followed his patron to war as a vassal; contributed to his ransom, or that of his children, if taken prisoners; and paid part of the costs of any lawsuit in which the patron might be engaged, or of his expenses in discharging honorable offices in the state. The relation on either side descended from father to son. It was esteemed a glory to a noble family to have a numerous clientage, and to increase that which it had inherited from its ancestors. The clients bore the clan-name* of their patron. Slaves were not numerous in the days of the kings. During the Republic, multitudes of captives were brought into the market by foreign wars; and at the close of that period, at least half the inhabitants of Roman territory were bondsmen.

17. Ancus Mar'tius conquered many Latin towns, and transported their citizens to Rome, where he assigned them the Aventine Hill as a residence. Of these new settlers some became clients of the nobility, but the wealthier class scorned this dependent condition, and relied upon the protection of the king. Hence arose a new order in the state, the *Plebs*, or commonalty, which was destined to become, in later times, equally important with the nobility. It included, beside the conquered

---

* A Patrician had at least three names: his own personal appellation, as Ca'ius, Marcus, or Lu'cius; the name of his clan, and the name of his family. Many Romans had a fourth name, derived from some personal peculiarity or memorable deed. Thus Pub'lius Corne'lius Scip'io Africa'nus belonged to the Cornelian *gens*, the Scipio family, and received a surname from his brilliant achievements in Africa. His clients bore the name Cornelius.

people, foreign settlers who came for trade, for refuge, or for employment in the army; clients whose protecting families had become extinct; and sons of patricians who had married wives of inferior rank. Ancus extended the Roman territory to the sea; built the port-town of Os′tia, and established salt-works in its vicinity; fortified the Janiculan Hill, opposite Rome, for a defense against the Etruscans; and constructed the Mamertine, the first Roman prison.

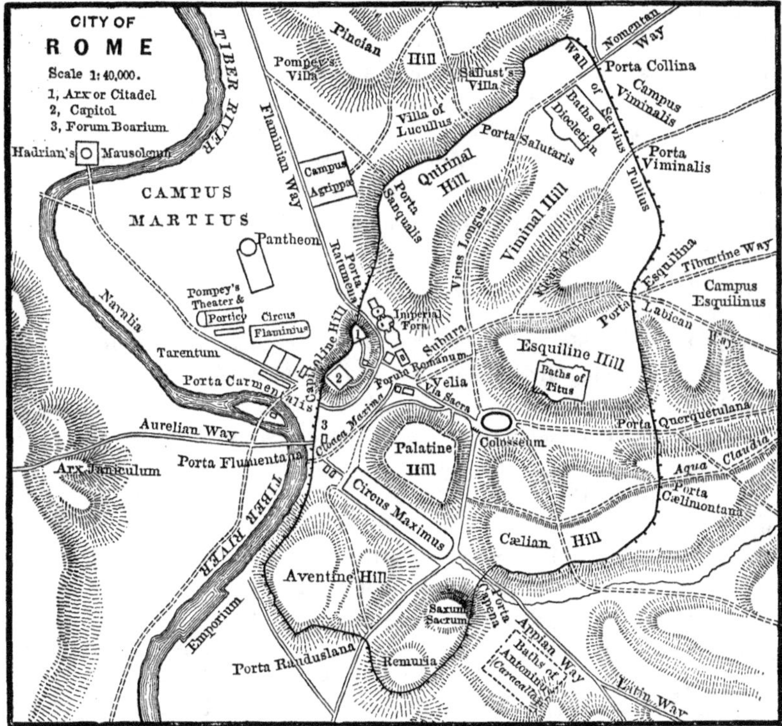

18. Lucius Tarquin′ius Priscus was of Greek origin, though he took his name from the Etruscan town Tarquinii, where he was born. The characteristics of his race were shown in the magnificent works with which he embellished Rome. He drained the lower parts of the city by a great system of sewers, and restrained the overflow of the Tiber by a wall of massive masonry, at the place where the Cloa′ca Maxima entered the river. In the valley thus redeemed from inundation he built the Forum, with its surrounding rows of porticos and shops; and constructed the Circus Maximus for the celebration of the Great Games, which had been founded by Romulus, and resembled in most of their features the athletic contests of the Greeks.

As a native of Etruria, Tarquin vowed the erection, upon the Capitoline, of a temple to Jupiter, Juno, and Minerva, the three deities who were worshiped together in every Etruscan city, and for this purpose he cleared away from that mountain all the holy places of the Sabine gods. The temple was built by his son. The wars of Tarquin against the Sabines, Latins, and Etruscans were usually victorious, and added largely to the population of Rome. From the noblest of the conquered peoples he formed three new half-tribes of fifty "houses" each, which he joined to the three old tribes of Ramnes, Tities, and Luceres, while he increased the number of Vestal Virgins from four to six, that each race might be equally represented. Tarquin was murdered by hired agents of the sons of Ancus Martius, who hoped thus to secure for themselves the throne of their father. But the Roman monarchy was strictly elective, not hereditary; their crime failed of its purpose, and Servius Tul'lius, an Etruscan general, and son-in-law of the murdered king, obtained the crown.

19. He made radical changes in the constitution, by giving to every free Roman the right of suffrage, though all offices in the government were still held by the nobles. The Greek cities of southern Italy were, at the same time, changing from aristocratic to popular forms of government, and there are many signs of Greek influence in Latium and Rome. The new popular assembly, *Comitia Centuria'ta,* was so called from the "centuries" in which the entire citizen-soldiery was enrolled. Wealth now acquired in Rome something of the power which had hitherto been reserved for rank. Every man who held property was bound to serve in the armies, and his military position was accurately graded by the amount of his possessions. Highest of all were the *Eq'uites,* or horsemen. These were divided into eighteen centuries, of which the first six — two for each original tribe — were wholly patrician, while the remaining twelve were wealthy and powerful plebeians.

The mass of the people enrolled for service on foot was divided into five classes. Those who were able to equip themselves in complete brazen armor fought in the front rank of the phalanx. Of this class there were eighty centuries: forty of younger men, from fifteen to forty-five years of age, who were the choicest of Roman infantry in the field; and forty of their elders, from forty-five to sixty, who were usually retained for the defense of the city. The second class were placed behind the first; they wore no coat of mail, and their shields were of wood instead of brass. The third class wore no greaves, and the fourth carried no shields. These three classes consisted of only twenty centuries each. The fifth and lowest military class did not serve in the phalanx, but formed the light-armed infantry, and provided themselves only with darts and slings. Below all the classes were a few centuries of the poorest people, who were not required to equip themselves for war. They were sometimes armed, at the public expense, on occasions of great loss or danger to the state; or they followed the army as supernumeraries, and were ready to take the weapons and places of those who fell.

20. Beside the patrician tribes of Ramnes, Tities, and Luceres, Servius made four tribes in the city and twenty-six in the country, consisting of land-owners without respect to rank. The meeting-place for the whole thirty was the Forum at Rome, while the centuries met without the city on the Field of Mars. The people assembled in the Forum had all the powers of self-government. They elected magistrates and levied taxes for the support of the state, duties which hitherto had belonged to the Comitia Curiata. Of the public lands on the Etruscan side of the Tiber, gained in his early wars, Servius assigned a certain portion to the plebeians, in full ownership. The patricians had leased these lands from the state for the pasturage of their flocks, and they were much exasperated by the new allotment.

21. Servius extended the bounds of the city far beyond the Roma Quadra′ta of the Palatine. The Esquiline, Cælian, and Aventine hills had already been occupied by surburban settlements, while the Capitoline, Quirinal, and Vim′inal were held by the Sabine tribes. These Seven Hills,* with a large space between and around them, were inclosed by Servius in a new wall, which lasted more than eight hundred years, until the time of the emperor Aurelian. Servius reigned forty-four years, B. C. 578–534. Desirous above all things for the continuance of his reformed institutions, he had determined to abdicate the throne, after causing the people, by a free and universal vote, to elect two magistrates who should rule but one year. Before the end of their term they were to provide, in like manner, for the peaceful choice of their successors; and thus Rome would have passed, by a bloodless revolution, to a popular government. The nobles, however, revolted against this infringement of their exclusive rights. Led by Tarquin, son of the first monarch of that name, and husband of the wicked Tullia, daughter of Servius, they murdered the beneficent king and placed their leader on the throne.

22. Tarquin, called "the Proud," set aside all the popular laws of Servius, and restored the privileges of the "houses"; but as soon as he felt secure in his power, he oppressed nobles and people alike. He compelled the poorer classes to toil upon the public works which his father had

---

* The name of the City of the Seven Mountains had been given to Rome when within much narrower limits. The *Septimontium* included only the Palatine, Esquiline, and Cælian, which were divided into smaller peaks or eminences, seven in all.

begun, and upon others which he himself originated. Such were the permanent stone seats of the Circus Maximus, a new system of sewers, and the great Temple of Jupiter on the Capitoline Hill. By wars or intrigues, Tarquin made himself supreme throughout Latium. But his insolence disgusted the patricians; he took away the property or lives of citizens without consulting the Senate, while he imposed upon them civil and military burdens beyond what the law permitted. The vile misconduct of his son Sextus led at last to a revolt, in which kingly government was overthrown. The Tarquins and all their clan were banished. The very name of king was thenceforth held in especial abhorrence at Rome. Only in one case was it tolerated. A "king for offering sacrifices" was appointed, that the gods might not miss their usual mediator with men; but this sacerdotal king was forbidden to hold any civil office.

RECAPITULATION.

Early history of Rome is largely fabulous. Three races in Italy, of whom the Etruscans, before the rise of Rome, were most powerful. Their cities, art, and religion. Rome was founded by Latins, but embraced a mixed population of Sabines, Etruscans, and others, which gave rise to the three tribes. Three hundred noble "houses" constituted the Senate and *Comitia Curiata.* Clientage. Formation of a commonalty under Ancus Martius. Buildings of Tarquinius Priscus. Free constitution of Servius Tullius. Division of the people into centuries, both as soldiers and citizens. Thirty tribes assemble in the Forum. Inclosure of the Seven Hills by the Tullian Wall. Tyranny of Tarquin the Proud. Royalty abolished at Rome. Supposed Chronology of the Kings: Romulus, B. C. 753–716; Numa, 716–673; Tullius Hostilius, 673–641; Ancus Martius, 641–616; L. Tarquinius Priscus, 616–578; Servius Tullius, 578–534; Tarquinius Superbus, 534–510.

RELIGION OF ROME.

23. Before passing to the history of the Republic, we glance at the religion of Rome. For the first 170 years from the foundation of the city, the Romans had no images of their gods. Idolatry has probably been, in every nation, a later corruption of an earlier and more spiritual worship. Roman religion was far less beautiful and varied in its conceptions than that of the Greeks.* It afforded but little inspiration to poetry or art, but it kept alive the homely household virtues, and regu-

---

* At a later period, when the Romans had become familiar with the literature of the Greeks, an attempt was made to unite the mythologies of the two nations. Some deities, like Apollo, were directly borrowed from the Greeks; in other cases, some resemblance of office or character caused the Greek and the Roman divinities to be considered the same. Thus Jupiter was identified with Zeus; Minerva, the thinking goddess—the Etruscan *Menerfa*—with Athena, etc. By order of the Delphic oracle or of the Sibylline Books, living serpents, sacred to Æsculapius, were brought from Epidaurus to Rome, to avert a pestilence, B. C. 293.

lated the transactions of the farm, the forum, and the shop, by principles drawn from a higher range of being.

The chief gods of the Romans were Jupiter and Mars. The former was supreme; but the latter was, throughout the early history of this warlike people, the central object of worship. March, the first month of their year, was consecrated to him, and, in almost all European languages, still bears his name. The great war festival occupied a large portion of the month. During its first few days the twelve *Salii*, or leapers, priests of Mars, who were chosen from the noblest families, passed through the streets singing, dancing, and beating their rods upon their brazen shields. Quirinus, under whose name Romulus was worshiped, was only a duplicate Mars, arising from the union of the two mythologies of the Romans and Sabines. He had, also, his twelve leapers, and was honored, in February, with similar ceremonies.

24. The celebrations of the several periods of the farmer's year were next in order to the war festival. The month of April was marked by days of sacrifice to the nourishing earth; to Ceres, the goddess of growth; to the patroness of flocks; and to Jupiter, the protector of vines; while a deprecatory offering was made to Rust, the enemy of crops. In May the Arval Brothers, a company of twelve priests, held their three days' festival in honor of Dea Dia, invoking her blessing in maintaining the fertility of the earth, and granting prosperity to the whole territory of Rome. August had its harvest festivals; October, its wine celebration in honor of Jupiter; December, its two thanksgivings for the treasures of the granary, its Saturnalia or seed-sowing on the 17th, and its celebration of the shortest day, which brought back the new sun. Sailors had their festivals in honor, respectively, of the gods of the river, the harbor, and the sea. The ceremonial year was closed with the singular Lu′perca′lia, or wolf festival, in which a certain order of priests, girdled with goat-skins, leaped about like wolves, or ran through the city scourging the spectators with knotted thongs; and by the Ter′mina′lia, or boundary-stone festival in honor of Ter′minus, the god of landmarks.

Janus, the double-faced god of beginnings, was a peculiarly Roman divinity. To him all gates and doors were sacred, as well as the morning, the opening of all solemnities, and the month (January) in which the labors of the husbandman began anew in southern Italy. Sacrifices were offered to him on twelve altars, and prayers at the beginning of every day. New-year's day was especially sacred to him, and was supposed to impart its character to the whole year. People were careful, therefore, to have their thoughts, words, and acts on that day pure, beneficent, and just. They greeted each other with gifts and good wishes, and performed some part of whatever work they had planned for the year; while they were much dispirited if any trifling accident occurred. A covered passage between the Palatine and Quirinal hills, *i. e.*, between the original Roman and Sabine cities, was known by the name of Janus. Armies going out or returning passed through it, and hence it was always open in time of war and closed in peace. The same ceremony was continued after the passage had ceased to be used, the triumphal gate having been constructed in the walls of Servius.

25. Vulcan, the god of fire and the forge, was honored by two festivals, the consecration of trumpets in May, and the Vol′cana′lia in August. Though of inferior rank to the divinities already mentioned, yet dearest of all to the Romans, were the gods of the hearth, the household, and store-room, and of the forest and field. Every house was a temple, and every meal a sacrifice to Vesta, the goddess of the hearth. Her temple was the hearth-stone of the city. There six chosen maidens, daughters of the most illustrious families, guarded the sacred fire, which was the symbol of the goddess, by night and day. Every house had over its main entrance a little chapel of the *La′res*, where the father of the family performed his devotions immediately on returning from any journey. The Lares were supposed to be the spirits of good men, especially the deceased ancestors of the family. Public Lares were the protecting spirits of the city; they were worshiped in a temple and numerous chapels, the latter being placed at the crossings of streets. There were also rural Lares, and *Lares Via′les*, who were worshiped by travelers.

26. Like all people in any degree affected by Greek culture, the Romans consulted the Delphic oracle. After the capture of Ve′ii (see § 57), they presented that shrine with a tenth of the spoils. Rome itself possessed only one oracle, that of Faunus (the favoring god), on the Aventine Hill. Several oracles of Fortune, Faunus, and Mars existed in Latium, but in none of them were audible responses given, by the mouth of inspired persons, as at Delphi. At Albu′nea, near Tibur, Faunus was consulted by the sacrifice of a sheep. The skin of the animal was spread upon the ground; the person seeking direction slept upon it, and believed that he learned the will of the god by visions and dreams. The Romans frequently resorted to the Greek oracles in southern Italy; and the most acceptable gift which the inhabitants of Magna Græcia could offer to their friends in Rome, was a palm-leaf inscribed with some utterance of the Cumæan sibyl, a priestess of Apollo at Cumæ, near Naples.

27. The Sibylline Books were believed to have been purchased by one of the Tarquins from a mysterious woman, who appeared at Rome offering nine volumes at an exorbitant price. The king refusing to purchase, the sibyl went away and destroyed three of the books; then brought back the remaining six, for which she asked the same amount of money.

The king again sent her away; she destroyed three more books, and demanded the whole price for the remaining three. The curiosity of Tarquin was aroused, and he bought the books, which were found to contain important revelations concerning the fate of Rome. They were kept in a stone chest under the temple of Jupiter Cap′itoli′nus. One of the four sacred colleges was charged with the care of them, and they were only consulted, by order of the Senate, on occasions of great public calamity.

28. The Romans probably learned from the Etruscans their various methods of divination — the interpretation of signs in the heavens, of thunder and lightning, of the flight or voice of birds, of the appearance of sacrifices, and of dreams. The legends ascribed to Tarquinius Priscus the introduction of Etruscan divinities and modes of worship into Rome. At a later time, the Senate provided by special decree for the cultivation of "Etruscan discipline" by young men of the highest birth, lest a science so important to the commonwealth should be corrupted by falling into the hands of low and mercenary persons.

The *Augurs* constituted the second of the sacred colleges; their number was gradually increased from three to sixteen; they were distinguished by a sacred dress and a curved staff, and were held in the highest honor. No public act of any kind could be performed without "taking the auguries" — no election held, no law passed, no war declared; for, by theory, the gods were the rulers of the state, and the magistrates merely their deputies. If, in the midst of the comitia, an augur, however falsely, declared that it thundered, the Assembly broke up at once. It must be admitted that the augurs often used their great power unfairly, in the political strife between patricians and plebeians. The latter, as originally foreigners (see § 17), were held to have no share in the gods of Rome, who thus became the exclusive patrons of the privileged class. When, by a change in the constitution, plebeians were at length elected to high offices, the augurs in several cases declared the election null, on the pretext that the auspices had been irregular; and as no one could appeal from their decision, their veto was absolute.

29. The College of Pontiffs was the most illustrious of the religious institutions attributed to the good king Numa. The pontiffs superintended all public worship according to their sacred books, and were required to give instruction to all who asked it, concerning the ceremonies with which the gods might be approached. Whenever sacred officers were to be appointed, or wills read, they convoked the Assembly. Certain cases of sacrilegious crime could only be judged by them; and in very early times, like the Hebrew scribes, they were the sole possessors of both civil and religious law. The highest magistrate, equally with private persons, submitted to their decrees, provided three members of the college agreed in the decision. They alone knew what days and hours might be used for the transaction of public business. The calendar was in their keeping, and—since these august and reverend dignitaries were only men—it is well known that they sometimes used their power to lengthen the year's office of a favorite consul, or to shorten that of one whom they disapproved. The title of Pon′tifex Maximus, or Supreme Pontiff, was adopted by the Roman emperors, and passed from them to the popes or bishops of modern Rome.

30. The fourth of the sacred colleges consisted of the *Fetia′les*, or heralds, who were the guardians of the public faith in all dealings with foreign nations. If war was to be declared, it was the duty of a herald to enter the enemy's country, and four times—once on either side of the Roman boundary, then to the first citizen whom he chanced to meet, and, finally, to the magistrates at the seat of government—to set forth the causes of complaint, and with great solemnity to call on Jupiter to give victory to those whose cause was just.

The priests of particular gods were called *Flamens*, or kindlers, because one of their principal duties was the offering of sacrifices by fire. Chief of them all was the Flamen Dialis, or priest of Jupiter; and next to him were the priests of Mars and Quirinus. Though the purity and dignity of the priestly life were guarded by many curious laws, the priest was not forbidden to hold civil offices. He was not allowed, however, to mount a horse, to look upon an army outside the walls, or, in early times, to leave the city for even a single night.

31. After the good king Servius Tullius had completed his census, he performed a solemn purification of the city and people. During the Republic, the same ceremony was repeated after every general registration, which took place once in five years. Sacrifices of a pig, a sheep, and an ox were offered; water was sprinkled from olive-branches, and certain substances were burned, whose smoke was supposed to have a cleansing effect. In like manner, farmers purified their fields, and shepherds their flocks. An army or a fleet always underwent lustration before setting out on any enterprise. In the case of the latter, altars were erected on the shore near which the ships were moored. The sacrifices were carried three times around the fleet, in a small boat, by the generals and priests, while prayers were offered aloud for the success of the expedition.

RECAPITULATION.

Roman religion less imaginative and more practical than the Greek. Jupiter, Mars, and Quirinus its chief divinities. Yearly festivals had reference chiefly to war and husbandry. Worship of Janus. Household gods. The Romans shared their belief in oracles with the Greeks; their arts of divination, with the Etruscans. Four Sacred Colleges: Pontiffs, Augurs, Heralds, and Keepers of the Sibylline Books. Priests might hold civil offices. Ceremonial cleansing of the city after every census; of armies and fleets before every expedition.

II. The Roman Republic.

32. The 480 years' history of the Roman Republic will be best understood if divided into four periods:

I. The Growth of the Constitution, B. C. 510–343.
II. Wars for the possession of Italy, B. C. 343–264.
III. Foreign Wars, by which Rome became the ruling power in the world, B. C. 264–133.
IV. Internal Commotions and Civil Wars, B. C. 133–31.

The leaders of the revolution which expelled the Tarquins, restored the laws of Servius and carried forward his plans, by causing the election of two chief magistrates, of whom one was probably a plebeian. The *consuls*, during their year of office, had all the power and dignity of kings. They were preceded in public by their guard of twelve lictors, bearing the *fasces*, or bundles of rods. Out of the city, when the consul was engaged in military command, an ax was bound up with the rods, in token of his absolute power over life and death.

33. For 150 years the Republic was involved in a struggle for existence, during which its power was much less than that of regal Rome. The Latins threw off their supremacy, and Lars Por′sena, the Etruscan king of Clu′sium, actually conquered the city, and received from the Senate an ivory throne, a golden crown, a scepter, and triumphal robe, in token of homage. In their further attempts upon Latium, the Etruscans were defeated, and Rome became independent, but with the loss of all her territories west of the Tiber. The Latins were defeated at the Lake Regillus, by the aid—so Roman minstrels related—of the twin deities, Castor and Pollux, who appeared at the head of the legions, in the form of two beautiful youths of more than mortal stature, mounted on white horses, and who were the first to break through into the enemy's camp. A temple was consequently built to them in the Forum, and they were regarded as the especial patrons of the Roman knights.

34. External dangers over, the patricians again made their power felt in the oppression of the common people. The first period of the Republic was absorbed in conflicts between the two great orders in the state—less attractive, certainly, than the romantic stories of the kingly age, or the stirring incidents of the later period of conquest. But the steps by which a great people has gained and established its freedom can never be without importance, especially to the only republic which has rivaled Rome in grandeur, in variety of interests, or in the multitude of races and languages included eventually within its limits.

35. The wealth of Rome hitherto had been chiefly derived from the products of the soil. The lands west of the Tiber were now lost, and all the rural district was open to invasion. Crops were ruined, farm buildings destroyed, cattle driven away. At the same time, through the losses and necessities of the government, taxes were greatly increased; and these were levied, not upon the reduced value of the property, but upon the scale of former assessments. To meet their dues, the poor were obliged to borrow money, at enormous rates of interest, from the rich. The nobles seized the opportunity to enforce to their full extent the cruel laws concerning debt, and the sufferings of the insolvent grew too grievous to be borne. Many sold themselves as slaves to discharge their obligations. Those who refused thus to sign away their own and their children's liberty were often imprisoned, loaded with chains, and starved or tortured by the cruelty of their creditors. The patrician castles, which commanded the hills of Rome, contained gloomy dungeons, which were the scenes of untold atrocities toward such as had the misfortune to incur the wrath of their owners.

36. Fifteen years after the expulsion of the kings, the plebeians, wearied out with a government which existed only for the rich, and imposed all its burdens on the poor, withdrew in a body to a hill beyond the Anio, and declared their intention of founding a new city, where they might govern themselves by more just and equal laws, B. C. 494. The patricians now perceived that they had gone too far. However much they hated the people, they had no idea of losing their services. They yielded, therefore, and received back the seceded plebeians on their own conditions. These were: (1.) Cancellation of claims against insolvent debtors; (2.) Liberation of all such who had been imprisoned or enslaved; (3.) Annual election of two *Tribunes*, whose duty it should be to defend the interests of the commons. The number of these officers was soon raised to five, and eventually to ten. Two plebeian *Æ'diles* were at the same time appointed, and charged with the superintendence of streets, buildings, markets, and public lands; of the public games and festivals, and of the general order of the city. They were judges in cases of small importance, like those of modern police courts; and they were eventually intrusted with the keeping of the decrees of the Senate, which had sometimes been tampered with by the patrician magistrates.

37. The scene of this first decisive battle of the people for their rights, was consecrated to Jupiter, and known in later years as the Sacred Mount (*Mons Sacer*). The Roman commons had thenceforth an important part in public affairs. To prevent suffering in future, Spurius Cassius, consul in the year following the secession, proposed a division among the plebeians of a certain part of the public lands, while the tithe of produce levied by the state upon the lands leased by the patricians, should be strictly collected and applied to the payment of the common people when they served as soldiers. Hitherto the troops had received no pay, while their burden of war expenses was great. The other consul opposed the law, and charged Cassius with seeking popularity that he might make himself a king. The law — the first of a long series of "Agrarian" enactments — was passed; but when the year of his consulship had expired, Cassius was brought to trial by his enemies, and condemned as a traitor. He was scourged and beheaded, and his house was razed to the ground, B. C. 485.

38. Having destroyed the leader, the patricians went on to rob the people of all the advantage of the law. They insisted on electing both consuls themselves, only requiring their confirmation by the popular assemblies; and with or without this confirmation, their candidates held supreme power, and refused to divide the public lands. The only resource of the commons was to withhold themselves from military service, and the tribunes now made their power felt by protecting them in refusing to enlist. The consuls defeated this measure by holding their recruiting stations outside of the city, while the jurisdiction of the tribunes was wholly within the walls. Though a man might keep himself safe within the protection of the tribunes, yet his lands were laid waste, his buildings burnt, and his cattle confiscated by order of the government. One last expedient remained. Though compelled to enlist, the soldiers could not be made to gain a battle; and considering the consul who led them, and the class to which he belonged, worse enemies than those whom they met in the field, they allowed themselves to be defeated by the Veientians.

39. The noble house of the Fa′bii, as champions of the nobility, had been for six successive years in possession of the consulship. They now saw the danger to Rome of longer opposition to the will of the people; and when Kæso Fabius, in the year 479 B. C., came into power, he insisted upon the execution of the Cassian law. The patricians refused with scorn, and the Fabii resolved to quit Rome. With their hundreds of clients, their families, and a few burghers who were attached to them by friendship and sympathy, they established a colony in Etruria, on the little river Crem′era, a few miles from the city. They promised to be no less loyal and valiant defenders of Roman interests, and to maintain with their own resources this advanced post, in the war then in progress against Veii. Two years from their migration, the settlement was surprised by the Veientians, and every man was put to death, B. C. 477.

40. The consuls still refused to comply with the Agrarian law, and at the expiration of their term were impeached by Genu′cius, one of the tribunes of the people. On the morning of the day appointed for the trial, Genucius was found murdered in his bed, B. C. 473. This treacherous act paralyzed the people for the moment, and the consuls proceeded with the enlistment of soldiers. Vo′lero Publi′lius, a strong and active commoner, refused to be enrolled; and in the tumult which ensued, the consuls with all their retinue were driven from the Forum.

The next year Volero was chosen tribune, and brought forward a law that the tribunes should thenceforth be elected by the commons alone in their tribes, instead of by the entire people in the centuries. This was designed to avoid the overwhelming vote of the clients of the great houses, who were obliged to obey the decrees of their patrons, and who often controlled the action of the general assembly. For a whole year the patricians contrived, by various delays, to prevent the passage of the bill. Ap′pius Clau′dius, one of the consuls, stationed himself with an armed force in the Forum to oppose it; and it was not until the plebeians, resorting in their turn to force, had seized the Capitol, and held it for some time under military guard, that the Publilian law was passed. This "second Great Charter of Roman liberties" gave the tribes not only the power of electing tribunes and ædiles, but of first discussing all questions which concerned the entire nation. It was a long step toward the gaining of equal rights by the commons, B. C. 471.

41. In the meanwhile, the Romans were carrying on wars with the Æqui and Volsci, two Oscan nations which had taken advantage of the changes in the Latin League, to extend their power to the cities on the Alban Mount and over the southern plain of Latium. Their forays extended to the very gates of Rome, driving the country people to take refuge, with their cattle, within the walls, where a plague then raging added the horrors of pestilence to those of war. It is probable that the civil conflicts in Rome had caused the exile of many citizens; and these, in most instances, joined the hostile nations. Rome was the champion of oligarchy among the cities of Italy, as Sparta was among those of Greece. The spirit of party was often stronger than patriotism; the sympathy between Roman and foreign aristocrats was greater than between patrician and plebeian at home; and thus an exiled noble was willing to become the destroyer of his country.

42. The story of Coriola′nus may be partly fictitious, but it truly illustrates the condition of the Republic at that period. Caius Marcius, a descendant of the fourth king of Rome, was the pride of the patricians for his warlike virtues, and had won his surname Coriolanus by capturing the Volscian town of Cori′oli by his individual gallantry. But he was bitterly opposed to the common people, and when he was about to be tried before the comitia for having opposed a distribution of corn, he fled and took refuge among the Volscians, whom he had formerly conquered. The king warmly welcomed him, and seized the first opportunity to stir up a new war with the Romans, that he might turn against them the arms of their best leader. When the Volscian army approached Rome, the Senate sent deputies to demand peace, but Caius refused all terms except such as were impossible for the Republic to grant. The priests and augurs next went to plead with him, but without effect.

At last the noble ladies of Rome, headed by Volum'nia, the mother of Caius, and his wife, Vergil'ia, with her young children, went out in a sad and solemn procession to plead for their sacred city. Coriolanus honored, above all, the mother to whose wise and faithful care he owed his greatness. He sprang to meet her with fitting reverence, but before she would receive his greeting, Volumnia exclaimed: "Let me know whether I stand, in thy camp, thy prisoner or thy mother; whether I am speaking to an enemy or to my son!" Her reproaches silenced Caius; the entreaties of his wife and children, and the tears of the noble ladies, moved him from his purpose. He exclaimed, "Mother, thine is the victory; thou hast saved Rome, but thou hast lost thy son!" He led away the Volscian army. Some say he fell a victim to their revenge; but others, that he lived on among them to extreme old age, and lamented, in the desolateness of his years of infirmity, the factious pride that had exiled him from wife, children, and native land.

43. In the meantime, Rome suffered another visitation of pestilence, in which thousands of people died daily in the streets. The Æquians and Volscians ravaged the country up to the walls of Rome; and in addition to their other miseries, the crowded multitude were threatened with starvation. Their civil grievances were not to be redressed by anything less than a thorough and radical reform. In the year 462 B. C., the tribune Terenti'lius Harsa proposed the appointment of a board of ten commissioners, half patrician and half plebeian, to revise the constitution, define the duties of consuls and tribunes, and frame a code of laws from the mass of decisions and precedents. This movement was the occasion for ten years of violent contention, during which Rome was several times near falling into the hands of the Volscians, and was once actually occupied by a band of exiles and slaves under a Sabine leader, Herdo'nius, who seized the Capitol and demanded the restoration of all banished citizens to their rights in Rome.

44. Chief of the exiles was Kæso Quinc'tius, son of the great Cincinna'tus, who had been expelled for raising riots in the Forum, to prevent any action of the people upon the Terentilian law. The invading party was defeated, and every man slain. The father of Kæso was then consul. In revenge for the fate of his son, he declared that the law should never pass while he was in office; and that he would immediately lead the entire citizen-soldiery out to war, thus preventing a meeting of the tribes. Nay more, the augurs were to accompany him, and so consecrate the ground of the encampment, that a lawful assembly could be held under the absolute power of the consuls, and repeal all the laws which had ever been enacted at Rome under the authority of the tribunes. At the close of his term, Cincinnatus declared that he would appoint a dictator, whose authority would supersede that of all other officers, patrician or plebeian. All these things could be done under the strict forms of the Roman constitution; but the Senate and the wiser patricians saw that the patience of the commons might be taxed too far, and persuaded Cincinnatus to forego so extreme an exercise of his power.

45. War with the Æquians went on, and treaties were only made to be broken. In the year 458 B. C., the entire Roman army was entrapped in a pass of the Alban Hills, surrounded by the enemy, and in imminent danger of destruction. In this crisis, Cincinnatus, who had retired from the consulship to resume his favorite toil of farming, was called to be dictator, with absolute power. The messengers of the Senate found him at his plow, in his little garden-plot across the Tiber. He left the plow in the furrow, hastened to Rome, levied a new army in a single day, went out and defeated the Æquians, and returned the next evening in triumph.

RECAPITULATION

Consuls are appointed with kingly power, but for a limited time. Rome subject to Porsena. The Latins are defeated at the Lake Regillus. Roman nobles oppress their debtors, and the poor secede. Tribunes of the people and ædiles are appointed. The first Agrarian Law is proposed by Cassius, B. C. 486. To avenge the tyranny of their consuls, the common soldiers refuse to fight. The Fabii take sides with the people, and are destroyed in their colony on the Cremera. The Publilian Laws give the election of officers to the people in their tribes, B. C. 471. War and pestilence. Ten years' debate upon the Terentilian Laws, which propose a revision of the constitution, B. C. 462–452. The Capitol seized by exiles and Sabines. Cincinnatus, as a noble, opposes the commons, but, as a general, saves Rome.

The Laws of the Twelve Tables.

46. The passage of the Terentilian law was delayed six years, but at length the nobles yielded the main point, and the *decemviri* were chosen. Though wholly patrician, they were men who enjoyed the confidence of both orders for their proved integrity. Both consuls and tribunes were superseded for the time, and full powers, constituent, legislative, and executive, were intrusted to the Ten. The laws of the Twelve Tables, which were the result of their labors, became the "source of all public and private right" at Rome for many centuries. During the debate upon the bill, commissioners had already been sent to Greece, to study the laws and constitution of the Hellenic states. They returned with an Ionian sophist, Hermodo′rus of Ephesus, who aided in explaining to the lawmakers whatever was obscure in the notes of the commissioners; and so valuable were his services, that he was honored with a statue in the Roman *comitium.*

47. Only a few points in this celebrated work of legislation can here be noticed. The laws of Rome gave to a father absolute right of property in his family. He might sell his son, his daughter, or even his wife. The latter act, indeed, was denounced as impious by the religious law, but no penalty was attached to it; the curse of the chief pontiff merely marked the guilty person for the wrathful judgments of Heaven. If a father desired to make his son free, the process was more difficult than the emancipation of a slave. The latter, if sold to another master, could be liberated at once, but a son thus sold and liberated returned to the possession of his father. This subjection could only end with the death of the parent, though the son himself might then be an old man. The Twelve Tables enacted that, if a father had three times sold his son, he lost all further control over him; but a son thus emancipated was considered as severed from all relationship with his father, and could no longer inherit his property. Women were all their lives considered as minors and wards. If their father died, they passed under the control of their brothers; or, if they married, they became the absolute property of their husbands. A widow might become the ward of her own son. Marriages between patricians and plebeians were declared unlawful, and children born in such had no claim upon their fathers' possessions.

48. The ten Law-givers visited with their heaviest penalties the defamation of character; and so stringent was their definition of libel, that neither poets nor historians dared even name the living except in terms of praise. It is much more difficult, therefore, to gain a true idea of public men in the history of Rome than of Greece, whose historians spoke with grand impartiality of men and measures, and the license of whose comic poets, though often used with insolent injustice, yet shows us all the weak points of character, and reveals the man as his contemporaries really saw him. The Roman historians, even when writing of the past, could often draw their materials only from funeral orations, or from the flattering verses of dependent poets, laid up among the records of great families.

49. The decemvirs, during their appointed year of office, completed ten tables of laws; and these, according to Roman ideas, were so just and so acceptable, that the assemblies willingly consented to renew the same form of government for another term, especially as the work of legislation was not quite complete. In the new decemvirate, Appius Claudius was re-elected, and his unscrupulous character now made itself felt in the tyrannical nature of the government. The people found that they had ten consuls instead of two, and the power of the Ten was unchecked by any popular tribune.

50. The domestic rights of the plebeians were rudely invaded. A fair maiden, Virginia, caught the eye of Appius as she went daily to school in the Forum, attended by her nurse. He declared that she was the slave of one of his clients, having been born of a slave-woman in his house, and sold to the wife of Virginius, who had no children of her own. The friends of Virginia and of the people resented this insolent falsehood with such indignation, that the consul's officers were compelled to release the maiden under bonds to appear the next day before his judgment-seat, where her lineage might be proved.

Virginius, her father, was with the army before Tus′culum. He was hastily summoned, and, riding all night, reached the city early in the morning. In the garb of a suppliant, he appeared in the Forum with his daughter and a great company of matrons and friends. But his plea was not heard. Appius judged the maiden to be, at least, considered a slave until her freedom could be proved, in direct violation of the law which he had himself enacted the year before, that every one should be regarded as free until proved a slave. Virginius perceived that no justice could be expected before such a tribunal. He only demanded one last word with his daughter; and having drawn her aside with her nurse into one of the stalls of the Forum, he seized a butcher's knife and plunged it into her heart, crying aloud, "Thus only, my child, can I keep thee free!" Then turning to the decemvir, he exclaimed, "On thy head be the curse of this innocent blood!" No one obeyed the consul's order to seize him. With the bloody knife in his hand, he rushed through the crowd, mounted his horse at the gate of the city, and rode to the camp.

51. The army of plebeians arose at his call and marched upon Rome. They entered and passed through the streets to the Aventine, calling upon the people, as they went, to elect ten tribunes and defend their rights. The other army, near Fide′næ, was aroused in the same manner by Icil′ius, the betrothed lover of Virginia. The common soldiers put aside those of the decemvirs who were with them, chose, likewise, ten tribunes, and marched to the city. The twenty tribunes appointed two of their number to act for the rest, and then leaving the Aventine guarded by a garrison, they passed out of the walls followed by the army, and as many of the people as could remove, and established themselves again on the Sacred Mount beyond the Anio.

52. The Senate, which had wavered, was now compelled to act. The seceders had declared that they would treat with no one but Valerius and Hora′tius, men whom they could trust. These were sent to hear their demands. The people required that the power of the tribunes should be restored, a right of appeal from the decision of the magistrates to the popular assembly established, and the decemvirs given up to be burnt, as nine friends of the commons had been, within the memory of men still living. This latter demand, caused only by the exasperation of the moment, was withdrawn upon maturer council; the others were granted, the decemvirs resigned, and the people returned to Rome, B. C. 449. A popular assembly was held, in which ten tribunes were elected, Virginius and Icilius being of the number. Two supreme magistrates were chosen by a free vote of the people, in the place of the decemvirate, and they were now first called consuls. Their powers were the same with those of the prætors, or generals, who had ruled from the expulsion of the kings to the appointment of the first decemvirate, except that an appeal might be made from their sentence to that of the comitia.

The first consuls under this new act were Valerius and Horatius. They went forth and gained so signal a victory over the Sabines, that Rome suffered no more incursions from that people for 150 years. Ancient custom and even law among the Romans honored victorious generals with a triumphal entry into the city on their return; but the Senate, whose duty it was to decree the triumph, regarding the consuls as false to the interests of their order, forbade any such honor to be paid them. Hereupon the people exerted their supreme authority, and commanded the consuls to "triumph" in spite of the Senate. (See §§ 109–111.) Appius Claudius and one of his colleagues were impeached and died in prison; the rest fled from Rome, and their property was confiscated.

53. A strong reaction now set in, in favor of the patricians; and so determined was their opposition to the new laws, that the people seceded again, but this time only to the Janiculum, west of the Tiber and opposite Rome. At last a law was passed legalizing marriage between the two orders. Instead of throwing open the consulship freely to the plebeians, it was agreed (B. C. 444) to divide its duties and dignities among five officers, of whom two, the censors, should be chosen only from the nobles, though by a free vote of the tribes, while the three military tribunes might be either patricians or plebeians. The censors were to hold office five years, the tribunes only one.

For some alleged defect in the auspices (see § 28), the first three tribunes were set aside, and for six years consuls were regularly appointed as before. In 438 B. C., tribunes were elected, and for three following years consuls again, showing the extreme difficulty with which the people gained their rights, even when conceded by law. In 433 B. C., an important law of Æmilius, the dictator, limited the duration of the censor's office to eighteen months, though he was still appointed only once in five years, thus leaving the place vacant a much greater time than it was filled.

54. The censors were invested with truly kingly splendor and extraordinary powers. They registered the citizens and their property, administered the revenues of the state, kept the rolls of the Senate, from which they erased all unworthy names, and added such as they considered fit. In this judgment of character they were guided solely by their own sense of duty. If a man was tyrannical to his wife and children, or cruel to his slaves, if he neglected his land, or wasted his fortune, or followed any dishonorable calling, he was degraded from his rank, whatever that might be. If a senator or a knight, he was deprived of his gold ring and purple-striped tunic; if a private citizen, he was expelled from the tribes and lost his vote. The censors were thus the guardians of morals, and their power extended to many matters which could hardly be reached by the general action of the law. The taking of every census was followed by a lustration, or ceremonial purifying of the people (see § 31). Hence, the five years which intervened between two elections of censors were called a *lustrum*, or 'greater year.

55. The Romans must have watched with interest, during the years 415 and 414 B. C., the movements of the great Athenian expedition against Syracuse. Had the brilliant schemes of Alcibiades been carried into effect, the Greeks would doubtless have become the leading power in western Europe; "Greece, and not Rome, might have conquered Carthage; Greek, instead of Latin, might have been at this day the principal element of the languages of Spain, of France, and of Italy; and the laws of Athens, rather than of Rome, might be the foundation of the law of the civilized world."

RECAPITULATION.

Decemviri chosen to make new laws for Rome. Absolute power of the *pater-familias*. Laws against libel make Roman history mere eulogium. Tyranny of the second decemvirate. Appius Claudius unjustly claims Virginia for a slave. The people secede, overthrow the decemvirate, and restore consuls and tribunes. The new consuls defeat the Sabines, and triumph in spite of the Senate. By another change of constitution, censors and military tribunes are chosen, instead of consuls. The censors have absolute power to correct public morals. The Athenians fail in their Sicilian expedition, B. C. 415, 414, and leave room for the supremacy of Rome.

CAPTURE OF ROME BY THE GAULS.

56. The Gauls were now beginning their terrible incursions from the north into the valley of the Po, thus absorbing the attention of the Etruscans; and the time favored a fresh attack of the Romans upon Veii, the nearest state across the Tiber. The war began B. C. 405, and lasted ten years. The necessity of keeping an armed force continually in the field, gave rise to the standing army, which ultimately made so essential a part of Roman power; and, at the same time, obliged the patricians to study the interests of the people. It was now agreed that the soldiers should be regularly paid, and money secured for this purpose by a careful collection of the rents for public lands. The number of military tribunes was doubled. Their chief, the præfect of the city, was a patrician, and chosen by that order, but the remaining five were elected from either or both classes, by a free vote of the popular assembly.

57. After ten years' warfare with varying success, Veii was taken (B. C. 396) by the dictator Camillus. It is said that on the very day of its surrender, Melpum, the Etruscan stronghold in the north, fell before the

Gauls. The loss of these two frontier fortresses began the rapid decline of Etrurian power. The joy of the Romans was commemorated by the whimsical custom, long continued, of concluding every festal game with a mock auction called the "Sale of Veientes." Cape′na, Fale′rii, Nep′ete, and Sunium were likewise conquered, and with their lands became possessions of Rome. Within half a century, the Etruscans lost to the Gauls all their possessions in Campania and north of the Apennines, and to the Romans, all between the Cimin′ian forests and the Tiber. The nation had already lost its force through unbounded excess in luxury. The nobles were enormously rich, while the people were poor and enslaved.

58. The war of the Romans against Volsin′ii was equally successful; but, by a sudden and terrible reverse, Rome was now doomed to suffer the fate which she too often inflicted. The Gauls, after conquering northern Etruria, overflowed the barrier of the Apennines and spread over central Italy. They met the entire Roman force near the little river Al′lia, and defeated it with great slaughter; then pushing on with irresistible power, they captured and burned the city. So overwhelming was the disaster, that the 16th of July, the date of the battle of the Allia, was pronounced a "black day" of ill-omen, on which no business could be safely transacted and no sacrifices acceptably offered.

59. The vestal virgins withdrew with the sacred fire to Cære, in Etruria; the mass of the people, with the fugitives from the conquered army, had taken refuge in Veii and other Etruscan towns; but the noblest of the patricians resolved to hold the Capitol. Those who were too old to fight, hoped to serve their country equally well by an heroic death. They repeated, after the pontifex maximus, a solemn imprecation,* devoting themselves and the army of the Gauls to death for the deliverance of Rome. Then, arrayed in their most magnificent apparel, holding their ivory scepters, and seated each upon his ivory throne at the door of his own house, they sat motionless while the tumult of plunder and pillage was going on around. The barbarians were struck with admiration of these venerable figures, and one of them began reverently to stroke the long white beard of Papir′ius. Enraged by this profaning touch, the old senator struck him with his ivory scepter. It was the signal for slaughter. The Gauls, recovering from their momentary awe, massacred the noble old men without delay.

60. The siege of the Capitol continued six or eight months. At one time it was nearly taken, by the enemy scaling the steep cliff by night. The garrison were asleep, but some geese sacred to Juno gave a timely alarm, and the citadel was saved. Marcus Manlius, who was the first to awaken, succeeded in throwing several of the first assailants down the cliff,

* For the probable form of this imprecation, see note, p. 276.

and thus maintained the fortress until his comrades could come to his aid. At length, though the garrison were nearly exhausted by hunger, the Gauls were equally ready to make terms, for they had heard that the Venetians were invading their northern possessions. A thousand pounds of gold were paid for the ransom of the city, and the barbarians retired. They were followed by Camillus, the conqueror of Veii and Falerii, who was now again dictator, and who, by cutting off straggling parties of the enemy, regained some portion of the rich booty which they were carrying away; but it is probably not true that he gained any important success over them, as was formerly believed.

61. A period of great distress followed the retreat of the Gauls. The farms, upon which the livelihood of so many people depended, had been laid waste; their fruit-trees, buildings, implements, stock and stores, even to the seed-corn needed for next year's sowing, had been burnt. Rome was a mass of rubbish, in which even the direction of the former streets could no longer be discerned. The government furnished roofing materials, and allowed wood and stone to be taken from the public forests and quarries, on condition that every person so aided would give security to complete his building within the year. But these pledges were often forfeited; and to meet the expense of rebuilding, as well as to pay the extraordinary taxes for restoring the fortress and the temples, money had to be borrowed, and the poor were again at the mercy of the rich. Innocent debtors were dragged from their homes, to toil as slaves in the shops or fields of their creditors.

Many chose to remain in the Etruscan towns where they had taken refuge, and even to make of Veii a new Rome for the plebeians, where they might live free from the overbearing rule of the patricians, and be themselves a privileged class. Though this wholesale secession was prevented, yet the numbers in Rome were so greatly diminished, that a mass of the conquered Etruscans were brought in to fill the vacant places. These were provided with Roman lands, were organized into four new tribes, and admitted to full civil rights. The "new people" formed more than a sixth part of the whole population of the reconstructed city.

62. No one could see without pity the distress of the people; but Marcus Manlius, the same whose alertness and presence of mind had saved the Capitol, had also reasons of his own for trying to relieve them. He was jealous of Camillus, and thought that his own services had not been duly rewarded. He sold at auction the best portion of his lands, and applied the proceeds to paying the debts of needy persons, thus delivering them from imprisonment and torture. He was rewarded by the unbounded gratitude of the poor; his house was continually thronged with partisans, to whom he spoke of the selfish cruelty of the nobles, in throwing the whole burden of the public calamity on others, and even accused them of embezzling the immense sums raised to replace the treasures of the temples, which had been borrowed to purchase the retreat of the Gauls.

63. For this charge Manlius was thrown into prison, and the people began to regard him as a martyr to their cause. On his release, he renewed his attacks upon the government. He fortified his house on the Capitoline, and with his party held the whole height in defiance of the authorities. His treason was so evident, that even the tribunes of the people took part with the patricians against him, and he was brought to trial before the popular assembly.

He appeared, followed by several comrades whose lives he had saved in battle, and by four hundred debtors whom he had rescued from the dungeon. He exhibited the spoils of thirty enemies slain with his own hand, and forty crowns or other honorary rewards received from his generals. He appealed to the gods, whose temples he had saved from pollution, and he bade the people look at the Capitol before they pronounced judgment. It was impossible to convict such a criminal in such a presence, for the very spot on the Capitol where Manlius had stood alone against the Gauls, was visible from the Forum. He was afterward condemned for treason and thrown from the Tarpeian Rock, the precipitous side of the Capitoline Hill, looking toward the Tiber.

64. The power of the patricians was only confirmed by this rash and selfish attempt to overthrow it. For seven years the distress of the people went on increasing; the commons lost heart, and their eldest men refused any longer to accept public office. Two younger men now came forward, who were destined, by their firm and wise procedure, to relieve in great measure the miseries of their class.

C. Licinius Stolo was of one of the oldest and wealthiest plebeian families, connected by many marriages with the nobles. Becoming tribune (B. C. 376), together with his friend, L. Sextius, he proposed a new set of laws, designed to remove both the poverty and the political wrongs under which the commons were suffering. (1.) To relieve immediate distress, it was proposed that the enormous interest already paid upon debts should be reckoned as so much defrayed of the principal, and should, therefore, be deducted from the sum still due. (2.) To prevent future poverty, the public lands, hitherto absorbed in great measure by the patricians, were to be thrown open equally to the plebeians, and no man was to be allowed to hold more than 500 *jugera*,* or to pasture more than 100 oxen and 500 sheep on the undivided portion. Further, to secure employment to the poor, a certain amount of free labor was required upon

* A *jugerum* was very nearly five-eighths of an acre.

every farm. (3.) Two consuls were to be elected, of whom one every year should be a plebeian.

65. The strongest objection to a plebeian consulship was on religious grounds; for high patricians held it an impiety to place in the supreme magistracy one who had no right to take the auspices, and whom they regarded as no true Roman. To attack this prejudice in the boldest manner, Licinius proposed to increase the number of keepers of the Sibylline Books from two to ten, and to appoint five of these from the plebeians. These laws were not passed without many years' violent opposition. At length they were ratified by the Senate and the Comitia Curiata (B. C. 367); and to celebrate this happy agreement between the two orders, a Temple of Concord was built upon the Capitoline Hill. At the same time, a new office, the prætorship, was instituted and confined to the patricians, comprising most of the civil and judicial duties which had hitherto belonged to the consuls, while the latter kept their absolute military power. The first plebeian consul under this arrangement was L. Sextius.

66. The restless and turbulent Gauls re-appeared in Latium, during the same year with the passing of the Licinian laws. They were defeated by the aged general Camillus, who had been six times military tribune and five times dictator. On their second invasion they encamped within five miles of the city, and struck terror, we may well believe, into the hearts of those who remembered the desolations of thirty years before; but, at length, they broke up their camp without fighting, and passed into Campania. On their return through Latium they were signally defeated. In 350 B. C., they spent the winter upon the Alban Mount, and joined the Greek pirates on the coast in ravaging the country, until they were dislodged by L. Furius Camillus, a son of the general.

They made a treaty B. C. 346, after which they never again appeared in Latium. They continued to be the ruling race between the Alps and the northern Apennines, and along the Adriatic as far south as the Abruz′zi. Many towns, like Milan, were held, however, by the Etruscans in a sort of independence, while the Gauls lived in unwalled villages. From their Tuscan subjects, the Gauls learned letters and the arts of civilized life, which spread from them, in a greater or less degree, to all the Alpine populations.

RECAPITULATION.

Veii taken B. C. 396, after a ten years' siege. Defeat of the Romans on the Allia, and capture of their city by the Gauls, B. C. 390. Massacre of the senators. Manlius saves the Capitol, during a seven months' siege. Rome in ruins. Distress of the poor. Treason of Manlius. The Licinian laws, passed after nine years' contest, relieve debtors and divide the public lands among the common people. The Gauls overrun central Italy, B. C. 361–346, but at length retire north of the Apennines.

SECOND PERIOD, B. C. 343–264.

67. From the political struggles which developed the Roman constitution, we turn to the series of foreign wars between Rome and her most powerful rival for the supremacy of southern Italy. The Samnites were a Sabine râce, settled as conquerors in the Oscan country. Their possessions were mostly inland, comprising the snow-covered mountain range which separates the Apulian from the Campanian plains, but they extended to the coast between Naples and Pæstum, where they included the once famous cities of Herculaneum and Pompeii.

The Samnites ranked with the Latins, as the most warlike races of Italy; but the conquests of the former, at the period to which we have now come, had been by far the more brilliant and extensive. In the decline both of Greek and Etruscan power in southern Italy (see Book III, § 90), they had gained control of the whole lower portion of the peninsula, except a few Greek colonies like Tarentum and Neapolis. But Latium, under the leadership of Rome, had advanced surely though slowly, securing each advantage by the formation of Roman colonies, bound by the strongest ties of obedience to the mother city, while the Samnite nation had no settled policy and no regularly constituted head. Each new settlement, therefore, divided and diminished their strength.

68. The conquerors of Cumæ and Capua adopted the luxurious habits of the Greeks and Etruscans, whom they had supplanted, but with whom they continued to live on friendly terms. The Greek-loving inhabitants of the coast dreaded their rude countrymen of the hills, almost as much as did the refined Hellenes themselves, and thus a great division took place in the Samnite stock. The civilized and Hellenized Samnites besought the aid of the Romans against the predatory hordes of their own race, who were constantly swooping down from the Samnian hills to ravage their fields. The Romans consented, on condition of their own supremacy being acknowledged throughout Campania, and their former treaty with Samnium was broken.

69. The First Samnite War began with the march of two Roman armies into Campania, while the Latin allies invaded the Pelignian country on the north. The Roman armies were victorious, and both consuls obtained a triumph. A large force was left, at the request of the Campanians, to guard their cities during the winter. The common soldiers were still burdened with poverty, and the prolonged absence from their farms occasioned serious suffering to their families.

In the second year of the war, mutinous plots were discovered, and a large body of the troops were sent home. On their way they released all the bondmen for debt whom they found working in the fields of their creditors, fortified a regular camp on the slope of the Alban Hills, and were joined by a large body of oppressed common people from the city. But when they met the army hastily raised by the patricians, and sent forth under Valerius the dictator — whose family had always been faithful friends to the people, and who was himself greatly beloved by all classes for his generous character, no less than his military glory — these men, whose revolt had been occasioned by real distress, and not by defect of loyalty, could not bring themselves to fight their fellow-citizens and the defenders of their common country. The two armies stood facing each other, until remorse on one side and pity on the other had overcome all mutual resentment; then, both pressing forward, they grasped hands or rushed into each others' arms with tears and demands for pardon. The just requirements of the soldiers were granted by the Senate, together with amnesty for their irregular proceedings, and this singular rebellion ended in a lasting peace.

70. The Latins, meanwhile, had been left to carry on the Samnite war by themselves, and their repeated successes encouraged them to assert their independence of Rome. The Romans now (B. C. 341) made peace with the Samnites, and, two years later, turned their arms against the Latins, who were strengthened by alliance with their late opponents, the Campanians and Volscians. The two consuls with their forces moved into Campania, and encamped in the plain of Capua, opposite the army of the three allies. Strict orders were issued against skirmishing or personal encounters, and disobedience was to be punished with death. Ignorant or heedless of the command, Titus Manlius, the consul's son, accepted a challenge from a Latin warrior, killed his opponent, and brought the spoils in triumph to lay at his father's feet. The consul turned away his face, and summoning his guards, ordered them to behead the young man before his tent, in the presence of all the soldiers. Roman discipline knew no ties of affection. Manlius, the father, was forever regarded with horror, but Manlius, the consul and general, was strictly obeyed as long as he commanded the armies of Rome.

71. The decisive battle in the Latin war took place at the foot of Vesuvius. The augurs, having taken the auspices as usual, declared that fate demanded the sacrifice of a general on one side and an army on the other. It was therefore made known to the Roman officers that, whichever portion of the army should begin to yield, the consul commanding in that quarter would devote himself to the gods of death and the grave, in order that the army which must perish might be that of the Latins.

Manlius led the Roman right; Publius Decius, the people's consul, the left. The battle was severe, and bravely fought on both sides; but, at length, the Latin right wing prevailed, and the Roman left began to give way. Decius instantly called the chief pontiff — for, as a plebeian, he himself was ignorant of the ceremonies by which the gods must be addressed —

and bade him dictate the form of words in which he was to devote himself to death. By the direction of the pontiff, he wrapped his toga around his face, set his feet upon a javelin, and repeated the imprecation.* Then sending his guard of lictors to the other consul to announce his fate, he mounted his horse, plunged into the host of the enemy, and was quickly slain. The Latins saw and understood the act, but they still fought fiercely, like men who struggled against fate. So equally matched were the main forces, that Manlius gained the day at last only by bringing on the poorer supernumeraries, whom he had armed to constitute a double reserve.

72. A second battle was much more easily won, and the Latins had no strength to rally for a third. The Latin League was wholly broken up, Roman law every-where took the place of local constitutions, and some cities even became Roman colonies. The Latins were one in race and language with Rome, and their transient hostility was exchanged for a close and permanent alliance. The battle under Mount Vesuvius was one of the most important in the history of Rome, for by securing the sovereignty of Latium, it opened the way to the conquest of the world.

73. For the next twelve years the Romans were unable to undertake any great foreign war. Italy was invaded by Alexander of Epirus, uncle of the great Macedonian conqueror, B. C. 332. His quarrel was with the Samnites, but if his success had been equal to his ambition, no engagements with the Romans would have prevented his overrunning the whole peninsula. He was defeated and slain, however, in 326 B. C., and the Romans immediately prepared for a renewed contest with the Samnites, which was to last twenty-two years, B. C. 326–304. The two chief states of Italy fought for sovereignty, and their allies included almost all the other nations in the peninsula.

The events of the first five years were too indecisive to be worth recording. The advantage was generally with the Romans, but the Samnite power was still unbroken, and was able, in 321 B. C., to inflict one of the most severe and disgraceful defeats that Roman arms had ever sustained.

* The form, which has been strictly preserved, may be of interest, as illustrating Roman ideas: "Thou Janus, thou Jupiter, thou Mars our father, thou Quirinus, thou Bellona; ye Lares, ye the nine gods, ye the gods of our fathers' land, ye whose power disposes both of us and of our enemies, and ye also, gods of the dead, I pray you, I humbly beseech you . . . . . that ye would prosper the people of Rome and the Quirites with all might and victory, and that ye would visit the enemies of the people of Rome . . . . . with terror, dismay, and death. And according to these words which I have now spoken, so do I now, on the behalf of the commonwealth of the Roman people . . . . . on behalf of the army, both the legions and the foreign aids . . . . . devote the legions and the foreign aids of our enemies, along with myself, to the gods of the dead and to the grave." It was deemed an impiety to ask for victory without making a sacrifice, for Nemesis avenged unmingled prosperity no less than crime.

The combined forces of Rome, led by the two consuls, were entrapped in a mountain-pass between Naples and Ben′even′tum, known as the "Caudine Forks." Half the soldiers fell in the fight which ensued; the rest surrendered, but were generously spared by Pontius, the Samnite general, on condition of an honorable peace being signed by the two consuls and by two tribunes of the people, who were present with the troops. The soldiers were then made to "pass under the yoke,"* in token of surrender, and were permitted to march away, without their arms, toward Rome. But the Senate, having got back its forces, refused to be bound by the agreement of the consuls. The signers of the treaty, stripped and bound, were given up to the vengeance of the Samnites, but Pontius refused to receive them. He did not choose to punish the innocent for the guilty, nor to justify the Roman government in taking all the advantage of the agreement, and refusing all the sacrifices.

74. The war went on six years without any very important event, until, in 315 B. C., the Samnites gained another great success at Lau′tulæ. Almost all the allies of Rome now deserted what seemed the losing cause. Campania revolted; the Ausonians and Volscians joined the Samnite alliance. But, in the following year, a still more severe and decisive battle gave victory to the Romans. The Samnites were crushed beyond all power of recovery. The war was continued, however, ten years longer, chiefly by the efforts of the Etruscans, Oscans, and Umbrians, to preserve the balance of power in Italy. But these efforts were never united, and the Romans were able to defeat them, one by one, until, in 304 B. C., the Samnites became subject to Rome, and all the other parties concluded a peace. Rome was now, without question, the first nation in Italy; and, considering the disputes which weakened the fragments of Alexander's empire, might almost be considered the greatest in the world. In intellectual culture, the Romans were still inferior to the conquered Samnites. Pontius, the Samnite general, was well versed in Greek philosophy, and in the elevation of his character far surpassed the proudest Romans of his time.

75. Near the close of the Second Samnite War, the Æqui, who had been for eighty years in a state of neutrality, took up arms against Rome; and immediately after the treaty of B. C. 304, the consuls marched 40,000 men into their territory. A sharp and severe struggle of fifty days resulted in the capture and destruction of forty-one towns. A large portion of the people were sold into slavery, and the rest became subjects of Rome. A few years later, however, they received the rights of citizens, were enrolled in the tribes, and served in the wars against the Samnites.

---

* *I. e.*, to march between two spears planted in the ground and surmounted by a third. Hence, our term "subjugation" = *sub jugum ire.*

76. The latter people busily employed the six years' interval between their second and third great struggle with Rome, in forming and strengthening the "Italian League." Etruscans, Umbrians, and Gauls, on the north, were allied with Lucanians, Apulians, most of the Greek cities, and the Samnites, on the south. Rome had the advantage in compactness, numbers, and wealth; her own or her allies' territory extended across Italy from the Mediterranean to the Adriatic, and divided the states of her enemies.

The war broke out in 298 B. C., but no important movement was made until, in 295 B. C., the combined armies of the four northern nations advanced toward Rome. The plan of the consuls was at once bold and sagacious. One army awaited the invaders, while another marched directly into Etruria. This movement exposed the weakness of the league, for the Etruscans and Umbrians, deserting their allies, drew off to defend their own territories. The Samnites and Gauls crossed the Apennines to Senti′num, where they were overtaken by the first Roman army. In the battle which followed, the Gallic war-chariots had nearly driven from the field the legions of Decius, the consul, when, remembering the example of his father at Vesuvius, he, likewise, devoted himself to the powers of death for the deliverance of Rome. The legions were at length triumphant; 25,000 of the enemy lay dead upon the field.

77. The Gauls now withdrew from the league, but the Samnites continued the war with unabated resolution. Twenty-eight years after his great victory at the Caudine Forks, Pontius again defeated a Roman army under Fabius Gur′ges. The Romans were so exasperated by this defeat where they were confident of victory, that they would have deprived the consul of his command, had not his old father, Fabius Maximus, offered to serve as his lieutenant.

A great victory was now gained, in which Pontius was captured, and made to walk, loaded with chains, in the triumph of the consul. When the procession reached the ascent to the Capitol, he was led aside and beheaded in the Mamertine prison — he who, thirty years before, had spared the lives and liberty of two Roman armies, and even generously released the officers when given over to his vengeance! This base treatment of a brave foe has been called the greatest stain in the Roman annals. The war was ended with the complete submission of Samnium, and the Romans established a colony of 20,000 people at Venu′sia, to hold the conquered territory in awe, B. C. 290.

78. In the same year, the consul, Curius Denta′tus, began and ended another war against the Sabines, who had come to the aid of their Samnite kinsmen. They were subdued, and their extensive country, rich in oil, wine, and forests of oak, fell into the possession of the Romans. The commons at Rome suffered greatly, nevertheless, from the burdens of the war. Their farms had been neglected during their absence with the army, and those who had the misfortune to have been taken prisoners, had to be ransomed at a cost ruinous to small fortunes.

Curius, the conqueror of the Sabines, proposed a new Agrarian law for the division of their lands among the poor of Rome. A political contest of several years ensued, during which the mass of the people seceded again to the Janiculum. A rumor of foreign invasion induced the Senate to yield and appoint Hortensius, a plebeian of ancient family, to be dictator. By his wise and conciliatory counsels, peace was restored. He convened all the people in a grove of oaks without the walls, and by the solemn oaths of the whole assembly passed the Hortensian laws, which ended the civil strife of Rome for 150 years. Every citizen received an allotment of land, and certain invidious marks of distinction between patricians and plebeians were effaced, B. C. 286.

RECAPITULATION.

The Hellenized Samnites ask the aid of Rome against their highland countrymen. The First Samnite War, B. C. 343–341, opens with success to the Romans. Sedition of troops in Campania. The Latins revolt against Rome and join the Campanians and Volscians. The Romans make peace and alliance with the Samnites for the Latin War, B. C. 340–338. In the battle of Vesuvius, Decius, the consul, devotes himself to death, and the Romans are victorious. The Latin League suppressed, and the supremacy of Rome established. An invasion of Italy by Alexander of Epirus, is followed by the Second Samnite War, B. C. 326–304. The Romans defeated at the Caudine Forks, B. C. 321, but at last completely victorious. They conquer the Æqui, B. C. 304. Third Samnite War, and Italian League against Rome, B. C. 298–290. Great victory at Sentinum over Gauls, Samnites, Etruscans, and Umbrians. Capture of Pontius, B. C. 292, and end of the Samnite wars. Sabine territories conquered and divided among the people, by Hortensian laws.

WAR WITH PYRRHUS.

79. Within three years (B. C. 283), the Romans were menaced by a new danger, in a powerful coalition formed by the Tarentines, and including nearly all the nations of Italy. The storm gathered swiftly and burst from all quarters at once. In the south, the Samnites, Lucanians, and Bruttians were in arms; in the north, the Etruscans and Umbrians, with hordes of Gallic mercenaries, were pouring into the field. Arre′tium alone stood firmly by the Roman alliance, and was besieged by an army of Etruscans and Gauls. The consul, Metel′lus, marching to its relief, was defeated with the total loss of his army. Embassadors, sent to remonstrate with the Seno′nian Gauls for the infringement of their treaty with Rome, were murdered, and their bodies hewed to pieces and cast out without burial. This outrage, which the laws of the rudest savages pronounced sacrilege, provoked a speedy vengeance. Dolabel′la, the consul, marched into the Gallic territory with his army, killed every man who was found, carried off the women and children as slaves, and reduced every village to a heap of ashes and rubbish.

80. The Boian Gauls took up arms to avenge their brethren, and, joining the Etruscans, met the Roman forces in the valley of the Tiber, near the little lake Vad′imon. They were defeated so thoroughly that very few escaped from the field. The consul Fabric′ius, the following year, defeated the Samnites, Lucanians, and Bruttians in several great battles, broke up the coalition in the south, and collected an amount of spoils which enabled him to pay all the war expenses of the year, and, beside allowing a liberal share to every soldier, to leave half a million of dollars in the treasury. Tarentum, the prime mover of the war, had never drawn a sword, but had left all its burdens and losses to her allies. To punish this passive but mischievous policy, a Roman fleet was now sent to cruise around the eastern and southern coasts of Italy. It was defeated and sunk by the Tarentines in their own harbor. They then seized Thurii, expelled the Roman garrison, and, in the name of all the Italian Greeks, sent to Pyrrhus, king of Epirus, for aid.

81. This accomplished and ambitious prince was glad of a new field of enterprise. He hastened into Italy with a well-appointed army of 25,500 men, drilled and equipped in the Macedonian fashion, and supplied with twenty elephants. The gay and self-indulgent Tarentines, quite willing that another should fight their battles for them, forgot their promises of service and subsidies; but Pyrrhus showed them that he was master by stopping the sports of the circus and theaters, and the banquets of the clubs, and keeping the citizens under arms from morning to night. Even with inferior forces he was able to defeat the Roman legions at Heracle′a, on the Siris. Seven times the Epirotes and Greeks were driven from the field, and seven times regained it; but when the last Italian reserve was engaged, Pyrrhus brought on his elephants, till then unknown in Italy, and they put to flight the Roman horse. The rout was complete; the Romans did not stay to defend their camp, but fled to Venu′sia, leaving Pyrrhus master of the field.

82. He was now joined by many allies, some of whom had even been subjects or friends of Rome; but the advantage of his victory was not sufficient to balance his loss in officers and men — losses the more serious as Greece was now overrun by the Gauls, and there was little hope of recruits. In these circumstances, Pyrrhus sent to Rome his embassador, Cin′eas, an orator of such brilliant talent, that he was said to have won more cities by his tongue than Pyrrhus by his sword. A large party was inclined to listen to his proposals of "peace, friendship, and alliance." But Appius Claudius — thirty years ago censor, now a blind old man — heard in his house that Rome was making peace, with a victorious enemy still upon Italian soil. He caused himself to be carried in a litter through the Forum to the Senate-house. When he arrived, all his sons and sons-in-law went out to meet him and lead him to his ancient place. All the Senate listened in breathless silence as the old man rose to speak, protesting against the dishonor of his country. When he ceased, it was voted that no peace should be made while any foreign foe was in Italy, and that the orator who had so nearly persuaded them should leave the city that very day.

83. The war went on between the consummate genius of Pyrrhus and the unconquerable will of the Roman people. They were fighting for existence, while Pyrrhus fought for glory; and though in every pitched battle he was victorious, fresh armies were always ready to oppose him. Still hoping to make peace with Rome, he refused to ransom or exchange the multitude of prisoners whom he had taken, but he allowed them all to return to Rome for the winter holidays — the Saturna′lia — on their simple promise to return if the Senate refused a treaty. The Senate refused, and every man returned. In his second campaign, Pyrrhus gained another brilliant victory, at As′culum, over the Romans and their allies. But his restless ambition now turned to a new field, and he departed into Sicily, where the Greek cities had implored his aid against the Carthaginians. Once master of that fertile island, he believed that he could attempt the conquest of Italy with better resources, and he left troops to hold Tarentum and Locri for his base of future operations in the peninsula.

84. In Sicily his genius and valor for a time drove all before him. The strong town of Eryx was taken, Pyrrhus himself being the first to mount the scaling-ladders. The Carthaginians implored peace, offering ships and money as the conditions of an alliance. Pyrrhus haughtily refused; but a reverse which he afterward suffered at Lilybæ′um, encouraged his enemies and alienated his allies. After two years he returned into Italy, pursued by a Carthaginian fleet, which defeated him with a loss of seventy ships. On landing, he was met by a body of Mamertines,* who had crossed the straits from Sicily, and whom he defeated only by a sharp and costly battle. He arrived at Tarentum with an army equal in numbers, but far inferior in character, to that with which he had come from Epirus four years earlier. His faithful Epirotes were slain, and in their places were ill-trained Italian mercenaries, who would serve only as long as pay and plunder abounded.

---

*The Mamertines, "Children of Mars," were a troop of Italian freebooters, formerly in the pay of Syracuse, but who had seized Messa′na and other fortresses in the north-east of Sicily, massacred the people, and made themselves independent.

85. Being in great want of money to satisfy these unruly followers, Pyrrhus yielded to the advice of his Epicure′an courtiers, and appropriated the treasures of the temple of Proser′pina, at Locri. The money was embarked by sea for Tarentum, but a storm drove the sacrilegious vessel back upon the coasts of Locri; and Pyrrhus was so affected by remorse, that he restored the gold and put to death the counselors. He believed that he was ever after haunted by the wrath of Proserpina, which dragged him down to ruin. The following year he was totally defeated near Beneventum, by Curius Dentatus, the consul. Toward the end of the year he passed over into Greece, still leaving a garrison at Tarentum, in token of his unconquered resolution to return.

During the first invasion by Pyrrhus, the Eighth Legion, stationed at Rhegium, and composed chiefly of Campanian mercenaries, had, like the Mamertines in Sicily, thrown off their allegiance, slaughtered the Greek inhabitants, and held the town as an independent military post. They were now reduced, and most of the garrison put to the sword; the rest, consisting of the original soldiers of the legion, were tried at Rome, scourged, and beheaded.

86. Roman supremacy was now speedily established both in northern and southern Italy. Picenum was conquered, and half her inhabitants were forcibly removed to the shores of the Gulf of Salerno. Umbria submitted B. C. 266, the chief cities of Etruria followed, and the entire peninsula south of the Macra and Rubicon became subject to Rome. Hitherto the Romans, like the Spartans, had prided themselves upon the homeliness of their manners. When the Samnites sent envoys to M. Curius to bespeak his kind offices with the Senate, and offer him a present of gold, they found the ex-consul seated by his fire and roasting turnips in the ashes, with a wooden platter before him. To their proffered gift he replied, "I count it my glory not to possess gold myself, but to have power over those who do."

The eleven years following the departure of Pyrrhus were a period of the greatest prosperity ever enjoyed by the common people of Rome, and the wealth arising from the conquest of Italy materially changed their manner of living. Every freeman received a fresh grant of seven *jugera* of land or a portion of money. The property of the displaced governments went, of course, to the Roman state, and thus valuable possessions of mines, quarries, forests, fisheries, and public lands were added to its domains. The administration of the public revenues demanded a greatly increased number of officials, and the rich, as well as the poor, profited by the results of war.

87. The new territories were secured by that system of colonies which, in later times, served to establish the Roman power from the Atlantic to the Euphrates. The colonies were of two kinds. Most favored were those composed of "Roman citizens," who retained all their rights as such, voting in the assembly, and being eligible to any office which they could have filled if remaining at Rome. Those who joined a "Latin colony," on the other hand, lost their civil rights in Rome, but they had privileges which attached them both by interest and affection to the mother city. Ostia, and the maritime colonies generally, were of the former and higher class. The great system of Roman roads, which ultimately intersected all western Europe, and may be seen to-day in their massive remains, owed its origin to Appius Claudius "the Blind," who when censor, in 312 B. C., constructed the Appian Way to connect Rome with her new dependency, Campania. He also built the first of the Roman aqueducts, to supply the poorer portion of the city with water.

88. The free-born plebeians of Rome now possessed half the high offices in the state, and even in the sacred colleges of pontiffs and augurs. They were admitted to the Senate when they had served as consuls, or had been appointed to be either prætors or ædiles. Appius Claudius, in his censorship, went still further, and placed upon the rolls of the Senate the names of some who had been born slaves, or who possessed no lands. He enrolled these two very numerous classes in the tribes as voters; and instead of assigning them to those of the city, where they almost exclusively belonged, he distributed them over all the districts, so that they might control all elections. To rescue Rome from the inevitable rule of the mob, his successors in the censorship confined these new votes to the city, thus giving them the control only of four tribes out of thirty-one, and so the danger was averted.

RECAPITULATION.

Coalitions in the north and south against the Romans. Siege of Arretium, and defeat of Metellus. War with the Senonian and Boian Gauls. Victories of Fabricius in the south. Pyrrhus comes to the aid of the Tarentines; defeats the Romans at Heraclea, Asculum, etc.; sends Cineas to Rome, whose persuasions are thwarted by Appius Claudius the Blind; passes into Sicily, and after two years returns to Epirus. All Italy subject to Rome. Increased wealth and luxury of the people. Many new colonies upon the conquered lands. Roads and aqueducts are constructed. Freedmen and non-possessors of land admitted to the suffrage by Appius Claudius.

THIRD PERIOD, B. C. 264–133.

89. The great commercial Republic of Carthage, though allied with Rome during the wars with Pyrrhus, had regarded with jealousy the steadily increasing power of the Italian state. The Roman people, on the other hand, had been so enriched by their recent wars, that they were eager for fresh plunder and a new allotment of conquered lands.

A slight and doubtful pretext was, therefore, sufficient to plunge the two nations into war. The Carthaginians had seized the citadel of Messana, under pretense of aiding the Mamertines against Hi′ero of Syracuse. The Romans had recently punished the buccaneers of Rhegium for precisely the same crime which the "Sons of Mars" had committed at Messana, but when the latter sought their aid against both Syracusans and Carthaginians, the temptation was too great; they accepted the disreputable alliance, and invaded Sicily with 20,000 men.

90. Having gained possession of Messana, they kept it for their own. The combined forces of Syracuse and Carthage, besieging the place, were defeated by Claudius, the consul; and Hiero, being distrustful of his African allies, returned home. The next year he made peace with the Romans, and continued until his death, nearly half a century later, their faithful friend and ally. Most of the Greek cities in Sicily followed his example. Hannibal,* son of Gisco, the Carthaginian general, could no longer meet the Romans in the field, but shut himself up in Agrigentum and was besieged. Hanno, attempting to relieve him, was decisively defeated; the city was taken, and its people were sold as slaves.

Hannibal, who escaped to Panor′mus (Palermo) with most of his troops, now carried the war upon the sea, and ravaged the defenseless coasts of Italy with a fleet of sixty vessels. The next year his lieutenant, Boö′des, with a naval detachment, met the consul, Scipio, at Lip′ara, and captured his whole squadron. Hannibal then set out with fifty ships to ravage the coasts of Italy again. But the Romans, wisely learning from their enemies, were now prepared to meet them on their own element. A Carthaginian quin′quereme (a vessel with five rows of oars) had been cast ashore on the coast of Bruttium. It was used as a model, and the Romans, who previously had had nothing greater than triremes, possessed, within two months, one hundred first-class war vessels. While the ships were building, the crews were trained on shore to their peculiar and complicated motions. In the very first encounter, Hannibal was defeated; in the second, off Mylæ, he lost fifty vessels, among them his magnificent flag-ship, which had formerly belonged to Pyrrhus.

91. In 259 B. C., Sardinia and Corsica were attacked, and the town of Ale′ria taken by the Romans. The following year, another great naval victory was gained off Ec′nomus, in Sicily; and the consuls, Manlius and Regulus, invaded Africa. They captured and fortified the town of Cly′pea, which they made their headquarters, and then proceeded to lay waste the lands of Carthage with fire and sword. The beautiful villas of the nobles

---

* N. B. Not the great Hannibal, who was son of Hamilcar, and hero of the *Second* Punic War. "Punic" is only another form of the adjective Phœnician, but is applied especially to the people of Carthage.

and merchants afforded inestimable spoils; and 20,000 persons, many of whom were of exalted rank, and accustomed to all the refinements of wealth, were dragged away as slaves.

In the winter, Manlius returned to Rome with half the army and all the plunder, while Regulus remained to prosecute the war. He defeated the Carthaginian generals, captured their camp, and overran the country at pleasure. More than three hundred walled villages or towns were taken. In vain the judges and nobles of Carthage cast their children into the brazen arms of Moloch, whence they rolled into the fiery furnace burning always before him. The hideous idol was not appeased, and the Roman general was equally implacable. To all embassies he refused peace, except on such intolerable terms that even disastrous war seemed better.

92. At the darkest moment, relief arrived in the person of a Spartan general, Xanthippus, who came with a body of Greek mercenaries. His military fame and the evident wisdom of his counsels inspired such confidence, that he was put in the place of the incompetent Punic commanders. With his 4,000 Greeks, added to the Carthaginian infantry and 100 elephants, he defeated and captured Regulus, and wholly destroyed the Roman army. A still more terrible disaster befell the fleet which had been sent to bring away the shattered remnants of the forces from Africa. A violent storm came on, and the southern coast of Sicily was strewn with the remains of 260 vessels and 100,000 men, B. C. 255.

The Romans, though nearly driven to despair of the republic, never relaxed their exertions, but equipped a new fleet, with which, the following year, they captured the important town of Panormus. This fleet was wrecked, B. C. 253, and the next two years were full of discouragements; but, in 250 B. C., a brilliant victory, won at Panormus by the proconsul Metellus, tended to restore the balance of the opposing forces. A hundred elephants, taken alive, were exhibited in the triumph of Metellus.

93. For the next eight years, the advantage was usually with the Carthaginians. Hamilcar Barca, the father of the great Hannibal, ravaged the coasts of Italy, and the Romans had no leader of equal genius to oppose to him. At last they rallied all their forces to put an end to the war. The wealthier citizens at their own expense fitted out a fleet of 200 ships, and the consul Luta′tius gained a decisive victory among the islands west of Sicily. This reverse, following twenty-three years of exhausting war, so disheartened the Carthaginians, that they agreed to abandon Sicily and all the neighboring islands, to pay 2,000 talents, and release all the Roman prisoners without ransom.

94. The First Punic War had lasted nearly twenty-four years, B. C. 264–241 inclusive. Rome emerged from it a great naval power, able to meet on equal terms the well-trained mariners who had hitherto ruled the western Mediterranean. Foreseeing that the struggle must be renewed, both parties spent the twenty-three years which followed in strenuous preparations. Rome seized upon Sardinia and Corsica; and Carthage, absorbed and weakened by a revolt of her mercenary troops, was compelled to submit, and even to pay a heavy fine for having presumed to remonstrate.

These islands, with Sicily, were placed under proconsular government, the system by which Rome afterward managed all her vast foreign possessions. The two consuls, on completing their year of office, divided the "provinces" between them by lot or agreement, and each held in his own, both military and civil control, while the finances were managed by quæstors responsible only to the Senate. When the provinces became numerous, the greater number were governed by pro-prætors. One-tenth of the whole produce of these conquered countries was claimed by Rome, beside a duty of five per cent on all imports and exports.

95. By the request of the western Greeks, Rome exerted her new naval power in clearing the Adriatic of the Illyrian pirates, who were ravaging its coasts and destroying its commerce. Their queen, Teuta, seized the Roman embassadors who were first sent into her country, killed two and imprisoned the third. In the war which immediately followed, she lost the greater part of her dominions, and was compelled to keep her corsairs within stricter limits for the future, beside paying a yearly tribute to her conquerors. In gratitude for this important service, the Romans were admitted to equal rights with the Hellenic race in the Isthmian Games and the Eleusinian Mysteries, B. C. 228.

96. While thus asserting her power in the Greek peninsula, Rome desired to extend her Italian dominion to its natural limit in the Alpine range. The Gauls were not slow in taking the alarm. Obtaining fresh forces from their kinsmen beyond the mountains, they advanced into central Italy, and, overrunning Etruria, threatened Rome again as in the days of Brennus. Three armies were quickly in the field to oppose them; and though one was routed, another, under the consul Æmil′ius, aided by Regulus,* who had unexpectedly arrived from Sardinia, gained a decisive victory which nearly destroyed the Gallic host. Within three years all Cisalpine Gaul submitted to Rome, B. C. 222. Mediola′num and Comum (Milan and Como), as well as Placen′tia, Parma, Mode′na, Man′tua, Vero′na, and Brix′ia, were occupied by Roman colonies, connected with the capital by the great military road called the Flaminian Way, and its continuations.

---

*Son of the Regulus who invaded Africa (§ 91), and who fell a victim to Carthaginian vengeance.

97. Carthage, meanwhile, had yielded only from necessity, and for a time, to the superior power of Rome. A large majority of her citizens were for renewing the war at the earliest possible moment; and to recruit her power and wealth, Hamilcar had devoted all his energies to the conquest of the Spanish peninsula, B. C. 236–228. After his death, his son-in-law, Has′drubal, organized and developed the resources of the country by building towns, encouraging trade and tillage, training the native tribes into efficient soldiers, and working the newly discovered silver mines, which, beside paying all the expenses of the province, were rapidly filling up the home treasury. Rome, with her command of the sea, secured from fear of invasion, saw without uneasiness the prosperity of her rival. But an item which no one could have foreseen, the genius of Hannibal, was now to be added to the resources of Carthage.

98. At nine years of age he had accompanied his father into Spain, and before the altar of his country's gods had taken a solemn oath of eternal and unrelenting enmity to Rome. The oath of the child had not been forgotten by the youth. At the age of eighteen he fought by his father's side in the battle where Hamilcar was slain; and during the following eight years of Hasdrubal's administration, that general intrusted his young brother-in-law with the command of most of his military enterprises. Upon the death of Hasdrubal, the army by acclamation placed Hannibal at its head, and the government at home neither could nor would annul the appointment.

Having confirmed his power in Spain by two years' war against the native tribes, Hannibal deliberately sought the quarrel with Rome to which he had devoted his life. The Greek city of Saguntum had placed itself under the protection of Rome. It was attacked by Hannibal, and taken after an obstinate defense of eight months. The Romans sent to Carthage to demand the surrender of the young general for this breach of the treaty. The reply was a declaration of war.

99. Leaving his brother Hasdrubal in charge of Spain, Hannibal prepared for a bolder movement than the Romans had foreseen. He knew that the great mountain-barrier of the Alps had already often been traversed by the Gauls, and he relied upon finding able guides among this people, who were mostly friendly to Carthage. He resolved, therefore, on the hitherto unprecedented feat of leading an army from Spain into Italy by land. Having offered, during the winter, solemn sacrifices and prayers for success, at the distant shrine of the Tyrian Hercules at Gades, he set forth from Carthagena, in the spring of 218 B. C., with an army of 90,000 foot, 12,000 horse, and a considerable number of elephants. The Spanish tribes between the Ebro and the Pyrenees were yet to be overcome. They resisted bravely, but were subdued, and a force of 11,000 men was left to hold them in subjection.

100. Having passed the Pyrenees, Hannibal advanced through friendly tribes of Gauls to the Rhone, which he crossed near the modern town of Orange, gaining an advance of three days upon the army of Scipio, the consul, who had intended to stop him. The passage of the Alps, with such a force, was one of the greatest military achievements of ancient times. The higher mountains were already obstructed by the snows of early autumn; hostile tribes contested his passage in narrow and dangerous defiles; and in two fierce battles, the army of Hannibal narrowly escaped total destruction. When, after fifteen days of toilsome and dangerous marching, he emerged into the plain of the Po, it was with scarcely more than one-fourth of the great army which had accompanied him from Carthagena.

101. The Insubrian Gauls welcomed Hannibal as their deliverer from the hated power of Rome. After a short period of rest in their hospitable country, he sought Scipio, and totally routed his forces in a battle on the Tici′nus. By a still greater victory on the Tre′bia, over the forces of the two consuls (Dec., 218 B. C.), Hannibal became master of northern Italy. All the Gauls who had wavered now hastened to join his standard; but the gain from this quarter was balanced by the irreparable loss of his elephants, and the severe suffering of his African and Spanish troops from the unwonted coldness of the winter.

In the spring of 217 B. C., he crossed the Apennines, and traversed the marshes of the Arno, a passage of tremendous difficulty, in which many of his beasts of burden perished. Again seeking battle, Hannibal passed the army of Flaminius at Arretium, and laid waste the country toward Peru′sia, thus provoking the consul to follow. When he had drawn the Roman army into a most perilous position, between precipitous cliffs and the Lake Thrasymene, he let loose his Gauls and Numidians to the attack. The defeat of the Romans was overwhelming: thousands were forced into the lake; thousands fell by the sword, among whom was Flaminius himself; and 15,000 prisoners remained in the hands of the enemy.

102. A panic seized Rome; the conqueror was instantly expected at her gates, and Fabius was elected dictator with unlimited powers. But Hannibal had sought to detach the Italian allies from Rome, by releasing without ransom all their prisoners whom he had taken. Wishing to give time for the disunion to take effect, he turned aside into Apulia, where he rested and recruited his troops worn by so many hardships.

It was already proved in three battles that the Carthaginian was irresistible in the field. The policy of Fabius, therefore, was to avoid a general engagement, while he annoyed and weakened his enemy by cutting off his foraging parties, and otherwise harassing his march. In vain Hannibal crossed the Apennines into the rich Campanian fields, plundering and destroying the crops; he could neither capture a town nor entice

Fabius into a battle. The latter fortified the Samnian mountain-passes, thinking to catch his enemy in a trap; but Hannibal eluded the snare and retired safe into Apulia, laden with abundant provision for the comfort of his winter-quarters.

103. Great discontent was felt at Rome with the cautious policy of the dictator, and, in the spring of 216 B. C., an army of nearly 90,000 men was led into Apulia by the two consuls Æmilius Paulus and Terentius Varro. They were met by Hannibal on the plain of the Aufidus, near the little town of Cannæ. The Carthaginians were inferior in numbers but superior in discipline, especially in the Numidian horsemen, who had always been victorious in an open field. Never had the Romans suffered so overwhelming a defeat. Their army was annihilated. From 40,000 to 50,000 men lay dead upon the plain, among whom were Æmilius the consul, eighty senators, and the flower of Roman knighthood. Varro, the other consul, with a small but resolute band, made his way in good order from the battle-field; the rest of the survivors were either dispersed or taken prisoners.

104. Southern Italy was now lost to Rome. Except the Roman colonies and the Greek cities held by Roman garrisons, all submitted to Hannibal. Capua opened her gates and became the winter-quarters of the African army. Philip of Macedon and Hieron′ymus of Syracuse made alliance with Carthage, and wars with these two powers divided the attention of the Romans. Still, beside keeping two armies in the foreign fields, they occupied every province of Italy with a separate force; and though too wise to meet Hannibal again in a general engagement, hemmed him in closely and cut off his supplies. The great general was now but faintly supported at home, and the ungenerous policy of Carthage probably deprived her of the conquest of Italy.

105. Three years, therefore, passed with no decisive events. In 212 B. C., Syracuse was taken by Marcellus after two years' siege. The attacks of the Romans had been long foiled by the skill of Archimedes, the philosopher, who is said to have burnt their ships at the distance of a bow-shot from the walls, by means of a combination of mirrors which concentrated the sun's rays. He constructed powerful engines, which, when attached to the walls, grappled the Roman ships and lifted them out of the water; and, in short, the brain of Archimedes was a better defense to Syracuse than the arms of all her soldiers. In the taking of the city, the philosopher was slain by some ignorant troopers; but Marcellus deeply regretted the event. He ordered him to be buried with high honors, and distinguished his family by many marks of friendship.

106. Hannibal had been long anxiously awaiting the arrival of his brother from Spain; but the generalship of the two Scipios, Cneius and Publius, who conducted the war in that country, and more especially the brilliant genius of the son of the latter, afterward known as Africanus, had detained Hasdrubal and involved him in many disasters, even the loss of his capital, Carthagena. At last, in 208 B. C., Hasdrubal left Spain to the care of two other generals, and striking out a new path, as his brother's route of eleven years before was now guarded by the Romans, he crossed the Pyrenees at their western extremity and plunged into the heart of Gaul. Many of the restless people flocked to his standard, and he "descended from the Alps like a rolling snow-ball, far greater than he came over the Pyrenees."

He found some of Hannibal's roads uninjured; the mountaineers made no effort to dispute his passage, and he arrived in Italy before he was expected, so that no Roman army was ready to receive him. He might, perhaps, have settled once for all the supremacy of Carthage by marching directly on Rome, for the resources of the Republic, both in men and money, had been drained to the utmost, and another Thrasymene or Cannæ would have ended her existence.

107. Hasdrubal lost time in the siege of Placentia, and his letter, describing to Hannibal his plan of operations, fell into the hands of Nero, the consul, who, by a rapid and secret march, joined his colleague at Sena with 7,000 men, leaving the main part of his army still facing Hannibal in the south. Hasdrubal was uninformed of the reinforcement of his enemy, but his quick ear caught one more trumpet-note than usual, at sunrise, in the Roman camp; and as he rode forth to reconnoiter, he discovered that the horses appeared over-driven, and the armor of the men stained. He therefore delayed until night-fall, and then moved to cross the river Metau′rus in search of a stronger position. But his guides betrayed him, and when morning dawned his worn and weary troops were still on the nearer side of the river, where they were soon overtaken by the foe. He made the best arrangement of his men which the crisis would admit, placing the ten elephants in front "like a line of moving fortresses," his veteran Spanish infantry on the right, the Ligurians in the center, and the Gauls on the left.

The battle was fiercely contested, for both armies felt that the decision of the day would be final, and that there was no hope for the vanquished. At last Nero, by a circuitous movement, fell upon the Spanish infantry, which had already borne the brunt of the fighting. Hasdrubal saw that the day was lost, and scorning to survive his men or to adorn a Roman triumph, he spurred his horse into the midst of a cohort, and died, sword in hand, B. C. 207.

108. The consul Nero returned to his camp before Hannibal had even discovered his absence. Hasdrubal's arrival in Italy, the battle and its result were first made known to the great general by seeing the ghastly head of his brother, which Nero had brutally ordered to be thrown within his lines. Hannibal read the tale of disaster in the terrible message, and groaned aloud that he recognized the fate of Carthage. Though he remained four years strongly posted in the mountain fastnesses of Bruttium, the issue of the war was already decided. In 204 B. C., the younger Scipio crossed into Africa, and the Carthaginians were compelled to recall Hannibal.

The final battle was fought at Zama, B. C. 202. The great Carthaginian displayed again his perfect generalship, but he had no longer his invincible cavalry, and his elephants were rendered useless by the skillful tactics of Scipio. He was defeated with the loss of 20,000 men slain, and an equal number of prisoners. The peace, concluded in the following year, took from Carthage all her possessions beyond the limits of Africa, and all the lands conquered from Numidia, whose king, Mas′sinis′sa, had rendered important aid to Scipio in the recent war. She surrendered, also, her fleet and elephants, promised a yearly tribute of 200 talents, and engaged to make no war without permission from Rome.

RECAPITULATION.

The First Punic War (B. C. 264-241) begins with the invasion of Sicily by the Romans, who are joined by many Greek cities, capture Messana and Agrigentum, equip a fleet upon a Carthaginian model, and gain many naval victories. They invade Africa, and ravage the lands of Carthage almost without opposition; but Xanthippus arrives with auxiliaries, defeats and captures Regulus. Five years of disaster to the Romans are followed by the great victory of Metellus at Palermo; and after eight years of again unsuccessful warfare, the victory of Lutatius among the Ægates ends the contest. During the peace which follows, Sardinia and Corsica are seized by the Romans, and placed under proconsular government; the Illyrian pirates are subdued, B. C. 229, 228; Cisalpine Gaul conquered, B. C. 225-222. The Second Punic War is begun, B. C. 218, by Hannibal. He crosses the Pyrenees and Alps, defeats the Romans on the Ticinus and the Trebia, and still more disastrously near the Lake Thrasymene and at Cannæ. Syracuse, though defended by the science of Archimedes, is captured by Marcellus. The three Scipios make successful war in Spain. Hasdrubal comes at last to the relief of his brother, but is defeated and slain on the Metaurus, B. C. 207. Hannibal is recalled to Africa, and finally defeated at Zama by Scipio Africanus, B. C. 202.

Extension of Roman Power.

109. A triumph was awarded to Scipio, who was received at Rome with unbounded enthusiasm. The *Triumph,* which was the highest reward a Roman general could attain, may here be described once for all. The victorious chief waited without the walls until the Senate had decided upon his claim to the honor. Several conditions were to be observed: the victory must have been over foreign and not domestic foes; it must have been, not the recovery of something lost, but an actual extension of Roman territory; the war must be completed and the army withdrawn from the field, for the soldiers were entitled to a share in the triumph of their general. The honor was limited to persons of consular or, at least, prætorian rank; an officer of lower grade might receive an *ovation*, in which he entered the city on foot, but the chariot was a mark of kingly state which could only be permitted to the highest.

110. If a triumph was decreed, a special vote of the people continued to the general his military command for the day within the walls, for without a suspension of the law, he must have laid it down on entering the gates. On the appointed day, he was met at the Triumphal Gate by the Senate and all the magistrates, in splendid apparel. Taking the lead of the procession, they were followed by a band of trumpeters, and a train of wagons laden with the spoils of the conquered countries, which were indicated by tablets inscribed in large letters with their names. Models in wood or ivory of the captured cities; pictures of mountains, rivers, or other natural features of the regions subdued; loads of gold, silver, precious stones, vases, statues, and whatever was most rich, curious, or admirable in the spoils of temples and palaces, made an important part of the display. Then came a band of flute players, preceding the white oxen destined for sacrifice, their horns gilded and adorned with wreaths of flowers and fillets of wool. Elephants and other strange animals from the conquered countries, were followed by a train of captive princes or leaders with their families, and a crowd of captives of inferior rank, loaded with fetters.

Then came the twelve lictors of the imperator in single file, their fasces wreathed in laurel; and, lastly, the triumphant general himself, in his circular chariot drawn by four horses. His robes glistened with golden embroidery; he bore a scepter, and upon his head was a wreath of Delphic laurel. A slave standing behind him held a crown of Etruscan gold; he was instructed to whisper from time to time in his master's ear, "Remember that thou art but a man." Behind the general rode his sons and lieutenants, and then came the entire army, their spears adorned with laurels—who either sang hymns of praise, or amused themselves and the by-standers with coarse jokes and doggerel verses at their general's expense. This rude license of speech was thought to neutralize the effect of overmuch flattery, which the Romans, like the modern Italians, were taught especially to dread. All the people, in gala dress, thronged the streets, and every temple and shrine were adorned with flowers.

111. As a terrible contrast to the joy of the day, just as the procession had nearly finished its course to the Capitol, some of the captured chiefs were led aside and put to death. When their execution was announced, the sacrifices were offered in the temple of the Capitoline Jupiter; the laurel crown of the general was placed in the lap of the image; a magnificent banquet was served, and the "triumphator" was escorted home, late in the evening, by a crowd of citizens bearing torches and pipes. The state presented him a site for a house, and at the entrance to this triumphal mansion, a laurel-wreathed statue of its founder perpetuated the memory of his glory to his latest descendants.

112. Carthage being stripped of her power and possessions, Rome became supreme in the western Mediterranean and the greater part of Spain. The confiscated lands of the Italian nations which had taken sides with Hannibal, afforded settlements for large bodies of veteran soldiers. The Cisalpine Gauls were still in revolt, under the lead of a Carthaginian general; but they were reduced by a ten years' war (B. C. 201–191), and afterward became Latinized with that wonderful facility which distinguishes their race.

113. The Alexandrine kingdoms in the East were all prematurely old and falling into decay. The campaigns of Flamininus against Philip of Macedon, B. C. 198, 197, have been already described. (See Book IV, §§ 81–83.) A new war for the protectorate of Greece was occasioned by the movements of Antiochus the Great. This ambitious and restless monarch not only welcomed to his court the now exiled Hannibal, but allied himself with the Ætolians and led an army to their aid. He had miscalculated the power of Rome, which met him promptly with much more than twice his numbers, defeated him once by land and twice by sea, and finally, in the great battle of Magnesia, in Lydia, shattered his forces, while beginning her own long career of Asiatic conquest. The lands conquered from Antiochus were divided between the friendly powers of Pergamus and Rhodes, and the example of their good fortune led many other nations to seek the Roman alliance.

114. For more than twenty years, Rome was occupied with continual wars in the west, against the brave and freedom-loving tribes of Spain and the Ligurian Alps, as well as with the natives of Corsica and Sardinia. The latter island was conquered, B. C. 176, by Sempronius Gracchus, who brought away so great a multitude of captives, that "Sardinians for sale" became a proverbial phrase in Rome for anything cheap and worthless.

Meanwhile, Philip V. had died in Macedon, and Perseus had succeeded to the throne. The final struggle of this prince with Rome, and its result in the battle of Pydna (B. C. 168), have been described in Book IV. Rome became for six centuries what Macedon had been only during one man's short career, the undisputed ruler of the civilized world. None except barbarians any longer hoped to resist her ascendency; and but for a few revolts, like those of the Achæans, the Carthaginians, and the Jews, her progress in absorbing the old states of Asia, Africa, and Europe was both peaceful and rapid.

115. After eighteen years of comparative tranquillity, it was resolved that the time had come for the complete extinction of Carthage. Cato, the censor, now eighty-four years of age, and the sternest of Roman legislators, declared that Rome could never be safe while her former rival was so near, so hostile, and so strong; and whenever he was called upon for his vote in the Senate, whatever might be the subject of debate, his unvarying reply was, "I vote that Carthage no longer be." The doomed city had more than fulfilled every condition of the treaty which closed the First Punic War, and still made many sacrifices for the sake of peace. But the last command of Rome was not intended to be obeyed. The Carthaginians were ordered to destroy their city, and remove to a situation farther from the sea. They refused, and a war began, in which, for four years, the brave spirit of the people sustained them without the faintest hope of victory.

116. Their fleet, their weapons, and their mines in Spain, Sardinia, and Elba had all been surrendered to the enemy. In two months 120 ships were built in the blockaded port, and a passage cut through the land to enable them to reach the sea. Public buildings were torn down to furnish timber and metal. Every living being toiled night and day at the defenses. An arsenal was established which daily produced 2,000 shields or weapons, and even the women contributed their long hair to make strings for the engines which hurled stones or arrows from the walls.

At length the Romans, under the consul Scipio Æmilia′nus, forced their way into the city. The people defended it house by house, and street by street, and days of carnage were still required to quench the pride of Carthage in ashes and blood. The city was fired in all directions, and when, after seventeen days, the flames were at last extinguished, nothing remained but shapeless heaps of rubbish. The territories of the Punic state became the "Province of Africa," whose capital was fixed at Utica. Roman traders flocked to the latter city, and took into their own hands the flourishing commerce of the coast.

117. In the same year, B. C. 146, L. Mum′mius, the consul, plundered and destroyed Corinth. Its walls and houses were leveled with the ground, and a curse was pronounced on whomsoever should build on its desolate site. Its commerce passed to Argos and Delos, while the care of the Isthmian Games was intrusted to Sicyon. The policy of Rome toward the Greeks was far more liberal than toward any other conquered people. Her firm and settled government was, indeed, preferable to the dissension and misrule which disfigured the later ages of Greece; and the Greeks themselves declared, in the words of Themistocles, that "ruin had averted ruin."

118. The natives of western Spain, intrenched among their mountains, still maintained a brave resistance to the power of Rome. The Lusitanians, who had never yet been conquered, were basely deceived by Serto′rius Galba, who enticed 7,000 of them from their strongholds by promising grants of fertile lands; and when, trusting the word of a Roman general, they had descended into the plain, he caused them to be treacherously surrounded, disarmed, and either massacred or enslaved.

Among the few who escaped was a youth named Viria′thus, who lived to become the leader and avenger of his people. The career of this guerrilla chief is full of stirring events. Issuing suddenly from a cleft in the mountains, he seven times defeated a Roman army with tremendous slaughter. In the last of these victories, the forces of Servilia′nus were entrapped in a narrow pass and completely surrounded. Absolute surrender was their only choice. Viriathus, however, preferring peace to vengeance, used his advantage with great moderation. He allowed his enemy to depart unhurt, on his solemn engagement to leave the Lusitanians henceforth unmolested in their own territories, and to recognize him, their chief, as a friend and ally of the Roman people.

119. The terms were ratified by the Senate, but only to be violated. On the renewal of the war, Viriathus sent three of his most trusted friends to remonstrate, and offer renewed terms of peace. The consul bribed these messengers, by promises of large rewards, to murder their chief. The crime was committed, and within a year Lusita′nia (Portugal) was added to the Roman dominions. Numantia, in the north, still held out against the besieging army of Qu. Pompe′ius. A severe winter caused great sickness and suffering in the legions, and Pompey offered peace on terms favorable to the Spaniards, but, according to Roman ideas, disgraceful to the besiegers. These were accepted, and the last payment but one had been made by the Numantines, when Pompey's successor in the consulship arrived at the camp. Being thus relieved from command, he denied that he had ever made the treaty, and persisted in his falsehood before the Senate.

The war went on six years, with no credit and frequent disgrace to the Romans, until Scipio Æmilianus, the greatest general of his own time, starved the city at last into surrender. Many of the Numantines, rather than fall into the hands of an enemy whose falsehood they had too often proved, set fire to their houses and perished among the burning ruins. The whole peninsula, except its northern coast, was now subject to Rome. It was divided into three provinces — Hither and Farther Spain, and Lusitania — and became eventually the most prosperous and best governed part of the Roman foreign possessions. The Lusitanian mountains were still haunted by brigands, and isolated country houses in that region had to be built like fortresses; yet the country was rich in corn and cattle, and occupied by a thriving and industrious people.

RECAPITULATION.

Rome, supreme in the western Mediterranean, makes war upon Philip V., of Macedon, and Antiochus the Great, of Syria. The battle of Magnesia, B. C. 190, lays the foundation of her power in Asia, and the battle of Pydna makes her the head of the civilized world. In the meanwhile, Sardinia is conquered, and wars carried on in Spain and Liguria. The third and last Punic War ends,

B. C. 146, with the destruction of Carthage. The same year, Corinth is destroyed by Mummius. Viriathus holds out nine years in western Spain; he is assassinated B. C. 140; Numantia is captured B. C. 133; and Spain divided into three Roman provinces.

FOURTH PERIOD, B. C. 133–30.

120. The possessions of Rome now extended from the Atlantic to the Ægean, and from the Atlas Mountains to the Pyrenees and Alps. But changes in the relations of rich and poor, governing and governed classes, in her own capital, now withdrew her attention for a while from foreign conquests, and led to important civil controversies. The old strife between patricians and plebeians was long ago at an end. Many plebeian houses had become noble through their members having held high offices in the state; and they had their clientage, their share in the public lands, their seat in the Senate, and their right of displaying waxen images of their ancestors in their houses or in funeral processions, equally with the oldest burghers of all. Freedmen were constantly admitted to the franchise.

121. The real cause of trouble was in the sufferings of the poor, who, since the formation of the last colony, in 177 B. C., had had no new allotment of lands. Rome was a "commonwealth of millionaires and beggars." The Licinian laws (see § 64) were practically set aside. Many rich proprietors held four times the amount of public land to which they were entitled; and instead of employing the required proportion of free labor, preferred to cultivate by means of gangs of slaves. The foreign wars, which formerly so frightfully reduced* the numbers of the common people, had now ceased; the labor market became over-stocked, and a mass of paupers, hungry, helpless, and hopeless, began to threaten serious danger to the state. The multitude of slaves, chiefly taken in war, more or less trained for fighting, and conscious of their strength, were a not less dangerous class. The best and wisest of the Romans saw the danger, and sought means to avert it. But among those who most deeply deplored the miseries of the people, a large party believed that nothing could be done.

122. In 133 B. C., the tribune Tiberius Gracchus, a son of the conqueror of Sardinia, and grandson of Scipio Africanus, brought forward a bill for reviving the provisions of the Licinian laws. The great amount of state lands which would thus become vacant, he proposed to divide among the poor; and to compensate the former occupants for their losses, by making them absolute owners of the 500 jugera of land which they could legally retain. This movement, apparently so just, was violently opposed. The leased lands had been, in some instances, three hundred

---

* During the seventeen years of the Second Punic War, the free citizens of Rome were diminished by one-fourth, and in Italy at large 300,000 people perished.

years in the same family. Buildings had been erected at great expense, and the property had been held or transferred as if in real ownership. The strong influence of the wealthy class was therefore made to bear against the bill; and when it was brought before the popular assembly, Octa′vius, a colleague of Gracchus in the tribuneship, interposed his veto and prevented the vote from being taken. But Gracchus moved the people to depose Octavius, and so carried the bill. Three commissioners, Tiberius Gracchus himself, his brother Caius, and his father-in-law, Appius Claudius, were appointed to examine into the extent of the abuse, and enforce the Agrarian laws.

123. Their task was difficult, and Tiberius had to content the people by continually bringing forward more and more popular measures. The kingdom of Pergamus, with its treasury, had just become the inheritance of the Romans. Gracchus proposed that the money should be distributed among the new land-holders, to provide implements and stock for their farms. Other proposals were for shortening the term of military service, for extending the privilege of jury to the common people, and for admitting the Italian allies to the rights of Roman citizens. The aristocratic party had declared from the beginning that this bold innovator should not escape their vengeance. His candidacy for a second tribuneship brought the opposition to a crisis. Tiberius was slain upon the steps of the Capitol, and his body thrown into the Tiber.

124. Though the reformer was dead, his reform went on. The party in power earnestly desired to relieve the public danger and distress, and, by order of the Senate, the commission continued the distribution of lands. A law proposed by Scipio Æmilianus, B. C. 129, withdrew the work from the hands of the commissioners, and placed it permanently in those of the consuls. The lands which were really public property were by this time distributed, and questions had arisen concerning territories which had been granted to Italian allies. "The greatest general and the greatest statesman of his age," Scipio saw as clearly and lamented as deeply as the Gracchi the needs of his country, and, with unselfishness equal to theirs, he sought to check the reform, when convinced that it had gone as far as justice would permit. But he, too, became a martyr to his efforts. Soon after the passage of his bill, and on the morning of the day appointed for his oration upon popular rights, he was found murdered in his bed.

125. Caius Gracchus returned from his quæstorship in Sardinia, B. C. 124, and became tribune of the people. His plans for relieving the poorer classes were more revolutionary than those of his brother, but many of them were most beneficent and widely reaching in their results. Colonies were formed, both in Italy and beyond the sea, to afford an outlet to the crowded and distressed population of Rome. Six thousand colonists were sent to the deserted site of Carthage; another company to Aquæ Sextiæ

(Aix), in southern Gaul; and a third, with the full "Roman right," to Narbo Martius (Narbonne′). The latter colony, though not founded until after the death of Caius, was equally a fruit of his policy. It was fostered by the commercial class, for the sake of its lucrative trade with Gaul and Britain.

A less beneficent though doubtless needed law, provided for the distribution of grain from the public stores, at less than half price, to all residents in the city who chose to apply for it. An extensive range of buildings, the Sempronian granaries, were erected to supply this demand. The result was the crowding within the walls of Rome of the whole mass of poor and inefficient people from the surrounding country, thus giving to the popular leaders a majority in the assembly, and the absolute control of the elections; creating, at the same time, that lazy, hungry, and disorderly mob which for five hundred years constituted the chief danger of the imperial city.

126. The lowest age for military service was fixed at seventeen years, and the cost of the soldier's equipment, which formerly had been deducted from his wages, was now defrayed by the government. Having thus won the poorer people, Caius drew to his side the plebeian aristocracy, by placing in their hands the collection of revenues in the provinces, thus creating the class of great merchants and bankers, hitherto scarcely known in Rome. The new "province of Asia" had been formed from the kingdom of Pergamus, and its name, like that of "Africa" given to the Carthaginian territory, doubtless implied that its limits were not considered as fixed. In accordance with the despotic principle that conquered or inherited lands were the private property of the state, the province was now loaded with taxes, and the privilege of collection was publicly sold at Rome to the highest bidder. The "publicans" amassed great fortunes, but the unhappy provincials were reduced to extreme distress.

127. Gracchus would have gone a step farther, and extended the full rights of Roman citizenship to all free Italians. But this liberal policy was equally hateful to the Senate and the commons. The former gained over his colleague, Liv′ius Drusus, who outbade Gracchus by proposing still more popular measures, which, however, were never meant to be fulfilled. Instead of two Italian colonies, composed only of citizens of good character, which had been planned by Gracchus, Drusus proposed twelve, to contain 3,000 settlers each. Caius had left the domain lands subject, as of old, to a yearly rent. Drusus abolished this, and left the lessees in absolute possession of their farms.

At the end of the second year, Caius lost his tribuneship, and the new consuls were opposed to him. His policy was now violently attacked, and especially the formation of the transmarine colonies. It was reported that African hyenas had dug up the newly placed boundary stones of Juno′nia, the successor of Carthage; and the priests declared that the gods in this way signified their displeasure at the attempt to rebuild an accursed city. The auguries were taken anew; a popular tumult arose, in which an attendant of the priests was killed. The next day the Forum was occupied by an armed force, and all the aristocratic party appeared with swords and shields. Caius and his former colleague, Ful′vius Flaccus, retired with their followers to the Aventine, the old stronghold of the commons. The nobility, with their Cretan mercenaries, stormed the mount; 250 persons of humble rank were slain, and the two leaders were pursued and put to death. Three thousand of their adherents were strangled in prison, by order of the Senate. Cornelia,* the mother of the Gracchi, was not permitted to wear mourning for the last and noblest of her sons; but the people honored their memory with statues, and on the sacred ground where they had fallen, sacrifices were offered as in temples of the gods.

128. Next to Egypt, the most important client-state of Rome was Numidia, which occupied nearly the same space with the modern province of Algeria. Massinissa, the Numidian king, had been rewarded for his faithful service in the Second Punic War, by a grant of the greater part of the Carthaginian territories. Micip′sa, his son, was now a feeble old man, who cared more for Greek philosophy than for affairs of state, and had dropped the control of his kingdom into the hands of his nephew, Jugur′tha, whom he raised by adoption to a level with his own sons. In his will he divided the civil, military, and judicial offices of the kingdom between the three princes.

After the old king's death, his sons, Adher′bal and Hiemp′sal, disputed the will, while Jugurtha boldly claimed the supreme and sole authority. Hiempsal was murdered by hired ruffians. Adherbal appealed in person to the Roman Senate, which had undertaken to guarantee his father's bequests. But Jugurtha had learned in the camps that every senator had his price; and his emissaries worked so skillfully, that the whole blame of the dispute and the murder was thrown upon the suppliant prince. A new division of the kingdom was ordered to be made, by Roman commissioners sent over for the purpose. Jugurtha received the fertile and populous region

* This illustrious lady was a daughter of Scipio Africanus, the greatest general save one, and, perhaps, the greatest character, whom Rome ever produced. Cornelia, after the early death of her husband, devoted herself to the education of her children, and was rewarded for her care by their perfect respect and love. After the death of Caius, she retired to Misenum, where her house became the resort of all the genius and learning of the age. Cornelia not only spoke her own language with the utmost elegance, but was well acquainted with Greek literature, and her letters to her sons are considered the purest specimens of Latin prose. She died in a good old age, and the people erected a statue to her memory, with the simple inscription, "Cornelia, the Mother of the Gracchi."

which was afterward known as Mauritania; Adherbal, with Cirta, the capital, had only a tract of sandy desert toward the east.

129. Jugurtha, however, was not satisfied; and failing by many insults to provoke his cousin to war, he at last besieged him in his capital, and in spite of lame remonstrances from Rome, captured and put him to death with cruel tortures, and ordered an indiscriminate massacre of all the inhabitants of the town. Of these, many were Italians. Even the base venality of the Roman government could no longer withstand the righteous indignation of the people. War was declared and an army promptly sent forward, which received the submission of many Numidian towns. But again the wily usurper was able to buy peace with African gold. He pretended to submit at discretion, but was re-instated in his kingdom upon paying a moderate fine and surrendering his war elephants, which he was soon permitted to redeem. Public indignation again broke out at Rome. Jugurtha was summoned to the city, to answer concerning the means by which he had obtained the peace. His cousin, Massi′va, took this opportunity to prefer his own claim to the kingdom of Massinissa; but he was assassinated by a confidant of Jugurtha, who immediately, with the aid of his master, escaped from Rome.

130. This new insult enraged the people beyond endurance. The Senate canceled the peace and dismissed Jugurtha from the city. His sarcastic remark in leaving expressed a melancholy truth: "If I had gold enough, I would buy the city itself." The war was renewed, but the army, equally demoralized with its chiefs, was wholly unfit for service. In attempting to besiege the treasure-town of Suthul, the incompetent commander suffered himself to be drawn off into the desert, where his whole army was routed and made to pass under the yoke. By the terms of surrender, Numidia was evacuated and the canceled peace renewed. The generals whose misconduct had led to this disgrace were tried at Rome and exiled, and with them Opim′ius, the head of the Numidian commission, and the real executioner of Caius Gracchus.

In token of the earnestness with which the war was now to be carried on, Qu. Metellus, a stern and upright patrician of the old school, was elected consul for the African campaign. Among his lieutenants was Caius Marius, the son of a Latin farmer, who had risen from the ranks by his sterling ability. He won the hearts of the soldiers by voluntarily sharing all their toils and privations; and through their reports to friends at home, his praise was in every mouth.

131. The wild tribes of the desert flocked to the standard of Jugurtha, whom they hailed as their deliverer from Roman domination; and with his swarms of fleet horsemen, he was able either to dictate the battle-field, or to vanish out of sight at any moment, when the combat seemed to be going against him. The Romans gained one or two victories, but no real advantage. An impression, doubtless false and unjust, sprang up at Rome, that the inaction of Metellus, like the reverses of his predecessors, was owing to a secret understanding with Jugurtha — or, at least, that he was prolonging the war to gratify his own love of power.

Availing himself of this prejudice, Marius returned to Rome, and was elected consul for the year 107 B. C. Instead of having his province allotted by the Senate, he was appointed by the people to the command in Africa. His election was really a revolution which gave power in the state to military talent, rather than to great wealth or noble birth. His quæstor in this expedition was L. Cornelius Sulla, a young nobleman distinguished chiefly hitherto by his unbounded licentiousness, but who, by energetic application to his duties, soon won the entire confidence and approbation of his commander. These two men stood, a few years later, in very different relations to each other, as alternate masters of the Roman world.

132. In spite of some daring adventures and the capture of several towns, the administration of Marius was not much more successful than that of Metellus. He continued in command as proconsul for the year 106 B. C.; and during the second winter, the real victory was gained by Sulla, who passed through the enemy's camp at great personal risk, and with consummate skill conducted a negotiation with King Bocchus, of Mauritania, for the surrender of Jugurtha. This notorious criminal was brought in chains to Rome, where, with his two sons, he adorned the triumph of Marius, Jan. 1, B. C. 104. A few days later, he perished with hunger in the lower dungeon of the Mamertine prison. A new peril now threatened Rome, and demanded unusual measures. In spite of a law to the contrary, Marius was reëlected to the consulship, and continued to hold that office five successive years, B. C. 104–100.

133. The Cimbri, a mingled horde of Celtic and Germanic tribes, had been dislodged in some unknown manner from their seats beyond the Danube, and were pressing upon the Roman frontier. Before the close of the Jugurthine War, they had four times defeated consular armies in Gaul and the Alpine regions. In the last of these defeats, at Orange, on the Rhone (B. C. 105), an army of 80,000 men had been destroyed, and all Italy was filled with terror. A new army was now on foot, and Marius, with his legate, Sulla, and many other able officers, hastened into Gaul. The Cimbri had turned aside into Spain, where, however, they met a brave resistance, and were soon driven back across the Pyrenees. In western Gaul nothing was able to resist their rapid course of conquest, until they arrived at the Belgian territory beyond the Seine. They were joined by a kindred tribe of Teuto′nes from the shores of the Baltic, and by three cantons of Helve′tii from the mountains of Switzerland. They now arranged a combined invasion of Italy, the Teutones to enter that country from Roman Gaul by the western passes of the Alps, while the Cimbri were to traverse the eastern passes from Switzerland.

134. It was the object of the consuls to prevent their junction, and for this purpose Marius awaited the Teutones on the Rhone, near its confluence with the Is'ara, while Catulus marched into northern Italy to meet the Cimbri. One of the greatest victories ever won by Roman arms was gained by the former, near Aix, B. C. 102. Three successive days the barbarians had assaulted the Roman camp, when, despairing of success, they resolved to leave it behind and continue their march into Italy.

Distrusting his new recruits, Marius would not suffer his men to be drawn from their intrenchments until the entire host had departed; and so great were the numbers, and so cumbrous the baggage of the barbarians, that they were six days in passing the Roman works. When they were gone, Marius broke up his camp and started in pursuit, still maintaining perfect order, and intrenching himself carefully every night. In the neighborhood of Aix he overtook the Teutones, and the pitched battle which was then fought ended in the complete destruction of the nation. The warriors who survived the combat put an end to their own lives; and their wives, preferring death to slavery, followed their example.

135. Meanwhile, the other division, less ably resisted, had advanced through the Brenner Pass and routed the army of Catulus near Trent. But the comfort and plenty of the Lombard plain were, for the moment, a better protection to Rome than the wisdom of her generals. The Cimbri went into winter-quarters, and Marius had time to recruit his army and hasten to join his colleague in the spring of 101 B. C. When the Cimbri ascended the valley of the Po, hoping to effect the proposed junction with their Teutonic comrades, they met, instead, the combined armies of Marius and Lutatius. The battle was fought at Vercel'læ, westward of Milan, July 30, 101 B. C. The barbarians were wholly defeated, and either slaughtered or enslaved; 14,000 were left dead upon the battle-field, and 60,000 were transferred to the slave-markets of Rome.

136. Marius was received at Rome with a brilliant triumph, in which he was hailed as a third Romulus and a second Camillus, and his name in libations was coupled with those of the gods. The common people rejoiced scarcely more for the victory over the barbarians than for that over the government. The triumph of their chosen general, the farmer's boy of Arpi'num, seemed to them a triumph of the untitled and unprivileged masses over the rich and favored few. Marius was elected to his sixth consulate, and if he had been as great a statesman as general, the Republic might even then have been exchanged for a monarchy.

But he had no matured policy, and no skill in adapting means to ends. He allied himself with two unprincipled demagogues, Saturni′nus and Glau′cia, to secure his election, and then abandoned them to the vengeance of the Senate, when their crimes had become too bold for endurance.

The government candidate for the consulship was assailed and beaten to death; and the party which procured the murder, proclaiming Saturninus its chief, broke open the prison doors and gave freedom and arms to both prisoners and slaves. This armed rabble fought the guards of Marius in the very market-place of the city; but it was driven at length to the Capitol, cut off from water, and forced to surrender. Without waiting the forms of trial, some young nobles climbed to the roof of the building where the rioters were imprisoned, tore off the tiles, and stoned them to death. In this disgraceful manner perished four high officers of the Roman people: a prætor, a quæstor, and two tribunes.

137. The beautiful island of Sicily was a second time the scene of a servile war, B. C. 102–99. Its fertility and importance as a grain market to Rome had attracted speculators, who farmed their vast estates by means of multitudes of slaves. In the First Servile War (B. C. 134–132), 200,000 rebels were in arms; the second taxed the best exertions of three successive consuls, and though it was ended, B. C. 99, in victory to Rome, the terror it had excited did not soon die away. The slaves not only outnumbered the ruling class, but surpassed it in strength, and even, in some rare instances, in military talent. They were treated with such inhuman cruelty, that they never lacked a motive for revolt, and thus the rural districts were always liable to outbreaks when the governing force was removed.

The Roman slave-code, it may be hoped, has never been equaled in barbarity by that of any civilized state. The slave was "nothing" in law; his master might torture or kill him with no other punishment than the loss of his property; and when, after such a victory as that of Vercellæ, captives could be bought, as we are told, for less than a dollar a head, that motive could have had no weight against the passion of revenge. Happily, society is sometimes better than its laws. Household servants commonly enjoyed the confidence and affection of their masters; physicians and teachers were usually Greek slaves, and their learning and talents caused them to be respected in spite of the misfortune of their condition.

RECAPITULATION.

Though plebeians enjoy political equality, the poor suffer for want of land and employment. Tiberius Gracchus passes the Agrarian laws, but becomes a martyr to his zeal for reform. Scipio Æmilianus, trying to moderate the Agrarian movement, is also murdered. Caius Gracchus founds colonies in Italy and abroad; provides for the poor by a public distribution of grain; gives to the rich plebeians the collection of provincial revenues, and thus creates a class of great bankers and publicans. He is opposed with armed violence and slain, B. C. 121. The crimes of Jugurtha occasion the Numidian war, B. C. 111-106. Metellus is succeeded in command by Marius, who becomes consul, B. C. 107. Jugurtha is captured by the address of Sulla. Marius defeats the Teutones in a great battle near Aix, B. C. 102; and the Cimbri, the next year, at Vercellæ. A sedition at Rome is followed by the death of several magistrates. Sicily is twice devastated by servile insurrections, B. C. 134-132, and B. C. 102-99.

The Social War.

138. Meanwhile, Rome was shaken by the efforts and death of another reformer, M. Livius Drusus, son of the opponent of Gracchus. As a noble, he was filled with shame for the corruptions of his order, and sought to revive the safest and best of the laws of the Gracchi, by giving the franchise to all Italians, and by taking the judicial power from the knights, who had greatly abused it. He was murdered at his own door by an unknown assassin, B. C. 91, and both of his laws repealed. The allies in the south and center of Italy, disappointed in all their hopes by the death of their champion, now flew to arms. Eight nations, the Marsi, Marrucini, Peligni, Vestini, Picenti′ni, Samnites, Apu′li, and Lucani, formed a federal republic under the name of *Italia*, chose two consuls, and fixed their capital at Corfin′ium, in the Apennines.

The first movements in the "Social War" were disastrous to Rome. L. Cæsar, the consul, Perper′na, his legate, and Postu′mius, a prætor, were defeated. A consular army under Cæpio was destroyed; Campania was overrun, and the northern Italians were almost ready to join the league. But a late concession saved Rome. The coveted rights of citizenship were conferred on all who had taken no part in the war, and on all who would now withdraw from it. The confederate ranks were thus divided; and, at length, even the Samnites and Lucanians, who were the last to submit, were won by a promise of all that they had asked.

139. The slow and cautious conduct of Marius in this war had been eclipsed by the brilliant activity of Sulla, who was now consul; and the Senate, choosing to consider the old general unequal to the hardships of a campaign, conferred the command against Mithridates upon the young patrician officer. The jealousy which had long ago supplanted the ancient confidence between Marius and Sulla, now broke out into violent opposition. To defeat his rival, Marius persuaded Rufus, the tribune, to propose a law for distributing the newly enfranchised Italians among all the tribes. The old citizens would thus be greatly outnumbered, and the appointment of Sulla reversed, for all the new voters regarded Marius as their friend and benefactor. The consuls interfered, but Marius and his ally occupied the Forum with an armed force, compelled the consuls to withdraw their interdict, passed the law by intimidation, and easily obtained a vote of the tribes appointing Marius to the command of the Pontic War.

140. This brutal interference with the forms of law was naturally met by an opposing force. The military tribunes sent by Marius to take command, in his name, of the army at Nola, were stoned to death by the soldiers of Sulla, who instantly marched upon Rome at the head of six legions. The city was unprepared for resistance; Sulla became its master, and Marius, with his son and partisans, fled. He wandered, a fugitive and outlaw, along the coast of southern Italy; now half starved in a wood, now buried all night to his chin in a swamp; again indebted for a few hours' sleep to the charity of a ship-master or to a peasant, who refused the reward offered by Sulla for the head of the outlaw, and enabled him to elude his pursuers.

At Mintur′næ he was sheltered by a woman to whom he had formerly rendered some kindness; but the officers of the town resolved to comply with the orders of the government at Rome, and with difficulty prevailed upon a Gallic or Cimbrian soldier to undertake the work of despatching him. But no sooner had the barbarian entered the room where the old general, unarmed and defenseless, lay upon a bed, than his courage failed, his drawn sword fell from his hand, and he rushed from the house, exclaiming, "I can not kill Caius Marius!"

141. The people of Minturnæ now took more generous counsel, and resolved not to destroy the deliverer of Italy. They provided him with a ship, and conducted him with good wishes to the sea, where he embarked for Africa. Here, too, he was warned by the governor to leave the country, or be treated as an enemy of Rome. But a revolution had by this time taken place in Rome itself, which favored the return of Marius. Cinna, one of the new consuls, was of the Marian party, and wished to enforce the laws of Rufus. The aristocrats armed, under the command of the other consul, Octavius, and a battle was fought in the Forum, in which Cinna was defeated and expelled from the city. Like Sulla, he appealed to the army; and as the army was now composed of Italians, who could not but favor that party which promised them supreme power in the Roman elections, the tide was turned against the aristocrats.

Marius returned, seized upon Ostia and other ports on the Latin coast, captured the corn ships, and thus starved Rome into surrender. This time the captured city was given up to a reign of terror. As Marius walked through the streets, his guards stabbed all persons whom he did not salute. Fresh lists were made out every day of those whom he either feared or hated, as victims for the dagger. Marius and Cinna declared themselves consuls for B. C. 86, in contempt of the usual form of election. But the unrelenting master of Rome did not long enjoy his seventh consulship, which he had all his life superstitiously expected, and now so unscrupulously obtained. He died on the eighteenth day of his magistracy, and in the seventy-first year of his age.

142. Sulla had brought the Mithridatic War to a victorious conclusion, having conducted five difficult and costly campaigns at his own expense, and recovered for Rome the revolted territories of Greece, Macedonia, and Asia Minor. But he never forgot that the Republic which he was serving had declared him a public enemy, confiscated his wealth, and murdered his best friends for their adherence to him. If his vengeance was delayed, it was only the more bitter and effectual. He now returned with a powerful army devotedly attached to his person, and laden with treasure collected from the conquered cities of Asia.

To disarm the enmity of the Italians, who formed the most valuable part of his opponents' forces, he proclaimed that he would not interfere with the rights of any citizen, old or new. He suffered no injury to be done to either the towns or fields of the Italians, and he made separate treaties with many of their cities, by which he guaranteed their full enjoyment of Roman privileges so long as they should favor his interests. The Samnites alone held out against Sulla, and in concert with the Marian party renewed their old hostilities. Cinna was murdered by his own troops, on his way to meet Sulla in Dalma′tia.

143. Landing at Brundis′ium, Sulla marched without opposition through Calabria, Apulia, and Campania; defeated one consul near Capua, and won over the entire army of the other by means of emissaries well supplied with gold. He was reinforced by three legions, under Cneius Pompey, and by the adherence of many distinguished citizens, among whom were Metellus Pius, Crassus, and Lucullus. He was still outnumbered by the Marians, who, in 82 B. C., brought into the field an army of 200,000 men, under the two consuls Papir′ius Carbo and the younger Marius. The latter was defeated, however, with great loss at Sacripor′tus, and took refuge in Præneste, where he had deposited his military chest, enriched by the treasures of the Capitoline temples. This town was blockaded, while Sulla marched upon Rome. Marius had secretly ordered his partisans in the city to put to death the most illustrious of the Cornelian faction; and thus perished the pontifex maximus, and many others whose sacred office or exalted character would, in more virtuous times, have made them secure from violence.

144. The army of Samnites and Lucanians, by the request of Marius, moved toward Rome, Telesi′nus, their leader, declaring that he would raze the city to the ground. A furious battle was fought near the Colline Gate, in which Sulla was victorious; and, with a cold-blooded ferocity too common in those fearful times, ordered 6,000 prisoners to be cut to pieces in the Campus Martius. Sulla was now master of Rome and of Italy, and his vengeance had begun. A "proscription list" of his enemies was exhibited in the Forum, and a reward of two talents was offered to all who would kill these outlawed persons, or even show the place of their concealment. As usual, private hatred and even the meanest avarice found indulgence under the name of political enmity. Any friend of Sulla was permitted to add names to the list; and as the property of the proscribed usually went to his accuser, the possession of a house, a field, or even a piece of silver plate was often enough to mark a man as a public enemy.

Sulla was appointed dictator, with unlimited power to "restore order to the Republic." The constitutional changes which he made, were designed to re-instate the Senate and nobles in the preëminence which they had enjoyed in the earliest years after the expulsion of the kings. He limited the sway of the tribunes of the people, and lowered the dignity of their office by prohibiting those who had held it from becoming consuls. Though himself a man of dissolute morals, Sulla clearly saw that the worst miseries of the Roman people proceeded from their own corruption, and he tried to check luxury and crime by the most stringent enactments. But the attempt was hopeless; the character of the nation was so far degraded that no rank or class was fit to rule, and its subjection to the will of a tyrant had become a necessity.

145. Sulla increased the number of the Senate by 300 new members chosen from the knights, all, of course, adherents of his own. He gained, also, a sort of body-guard, by giving the rights of citizenship to 10,000 slaves of those whom he had proscribed. These freedmen all received his own clan-name, Cornelius, and became his clients. He rewarded his veterans with the confiscated lands of the Marian party, thus replacing honest and industrious farmers with too often lawless and thriftless military communities. When Sulla had held the dictatorship three years, he surprised the world by suddenly resigning it, and retiring to his country-seat at Pute′oli. Here he devoted his days to the amusements of literature, mingled, unhappily, with less ennobling pleasures. He died B. C. 78, the year following his abdication. Two days before his death he completed the history of his own life and times, in twenty-two volumes, in which he recorded the prediction of a Chaldæan soothsayer, that he should die, after a happy life, at the very height of his prosperity.

146. A remnant of the Marian faction still held out in the west of Spain. Sertorius had been sent to command that province, chiefly because, as the most honest and keen-sighted of the Marians, he was troublesome to his brother officers. During the proscription by Sulla, he was joined by many exiles, who aided him in drilling the native troops. Though driven for a time into Africa by the proconsul An′nius, he returned, upon the invitation of the Lusitanians, with a Libyan and Moorish army, which defeated the fleet of Sulla in the Straits of Gibraltar, and his land forces near the Guadalquivir. All Roman Spain became subject to Sertorius. With the aid of Cilician pirates, he captured the islands of Ivi′ca and Formente′ra. He formed a government, in which the senate was composed only of Romans; but he distinguished the native Spaniards by many marks of favor, and won their confidence not only by his brilliant genius, but by his perfect justice in the administration of their affairs.

147. Metellus, Sulla's colleague in the consulship, who commanded his armies in Spain, was completely baffled by the unwearied activity and superior knowledge of the country displayed by Sertorius. At length Cneius Pompey, who had already, in his thirtieth year, gained the title of Great, and the honor of a triumph for his victories over the allies of the Marians in Africa, was sent into Spain with the title of proconsul, to share the command with Metellus. His military skill far surpassed that of his predecessors, but for five years the war was still dragged out with more loss and vexation than success.

At last, Sertorius was murdered by one of his own officers, a man of high birth, who envied the ascendency of genius and integrity, and hoped by removing his general to open the way to his own advancement. He was totally defeated and captured by Pompey in the first battle which he fought as commander-in-chief; and though he tried to save his life by giving up the papers of Sertorius, and thus betraying the secrets of his party in Rome, he was ordered to instant execution, B. C. 72.

148. The Spanish war was now ended, but a nearer and greater danger threatened Rome. The pride and luxury fed by foreign conquest had brought no increase of refinement to the common people; and their favorite amusement for festal days was to see the bravest captives, taken in war and trained for the purpose, slaughter each other in the amphitheater. The ædiles, who provided the public shows, vied with each other in the numbers and training of the gladiators, whom they either bought or hired from their owners for exhibition. Among the unhappy men who were under training in the school at Capua, was a Thracian peasant named Spar′tacus. His soul revolted against the beastly fate to which he was doomed, and he communicated his spirit to seventy of his comrades. Forcibly breaking bounds, they passed out at the gates of Capua, seized upon the road some wagon-loads of gladiators' weapons, and took refuge in an extinct crater of Vesuvius. They defeated 3,000 soldiers who besieged them, and armed themselves more effectively with the spoils of the slain.

Spartacus proclaimed freedom to all slaves who would join him. The half-savage herdsmen of the Bruttian and Lucanian mountains sprang to arms at his call, and the number of insurgents quickly rose to 40,000. They defeated two legions under the prætor Varinius, stormed and plundered Thurii and Metapon′tum, Nola and Nuce′ria, and many other towns of southern Italy. In the second year their forces were increased to 100,000 men, and they defeated successively two consuls, two prætors, and the governor of Cisalpine Gaul. All Italy, from the Alps to the Straits of Messana, quaked at the name of Spartacus, as it had done, more than a hundred years before, at that of Hannibal; but it only proved the decay of Roman character, that a mere bandit chief could accomplish what had once taxed the genius of the greatest general whom the world had yet produced.

149. Spartacus, however, saw clearly that in the end the organized power and resources of Rome must be superior to his own, and he only proposed to his followers to fight their way to and beyond the Alps, and then disperse to their homes; but the insurgents, spoiled with success, refused to leave Italy, and turned again to the south. Their winter-quarters, near Thurii, were like an immense fair crowded with the plunder of the whole peninsula, which merchants from far and near assembled to buy. Spartacus refused gold or silver, and took in exchange only iron or brass, which he converted into weapons of war by means of foundries established in his camp. In the panic which pervaded Rome, no one was willing to offer himself for the office of prætor. At length, Licinius Crassus accepted the appointment, and led eight legions into the field.

150. Spartacus was twice defeated, and driven to the southern point of Bruttium. Thence he tried to escape into Sicily, where the servile war was still smoldering and ready to be rekindled, and where, by holding the grain fields, he could soon have raised a bread-riot among the hungry mob of Rome. But the Cilician pirates, who had engaged to transport him, proved treacherous; and his attempt to convey his army across the straits on rafts and wicker boats was ineffectual. He then, in despair, broke the lines of Crassus, and once more threw Rome into great consternation.

But the same jealousies which had scattered the forces of Greeks and Romans, doomed the barbarians, also, to destruction. Thirty thousand Gauls separated themselves from Spartacus and his Thracians, and were totally destroyed near Crotona. The final encounter took place on the head-waters of the Silarus. Spartacus fell desperately fighting, and his army was destroyed. Only 5,000 of his men made their way to the north of Italy, where they were met by Pompey on his return from Spain, and all put to the sword. The 6,000 prisoners taken by Crassus were crucified along the Appian Way.

151. The two triumphant generals, Pompey and Crassus, demanded the consulship as their reward. To attain this, it was needful to set aside some of the Sullæan laws, for Pompey had neither reached the required age nor passed through the preliminary offices. But the deliverers of Rome could not ask in vain. On Dec. 31, B. C. 71, Pompey triumphed a second time for his victories in Spain; the next day, Jan. 1, B. C. 70, he entered on the duties of his consulship with Licinius Crassus. Though formerly a chief instrument of the oligarchy under Sulla, Pompey now attached himself to the democratic party, more especially to the wealthy middle class. He restored to the tribunes of the people the power which Sulla had taken away, and caused judges to be chosen no longer exclusively from the Senate, but in equal proportions from the Senate, the knights, and the tribunes of the treasury — a class of moneyed men who collected and paid the revenues due to the soldiers.

Reform in the government of the provinces was a rallying cry of the new party, and the year of Pompey's consulate was marked by the prosecution of Verres, ex-prætor of Syracuse, for his shameless robbery of the province of Sicily. The impeachment was conducted by Marcus Tullius Cicero, the great lawyer and orator, whose wonderful learning and eloquence had already made him illustrious. Cicero was allowed one hundred and ten days to collect evidence of Verres's guilt. In less than half the time he returned from Sicily, followed by a long train of witnesses, whose fortunes had been ruined by the fraud and inhumanity of the prætor. Verres himself had been heard to boast that he had amassed wealth enough to support a life-time of luxury, even if he should spend two-thirds of his ill-gotten gains in hushing inquiry or in buying a pardon; and the unhappy provincials plainly declared that, if he were acquitted, they would petition the Senate to repeal all the laws against official injustice, that in future their governors might, at least, only plunder to enrich themselves, and not to bribe their judges. But Verres was condemned, and not even awaiting his sentence, escaped with his treasures to Massilia.

152. At the end of his consulship, Pompey did not accept a province, but remained quietly in Rome, taking no part in public affairs. An increasing danger soon demanded the exercise of his talents. Since the destruction of the naval power of Carthage, Syria, and Egypt, the pirates of the Cilician coast had cruised unchecked throughout the Mediterranean, and had even been encouraged by Mithridates and Sertorius in their enmity against Rome. They captured the corn-ships, plundered the wealthiest cities, and even attacked Roman dignity in its most imposing form, by carrying off great magistrates, with their trains of attendants, from the Appian Way.

The crisis demanded extraordinary measures, and, in B. C. 67, Pompey was intrusted with absolute and irresponsible control of the Mediterranean, with a district extending fifty miles inland from its coasts, and with unlimited command of ships, money, and men. The price of provisions fell instantly upon his appointment, showing the confidence which his great ability had inspired. In forty days he had swept the western sea, and restored the broken communication between Italy, Africa, and Spain. Then sailing from Brundisium, he cleared the sea to the eastward, hunting the corsairs from all their inlets by means of the several squadrons under his fifteen lieutenants, and winning many to voluntary submission by his merciful treatment of the prisoners who fell into his hands.

The final battle took place near the Cilician coast, above which, on the heights of Mount Taurus, the pirates had placed their families and their plunder. They were defeated; 10,000 men were slain, their arsenals, magazines, and 1,300 vessels destroyed, while 400 ships and 20,000 prisoners were taken. Pompey showed no less wisdom in disposing of his captives than energy in defeating them. They were settled in isolated towns, and provided with honest employment; and as a result of the short and decisive conflict of three months, the Mediterranean remained safe and open to peaceful traffic for many years.

153. The Mithridatic War, though conducted with great ability by Lucullus, had become disastrous to the Romans; and a new law, proposed by Manil′ius, now extended Pompey's jurisdiction over all the forces in Asia, with power to make war, peace, or alliance with the several kings at his own discretion. Within a year, B. C. 66, he received the submission of the king of Armenia, and drove Mithridates beyond the Cau′casus. He deposed the last of the Seleucidæ, and placed Syria, as well as Pontus and Bithynia, under provincial management.

As centers of Roman or Greek civilization, he founded thirty-nine new cities, beside rebuilding or reviving many old ones. Among the former was Nicop′olis—"the city of victory"—which he caused to be built as a home for his veteran soldiers, on the site of the decisive overthrow of Mithridates. He subdued Phœnicia and Palestine, B. C. 63, captured the temple-fortress of Jerusalem by a siege of three months, and established Hyrcanus as "high priest and ruler of the people." The next year he returned to Italy in a long triumphal procession.

RECAPITULATION.

Death of Drusus is followed by the Social War, in the victorious ending of which Sulla gains great glory. Marius interferes by violence with his appointment to command in the war against Pontus. Sulla overpowers the city by his legions, and Marius becomes an exile. After Sulla's departure he returns, captures Rome, and massacres his opponents, but dies soon after the beginning of his seventh consulship. Sulla, returning triumphant from the East, defeats the new consuls and their allies, and by his proscriptions makes havoc with life and property at Rome. As dictator, he restores the aristocratic government of the early Republic. He dies in retirement, B. C. 78. Sertorius, ten years sovereign in Spain, is opposed by Pompey, and murdered, B. C. 72. War of the gladiators, under Spartacus, fills all Italy with terror, B. C. 73–71. It is ended by Crassus, who, with Pompey the Great, becomes consul for B. C. 70. Cicero impeaches Verres for extortion in Sicily. Pompey, intrusted with extraordinary powers by the Gabinian law, destroys the Cilician pirates; then completes the Pontic War, and establishes Roman dominion in western Asia.

Conquests of Julius Cæsar.

154. Rome, meanwhile, had narrowly escaped ruin from the iniquitous schemes of one of her own nobles. L. Ser′gius Catili′na, a man of ancient family, but worthless character and ruined fortunes, seized the time when all the troops were absent from Italy, to plot with other nobles, as wicked and turbulent as himself, for the overthrow of the government. The new consuls were to be murdered on the day of their inauguration. Catiline and Autro′nius were to take the supreme command in Italy, and Piso was to lead an army into Spain. The first plot failed through the imprudence of its leader; but a second, of still bolder and more comprehensive character, was formed. Eleven senators were drawn into the conspiracy; magazines of arms were formed, and troops levied in various parts of the peninsula. The wide-spread discontent of the people with the existing government aided the success of the movement; and, in the end, slaves, gladiators, and even criminals from the common prisons, were to be liberated and armed.

The secret was kept by a vast number of persons for eighteen months, but the main features of the plot were at length made known to Cicero, then consul, and by his vigilance and prudence it was completely foiled. He confronted Catiline in the Senate — where the arch conspirator had the boldness to take his usual place — with an oration, in which he laid open with unsparing vehemence the minutest circumstances of the plot. The convicted ringleader fled from Rome in the night, and placed himself at the head of his two legions, hoping yet to strike an effective blow before the levies ordered by the Senate could be fit for service. His chief accomplices were seized and strangled in prison, by order of the Senate, while he himself was followed and defeated in Etruria by the proconsul Antonius. The battle was decisive. Catiline fell fighting far in advance of his troops, and 3,000 of his followers perished with him. No free Roman was taken alive. B. C. 62.

155. Though this daring conspiracy was thus happily crushed, the weakness and disorder of society alarmed the best and wisest citizens. It was feared that some man of commanding talent might yet succeed where Catiline had failed, and overthrow the liberties of Rome. Pompey, now returning with his victorious legions from the East, was the immediate object of dread to the Senate and aristocratic party. But he quieted apprehension by disbanding his army as soon as he touched the soil of Italy, and proceeded slowly to Rome accompanied by only a few friends. They could not refuse his claim to a triumph, and from the number and extent of his victories, this pageant was the most imposing that Rome had ever seen. Although there was no army to lengthen the procession, it occupied two days in passing through the city. The inscriptions enumerated 22 kings and 12,000,000 of people as conquered; 800 ships, nearly 900 towns, and 1,000 fortresses taken; and the Roman revenues nearly doubled.

By an unusual act of clemency, Pompey spared the lives of all his captives, and dismissed to their homes all except Aristobulus, of Judæa, and the young Tigranes, of Armenia, who were detained lest they should stir up revolts in their respective countries. But though the aristocrats of the Senate had taken part in the public honors paid to Pompey, they could not forget that his appointment in the East had been in defiance of their opposition. His demands of allotments of land to his veterans, and for himself a second consulship and the ratification of his official acts, were refused; and Pompey, to redeem his pledges to his soldiers, now made an alliance with an abler man, and one far more dangerous to the old order of things—if the Senate could but have foreseen it—than himself. B. C. 60.

156. Caius Julius Cæsar had been proscribed in his eighteenth year, because he had refused to put away his young wife, Cornelia, the daughter of Cinna, at the command of Sulla. He was for a time a fugitive in danger of death, but his friends at length, with great difficulty, procured his pardon from the dictator, on the plea of his youth and insignificance. Sulla was more discerning; he remarked, "That boy will some day be the ruin of the aristocracy, for there are many Marii in him."

Upon the death of his aunt Julia, the widow of Marius, Cæsar defied the law which had pronounced her husband an enemy of the state, by causing his waxen image to be carried in the funeral procession. It was welcomed by the people with loud acclamations. In his ædileship, three years later—which, in the magnificence of the games celebrated, and the buildings erected at his own expense, surpassed all that had preceded it—Cæsar ventured upon a bolder step. He replaced in the Capitol, during one night, the statues of Marius, and the representations of his victories in Africa and Gaul, which had been removed by Sulla. When morning dawned, the common people and the veterans of Marius wept and shouted for joy at the re-appearance of the well-known features, and greeted Cæsar with rapturous applause. Though formally accused in the Senate of violating a law, he could not be condemned against the voice of the people.

157. Dignities and honors followed in rapid succession. He became pontifex maximus in 63 B. C.; prætor, in 62; and at the end of his prætorship he obtained the government of Farther Spain. In this first military command he acquired not only wealth for himself and his soldiers, but great reputation by subduing the Lusitanian mountaineers. On his return, he desired both a triumph and the consulship; but he could not obtain the one if he entered the city before it was decreed, nor the other without being personally present at the approaching election; so he abandoned the showy for the solid advantage, and was duly chosen consul, with Bib′ulus, a tool of the Senate, for his colleague.

158. He now managed to detach Pompey from the senatorial party, and form with him and Crassus a *triumvirate*, which, though only a secret agreement, not a public magistracy, ruled the Roman world for several years. The power of Crassus was due to his enormous wealth; that of Pompey, to his great military services; and that of Cæsar, to his unequaled genius and unbounded popularity. Their combined influence was soon felt in the official acts of Cæsar. He brought forward an Agrarian law for dividing the rich public lands of Campania among the poorest citizens. It was passed against the violent opposition of Bibulus and all the aristocratic party; a commission of twenty, with Pompey and Crassus at its head, was appointed to divide the lands, and the veterans thus obtained most of their claims.

The defeated consul, who had declared that he would rather die than yield, now shut himself up in his house, and never re-appeared in public until his year of office had expired. Cæsar obtained a ratification of all Pompey's acts in Asia, and, at the same time, attached the equites to his party, by giving them more favorable terms in farming the provincial revenues. At the close of his consulship he obtained the government of Illyricum and Gaul, on both sides of the Alps, for a term of five years, with a general commission to "protect the friends and allies of the Roman people."

159. The religious and national bond between the many Celtic tribes which inhabited the ancient territories of Britain, Belgium, France, Switzerland, and a part of Spain, was strong enough to unite them, now and then, in resistance to their common enemies, the Germans on the north and the Romans on the south, but not strong enough to prevent rivalries among themselves, which often gave the foreign power room to interfere in their affairs. The Roman province, founded B. C. 121, now extended northward along the Rhone as far as Geneva; and a great emigration of Germans had occupied territories west of the Rhine, from the neighborhood of the modern Strasbourg to the German Ocean.

160. During his first summer in Gaul, Cæsar, by the extraordinary swiftness and decision of his movements, subdued two nations and established

Roman supremacy in the center of the country. The Helvetii, who lived between Lake Geneva and the Jura, finding themselves in too narrow quarters, had resolved to emigrate and conquer new habitations to the westward. They burned their twelve towns and four hundred villages, and assembled at Geneva to the number of 368,000 persons, men, women, and children, intending to pass through the Roman province into western Gaul. Cæsar prevented this move by a wall nineteen miles in length, which he extended along the left bank of the Rhone; and bringing up three legions from Italy, he followed the Helvetians along their second route, and defeated them near Bibrac′te. The remnant of the nation — less than one-third of the number on their muster-rolls when the migration began — were ordered back to their native hills.

The Seq′uani, a Celtic tribe north of the Helvetii, had called in Ario-vis′tus, the most powerful of the German chiefs, against their rivals the Ædui, who were styled allies and kinsmen of the Romans. Having subdued the Ædui, Ariovistus turned upon his late allies, and demanded two-thirds of their lands in payment for his services. All the Gauls begged aid of Cæsar, who met the German prince near the Rhine, in what is now Alsace. So great was the fame of Ariovistus and his gigantic barbarians, who for fourteen years had not slept under a roof, that the Roman soldiers were afraid to fight; and though shamed out of their cowardice by the stirring appeal of their general, every man made his will before going into battle. The result of the combat was the complete destruction of the German host, only Ariovistus and a few followers escaping across the Rhine.

161. The second year, Cæsar conquered the Belgians north of the Seine, and the Senate decreed a public thanksgiving of fifteen days for the subjugation of Gaul. His lieutenant, Decimus Brutus, fought the first naval battle on the Atlantic, with the high-built sailing vessels of the Celts. The maritime tribes revolting the following winter, were subdued; and but for a few brief rebellions, the territories of France and Belgium remained under Roman dominion. Cæsar repaired each winter to his province of Cisalpine Gaul, to watch affairs in Italy. In 56 B. C., he had to reconcile Pompey with Crassus, and re-arrange, in his camp at Luca, the affairs of the triumvirate.

It was agreed that Pompey and Crassus should be consuls the next year, and that, after their term had expired, the former should govern Spain, and the latter Asia, while the proconsular government of Cæsar in Gaul should be prolonged to a second term of five years. In choosing the most arduous and least lucrative province for himself, Cæsar wished to begin the execution of his great scheme for civilizing the West, and organizing the whole Roman dominion into one compact state. The revolution begun by the Gracchi was not yet completed, and it was easy to see that the strife of parties must come again to the sword, as it had in the time of Marius and Sulla. In such a case, Cæsar desired to be near Italy, and to have an army trained to perfect discipline and devotion to himself.

162. In the fourth year, B. C. 55, he threw a bridge across the Rhine and invaded Germany. Late in the autumn, he made a reconnoitering expedition to Britain, and received hostages from the tribes. This time the Senate decreed twenty days' thanksgiving, though Cato stoutly insisted that Cæsar ought, rather, to be given up to the vengeance of the barbarians, to avert the anger of the gods for his having seized the German embassadors. The next year, B. C. 54, Cæsar again invaded Britain with five legions. Notwithstanding the brave resistance of a native chief, Cas′sivelau′nus, he penetrated north of the Thames, took hostages, and imposed tribute; but he left no military posts to hold the island in subjection.

A formidable revolt of the Gauls, the following winter, destroyed one of the six divisions of the Roman army, and imperiled another, commanded by Quintus Cicero, brother of the orator. Cæsar came to its relief, defeated 60,000 of the enemy, and restored quietness to the north. The Germans having aided in this revolt, he again crossed the Rhine near Coblentz, in the summer of 53 B. C. He fought no battles, for the people took refuge among their wooded hills; but the invasion served, as before, to make an imposing display of Roman power.

163. The following year, Gaul was every-where in a blaze of revolt, and the campaign was the most difficult and brilliant of all Cæsar's operations. Ver′cinget′orix, king of the Arver′ni, and the ablest of the Gallic chieftains, stirred up all the tribes, and nearly wrested the country from Roman control. While Cæsar was besieging him in Ale′sia, a Gallic army of more than a quarter of a million of men encamped around the Romans and besieged them in turn. But the genius of the proconsul surmounted even this crisis. He kept down all attempts at sortie, while he defeated the outer army; then forced the town to surrender, and captured Vercingetorix himself. Six years later, the Gallic chief adorned the triumph of Cæsar, and was then executed in the Mamertine prison at the foot of the Capitol. The Gauls now saw that resistance was hopeless. The firm and skillful management of Cæsar in pacifying the country and organizing the Roman rule, completed the work that his brilliant victories had prepared; and by the year 50 B. C., Gaul was at peace.

164. Meanwhile, Crassus, fearing that his colleagues would reap all the warlike glory of the league, undertook, after plundering the temples of the East, to make war against Parthia — a war unprovoked by the enemy, unauthorized by the Senate, and unwarranted by his own abilities. Contrary to advice, he plunged into the hot and sandy desert east of the Euphrates, lost the greater part of his army in a battle near Carrhæ (the Haran of Abraham), and was himself slain, soon after, by the treachery of the Parthian general, B. C. 53.

Pompey, now sole consul, no longer pretended any friendship for Cæsar. The conqueror of Mithridates and the Cilician pirates did not fancy that he could be eclipsed by any man; and the relationship between them was lately dissolved by the death of Julia, the daughter of Cæsar, who had been the wife of Pompey. The enemies of the former obtained a decree of the Senate requiring him to surrender his proconsular power, and return to Rome before becoming candidate for a second consulship. Cato had declared that he would prosecute Cæsar for capital offenses as soon as he should resign his command.

It could hardly have been expected that the governor of Gaul would quit his devoted legions, and all the treasures of the conquered province, to place himself unarmed at the mercy of his enemies. Such virtue had been known in the days of Curtius, but self-surrender for the public good had ceased to be fashionable at Rome. Moreover, Cæsar may well have doubted whether the sacrifice of his life would promote the public interests. The Romans required a master; and his own plans for building up a great empire from the scattered fragments of provinces, by extending equal rights to all the conquered peoples, were doubtless the most enlarged and beneficent that had yet been formed. He believed that the great interests of Rome were consistent with his own.

165. His enemies lost no opportunity to deprive him of resources. Under pretext of a war with Parthia, the two former colleagues of Crassus were required to furnish each one legion to be sent to Asia. Pompey had formerly lent a legion to Cæsar, and now demanded its return. Cæsar dismissed the two legions, giving to each man his share of the treasure which was to be distributed at his approaching triumph. He wrote at the same time to the Senate, offering to resign his command if Pompey would do the same, but not otherwise. The two legions were kept in Italy. After a violent debate, it was enacted that Cæsar should, without conditions, disband his army on a certain day, under penalty of being declared an enemy of the state. The tribunes, Antonius and Cassius, vetoed the motion, but their veto was set aside; and believing their lives in danger, they fled to Cæsar's camp at Raven′na.

RECAPITULATION.

Catiline's deep-laid conspiracy is defeated by Cicero, and its leader slain in battle. Pompey disbands his army and triumphs for his conquests in Asia. He forms with Cæsar, now consul, and Crassus, the first triumvirate. The next year, B. C. 58, Cæsar, as proconsul, assumes the command in Gaul; subdues the Helvetii and the Germans, under Ariovistus, in one campaign; afterward conquers the Belgæ; twice bridges the Rhine and ravages Germany; twice invades Britain; suppresses revolts in Gaul, and organizes the whole country into a peaceful and permanent part of the Roman dominion. Crassus, in Asia, is overwhelmingly defeated, with the loss of his army and his life, B. C. 53. Pompey breaks with Cæsar, and becomes the champion of the Senate.

Cæsar Master of Rome.

166. It was time for decisive action. Cæsar crossed the Rubicon, a little river which separated his province from Roman Italy, and advanced with one legion, the troops in Gaul having received orders to follow without delay. To enter the country without resigning his command was itself a declaration of war. Panic seized Rome, and the Senate fled, leaving the public treasures behind. Fifteen thousand recruits, destined for Pompey's army, seized their officers and handed them over, with themselves and the town Corfin'ium, where they were quartered, to Cæsar. Other bodies of recruits followed their example. Pompey, having lost more than half his ten legions, retired to Brundisium; and though besieged by Cæsar, succeeded in escaping with 25,000 men to Greece.

The Roman world was now really divided between the two generals. Pompey controlled Spain, Africa, and the East, and hoped, by commanding the sea and the corn islands, to starve Italy into surrender. Cæsar had only Italy, Illyricum, and Gaul. If Pompey had acted with energy, he might speedily have created an army in the East and regained Rome, but by delay he allowed Cæsar to attack his provinces in detail, and wrest the entire empire from his grasp. The emigrated nobles assembled themselves at Thessalonica and re-organized a senate, in which they made a vain show of keeping up the constitutional forms, while, by their petty jealousies, they hampered every movement of their general-in-chief.

167. Cu'rio, the ablest of Cæsar's lieutenants, captured Sicily, and thus averted famine from Rome. In Africa he was less fortunate. Drawn into an unexpected combat with the whole army of King Juba, he was defeated, and chose to be slain rather than meet his general in disgrace. Instead of the anarchy and general proscription which his enemies had predicted, Cæsar soon restored order in Italy, and universal confidence, by the moderation and forbearance of his conduct. Friends and foes were equally protected. The moneyed class, which had most to gain from a settled government, came over to the side of Cæsar, and the "rich lords resumed their daily task of writing their rent-rolls."

His first foreign enterprise was against Spain, where Pompey had seven legions. It was conquered by a severe and toilsome campaign of forty days. Returning through Gaul, Cæsar received the surrender of Massilia, and learned of his appointment to the dictatorship at Rome. He held this high office only eleven days, but long enough to preside at the election of consuls, in which he himself, of course, received the greatest number of votes; to pass laws relieving debtors, and restoring to the enjoyment of their estates the descendants of those whom Sulla had proscribed; and to begin his scheme of consolidating the provinces, by granting the full rights of Roman citizenship to the Gauls.

168. As consul, he then led his army to Brundisium and crossed into Greece. Pompey had assembled from the eastern countries a great army and fleet, the latter of which commanded the sea, and seemed to forbid the passage of Cæsar. But Bibulus, the admiral, confiding in his superior numbers and the wintry season, was off his guard until seven legions were landed in Epirus. The attempt to capture Pompey's camp and treasures, at Dyrra′chium, failed; but the vain confidence inspired by their partial success, in the proud and frivolous young nobles of the refugee party, eventually proved their ruin.

Cæsar was, indeed, in a perilous position; his fleet was destroyed, and he was cut off in a hostile country where food must soon fail. Nevertheless, with his usual good fortune or consummate skill, he contrived to draw his victorious enemy after him to the interior of the country, where Pompey's fleet gave him no advantage, and then to choose his own battle-field at Pharsa′lia, in Thessaly. The army of Pompey, in horse and foot, numbered 54,000 men; that of Cæsar, scarcely more than 22,000. The former was abundantly supplied both with provisions and military materials, while the latter was near the point of starvation, and compelled to stake its existence on one desperate venture. So certain did the result appear, that the patricians in Pompey's camp were already disputing among themselves the succession to Cæsar's pontificate.

169. On the 9th of August, B. C. 48, the Pompeians crossed the river which separated the two camps, and with their cavalry commenced the attack. Cæsar's horsemen were driven in, but a picked troop of his legionaries, tried on a hundred Gallic fields, unexpectedly charged the assailants. Their orders were to aim their javelins at the enemies' faces. Confused by this novel attack, the cavalry turned and fled; and Pompey, who had been urged by the reproaches of his self-appointed counselors to give battle, contrary to his better judgment, and who had never shared their confidence, did not wait to see the general attack, but galloped away to his camp.

His army was completely routed; 15,000 lay dead upon the field, and 20,000 surrendered on the morning after the battle. Many of the aristocracy hastened to make their peace with the conqueror; the "irreconcilables" either betook themselves to the mountains or the sea, to carry on for years a predatory warfare; or to Africa, where King Juba, of Numidia, perceiving that Cæsar's consolidating policy would deprive him of his kingdom, still stood firmly on the Pompeian side. The other client-states withdrew their quotas of ships and men as soon as they saw that Pompey's cause was lost.

170. Pompey fled to Egypt. The young queen, Cleopatra, was now in Syria, having been driven from her kingdom by her brother's guardian, Pothi′nus, who was with an army holding the eastern frontier against her.

The perfidious statesmen who surrounded the king, sent out a boat inviting the illustrious fugitive to land; but just as he had reached the shore, he was stabbed by a former centurion of his own, who was now in the service of Ptolemy. Pompey perceived his fate; without a word, he covered his face with his toga, and submitted to the swords of his executioners. His head was cut off, and his body cast out upon the sand, where it was buried by one of his own attendants.

Cæsar soon arrived in pursuit; but when the ghastly head was presented to him, he turned away weeping, and ordered the murderers to be put to death. He remained five months at Alexandria, regulating the affairs of the kingdom, which he secured to Cleopatra jointly with her brother. He thus became involved in war with the people, and in a naval battle was once compelled to save his life by swimming from ship to ship, holding his sword in his teeth, and the manuscript of his Commentaries upon the Gallic Wars in one hand over his head. He was victorious at last, and Ptolemy was drowned in the Nile.

171. Cæsar then turned rapidly toward Asia Minor, where Pharnaces of Pontus was trying to regain his father's lost dominions. The Roman army had been defeated at Nicopolis with great loss, but Cæsar won a decisive victory at Zie'la, and finished the campaign in five days. It was on this occasion that he sent to the Senate his memorable dispatch, "Veni, vidi, vici." * The presence of the chief made a similar transformation of the war in Africa. The Pompeian party had re-established its senate at Utica, and during Cæsar's long delay in Egypt had raised an army fully equal to that which had been conquered at Pharsalia.

In attempting to carry the war into Africa, Cæsar met an unexpected obstacle in a mutiny of his veterans in southern Italy. Wearied out with the unusual hardships of their last campaigns, and imagining that their general could do nothing without them, they refused to embark for Sicily, and commenced their march toward Rome. Having provided for the security of the city, Cæsar suddenly appeared among the legions, and demanded to know what they wanted. Cries of "discharge!" were heard on every hand. He took them instantly at their word; and then addressing them as "citizens," not as "soldiers," promised them, at his approaching triumph, their full share in the treasure and lands which he had destined for his faithful followers, though in the triumph itself they could, of course, have no part.

His presence and his voice revived their old affection; they stood mute and ashamed at the sudden severing of the bond which had been their only glory in the past. At length they began to beg, even with tears, that they might be restored to favor, and honored again with the name of

---

* I came, I saw, I conquered.

"Cæsar's soldiers." After some delay their prayer was granted; the ring-leaders were only punished by a reduction of one-third in their triumphal presents, and the revolt was at an end.

172. The campaign in Africa was not less difficult than the one in Greece. The Pompeians were well supplied with cavalry and elephants, and were able to fight on fields of their own choosing. They gained a battle near Rus′pina, but in the more decisive conflict at Thapsus, they were completely overthrown. The soldiers of Cæsar disregarded his orders to spare their fellow-citizens; they were determined to obtain rest from war at any cost of Roman blood, and 50,000 Pompeians were left dead upon the battle-field. Cæsar was now master of all Africa. Cato, commanding at Utica, provided for the safety of his friends either by flight or surrender; then shutting himself in his room, read all night the treatise of Plato on the Immortality of the Soul, and toward morning killed himself with his own sword.

173. Cæsar returned to Rome in possession of absolute power. Instead of the proscriptions, which, in similar circumstances, had marked the return of Marius and Sulla, he proclaimed amnesty to all, and sought to avail himself of the wisdom of all parties in reorganizing civil affairs. As he had never triumphed, he now celebrated four days for his victories in Gaul, Egypt, Pontus, and Numidia; but the rejoicings were only for the conquest of foreign foes, for it was regarded as unseemly to triumph over Roman citizens. Twenty thousand tables were spread in the streets and public squares, gifts of grain and money were distributed among soldiers and people, and the games were celebrated with a splendor never before approached.

Coin of Cæsar, enlarged twice the size.

Cæsar now applied himself with diligence to regulate the disorders of the state; and the benefit of one, at least, of his provisions is felt even to the present day. The reckoning of time, through the carelessness or corruption of the pontiffs (see § 29), had fallen into hopeless confusion: harvest festivals took place in spring, and those of the late vintage at midsummer. Cæsar, as chief pontiff, reformed the calendar, by adding ninety days to the current year, and then, with the aid of an Alexandrian astronomer, adapted the reckoning to the sun's course. He made the Roman year consist of 365 days, and added a day every fourth year. The Julian Calendar, with only one emendation,* is that which we now follow. In acknowledgment of his service in this matter, the Senate ordered the month of Cæsar's birth to be called henceforth from his clan-name, July. His successor, Augustus, on occasion of some trifling improvement in the calendar, gave his own surname to the following month.

174. The Pompeians made one more rally in Spain, but they were defeated and overthrown by Cæsar, in the severe and decisive battle of Munda, March 17, B, C. 45. Cneius Pompey, the younger, was slain; his brother Sextus soon submitted, and received the family estates. He was proscribed during the disorders which followed the death of Cæsar, and for eight years kept up a piratical warfare upon the sea. Having settled the affairs of Spain, Cæsar celebrated a fifth triumph, and was loaded by the servile Senate with unlimited powers and dignities. He became dictator and censor for life, the latter office now receiving its new title, præfecture of morals. He was permitted to make peace or war without consulting either Senate or people. In his highest and most distinctive power, that of perpetual imperator, he was to name his successor. His person was declared sacred, and all the senators bound themselves by oath to watch over his safety. His statues were ordered to be placed in all the temples, and his name in civil oaths was associated with those of the gods.

175. Cæsar availed himself of his unprecedented power to plan many great works of general utility. He projected a much-needed digest of Roman laws, and the founding of a Latin and Greek library on the model of that of Alexandria, which had been almost destroyed by fire during the recent siege. He proposed to turn the course of the Tiber, so as at once to drain the Pontine marshes, to add to the city an extensive tract of land available for building, and to connect with Rome the large and convenient port of Terraci'na, instead of the inferior one of Ostia.

Above all, he desired to substitute a great Mediterranean empire for the mere city government which, for more than a hundred years, had ruled Italy and the world. To atone for the narrow policy of municipal Rome, he rebuilt the two great commercial cities, Carthage and Corinth, which Roman jealousy had demolished; and he effaced, as far as possible, the distinctions between Italy and the provinces. In the many colonies which he founded in Europe, Asia, and Africa, he provided homes for 80,000 emigrants, mostly from the crowded tenement houses of Rome itself. His plans embraced the varied interests of every class and nation within the empire, and aimed to reach, by the union of all, a higher civilization than either had attained alone. In the wildest regions of Germany, Dalmatia, or Spain, the Roman soldier was followed by the Greek school-master and the Jewish trader.

---

* That of Pope Gregory XIII., A. D. 1582.

176. Though occupying the highest rank as a general, Cæsar was more a statesman than a warrior, and desired to base his government, not upon military power, but upon the confidence of the people. He was already in his fortieth year when he first assumed the command of an army. Still, his great works as a ruler had all to be executed in the brief intervals of military affairs. The five and a half years which followed his accession to supreme power were occupied by seven important campaigns; and he was about undertaking an expedition against Parthia, to avenge the overthrow of Crassus, when a violent death ended his career. It is said that he desired, before his departure, to receive the title of king.

A conspiracy had already been formed among his personal enemies. It was now strengthened by the accession of several honest republicans, who dreamed that the death of the dictator would restore freedom to the state. At the festival of the Lupercalia, Feb. 15, B. C. 44, the crown was offered to Cæsar, by Antony, his colleague in the consulship; but, perceiving the consternation of the people, he declined it. On the 15th of the following month, in spite of many warnings, Cæsar repaired to the Senate-house. He had just taken his seat, when one of the conspirators stooped and touched his robe. At this signal, Casca stabbed him in the shoulder; the others thronged around with their drawn swords or daggers.

Instead of the flattering crowd, nothing but murderous faces and the gleam of steel met his eye on every side. Still he stood at bay, wounding one assailant with his stylus, throwing back another, and disarming a third, until he received a wound from the hand of Brutus, whom, though an adherent of Pompey, he had honored with his confidence and loaded with benefits. Then drawing his mantle about him, with the reproachful exclamation, "And *thou*, Brutus!" he fell at the base of Pompey's statue and expired.

177. Brutus, raising aloft his bloody dagger, cried aloud to Cicero, "Rejoice, father of our country, for Rome is free!" Never was rejoicing more unfounded. If Brutus and his accomplices could have restored to the Roman people the simple and self-denying virtues of the olden time, Rome would indeed have been free. But Cæsar understood the times better than his assassins. In cutting off the only man who was capable of ruling with clear insight, firmness, and beneficence, they had plunged the state again into the horrors of civil war, and made it the easy prey of a less able and less liberal despot. Senate and people were at first paralyzed by the suddenness of the change, and by fear of a return to the old scenes of proscription. Antony, now sole consul, had time to possess himself of Cæsar's papers and treasures; and by his funeral oration over the body of the dictator—especially by reading his will, in which all the Roman people were remembered with great liberality—he roused the indignant passions of the crowd against the murderers.

Antony was for a time the most popular man in Rome, but a rival soon appeared in the person of Octavia′nus, the grand-nephew and adopted son of Julius Cæsar. This young man, who had been educated with great care under the eye of his adoptive father, arrived from the camp at Apollonia and claimed his inheritance, out of which he carefully distributed the legacies to soldiers and people. Cicero was led to look upon him as the hope of the state, and in his third great series of orations, called the Philip′pics, he destroyed the popularity of Antony and his influence with the Senate. Two of Antony's legions deserted to Octavian, and Antony himself, in two battles, was routed and driven across the Alps.

178. The two consuls for the year 43 B. C. were slain in the battle before Mu′tina. Octavian, returning to Rome, compelled the popular assembly to elect him to that office, though he was only nineteen years of age. He was appointed to carry on the war against Antony, who had now been joined by Lepidus—formerly master of the horse to Julius Cæsar—and was now descending from the Alps with a formidable army of seventeen legions. But the Senate, almost equally afraid of Antony and Octavian, revoked the outlawry of the former; and the latter, disgusted with its vacillations, resolved upon a league with the two commanders, whose forces alone could give him victory over the assassins.

On a small island in the Reno, near Bono′nia (Bologna), the three met, and the Second Triumvirate, of Antony, Cæsar Octavianus, and Lepidus, was then formed, B. C. 43, proposing to share between them for five years the government of the Roman world. A proscription followed, in which Cicero, though the friend of Cæsar, was sacrificed to the hatred of Antony. The illustrious orator was murdered near his own villa at For′miæ, and his head and right hand were nailed to the rostrum at Rome, from which he had so often discoursed of the sacred rights of citizens. Two thousand knights and three hundred senators perished in this proscription. Those who could escape took refuge with Sextus Pompey in Sicily, or with Brutus and Cassius in Greece.

179. Antony and Octavian crossed the Adriatic, and defeated the last of the conspirators in two battles at Philippi, in the autumn of 42 B. C. Both Brutus and Cassius ended their lives by suicide. Cæsar returned to Italy, where a new civil war was stirred up by Fulvia, the wife of Antony, and Lucius, his brother. Lucius Antonius threw himself into Perusia, where he was besieged and taken by Octavian. The common citizens were spared, but 300 or 400 nobles were slain at the altar of Julius Cæsar, on the anniversary of his death, March 15, B. C. 40. Fulvia died in Greece, and a new agreement between the triumvirs, called the Peace of Brundisium, was sealed by the marriage of Antony with Octavia, the sister of the younger Cæsar.

In the new division of the civilized world, Antony received the East; Octavian, Italy and Spain; and Lepidus, Africa. Sextus Pompey, whose fleets, commanding the sea, threatened the capital with famine, was admitted, next year, to a sort of partnership with the triumvirate, in which he received the islands of the western Mediterranean, on condition of his supplying Rome with grain. The conditions of this treaty were never fulfilled, and a two years' war between Pompey and Octavian was the result. It was ended B. C. 36, by a great sea-fight off Nau′lochus. Agrippa, the intimate friend of Cæsar, routed the forces of Pompey, who fled in despair to Asia, and the following year was captured and put to death. His land forces, deserted by their leader, prevailed upon Lepidus to become their general, and declare war against Octavian. But the young Cæsar acted with an intrepidity worthy of his name. He went unarmed and almost alone into the camp of Lepidus, and by his eloquence persuaded them to desert their unworthy commander and be faithful to himself.

180. Lepidus being degraded, the two remaining members of the triumvirate continued three years at the head of affairs. But an alliance so purely selfish could not be permanent. Antony neglected his noble wife for the enchantments of the Egyptian queen, on whom he bestowed Phœnicia, Cœle-Syria, and other dominions of Rome. He wasted the forces committed to him in expeditions which resulted only in loss and disgrace; and he laid aside the simple dignity of a Roman citizen for the arrogant ceremony of an Eastern monarch.

In 32 B. C., war was declared against Cleopatra, and in September of the following year the forces of the two triumvirs met off Actium, in Acarnania. Antony had collected a vast fleet and army; but his officers, disgusted by his weak self-indulgence, were ready to be drawn over to the side of Octavian. Disheartened by many desertions, Antony took no active part in the battle, but while those of his forces who still faithfully adhered to him were fighting bravely in his defense, he drew off with a portion of his fleet, and followed Cleopatra to Egypt. His land army, after waiting a week for its fugitive commander, surrendered to Octavian.

From this moment Cæsar was master of the Roman world. The final blow was given the next year in Egypt, where Antony was defeated before Alexandria, and deserted by his fleet and army. Cleopatra negotiated to betray him, but when she found that Octavian wanted to capture her, that she might adorn his triumph, she ended her life by the poison of an asp. Antony, in despair, had already killed himself, and Egypt became a Roman province. Octavian, returning to Rome the following year, celebrated a three-fold triumph, and the gates of Janus were closed the third time, in token of universal peace, B. C. 29.

RECAPITULATION.

Cæsar crosses the Rubicon, and in three months becomes master of Italy. He subdues the Pompeians in Spain, becomes dictator, and afterward consul; pursues Pompey into Greece; is defeated at Dyrrhachium, but victorious at Pharsalia,

B. C. 48. Pompey is slain in Egypt. Cæsar re-establishes Cleopatra under the Roman protectorate; re-conquers Pontus; quells a mutiny in his Gallic legions, and overthrows the Pompeians at Thapsus, in Africa. He celebrates four triumphs at Rome; reforms the calendar; finally crushes the Pompeians in Spain; is invested with sovereign powers, and organizes a cosmopolitan empire. On the eve of departure for Asia, he is murdered in the Senate-house by sixty conspirators. Antony aims to succeed him, but Octavian receives his inheritance. Antony, Octavian, and Lepidus form the Second Triumvirate, B. C. 43. In the proscription which follows, Cicero is killed. Brutus and Cassius are defeated at Philippi, B. C. 42. A dispute in the triumvirate is ended by the Peace of Brundisium, and the marriage of Antony and Octavia. Lepidus is degraded from the triumvirate, B. C. 35; the two remaining colleagues quarrel, and the battle of Actium makes Octavian supreme ruler of the empire, B. C. 31.

III. The Roman Empire.

181. First Period, B. C. 31–A. D. 192. The empire founded by Cæsar Octavianus was an absolute monarchy under the form of a republic. Many of the high offices, which had been borne by different persons, were now concentrated in one; but he declined the name dictator, which had been abused by Marius and Sulla, and was careful to be elected only for limited periods, and in the regular manner. The title Imperator, which he bore for life, had always belonged to generals of consular rank during the time of their command. The name Augustus, by which he is henceforth to be known, was a title of honor bestowed by the Senate, and made hereditary in his family. As chief, or "Prince of the Senate," he had the right to introduce subjects for discussion; and as pontifex maximus, or high priest of the state, he had a controlling influence in all sacred affairs.

He lived in the style of a wealthy senator in his house on the Palatine, walked abroad without retinue, and carefully avoided kingly pomp. The popular assemblies still appointed consuls, prætors, quæstors, ædiles, and tribunes, but the successful candidate was always recommended by the emperor, if he did not himself accept the appointment. These old-fashioned dignities were now little more than empty names, the real power having passed, under Augustus himself, to new officers, especially to the præfect of the city and the commander of the Prætorian Guard.* The people, meanwhile, were satisfied with liberal distributions of corn, wine, and oil, and amused by a constant succession of games.

182. In seven centuries the Roman dominion had grown from the few acres on the Palatine Hill, to embrace the Mediterranean with all its coasts, from the Atlantic to the Euphrates, and from the African Desert to the Rhine, the Danube, and the Euxine. The twenty-seven provinces,

---

* This guard consisted of 10,000 Italian soldiers, quartered near Rome for the security of the emperor's person. And so great was its influence, that, in the later days of the empire, it often assumed to dispose of the crown without reference to Senate or people.

reorganized by Augustus, were divided between himself and the Senate according to their condition. Those which were securely at peace were called Senatorial Provinces, and governed by proconsuls appointed by the legislative body; those which demanded the presence of an army were Imperial Provinces, and were managed either by the emperor in person or by his legates.

The standing army, which maintained order in the entire empire, consisted, in the time of Augustus, of twenty-five legions, each legion numbering, in horse, foot, and artillery, a little less than 7,000 men. This force of 175,000 was distributed along the Rhine, the Danube, and the Euphrates, or in Britain, Spain, and Africa, according to the danger from the outer barbarians. While internal peace was maintained by the wise management of Augustus, the natural boundaries of the empire above mentioned were only gained and kept by active war. Northern and northwestern Spain, the Alpine provinces of Rhætia and Vindelic′ia, and the Danubian countries Nor′icum, Panno′nia, and Mœ′sia, required almost unremitted warfare of more than twenty years, B. C. 12–A. D. 9.

183. The Germans, east of the Rhine and north of the Danube, though often defeated, were never subdued. Drusus, a step-son of Augustus, was the first Roman general who descended the Rhine to the German Ocean. He built two bridges and more than fifty fortresses along the river, and imposed a tribute upon the Frisians north of its mouth. Drusus died in his third campaign, B. C. 9, and was succeeded by his brother Tiberius, who after many years, A. D. 4, seemed to have subdued the tribes between the Rhine and the Elbe.

Coin of Drusus, twice the size of the original.

But his successor, Qu. Varus, attempted to establish the same arrogant and arbitrary rule which he had exercised over the slavish Syrians—a people crushed by nearly two thousand years of despotism, Assyrian, Egyptian, Persian, and Macedonian. The free-spirited Germans rose in revolt, under their princely leader, Armin′ius (Herman). Arminius had been educated at Rome, and had thoroughly learned the tactics of the legions; but Roman refinement never weakened his German fidelity to fatherland. Private wrong was now added to national oppression, and he deeply laid and firmly executed his plan for the destruction of the Roman army and the deliverance of Germany.

184. Varus was enticed into the broken and difficult country of the Teutoberg′er Wald, at a season when heavy rains had increased the marshiness of the ground. Barricades of fallen trees blocked his way, and, in a narrow valley, a hail-storm of javelins burst upon his legions from the hosts of Arminius. On the next day the battle was renewed, and the Romans were literally destroyed, for all the captives were sacrificed upon the altars of the old German divinities. The garrisons throughout the country were put to the sword, and within a few weeks not a Roman foot remained on German soil.

The news of the disaster struck Rome with terror. The superstitious believed that supernatural portents had accompanied the event. The temple of Mars was struck by a thunderbolt, comets blazed in the sky, and spears of fire darted from the northward into the prætorian camp. A statue of Victory, which had stood on the Italian frontier looking toward Germany, turned of its own accord and faced toward Rome. Augustus, in his grief, heightened by the weakness of old age, used for months to beat his head against the wall, exclaiming, "Quintilius Varus, give me back my legions!"

By the revolt of Arminius, Germany was once and forever freed. Roman armies were led thither by Germanicus and the younger Drusus, but they gained no permanent advantages; and by the will of Augustus and the policy of his successors, the Rhine continued to be regarded as the frontier until, five centuries later, the tide of conquest turned in the other direction, and the Teutonic races divided the Roman Empire into the kingdoms of modern Europe.

185. The reign of Augustus was a refreshing contrast to the century of revolution which had preceded it, for the security and prosperity that were felt throughout the empire. Commerce revived, agriculture was greatly improved, and the imperial city was adorned with temples, porticos, and other new and magnificent buildings. Augustus could truly boast that he "found Rome of brick and left it of marble." A more lasting glory surrounds his name from the literary brilliancy of his court. Livy, the historian, and Virgil, Horace, Ovid, Tibul′lus, with other poets, enjoyed his patronage and celebrated his achievements; and in allusion to this, the brightest period of every nation's literature is commonly called its "Augustan Age." Augustus had no son, and his choice of an heir fell upon Tiberius, the son of his wife, Livia, by a former marriage. By the same arrangement, Germanicus, the son of Drusus, was adopted by Tiberius, and married to Agrippi′na, granddaughter of Augustus.

186. In the 77th year of his age, Augustus closed his long and wonderfully prosperous reign of forty-five years, A. D. 14. The Senate and people submitted to his appointed successor. The army would more willingly have proclaimed its idolized general Germanicus, but the younger prince

ROMAN FORUM, UNDER THE EMPERORS.

Temple of Juno Moneta. Temple of Jupiter Tonans. Julian Basilica. Temple of Saturn. Arch of Tiberius. Tabularium, or Hall of Records. Temple of Vespasian. Milliarium and Rostra. Temple of Concord. Statue of Domitian. Arch of Septimius Severus. Temple of Jupiter Capitolinus. Mamertine Prison.

absolutely refused to sanction the act. Tiberius, so far from prizing his fidelity, never forgave his popularity; and the court soon understood that the surest way to gain the favor of the emperor was to ill-treat his adopted son.

The policy of Tiberius was that of many another cowardly and suspicious tyrant. Conscious of his own unworthiness, either by birth or genius, of the high place he filled, he saw a rival in every possessor of great talent or even exalted virtue. He was afraid to call to his assistance the great patricians or the princes of the Julian house, and he regarded his own relations with unmingled jealousy. As he found it impossible, however, to administer alone all the world-embracing affairs of such an empire, he raised to the post of prætorian præfect a Volsinian knight, Seja'nus, whom he fancied too mean to be dangerous, but who became, in fact, the master of the whole dominion.

187. Germanicus, meanwhile, conducted three campaigns, A. D. 14–17; and, after several disasters, gained some important victories over Arminius, between the Rhine and the Elbe. He was recalled A. D. 17, to receive the honor of a triumph, and was met, twenty miles from Rome, by an enthusiastic multitude which had poured forth to welcome him. He was, indeed, dangerously dear both to his legions and to the common people; and though he believed that in one year more he could complete the conquest of Germany, he was now transferred to another army and to the eastern wars. In his new command he settled the affairs of Armenia, and organized Cappadocia as a province; but he died A. D. 19, near Antioch in Syria, believing himself poisoned by Piso, a subordinate, who had been sent by the emperor with express orders to thwart and injure his chief.

188. Drusus, the son of Tiberius, was poisoned by order of Sejanus, who had the boldness to request permission of the emperor to marry the widow of his victim. This was refused; but Tiberius, still blinded to the marvelous ambition of the wretch who ruled him, consented to retire to Capreæ, and leave Rome in the hands of Sejanus. His time was now given up to swinish excesses, while his worthless lieutenant maintained for five years a riot of misrule. His wicked schemes did not spare the best or noblest of the imperial family; but, at length, he perceived his master's suspicion directed toward him, and prepared to anticipate the blow by assassinating Tiberius himself. His plot was discovered, and he was suddenly seized and executed, A. D. 31.

The fall of this unworthy favorite took from Tiberius the only man whom he had ever trusted, and henceforth all were equally the objects of his fierce and cruel jealousy. Agrippina, the noble wife, as well as Nero, Drusus, and Livil'la, the unworthy sons and daughter of Germanicus, were put to death by his orders. Unlike Augustus, who scrupulously kept within the forms of law, he usurped the right to condemn without trial all who were obnoxious to him; and he extended the definition of treason to words and even thoughts. From his island retreat in the beautiful Bay of Naples, he issued destruction to men, women, and even innocent children who had the misfortune to be of sufficiently noble birth to attract his attention. It was a relief to the world when he died from illness, A. D. 37, at the age of seventy-eight.

189. Tiberius had appointed no successor, but Senate, soldiers, and people united in the choice of Caius Cæsar, the only surviving son of Germanicus and Agrippina. In his childhood he had been the pet of the legions in Germany, and from the little military boots (*caligæ*) which he wore to please them, he acquired the nickname *Caligula*. This childish appellation is the name by which he is commonly known in history. Caligula was now twenty-six years of age, and was considered to be of a mild and generous disposition. The first months of his reign justified the impression. He released the prisoners and recalled the exiles of Tiberius, and he restored power to the regular magistrates and the popular assemblies. But his weak head was turned by the possession of absolute power, and of the enormous wealth hoarded by Tiberius. In unbounded self-indulgence, he extinguished the last spark of reason, and exerted his tremendous power only for mischief, and in the most wild and reckless manner. Choosing to be considered as a god, he built a temple to himself, under the name of Jupiter Latiaris; and so servile was Rome now become, that her noblest citizens purchased the honor of officiating as priests to this worthless divinity.

The worst abuse of absolute power was shown in contempt for human life. When the supply of criminals for the public games was exhausted, the emperor ordered spectators, taken at random from the crowd, to be thrown to the beasts; and lest they should curse him in their last agonies, their tongues were first cut out. But this mad career of despotism worked its own destruction; for, in the fourth year of his reign, and the thirtieth of his age, Caius Cæsar was murdered by two of his guards.

190. The Roman world being thus suddenly without a master, the prætorians took upon themselves to decide its fate. Finding Claudius, the uncle of Caligula, a weak and timid old man, hiding himself in the palace, they saluted him as emperor, and hurried him away to their camp, where he received the oaths of allegiance. Considered from childhood as lacking in intellect, Claudius had been treated by his relatives with a contempt, and by his servants with a harshness and cruelty, which only increased the natural irresoluteness of his character. Yet, though feeble, he was a good and honest man, and the evil wrought in his reign was the work of others. His infamous wife, Messali′na, gratified her jealousy and revenge at the expense of the noblest in the state, especially the imperial princesses, without even a show of legal formality. At last she was executed for her crimes, and the emperor procured a law from the Senate which enabled him to marry his niece, Agrippina.

This princess appears to advantage only when compared with her predecessor. She recalled Seneca, the philosopher, from exile, and made him the tutor of her son, Nero. She protected many who were unjustly accused, and she advanced to power the faithful Burrhus, who proved a better servant, both to herself and her son, than either deserved. At the same time, Agrippina persuaded her husband to set aside his own son, Britan′nicus, in favor of her son by a former marriage. This youth bore his father's name, L. Domitius Ahenobar′bus, but by the emperor's adoption he became Nero Claudius Cæsar Drusus Germanicus. By the first of these names he is known in history as one of the most wicked of tyrants. Having gained all that she hoped from the weak compliance of Claudius, Agrippina poisoned him, and presented her son to the prætorian guards as their imperator. Some, it is said, cried out, "Where is Britannicus?" but there was no serious resistance, and the new emperor was accepted by the Senate, the people, and the provinces.

191. For the first five years, under the wise and honest administration of Seneca and Burrhus, the Romans believed that the golden age had returned. Taxes were remitted; lands were allotted to the needy and deserving. The *delators,* that infamous class of people who made their living by accusing others of crime, were suppressed or banished. The Roman arms prospered in Armenia, under the able command of Cor′bulo, who captured the two capitals, Artax′ata and Tigranocerta, and completely subdued the kingdom. In Germany all was quiet, and the legions on the lower Rhine had leisure to complete the embankments which protected the land from inundation.

None of this prosperity was due, however, to the character of Nero, who was a sensual and cruel tyrant even from his youth. In the second year of his reign he poisoned his foster-brother, Britannicus. A few years later, he murdered his mother, his wife, and the too faithful Burrhus, cast off the influence of Seneca, and thenceforth gave free course to his tyrannical caprices. He encouraged the informants again, and filled his treasury with the confiscated property of their victims.

192. He persecuted both Jews and Christians, charging upon the latter the great fire at Rome, which he was more than suspected of having himself caused to be kindled. By this terrible conflagration, ten of the fourteen wards, or "regions," of the city were made uninhabitable. Nero watched the burning from a tower on the Esquiline, while, in the dress of an actor, he chanted the "Sack of Troy." Whether or not he had ordered the destruction of Rome in consequence of his disgust with its narrow and winding streets, he wisely availed himself of the opportunity to rebuild it in more regular and spacious proportions. The houses were constructed of stone, and rendered fire-proof; each was surrounded with balconies, and separated from other houses by lanes of considerable width, while a plentiful supply of water was introduced into every tenement.

The palace of Nero having been destroyed, he built his Golden House on a scale of magnitude and splendor which Rome had never seen. The porticos which surrounded it were three miles in length; within their bounds were parks, gardens, and a lake which filled the valley afterward occupied by the Flavian Amphitheater. The chambers of this imperial mansion were gilded and inlaid with gems. The least of its ornaments, though probably the greatest of its objects, was a colossal statue of Nero himself, 120 feet in height.

193. Nero desired to be praised as a musician and a charioteer, and so far forgot his imperial dignity as to appear as an actor in the theaters. He gained prizes at the Olympic Games, A. D. 67, which had been delayed two years that he might be present. He took part, also, in the vocal performances at the Isthmian Games, on which occasion he ordered the death of a singer whose voice drowned his own. On his return, he entered Rome through a breach in the walls, after the ancient Hellenic custom; but the 1,800 garlands with which he had been laden by the servile Greeks, showed the decline of the old heroic spirit, rather than the glory of the victor.

194. The impositions of Nero caused revolts in the provinces, and, among others, Vespasian, the future emperor, was sent to pacify Judæa. But Nero was jealous of his most able and faithful officers. Cor′bulo, the conqueror of Armenia, Rufus and Scribo′nius, the commanders in Germany, were recalled, and avoided public execution only by putting themselves to death. All the generals on the frontier perceived that they could escape a similar fate only by timely revolt, and insurrections broke out at once in Germany, Gaul, Africa, and Spain. The conspirators agreed, at length, in the choice of Galba, the governor of Hither Spain, as their leader and emperor.

Nero perceived that resistance was hopeless. Deserted by the prætorians and all his courtiers, he fled from his Golden House and hid himself in the cottage of Phaon, his former slave, a few miles from the city. After spending a night and part of a day in an agony of terror, he summoned courage to end his own life, just as he heard the tramp of the horsemen who were coming to take him. He was but thirty years of age, and had reigned nearly fourteen years. With him expired the line of Augustus. The imperial power never again remained so long in any one family as it had among the members, by adoption or otherwise, of the Julian house.

RECAPITULATION.

Augustus (B. C. 30–A. D. 14) combines in himself all the dignities of the Republic, but carefully avoids the appearance of royalty. He leaves the peaceful provinces to the Senate, but assumes the command of those which are at war. The Germans, under Arminius, revolt and destroy the legions of Varus. The "Augustan Age" is distinguished for prosperity and enlightenment. Tiberius (A. D. 14–37) succeeds Augustus, but Sejanus rules the empire. Germanicus and many others are persecuted and put to death. Caius Cæsar (Caligula, A. D. 37–41) begins well, but, soon spoiled by power, exhibits "the awful spectacle of a madman, master of the civilized world." He is succeeded by his uncle Claudius (A. D. 41–54), a weak but honest man. Agrippina, having poisoned him, makes her son Nero emperor (A. D. 54–68). Upon the death of his instructors, he proves a reckless and cruel tyrant. He rebuilds Rome with unprecedented magnificence after the great fire. Having caused the death of his best generals, he kills himself only in time to escape the vengeance of his people.

DECLINE OF THE EMPIRE.

195. Galba, the most distinguished general of his time, had gained the favor of the emperor Claudius by refusing to assume the crown upon the death of Caligula. He had proved his ability and worth by his wise and just administration of the province of Africa, and had been honored at Rome with the highest dignities to which his patrician birth and eminent services entitled him. He was now more than seventy years of age, but learning that Nero had sent orders for his death, he resolved to rid the world of a tyrant by accepting the crown. He was a Roman of the ancient style, and the luxurious prætorians were equally disgusted with his strict discipline and his sparing distribution of money. By adopting Piso as his successor, he disappointed Otho, who easily raised a revolt against him, and the aged emperor and his adopted son were slain in the Forum, Jan. 15, A. D. 69.

196. Otho, the early favorite of Nero, had for ten years been governor of Lusitania. He was acknowledged, on the death of Galba, by the Senate and most of the provinces, but the legions in Germany had already (Jan. 3, 69) proclaimed their own general, Vitel'lius. The armies of the two generals met near the confluence of the Adda and the Po. Otho was defeated, and died by his own hand. Vitellius, having gained a crown by the skill and energy of his officers, lost it by his own unworthiness. Without the courage or ability of his predecessors, he surpassed them in contemptible self-indulgence. Vespasian, commander in Judæa, in revolting against this monster, was hailed by the acclamations of all good people, and supported by all the legions of the East. He took possession of Egypt, the grain-market of Rome, and sent his lieutenants into Italy. This time the generals of Vitellius were defeated on the Po, the capital was taken by assault, and the disgraced emperor put to death.

197. During the reign of Vespasian, order and prosperity succeeded to the storms which had convulsed the empire. The old discipline was revived, the revenues were re-organized, the capital was beautified, and the people employed by the construction of such great works as the Coliseum and the Temple of Peace. The space inclosed by Nero for his own enjoyment, was thrown open by Vespasian to the use of the people; and the materials of the Golden House served to enrich many public buildings. The revolt of the Batavians and other tribes on the lower Rhine was suppressed, A. D. 70; the Jewish War of Independence was finally subdued, the Holy City taken, and the people dispersed. Agric′ola completed the subjugation of Britain as far as the Tyne and the Solway, which he connected by earthworks and a chain of forts.

198. Titus, the son of Vespasian, having proved his military talent during the reign of his father, by the capture of Jerusalem, had been rewarded by a triumph, and by the title of Cæsar, which implied his association in the government. At the death of Vespasian, he became sole emperor without opposition. Whatever may have been his personal faults, Titus distinguished himself as a ruler by sincere and constant efforts to promote the happiness of his people. Recollecting, one evening, that he had performed no act of kindness, he exclaimed that he had lost a day.

The circumstances of his reign made peculiar demands upon the emperor's benevolence. The beautiful Campanian towns, Hercula′neum and Pompe′ii, were destroyed by a sudden eruption of Vesuvius. A fire raged again three days and nights at Rome, followed by a general and fatal pestilence. Titus assumed the pecuniary loss as his own, and even sold the ornaments of his palace to defray the expense of rebuilding the ruined houses. He established public baths on the site of Nero's gardens on the Esquiline, and completed the Coliseum, or Flavian Amphitheater, which he dedicated by a festival of a hundred days, including combats of 5,000 wild beasts. After a reign of but little more than two years, Titus died of a fever, having named his brother as his successor, A. D. 81.

199. Domitian was regarded by the people with more favor than he deserved, on account of the virtues of his father and brother. His nature was morose and jealous; and when his ill-success in military matters began to be contrasted with the victories of his predecessors, he became cruel and tyrannical, reviving the false accusations, forfeitures, and death-penalties of the reign of Nero. He was partially successful in his wars in Germany, but he was defeated on the Danube with great disaster, and even consented to pay an annual tribute to the Dacians, to keep them from invading Mœsia. When the cruelties of Domitian began to excite the fears of his servants, he was murdered, Sept. 18, A. D. 96.

200. The Senate now asserted a power which it had failed to exercise since the days of Augustus, by naming Nerva as sovereign. He was a childless old man, but he chose for his successor M. Ul′pius Traja′nus, a general whose vigor and ability, already shown in war, promised well for the interests of the state. It was henceforth considered the duty of the emperor to select from all his subjects the man most fit to rule, without reference to his own family, and the heir thus adopted bore the name of Cæsar. The mild, beneficent, and economical government of Nerva afforded a pleasing contrast to the severe and sanguinary rule of Domitian. Upon his death, which occurred A. D. 98, his adopted heir was immediately recognized as emperor.

201. Trajan was born in Spain, and his youth had been passed in military service. The Romans regarded him as the best of all their emperors. In personal character he was brave and generous, diligent and modest; in his policy as a ruler he was both wise and liberal. He scrupulously regarded the rights and dignities of the Senate, and treated its members as his equals. He was most diligent in hearing causes that were presented for his judgment, and in corresponding with the governors of provinces, who consulted him on all important affairs in their administration.

He managed the finances so well, that, without oppressive taxes or unjust confiscations, he always had means for the construction of roads, bridges, and aqueducts; for loans to persons whose estates had been injured by earthquakes or tempests; and for public buildings in Rome and all the provinces. The Ulpian Library and the great "Forum of Trajan," for the better transaction of public business, among many other useful and elegant works, bore witness to his liberality. The reign of Trajan was a literary epoch only second to that of Augustus. The great historian Tacitus, the younger Pliny, Plutarch, Sueto′nius, and Epicte′tus, the slave-philosopher, were all living at this time.

202. Augustus had enjoined his heirs to regard the Rhine, the Danube, and the Euphrates as the limits of their dominion. Trajan, however, desiring to throw off the disgraceful tribute which Domitian had promised to the Dacians, made war twice against their king, Deceb′alus. He was completely victorious; the king was slain, and his country became a Roman province guarded by colonies and forts. On his return, A. D. 105, Trajan celebrated a triumph, and exhibited games during 123 days. It is said that 11,000 wild beasts were slaughtered in these spectacles, and that 10,000 gladiators, mostly Dacian prisoners, killed each other "to make a Roman holiday."

In the later years of this reign, the Roman and the Parthian empires came into conflict for the control of Armenia. Trajan quickly reduced the latter country to a Roman province, and, in subsequent campaigns, he wrested from the Parthians the ancient countries of Mesopotamia and Assyria. Trajan died in Cilicia, A. D. 117. His ashes were conveyed to Rome in a golden urn, and placed under the column which bears his name.

203. Ha′drian began his reign by surrendering the Asiatic conquests of Trajan. During the twenty years of almost unbroken peace which marked his administration, Hadrian visited the remotest corners of his empire, studied the wants and interests of his people, and tried impartially to secure the best good of all. York in England, Athens, Antioch, and Alexandria shared with Rome the honors of an imperial capital; and each had its part of those great architectural works which, in some cases, still exist to commemorate the glory of Hadrian. A revolt of the Jews, A. D. 131–135, was ended with the banishment from Palestine of the last remnants of their race. A Roman colony, Æ′lia Capitolina, was founded upon the site of Jerusalem, to which the Christians, expelled by Titus, were freely admitted with the first of their Gentile bishops. Of all the benefits which Hadrian conferred upon the empire, the greatest, perhaps, was his choice of a successor.

204. T. Aurelius Antoni′nus came to the throne. A. D. 138. His uneventful reign presents the rare example in Roman annals of twenty-three years' undisturbed tranquillity, and is a striking example of the truth of the saying, "Happy is the people that has no history." The happiness of his great family, for so he regarded his subjects, was the ruling purpose of his life. In Britain, the Roman boundary was pushed to its farthest northern limit during this reign, and guarded by the "Wall of Antoninus," extending from the Frith of Forth to the Clyde.

Marcus Aurelius, the nephew of Hadrian, who, together with L. Verus, had been adopted by Antoninus, assumed the latter's name* with his crown. He resembled his adoptive father in his love of religion, justice, and peace; but his reign was far less happy, owing to calamities which were beyond his power to avert. The barbarians north of the Danube began to be crowded by a new and great immigration from the steppes of Asia. The Scythic hordes, broken up from their ancient seats, we know not by what impulse or necessity, had thrown themselves upon the Germans, and these were driven across the Roman frontier, even into Italy, which they ravaged as far as Aquilei′a, on the Adriatic. The two emperors proceeded against them. Verus died in the Venetian country A. D. 169, but Aurelius remained at his post on the Danube, summer and winter, for three

* Of the two Antonines, the first is commonly called Antoninus Pius; the second, Marcus Antoninus.

years. He gained a great victory over the Quadi, A. D. 174. A sudden storm, occurring during the battle, decided the result. The pagans attributed it to an intervention of Jupiter Pluvius; but the Christians, to the prayers of Christian soldiers in the "Thundering Legion."

During the first years of the reign of Aurelius, the Parthians made a formidable attack upon the eastern provinces, destroyed an entire legion, and ravaged all Syria. The general Avidius Cassius, being sent against them as the lieutenant of Verus, more than made good the Roman losses, for he extended the boundary of the empire again to the Tigris. But after the death of Verus, Cassius was led to proclaim himself emperor, and gained possession of most of the Asiatic provinces. Before Aurelius could arrive in the East, the rebel chief was slain by his own officers, after a reign of three months. Aurelius caused his papers to be burnt without reading them, and suffered no man to be punished for his part in the rebellion.

The elevation and self-control which distinguished the emperor were owing, in great measure, to the Stoic philosophy which he studied from his twelfth year. The only blot on his character is the persecution of the Christians, which was doubtless instigated by the harsh and arrogant Stoics who surrounded him. Justin Martyr at Rome, the venerable Polycarp at Smyrna, and multitudes of less illustrious disciples at Vienna and Lyons, suffered death for their fidelity to their religion, A. D. 167–177. Marcus Aurelius died in Pannonia, A. D. 180.

205. Deceived by the youthful promise of his only son, Aurelius had associated Com′modus with him in the government at the age of fifteen. If the young prince could have enjoyed many years of training under the wise and virtuous care of his father, he might indeed have become all that was hoped of him. But the untimely death of the good Aurelius left his son at seventeen a weak, self-indulgent youth, easily controled by worthless associates. For three years the government continued in the course which Aurelius had marked out for it. But, A. D. 183, a plot for the murder of Commodus was detected, and many senators were believed to be involved. His revengeful nature, stimulated by fear, now made him a monster of tyranny. His only use of imperial power was to issue warrants for the death of all whom he suspected. Vain of his strength and skill, he assumed the name of the Roman Hercules, and exhibited himself in the amphitheater as a marksman and gladiator. At last, some of the intended victims of his proscriptions avoided their own destruction by strangling him in his bed-chamber, after he had reigned twelve years and nine months, A. D. 192.

206. The decline of the empire, which had been delayed by the Five Good Emperors — Nerva, Trajan, Hadrian, and the two Antonines — proceeded with frightful rapidity under Commodus. The armies in the provinces, tired of discipline, broke up into petty bands which robbed and murdered on their own account. One historian tells us that Peren′-nis, the prætorian præfect, was deposed and slain, with his wife and children, upon the demand of 1,500 insurgent soldiers who had marched unresisted from Britain to Rome. Society was as thoroughly demoralized as the army. Except among the despised and persecuted Christians, purity of life was scarcely to be found. Poverty was creeping upon the nations through the decline of industry, but luxury and self-indulgence were more wildly excessive than ever.

RECAPITULATION.

Galba (A. D. 68, 69) offends his guards by his strict economy, and is murdered after seven months. Otho, three months emperor, is defeated by Vitellius, who reigns from April to December, A. D. 69. Vespasian (A. D. 69–79) restores peace, order, and prosperity. In his reign Jerusalem is destroyed. The short but beneficent reign of Titus (A. D. 79–81) is disturbed by great calamities—earthquake, fire, and pestilence. Domitian (A. D. 81–96) is a gloomy tyrant, disgraced abroad and detested at home. Nerva (A. D. 96–98) restores confidence, and chooses for his successor Trajan (A. D. 98–117), who is called the best and ablest of all the emperors. He gains victories north of the Danube and east of the Euphrates, thus extending the empire to the utmost limits which it ever attains. Hadrian (A. D. 117–138) visits every portion of his dominions, and diffuses every-where the blessings of peace and good government. Antoninus Pius (A. D. 138–161) enjoys a reign of unexampled tranquillity. Marcus Aurelius (A. D. 161–180), though a peaceful philosopher by choice, is involved by necessity in many wars. He generously forgives the rebellion led by Cassius, but permits a persecution of the Christians, at the instance of the Stoics. Commodus (A. D. 180–193), exasperated by a plot against his life, becomes a revengeful tyrant, and under his reckless misrule all order, industry, and safety vanish from the empire.

SECOND PERIOD, A. D. 193–284.

207. By their unchecked disorders, the soldiers had learned their power, and now assumed to set up and put down emperors at their will. The murderers of Commodus proceeded to the house of Per′tinax, præfect of the city, and offered him the crown. He was a good old man, one of the few surviving friends of Marcus Antoninus, and one to whose care the young prince Commodus had been committed. He reluctantly accepted the dangerous honor, and the result justified his fears. The economy and order which he attempted to introduce, disgusted equally the amusement-loving citizens and the turbulent and grasping soldiers. Pertinax was murdered in his own palace by the prætorians, March 28, A. D. 193, after a reign of less than three months. The guards now put up the imperial crown at public auction, and sold it to Did′ius Julia′nus, a wealthy senator, for $15,000,000. The Senate acknowledged him, and he reigned more than two months at Rome. But the armies in Britain, Pannonia, and Syria, not so much offended by the scandalous insolence as encouraged by the example of their comrades at the capital, set up their own leaders, Albi′nus, Seve′rus, and Niger, as emperors.

208. Severus arrived first at Rome, gained over the prætorians by promises of donatives, and was acknowledged by the Senate. Julianus was deserted and slain in his palace. The first imperial act of Severus was to disarm the prætorians, and to banish them to a distance of 100 miles from the capital. He defeated his two rivals, the one at Cyzicus and Issus, and the other near Lyons (Lugdu′num), in Gaul; and by their death became undisputed master of the empire. Instead of the old prætorians, he garrisoned Rome with 40,000 troops chosen from the legions, and their chief, the prætorian præfect, became, next the sovereign, the most powerful person in the world; for, beside his military command, he had control of the public treasury, and great influence in the making and enforcing of the laws. Severus was an able and successful general. He extended the empire eastward by the capture of the Parthian capital, and the conquest of Adiabe′ne; and northward, by his wars against the Caledonians. He died at York, the Roman capital of Britain, A. D. 211, having reigned eighteen years.

209. The two sons of Severus, Caracal′la and Geta, had been associated by their father in his imperial dignity, and reigned together a year after his death. Then their mutual hatred broke out afresh, and after a vain attempt to divide the empire between them, Caracalla murdered Geta in the arms of their mother. In the five years of his sole reign, he proved one of the worst tyrants that Rome had known. Under the pretext of exterminating the "friends of Geta," he massacred 20,000 persons, some of whom were the most virtuous and illustrious in the empire. Goaded by his restless conscience, Caracalla then quitted Rome, and wandered through all the eastern and northern provinces, followed every-where by a track of poverty, desolation, and death. At last he plunged into a war with Parthia, in which he had some success; but before his second campaign he was murdered by Macri′nus, his prætorian præfect, whom the guards proclaimed emperor.

210. Macrinus bestowed the title of Cæsar upon his son, and then hastened to follow up Caracalla's victories over the Parthians. He encountered the Eastern monarch near Nis′ibis, and suffered a shameful defeat, which forced him to retire into Syria. The soldiers were now tired of their chosen imperator, whose severity of discipline was an unwelcome change from the reckless liberality of Caracalla. Julia Mæsa, sister-in-law of Severus, persuaded one division of the army to accept as their prince her grandson, Bassia′nus, whom she declared to be a son of Caracalla. He is more commonly called Elagab′alus, from the Syrian sun-god to whose priesthood he had been dedicated as a child. The wealth which Mæsa had hoarded during her residence at her sister's court materially aided to convince the soldiers. A body of troops, sent to quell the insurrection, were also, in great measure, gained over to her wishes. A battle was fought near Antioch, in which Macrinus was defeated, and eventually slain, after a reign of fourteen months.

211. Elagabalus, or his ministers, hastened to send a letter to the Senate, in which he loaded himself with all the high-sounding titles of Cæsar, Imperator, son of Antoninus, grandson of Severus, Pius, Felix, Augustus, etc. The Romans passively admitted his claims, and the Arval Brothers offered their annual vows for his health and safety under all these names. The Syrian boy, who, at the age of fourteen, found himself thus clothed with imperial honors, was the most contemptible of all the tyrants that ever afflicted the Roman world. His days and nights were given up to gluttonous feasting and loathsome excesses.

The decorous and solemn rites of Roman religion were replaced by degrading sorceries, which were believed to be accompanied in secret by human sacrifices. The Syrian sun-god was placed above Jupiter Capitolinus himself, and all that was sacred or honorable in the eyes of the people became the object of insult and profanation. The emperor had been persuaded to confer the title of Cæsar on his cousin, Alexander Severus; but perceiving that this good prince soon surpassed him in the respect of the army, he sought to procure his death. A second attempt was fatal to Elagabalus. The prætorians murdered him and cast him into the Tiber.

212. Alexander Severus, now in his seventeenth year, was acknowledged with joy by the soldiers and the Senate. His blameless life and lofty and beneficent aims present a bright, refreshing contrast to the long annals of Roman degradation. Purity and economy returned to public affairs; wise and virtuous men received the highest offices; the Senate was treated with a deference which belonged to its ancient dignity, rather than to its recent base compliance with the whims of the army. If the power of Alexander had been as great as his designs were pure, the world might have been benefited.

A great revolution, about this time, changed the condition of Asia. The new Persian monarchy, under Artaxerxes, the grandson of Sassan, had overthrown the Parthian empire, and now aimed at the recovery of all the dominions of Darius Hystaspes. Artaxerxes actually sent an embassy to Alexander Severus, demanding the restitution to Persia of her ancient provinces between the Ægean and the Euphrates. The reply was a declaration of war. Alexander in person met the forces of Artaxerxes in the plain east of the Euphrates, and defeated them in a great battle, A. D. 232.

Hearing that the Germans were plundering Gaul, he hastened to make peace and returned to Rome. The next year he set out for Germany; but before he could begin his military operations there, he was murdered by a small band of mutinous soldiers. The virtues of Alexander were largely owing to the watchful care of his mother, in guarding his childhood from the wickedness with which he was surrounded. The prince repaid her vigilance by the most dutiful and tender regard; and it is said that her over-cautious and economical policy, which led him to withhold gifts of money demanded by the army, occasioned his death.

213. The ringleader of the mutiny was Max′imin, a Thracian peasant—a brutal and illiterate ruffian, yet with enough natural ability to cause him to be chosen emperor by his comrades. Three years this savage ruled the world, his only policy being hatred toward the noble and covetousness toward the rich; until the people of Africa, roused to fury by the extortions of his agents, revolted and crowned their proconsul, Gor′dian, and his son. The two Gordians were slain within a month; but the Senate supplied their place by two of its own number, and with unwonted spirit prepared for the defense of Italy. Maximin marched from his winter-quarters on the Danube, but he had advanced no farther than Aquileia when he was murdered in his tent by his own soldiers.

214. Though the legions had destroyed the emperor of their choice, they had no intention of yielding to that of the Senate. They murdered Pupie′nus and Balbi′nus within six weeks of their triumph over Maximin, and bestowed the imperial robes upon a younger Gordian, the grandson of the former proconsul of Africa. This boy of twelve years was intended, of course, to be a mere tool of his ministers. Timesith′eus, the prætorian præfect, was an able officer, and, so long as he lived, vigorously upheld the imperial power against Persian assaults and African insurrections. He was succeeded in command by Philip the Arabian, who artfully procured the death of the young emperor, and assumed the purple himself. He wrote to the Senate that Gordian had died of disease, and requested that divine honors should be paid to his memory.

215. Among the few events recorded of the five years (A. D. 244–249) of Philip's reign, is the celebration of the "Secular Games" at Rome, upon the completion of a thousand years from the building of the city, April 21, A. D. 248. Rival emperors were set up by the Syrians, and by the army in Mœsia and Pannonia. Decius, a senator, was sent by Philip to appease the latter. Their mock-emperor was already dead, but the soldiers, believing their guilt too great to be forgiven by Philip, thronged around Decius with tumultuous cries of "Death or the purple!" The loyal officer, with a hundred swords at his throat, was compelled to be crowned, and to consent to lead his rebellious army into Italy. He wrote to assure his master that he was only acting a part, and would resign his mock-sovereignty as soon as he could escape his troublesome subjects. But Philip did not believe these professions of loyalty. He marched to meet the insurgents at Verona, was defeated and slain, Sept., A. D. 249.

216. The two years' reign of Decius (A. D. 249–251) was marked by two widely different attempts to restore the ancient religion and morality of Rome — the revival of the censorship and the persecution of the Christians. It was deeply felt that the calamities of the empire were due to the corruption of its people. But the first measure produced no effect, while the second only aroused the evil passions of men, and occasioned untold misery. The bishops of Antioch, Jerusalem, and Rome became martyrs, and Alexandria was the scene of a frightful massacre. Another calamity, for which Decius was not responsible, was the first great incursion of the Goths, who ravaged the provinces of Mœsia and Thrace south of the Danube. Decius was defeated by them in A. D. 250; and the next year, in attempting to cut off their retreat, he lost his life in a great battle.

217. Gallus, an able general, was crowned by the Senate, Hostilia′nus, the son of Decius, being associated with him in the imperial dignity. Calamities thickened; pestilence raged in Rome, and fresh swarms of barbarians, only encouraged by the successes of the Goths, and the sums of money which had been paid them as the price of peace, ravaged the Danubian provinces. Hostilianus died of the plague, and the distress of the people led them to unjust accusations of the emperor. Æmilianus having defeated an army of the invaders, was proclaimed as sovereign by his troops, and, marching into Italy, defeated Gallus and his son at Interam′na. Æmilian was acknowledged by the Senate, but his reign was short. Valerian, a noble and virtuous officer, had been sent by Gallus to bring the Gallic and German legions to his aid. He arrived too late to save his master, but he defeated Æmilian near the scene of his former victory, and himself received the allegiance of Senate and people.

It was no enviable distinction, for the causes that were tending to the destruction of the empire were more numerous and fiercely active than ever. The Franks from the lower Rhine, the Aleman′ni from southern Germany, ravaged Italy, Gaul, and Spain, and even crossed the straits into Africa. The Goths had made themselves fleets from the forests of the Euxine, with which they devastated the coasts of Asia Minor and Greece, capturing and burning innumerable cities, among which were Cyzicus, Chalcedon, Ephesus, and even Corinth and Athens. The new Persian kingdom of the Sassanidæ had increased in power. Its second monarch, Sapor, conquered Armenia, and overran the Roman provinces in the East. He defeated and captured Valerian in a battle near the Euphrates, and gratified his pride by a spectacle which no monarch before had ever been able to exhibit — a Roman emperor, loaded with chains but clothed in purple, a perpetual captive at his court.

The government being thus overwhelmed with calamities, various pretenders claimed the sovereignty of the several fragments of the empire. These adventurers were known in general as the "Thirty Tyrants." Their reigns were usually too short or too insignificant to be worthy of mention. Palmyra continued to be the royal seat of Odena'tus, and after his death, of his widow, Zenob'ia, for ten years, A. D. 264–273, inclusive. Pos'thumus established a kingdom in Gaul, which lasted seventeen years. Valerian, before his disasters in the East, had associated with him, in the cares of empire, his son Gallie'nus; but that prince could attempt little more than the defense of Italy. Aure'olus, commanding on the upper Danube, assumed the imperial title and crossed the Alps. He was defeated by Gallienus, and besieged in Milan. Through his arts, Gallienus was slain by his own soldiers; but they conferred the purple on a more honest man and better general, whom the murdered prince had named in his dying moments. Milan was taken and Aureolus put to death.

218. Though the Roman Empire seemed to be doomed to destruction, equally by disunion within and the attacks of barbarians from without, its final disruption was delayed by a succession of able emperors. Claudius, who succeeded Gallienus, A. D. 268, vanquished the Alemanni in Italy, and the Goths in Mœsia. Aurelian (A. D. 270–275) again routed the Goths in Pannonia; and then recalling the advice of Augustus, he ceded to the barbarians the provinces north of the Danube, removing the Roman inhabitants to Mœsia. He made a war against Zenobia, which ended in the capture of the "Queen of the East," and the overthrow of her kingdom. A still more difficult enterprise awaited Aurelian in the west, where Tet'ricus, the last successor of Posthumus, had united Gaul, Spain, and Britain into one powerful monarchy. But he was conquered, and the empire was again established on the borders of the Atlantic, A. D. 274.

Aurelian was about to turn his victorious arms against the Persians, when he was assassinated by several of his officers, owing to a plot formed by his secretary, Mnes'theus. The army, indignant at the crime, applied to the Senate for a new emperor, instead of permitting any general to seize the crown. The Senate, after six months' hesitation, during which the soldiers respectfully waited, named M. Claudius Tac'itus, a senator of vast wealth and blameless character. He would gladly have declined the laborious and perilous position, on account of his age and infirmities; but the Senate insisted, and Tacitus was crowned. All the acts of his short reign were directed to the improvement of morals, and the establishment of law and order throughout the empire. He was called away to Asia Minor, where a troop of Goths, engaged by Aurelian to serve in his Eastern expedition, were committing disorders for want of pay. They were expelled; but Tacitus, enfeebled by old age, sank under the exertion, and he died two hundred days from his accession to the throne, A. D. 276.

219. Florian, brother of Tacitus, assumed the purple at Rome, while the army in the East proclaimed Probus, their general. The soldiers of

Florian, however, refused to fight their comrades, and, after three months, put their leader to death. Probus, thus undisputed master of the Roman world, was an able general and a wise and beneficent sovereign. He not only drove the Germans out of Gaul, subdued the Sarmatians, and terrified the Goths into peaceable behavior, but he provided for the security of his extended frontier by settling the border provinces with numerous colonies of barbarians, who, becoming civilized, made a barrier against further incursions of their countrymen. He wished, also, to improve waste lands by the draining of marshes and the planting of vines, and to employ in these works the dangerous leisure of his soldiers. But the legionaries did not share the thrifty policy of their emperor. They mutinied at Sir′mium, and by another murder ended the beneficent reign of Probus, A. D. 282.

220. Carus, the prætorian præfect, was hailed as emperor by the army, and conferred the title of Cæsar on his two sons, Cari′nus and Nume′rian. Leaving the former to govern the West, Carus, with Numerian, turned toward the East; first gained a great victory over the Sarmatians in Illyricum, and then proceeded to overrun Mesopotamia, and capture the two great cities of Seleucia and Ctes′iphon. He had advanced beyond the Tigris, and seemed about to overthrow the Persian kingdom, when he suddenly died, whether by lightning, by disease, or by the dagger, historians are not agreed.

Coin of Diocletian, enlarged twice the size.

His son Numerian yielded to the superstitious fears of his soldiers, and withdrew within the Roman boundaries. On the retreat he was murdered by his father-in-law, who was also prætorian præfect, and who hoped to conceal the crime until he could reap the fruits of it. But the army discovered the death of their beloved emperor, and set up Diocle′tian, the captain of the body-guards, to avenge and succeed him.

Carinus, meanwhile, reigning in the West, was dazzling the Roman world by expensive games, and insulting it by his profligacy. Hearing of the murder and usurpation, he marched with a large and well-disciplined army to meet Diocletian, and joined battle near Margus, in upper Mœsia. The Western troops were victorious, but Carinus, while leading the pursuit, was slain by one of his own officers. His followers came to an agreement with those of Diocletian, who was universally hailed as emperor.

221. His accession began a new period in the empire, when the power of the sovereigns became more absolute, ceasing to be checked either by the lawful authority of the Senate or the insolence of the soldiers. During the ninety-two years which had elapsed since the death of Commodus, the legions had claimed the privilege, not only of raising to the imperial power whomsoever they might choose, but of removing the object of their choice whenever he ceased to content them. No general who desired to be emperor dared stint his donatives, or enforce the needful severity of discipline. But for the almost constant danger from barbarians without, the army, which was the real tyrant of the Roman world, might have already put an end to all order, peace, and civil government.

RECAPITULATION.

Pertinax (A. D. 193) is crowned and murdered by the prætorians, who then sell the throne to Julianus. Severus (A. D. 193–211) buys the adhesion of the guards, and having gained the imperial power, disarms and expels them. He enlarges his dominions by conquests both in the east and west. Caracalla murders his brother, and misgoverns the empire six years, A. D. 211–217. Macrinus (A. D. 217, 218) gains and loses his crown by violence. Elagabalus (A. D. 218–222) introduces Syrian manners and worship into Rome. He is succeeded by his cousin, Alexander Severus (A. D. 222–235), who gains a great victory over the new Persian empire of the Sassanidæ, but is afterward slain in Germany during a mutiny of his troops. Maximin (A. D. 235–238), a Thracian, is set up, and in three years put down, by his comrades in the army. The two Gordians reign less than a month, Pupienus and Balbinus about six weeks, when a younger Gordian (A. D. 238–244) is invested with the purple at the age of twelve. He loses his life through the arts of Philip the Arab, who becomes emperor, and celebrates, A. D. 248, the thousandth year of the existence of Rome. Decius, being sent to quell a revolt in Pannonia, is crowned by the soldiers, A. D. 249, and Philip is slain. Two great calamities mark the reign of Decius: a persecution of Christians and an incursion of Goths. Gallus (A. D. 251–253) is deposed by Æmilianus, who is soon superseded by Valerian (A. D. 254–260). The whole empire is overrun by Gothic and German invaders. Valerian, in his wars in the East, is captured, and spends the last seven years of his life at Sapor's court. "Thirty Tyrants" spring up in various parts of the empire. Gallienus reigns in Italy, first with his father. Valerian, and afterward alone, A. D. 254–268. He is slain through the management of a pretender, Aureolus, but is succeeded by Claudius (A. D. 268–270), who defeats the barbarians. Aurelian (A. D. 270–275) makes the Danube again the northern boundary of the empire; subdues Zenobia in the east and Tetricus in the west; is murdered on his way to Persia. Tacitus (A. D. 275, 276), being appointed by the Senate, reigns two hundred days. Florian, his brother, is deposed by his own troops. Probus (A. D. 276–282) restores security by a wise and energetic reign. Carus gains great victories in the East; but after his sudden death, his son Numerian abandons his conquests. Numerian is slain in the East, Carinus in the West, and Diocletian becomes emperor.

THIRD PERIOD, A. D. 284–395.

222. Under the firm and wise policy of Diocletian, the Roman world entered upon a century of greater vigor and security. The empire being too large to be administered by a single head, Diocletian conferred equal power upon his friend and comrade Maxim′ian, with the title of Augustus. A few years later, two Cæsars, Gale′rius and Constan′tius, were added to the imperial college, each being associated, as adopted son and successor, with one of the emperors. To the Cæsars were assigned the more exposed provinces, which needed an active and vigilant administration, while the Augusti kept to themselves the old and settled portions of the empire. Constantius had Gaul, Spain, Britain, and the whole frontier of the Rhine; Galerius had Noricum, Pannonia, and Mœsia, with the defenses of the Danube; while Maximian governed Italy and Africa, and Diocletian retained for himself Thrace, Macedonia, Egypt, and the East. Though allotted thus to its several rulers, the empire was not divided. The four princes governed in consultation, and were equally honored in all parts of the realm.

223. In A. D. 286, a naval chief, Carau′sius, being intrusted with a powerful fleet for the defense of the British and Gallic coasts against the Franks, gained over the troops in Britain, seized the island, and set up an independent government. He built new ships, and soon became master of the Western seas. Diocletian and Maximian, after vain attempts to break his power, were compelled to acknowledge him as their colleague in the empire, A. D. 287. Constantius, upon becoming Cæsar, made war, A. D. 292, upon this new Augustus; captured Boulogne after a long and severe siege, and was preparing to invade Britain, when Carausius was killed by his chief officer, Allec′tus.

Constantius landed, three years later, in Britain, and by a battle near London recovered the island. He afterward drove the Alemanni out of Gaul, and settled his captives in colonies upon the lands depopulated by their ravages. At the same time, Maximian quelled a formidable revolt of the Moors in Africa; and Diocletian, by a siege of eight months, captured Alexandria, where a rival emperor had usurped the throne, and punished the rebellious city by a massacre in which many thousands perished. The Cæsar Galerius made war against the Persians for the recovery of Armenia, which they had taken from Tirida′tes, the vassal of Rome. He was defeated near Carrhæ, on the very scene of the overthrow of Crassus, more than three centuries before; but he retrieved this misfortune by a great victory over King Narses, followed by an advantageous peace.

224. The system of Diocletian was thus effective and prosperous, as far as it concerned the foreign enemies of the state; but the expenses of four imperial courts, with the immense number of soldiers and officials, imposed heavy burdens upon the people. The wretched tax-payers were often tortured to enforce payments which they were unable to make. The civil wars of the preceding centuries had deprived extensive districts of inhabitants; and the productions of the earth and of human industry had ceased.

225. The greatest blot upon the memory of Diocletian is the persecution of Christians in the last year of his reign. Every province and every great city of the empire had now heard the doctrines of Christ, and the church in Rome numbered 50,000 members. In an age of turbulence and corruption, Christians were every-where distinguished as the most orderly, industrious, loyal, and honest members of the community. Their refusal to worship the image of the emperor, which was an essential part of the Roman religion, had brought upon them several local persecutions, but none so widely extended and severe as that of Diocletian. The edict requiring uniformity of worship was issued A. D. 303. Instantly the cruel passions of the pagans were let loose from restraint. Innocent blood flowed in every province. Whoever had either malice or covetousness to indulge, had only to accuse his enemy of being a Christian, and to be rewarded with half the confiscated goods. In the extreme west, Constantius protected those of the "new religion," but elsewhere there was no appeal from the atrocious cruelties sanctioned by courts of law.

226. Of the many acts by which Diocletian abased the authority of the Senate, the most effective was the removal of the center of government from the ancient city on the Tiber. His own official residence was at Nicomedia; that of Maximian, at Milan; while Constantius held a provincial court at York, and Galerius at Sirmium, on the Savus. The Senate thus became the mere council of a provincial town. Imperial edicts took the place of the laws which had formerly received its sanction. The insolent prætorians were, at the same time, replaced by the "Jovian" and "Herculean Guards"; and their præfect, who had been a rival of the emperor, became merely an officer of the palace. Diocletian, however, celebrated the twentieth year of his reign, and his numerous victories, by a triumphal entry into Rome; and this was the last "triumph" which the ancient capital ever beheld.

227. The next year, A. D. 305, Diocletian, worn out with the cares of empire, formally abdicated his power, and compelled Maximian to do the same. The two Cæsars now became Augusti, and two new candidates, Maximin and Severus, were appointed by Galerius to the former title. The legions in Britain were dissatisfied, however, by seeing the choice of a successor taken away from their own imperator; and upon the death of Constantius, A. D. 306, they immediately proclaimed Con′stantine, his son. He was acknowledged as Cæsar by Galerius, who conferred the rank of Augustus on Severus.

But, the next year, Maxen′tius, son of Maximian, was declared emperor by the Senate and people of Rome, and his father resumed the purple, which he had unwillingly laid aside at the command of Diocletian. Severus, attempting to crush this insurrection, was taken captive at Ravenna, and privately put to death. Galerius now conferred the imperial dignity on Licinius, and for two years the Roman world was peaceably governed by six masters: Constantine, Maximian, and Maxentius in the West; Galerius, Maximin, and Licinius in the East.

228. The peace was first broken by the dissensions of Maximian and his son. The elder emperor fled from Rome, and was well received by Constantine, who had married his daughter. Before long, however, Maximian entered again into plots with Maxentius for the ruin of Constantine; which becoming known to their intended victim, he returned promptly from his campaign on the Rhine, besieged his father-in-law in Massilia, and put him to death, A. D. 310. Galerius died the next year at Nicomedia, and the empire was again divided into four parts, of which Constantine ruled the extreme west; Maxentius, Italy and Africa; Licinius, Illyricum and Thrace; Maximin, Egypt and Asia.

The cruel and rapacious character of Maxentius wearied out his subjects, who sent deputies from Rome, beseeching Constantine to come and be their sovereign. This great general had won the love of his followers, not less by his firm and successful dealings with the barbarians, than by his liberal protection of the Christians, whose virtues he esteemed, and whose rights of conscience he respected. On his march toward Italy, it is said that he beheld a vision. A flaming cross appeared in the heavens, bearing in Greek the inscription, "By this, conquer!" Thenceforth, the cross replaced the pagan symbols which had been carried at the head of the legions; and the omen, if such it was, was amply fulfilled.

229. Constantine passed the Alps, A. D. 312, defeated the troops of Maxentius near Turin, captured Verona after an obstinate siege and battle, and encountered his rival in a final combat before the gates of Rome. In the battle of the Mil′vian Bridge, Maxentius was defeated and drowned. The following year, Maximin was defeated by Licinius, in a great battle at Heraclea, on the Propontis, and put an end to his life at Tarsus, in Cilicia. Constantine and Licinius, in a series of battles, divided the world between them. The river Strymon and the Ægean became the boundaries between the Eastern and Western empires. Two sons of Constantine and one of Licinius received the title of Cæsar. Crispus, on the Rhine, gained a victory over the Franks and Alemanni; and Constantine, on the Danube, executed a terrible vengeance upon the Goths, who had invaded the Roman territory.

230. After seven years' peace, war broke out between the emperors, in A. D. 322. Licinius was defeated near Hadriano′ple, besieged in Byzantium, and finally overthrown upon the Heights of Scuta′ri, overlooking the latter city. His death made Constantine the sole ruler of the civilized world. His great dominion received a new constitution suitable to its magnitude. The seat of government was fixed upon the confines of Europe and Asia, in the new and magnificent city bearing the emperor's name, which he built upon the ruins of the Greek Byzantium. The whole empire was divided into four *præfectures*, which nearly corresponded to the dominions of the four emperors, A. D. 311. (§ 228.) Each præfecture was divided into *dioceses*, and each diocese into proconsular governments, or *presidencies*.

This subdivision of the empire gave rise to three ranks of officials, somewhat resembling the nobility of modern Europe. The republican form of government, so ostentatiously cherished by Augustus, had now disappeared, and in its place was the elaborate ceremony of an Oriental court. Even the 10,000 spies, known as the "King's Eyes," were maintained as of old by Xerxes and Darius. A standing army of 645,000 men was kept upon the frontier; but as Roman citizens were now averse to military service, the legions were largely composed of barbarian mercenaries. The Franks, especially, had great importance, both in the court and camp of Constantine.

231. The great event of this reign was the admission of Christianity as, in a certain sense, the religion of the state. The Edict of Milan, A. D. 313, guaranteed to the hitherto persecuted people perfect security and respect; that of A. D. 324 exhorted all subjects of the empire to follow the example of their sovereign, and become Christians. Heathenism was not yet proscribed. Constantine was pontifex maximus, and must, on certain occasions, have offered sacrifices to the fabulous gods of Rome. It was only in his last days that he received Christian baptism; but he presided in the first General Council of the Church at Nice, in Bithynia, A. D. 325, to which he had convened bishops from all parts of the empire, to decide certain disputed matters of faith. Though he treated the assembled fathers with every mark of reverence, he refused to persecute Arius and his followers, the Alexandrian heretics, whom the Council condemned.

232. Crispus, the eldest son of Constantine, who had been named Cæsar at the age of seventeen, was the idol of the people, but an object of jealousy to his father, who suspected him of treasonable designs. Whether the charges against him were true, we have no means of knowing. He was seized during the festivities in Rome, in honor of the twentieth year of his father's reign, tried secretly, and put to death. The last years of Constantine were disturbed by fresh movements of the barbarians north of the Danube. The Sarmatians, being attacked by the Goths, implored the aid of the Romans. Constantine was defeated in one battle with the invaders, but in the next he was victorious, and 100,000 Goths, driven into the mountains, perished with cold and hunger. In the division of spoils, the Sarmatians were dissatisfied, and revenged themselves by making inroads upon the Roman dominions. In succeeding wars they were defeated and scattered; 300,000 were received as vassals of the empire, and settled in military colonies in Pannonia, Thrace, Macedonia, and Italy.

233. Hoping to secure peace to the empire after his death, Constantine assigned its different parts to his three sons and two nephews, whom he had carefully educated for their great responsibilities. But his care was unavailing. Immediately upon his decease, A. D. 337, Constantius, his second son, being nearest, seized the capital, and ordered a massacre of all whose birth or power could give them any hopes of obtaining the sovereignty. Of his own relatives, only two cousins, Gallus and Julian, escaped. The three sons of Constantine then divided the empire between them. Constantine II., the eldest, received the capital, together with Gaul, Spain, and Britain; Constantius had Thrace and the East; Constans, Italy, Africa, and western Illyricum.

The reign of Constantius was occupied by a disastrous war with Persia. The pagan Armenians revolted upon the death of their king, Tiridates — a "friend of the Romans," who had established Christian worship in his dominions — and opened their gates to the Persians. The son of Tiridates sought the aid of Constantius, who succeeded in restoring the prince Chos′roes to his dominions. The fortress of Nisibis, which was esteemed the bulwark of the East, withstood three memorable sieges by the Persians; but the Roman armies were defeated in nine pitched battles, and the raids of the Persian cavalry extended even to the Mediterranean, where they captured and plundered Antioch.

234. In the meanwhile, discord had broken out between the emperors in the West, and Constantine II., invading the dominions of his brother Constans, was defeated and slain near Aquileia. Constans seized his provinces, and reigned ten years (A. D. 340–350) over two-thirds of his father's empire. Magnentius, an officer in Gaul, then assumed the purple, and Constans was slain. Constantius, recalled from his Persian wars, defeated Magnentius in a toilsome campaign on the Danube; received the submission of Rome and the Italian cities; and finally, by a great battle among the Cottian Alps, ended the rebellion with the life of the usurper, A. D. 353. Sixteen years after the death of the great Constantine, the empire was thus reunited under one sovereign. Gallus, the cousin of Constantius, had been taken from prison to receive the title of Cæsar and the government of the East. But he proved wholly unfit to rule; he treated with insult the embassador of his cousin, and even caused him to be murdered by the mob of Antioch. Gallus was thereupon recalled, and put to death at Pola, in Is′tria.

RECAPITULATION.

Diocletian (A. D. 284–305) associates Maximian as "Augustus," and Galerius and Constantius as "Cæsars," with himself in the management of the empire. Constantius overthrows the sovereignty of Carausius in Britain and northern Gaul. Galerius gains victories in Asia; Diocletian, in Egypt; and Maximian, in Africa. The new system is efficient abroad, but oppressive at home. Christians are severely persecuted. Seat of government removed from Rome. Diocletian and Maximian resign, A. D. 305. Galerius (A. D. 305–311) and Constantius (A. D. 305, 306) become emperors; Severus and Maximin, Cæsars. Constantine the Great (A. D. 306–337), succeeding his father, Constantius, eventually conquers Maximian, who has resumed the purple, and Maxentius (A. D. 312), who has been proclaimed at Rome, and reigns over the Western empire. Licinius (A. D. 307–323), after the death of Galerius, conquers Maximin, and reigns east of the Ægean. Constantine conquers Licinius, A. D. 323, and becomes sole emperor. Fixes his court at Constantinople; reorganizes the government; makes Christianity the religion of the state; has wars with the Goths; and establishes military colonies of Sarmatians within the bounds of the empire. After his death, his three sons destroy their kinsmen, and divide the dominion between them. While Constantius II. is at war with Persia, his brother, Constantine II., is slain by Constans, who is himself deposed, after ten years, by Magnentius. Constantius, returning from the East, A. D. 350, defeats Magnentius, and reigns over his father's entire dominion, A. D. 353-361.

Extinction of Paganism.

235. Julian, the younger brother of Gallus, was permitted to pursue his favorite studies at Athens, until, A. D. 355, he was called to the court of Milan, dignified with the title of Cæsar, and intrusted with the government of Gaul. His conduct displayed great energy and talent. He severely defeated the Alemanni, in the battle of Strasbourg; drove the Franks from their castles on the Meuse; and in three invasions of Germany, liberated 20,000 Roman captives. He rebuilt the cities of Gaul which the barbarians had destroyed; adorned Paris, his winter residence, with a palace, theater, and baths; imported grain from Britain for the sustenance of the people; and protected agriculture, manufactures, and commerce.

Constantius became jealous of his cousin's fame, and sought to disarm and disgrace him, by ordering the greater part of the Gallic army to the East. Julian was preparing to send away his devoted followers, but the soldiers mutinied, proclaimed him emperor, and forced him to assume the purple robe. An embassy to Constantius was contemptuously dismissed; and Julian, after again chastising the Franks, and improving the defenses of the German frontier, set forth to decide the question by actual war. Penetrating the Black Forest as far as the Danube, he descended that river with a captured fleet, surprised Sirmium, and was received with acclamations by the people. He sent letters justifying his conduct to the principal cities of the empire, especially to the senates of Athens and Rome; and he was invested by the latter with the imperial titles which it alone could legally bestow. The sudden death of Constantius, at Tarsus, Nov., A. D. 361, ended the uncertainty. All Constantinople poured forth to welcome Julian, at a distance of sixty miles from the capital, and soldiers and people throughout the empire accepted him as their head.

236. His first acts were to retrench the Oriental luxury of the palace, to punish the officers of Constantius who had oppressed the people, and to dismiss the 10,000 spies. A philosopher by choice, and an emperor only by compulsion, Julian prided himself upon the frugal simplicity of his habits, and professed himself merely the "servant of the Republic." He is known in history by the unhappy name of "Julian the Apostate." Incensed against the *Christian* cousins who had murdered his entire family, he extended his hatred to the faith which they so unworthily professed. He publicly renounced Christianity, and placed himself and his empire under the protection of the "Immortal Gods."

To spite the Christians, he patronized the Jews, and attempted to rebuild their Temple at Jerusalem; but he was thwarted by balls of fire breaking out near the foundation, which made it impossible for the workmen to approach.* He excluded all Christians from the schools of grammar and rhetoric, hoping thus to degrade them in intellectual rank, and weaken them in controversy. He, however, disappointed the pagan zealots by proclaiming toleration to all parties. In the spring of A. D. 363, Julian departed with a great army for the East, where the ravages of the Persian king had for four years met with little resistance. He gained an important victory over the Persians at Ctesiphon, but in a subsequent skirmish he was mortally wounded, and died, June, A. D. 363, after a reign of only sixteen months.

237. Jovian, the captain of the life-guards, was saluted as Augustus by the generals of Julian. He obtained peace with the Persian king by ceding the five provinces east of the Tigris, and then conducted a difficult retreat to the capital. The principal act of his reign was the re-establishment of Christian worship and of universal tolerance. He died, Feb., A. D. 364, after a reign of eight months. The civil and military officers of the empire met at Nicæa, and chose for their sovereign Valentin′ian, a Christian and a brave soldier, who had distinguished himself by service both on the Tigris and the Rhine. His brother Valens was made his colleague, with the command of the East, extending from the lower Danube to the boundaries of Persia.

238. Valentinian fixed his capital at Milan, which alternated with Rheims and Treves as his headquarters. He signally defeated the Alemanni, and guarded the Rhine by a new series of forts. The coasts of western Europe now began to be overrun by piratical Saxons, while the Picts and Scots swept over all the cultivated fields of southern Britain, from the Wall of Antoninus to the coast of Kent. Theodo′sius, father of the future emperor of that name, led a veteran army to the relief of the Britons, and afterward gained among the Orkneys a great naval victory over the Saxons.

---

* So says Ammia′nus Marcelli′nus, an honest and usually trustworthy historian, contemporary with Julian, and probably a pagan.

Having defeated the Alemanni on the upper Danube, Theodosius was next sent into Africa to quell a revolt of the Moors and provincials, provoked by the extortions of Count Roma′nus. Firmus, the chief of the Moors, was as wily as Jugurtha, but Theodosius showed all the skill of Metellus or of Scipio. He imprisoned Romanus and restored order to the province; but he was rewarded only by unjust suspicions and a military execution, A. D. 376. Valentinian was already dead (Nov., A. D. 375), and the ministers who surrounded his son disguised the truth to suit their own purposes.

239. Valens, meanwhile reigning in the East, was far inferior to his brother in firmness and beneficence of character. At the beginning of his reign, Proco′pius, a kinsman of Julian, gained possession of Constantinople, and kept it several months as nominal emperor. He was captured at last, and suffered a cruel death in the camp of Valens. The great event of this period was the irruption of a new and terrible race of savages from northern Asia. The Huns were more hideous, cruel, and implacable than even the fiercest of the barbarians hitherto known to the Romans. The Great Wall, which still divides China from Mongolia, had been erected as a barrier against their inroads; but their attention was now turned to the westward, where the Goths, north of the Black Sea, were the first to feel their power.

The great Gothic kingdom of Her′manric extended from the Danube and Euxine to the Baltic, and embraced many kindred tribes, of which the eastern or Ostro-Goths, and the western or Visi-Goths were most important. The former were conquered by the Huns; the latter besought permission from Valens to settle on the waste lands south of the Danube, and become subjects of the empire. Their request was granted, and a million of men, women, and children crossed the river. But the Roman commissioners who were charged with receiving and feeding this starving multitude, seized the opportunity to make their own fortunes, at the expense of their honor and of the safety of the empire.

The Goths had been required to give up their arms, but they purchased of these officers permission to retain them. The food which was served to them was of the vilest quality and most extravagant price. Discontent broke out among the turbulent and armed host. The Gothic warriors marched upon Marcianop′olis, defeated the army which was sent to defend it, and laid waste all Thrace with fire and sword. Instead of pacifying the Goths by a just punishment of the offenders, and by pledges of justice for the future, Valens sent for aid to his nephew Gratian, and advanced with his army to fight with the barbarians. In a battle near Hadrianople he was slain, and two-thirds of his army perished, A. D. 378.

240. Gratian, the son of Valentinian, had been three years emperor of the West, and now became sole sovereign of the dominions of Augustus.

He chose, however, for a colleague, the general Theodosius, to whom he committed the empire of Valens, with the addition of the province of Illyricum. The youth of Gratian was adorned by a fair promise of all the virtues; but as soon as his excellent instructors left him, he proved himself weak and wholly unfit for command. Bad men gained and abused his confidence.

Maximus, in Britain, revolted, and passed over into Gaul with an army. Instead of fighting, Gratian fled from Paris; his armies deserted to the enemy, and the fugitive emperor was overtaken and slain at Lyons, A. D. 383. He had already, on his accession, shared the imperial dignity with his brother, Valentinian II., then only five years of age. Maximus, being in actual possession of the countries west of the Alps, was acknowledged by Theodosius, on condition of the young Valentinian being left in secure possession of Italy and Africa. The sovereign of Gaul, Spain, and Britain soon became strong enough to break his word. He invaded Italy, and the young emperor, with Justi′na his mother, fled to the court of Theodosius for protection. The emperor of the East marched to attack Maximus, whom he defeated and caused to be executed as a traitor, and established Valentinian II. in the sovereignty of the whole Western empire.

241. The young sovereign of the West proved as weak as his brother. He fell under the control of an officer of his own, a Frank named Arbogas′tes; and when he attempted to shake off the yoke, the too powerful servant murdered his master and set up an emperor of his own choosing. Euge′nius reigned two years (A. D. 392–394), as the tool of Arbogastes; but Theodosius at length defeated his army near Aquileia, and put him to death.

For four months the Roman world was united, for the last time, under one sovereign. Theodosius the Great well deserved the title by which he is known in history. His vigorous and prudent management changed the Goths from dangerous enemies into powerful friends. Great colonies of Visi-Goths were formed in Thrace, and of Ostro-Goths in Asia Minor; and 40,000 of their warriors were employed in the armies of the emperor. If later monarchs had acted with the wisdom and firmness of Theodosius, these recruits might have added great strength to the then declining empire. They were, in fact, a chief occasion of its fall.

242. This reign is marked by the extinction of the old pagan worship. The temples were destroyed, and all sacrifices or divinations forbidden. The Egyptians believed that Serapis would avenge any profanation of his temple at Alexandria; but when a soldier, climbing to the head of the colossal idol, smote its cheek with his battle-ax, the popular faith was shaken, and it was admitted that a god who could not defend himself was no longer to be worshiped. Arians and other Christian heretics were persecuted with scarcely less rigor than the pagans; for they were forbidden to preach, ordain ministers, or hold meetings for public worship. The penalties inflicted by Theodosius were nothing more than fines and civil disabilities; but his contemporary, Maximus, is said to have been the "first Christian prince who shed the blood of his Christian subjects for their religious opinions."

The power and dignity of the Church at this time is shown by the conduct of Ambro′sius, Archbishop of Milan. Theodosius had ordered a general massacre of the people of Thessalonica, as a punishment for a wanton tumult which had arisen in their circus, during which a Gothic general and several of his officers had been killed. Several thousands of persons, the innocent with the guilty, were slaughtered by barbarian troops sent thither for the purpose. When the emperor, who was then at Milan, went as usual to church, Ambrosius met him at the door, and refused to admit him to any of the offices of religion until he should publicly confess his guilt. The interdict continued eight months; but, at length, the master of the civilized world, in the garb of the humblest suppliant, implored pardon in the presence of all the congregation, and was restored, at Christmas, A. D. 390, to the communion of the Church.

Before his death, Theodosius divided his great dominions between his two sons, giving the East to Arcadius, and the West to Hono′rius. The latter, who was only eleven years of age, was placed under the guardianship of the Vandal general Stil′icho, who had married a niece of the great emperor. Theodosius died at Milan, Jan. 17, A. D. 395.

RECAPITULATION.

Julian administers Gaul and invades Germany with great energy and success. He incurs the jealousy of his cousin, and is declared emperor by his troops. Constantius dies, and Julian (A. D. 361-363), now universally acknowledged, restores paganism. He is killed in an Eastern campaign, and is succeeded by Jovian, who withdraws west of the Tigris. On the death of Jovian, A. D. 364, Valentinian (A. D. 364-375) is chosen by the court and army, and assigns the Eastern empire to his brother Valens. The general Theodosius gains important victories over Saxons, Picts, Scots, and Moors. Procopius usurps for a time the Eastern capital, and the empire is threatened by both Huns and Goths. In war with the latter, Valens is slain. Gratian (A. D. 375-383), son of Valentinian, confers the Eastern empire upon the younger Theodosius (A. D. 379-395). He is himself dethroned by Maximus, who becomes sovereign of Gaul, Spain, and Britain, and even expels the brother of Gratian (A. D. 387) from Italy. Theodosius destroys Maximus, and restores Valentinian II. as emperor of the West; but this young monarch is soon murdered by Arbogastes. Eugenius reigns two years, A. D. 392-394. Theodosius defeats him, and rules the united empire four months. He conciliates the Goths; abolishes pagan rites; persecutes heretics; does penance at Milan; divides the empire between Arcadius and Honorius.

FOURTH PERIOD, A. D. 395–476.

243. The empire east of the Adriatic continued more than a thousand years from the accession of Arcadius, and its records belong to Mediæval History. From the death of the great Theodosius, the division of the two empires was complete. Rufi′nus, the minister of Arcadius, bore a mortal enmity to Stilicho, the guardian of Honorius; and for the sake of revenge, he let loose the Goths upon the Western empire. Al′aric, the Visi-Goth, was made master-general of the Eastern armies in Illyricum. At the same time, he was elected to be king of his own countrymen, and it is uncertain in which character he invaded Italy, A. D. 400–403. Honorius was driven from Milan, but Stilicho defeated the invader at Pollen′tia, and afterward at Verona, and persuaded him, by promises of lands for his followers, to withdraw from Italy.

During the rejoicings at Rome on account of his retreat, an incident occurred which marks the progress of Christianity in the declining empire. Telem′achus, a monk, entered the arena of the Coliseum and attempted to separate the gladiators, protesting, in the name of Christ, against their inhuman combat. He was stoned to death by the crowd; but their remorse bestowed upon him the honors of a martyr; and the emperor, who was present, made a law abolishing forever the shedding of human blood for public sport.

244. Honorius transferred his capital from Milan to the impregnable fortress among the marshes of Ravenna, which continued three centuries to be the seat of government for Italy. A fresh invasion from Germany, led by the pagan Radagai′sus, devastated western Italy. Gaul was, at the same time, overrun by a mingled horde of Vandals, Suevi, Alani, and Burgundians; and from that moment the Roman Empire may be said to have fallen in the countries beyond the Alps. The army in Britain revolted; and after electing and murdering two emperors, set up Constantine, who led them into Gaul, defeated the German invaders, passed into Spain, and established a kind of sovereignty over the three western countries of Europe.

Meanwhile, Stilicho was disgraced and slain, through the intrigues of his enemy, Olympius. While the barbarian auxiliaries in his army were lamenting his death, they were enraged by a massacre of their wives and children, who had been kept as hostages in the various cities of Italy. This insane act of cruelty sealed the fate of Rome. The barbarians, freed from either the duty or necessity of obeying Honorius, flocked to the camp of Alaric, in Illyricum, and urged him to invade Italy. The Visi-Goth had injuries of his own to avenge. He passed the Alps and the Po, and, after a rapid march, pitched his camp upon the Tiber. Rome was reduced to starvation. Thousands died of famine, and thousands more from the pestilence which it occasioned. At length, Alaric accepted the terms offered by the Senate, and retired, upon the payment of an enormous ransom, A. D. 408.

245. His brother-in-law, Adolphus, now joined him with a troop of Huns and Goths. Alaric offered peace to the court of Ravenna, on condition of receiving lands for his followers, between the Danube and the Adriatic. His demands being refused, he again marched upon Rome, and set up an emperor of his own choosing, in At′talus, præfect of the city. Ravenna was only saved from his attack by a reinforcement from Theodosius II., now emperor of the East. Africa was likewise delivered by the vigilance of Count Herac′lian. But Alaric was soon tired of his puppet-king. He deposed him, and again sought peace with Honorius. The treaty failed through the ill-will of Sarus, a Goth in the imperial service, who was a bitter enemy and rival of Alaric.

The king of the Visi-Goths now turned a third time, and with relentless rage, upon Rome. The Eternal City was taken, Aug. 10, A. D. 410, and for six days was given up to the horrible scenes of murder and pillage. Though greatly reduced in power, Rome had never lost her dignity, or the wealth of her old patrician houses. These were now ransacked; gold, jewels, and silken garments, Grecian sculptures and paintings, and the choicest spoils of conquered countries, brought home in triumph by ancestors of the present families, went to enrich the Gothic and Scythic hordes, who were so ignorant of the value of their plunder, that exquisite vases were often divided by a stroke of a battle-ax, and their fragments distributed among the common soldiers. Only the churches and their property were respected, for Alaric declared that he waged war with the Romans, and not with the apostles.

246. At length the king of the Goths withdrew, laden with spoils, along the Appian Way, meditating the conquest of Sicily and Africa. Storms, however, destroyed his hastily constructed fleet, and a sudden death terminated his career of conquest. He was buried in the channel of the little river Busenti′nus, and his sepulcher was adorned by his followers with the treasures of Rome. Adolphus, his successor, made peace with Honorius, and received the hand of the imperial princess Placid′ia, who had been taken prisoner during the siege. Her bridal gifts consisted of the spoils of her country. Adolphus retired into Gaul, and then into Spain, where he founded the kingdom of the Visi-Goths, as a dependency upon the Western empire.

Constantine was driven out of Spain, and captured at Arles, by Constantius, who was rewarded for his distinguished services by a marriage with Placidia, after the death of her Gothic husband, and by the imperial titles which he bore as the colleague of her brother. He reigned but seven months, and after his death Placidia quarreled with Honorius, and took refuge with her nephew at Constantinople. In a few months the emperor of the West ended a disgraceful reign of twenty-eight years, A. D. 423. John, his secretary, usurped the throne; but Theodosius II. sent a fleet and army to enforce the claims of his cousin, the son of Placidia, and the troops in Ravenna were easily persuaded to surrender their upstart emperor. John was beheaded at Aquileia, A. D. 425.

247. Valentinian III. was a child of six years. The Western empire was therefore placed under the regency of his mother, Placidia, who continued to rule it for a quarter of a century, while the military command was held by Aë′tius and Boniface. Unhappily, these two generals were enemies. The malicious falsehoods of Aëtius led Boniface into rebellion, and lost Africa to the empire. Gen′seric, king of the Vandals in Spain, willingly accepted the invitation of Boniface, and crossed the straits with 50,000 men. The Moors immediately joined his army; the Donatists* hailed him as their deliverer from persecution.

Too late, Boniface discovered his mistake, and returned to his allegiance. All Roman Africa, except Carthage, Cirta, and Hippo Regius, had passed over to the Vandals. Forces were sent from Constantinople to aid those of Italy; but the combined armies were defeated, and Boniface was compelled to abandon Africa, taking with him all the Roman inhabitants who were able to leave. The countries on the Danube had been ceded to the Eastern empire, in return for the aid of Theodosius II., in placing Valentinian III. upon his throne. Britain, unprotected by the Roman armies, had thrown off her allegiance, and had for forty years no government except that of the clergy, the nobles, and the magistrates of the towns. The Goths were settled permanently in south-western Gaul; the Burgundians in the east, and the Franks in the north of the same country; and except a small tract in southern Gaul, the Western empire now included only Italy and the region of the western Alps.

248. Aëtius defended the Gallic province against the Visi-Goths on one side, and the Franks on the other, until the latter called in a new and more terrible ally than all previous invaders, in At′tila, king of the Huns. This savage chief was known to the terror-stricken world of his time, as the Scourge of God. He had subdued to his authority all the barbarians between the Baltic and the Euxine, the Rhine and the Volga, and his army of 700,000 men was officered by a host of subject kings. He had been for nine years ravaging the Eastern empire to the very walls of Constantinople, and had only retired upon the promise of an enormous annual tribute, and the immediate payment of 6,000 pounds of gold. He now invaded Gaul, in behalf of a Frankish king who had been driven beyond the Rhine, and had sought his aid.

* A very numerous sect in Africa, opposed by Augustine, Bishop of Hippo, and by an edict of Honorius.

Theod'oric, the son of Alaric, now king of the Visi-Goths, had allied himself with the Romans, and their united armies came up with Attila, just as he had effected the capture of Orleans by battering down its walls. The Hun instantly drew off his hordes from the plunder of the city, and retreated across the Seine to the plains about Chalons', where his Scythian cavalry could operate to better advantage. Then followed one of the most memorable battles in the history of the world. The aged king Theodoric was slain, but the victory was gained by the valor of his subjects. Attila was driven to his circle of wagons, and only the darkness of night prevented the total destruction of his hosts.

This was the last victory ever achieved in the name of the Western empire. It settled the great question, whether modern Europe should be Teuton or Tartar. The Goths were already Christian; their rude energy was well adapted to the laws and institutions of civilized life. The Huns were savage, heathen, destructive; mighty to ravage and desolate, but never, in their greatest power and wealth, known to build and organize a state. Most of what is admirable in European history would have been reversed by a different result of the battle of Chalons.

249. Attila retreated beyond the Rhine. Two years later, he descended into north-eastern Italy, reduced Aquileia, Alti'num, Concordia, and Padua to heaps of ashes, and plundered Pavia and Milan. The fugitives from the old territory of the Veneti took refuge upon the hundred low islets at the head of the Adriatic, and laid, in poverty and industry, the foundations of the Republic of Venice. While he was diverted from his threatened march upon Rome, by the intercessions of Pope Leo, Attila suddenly died, and his kingdom fell to pieces even more rapidly than it had been built up. Two of his sons perished in battle. Irnac, the youngest, retired into Scythia. Valentinian showed his relief from apprehension by murdering Aëtius with his own hand. Having in many ways disgusted and offended his subjects, he was himself assassinated in March, A. D. 455.

Maximus, his murderer, assumed the purple, but he continued in power less than three months. Eudox'ia, the widow of Valentinian, called in the aid of Genseric, the Vandal king of Africa, who, commanding the Mediterranean with his fleets, was only too eager for the spoils of Italy. The Romans, as soon as he had landed in Ostia, put to death their unworthy emperor; but this execution failed to appease the barbarian. Fourteen days the Eternal City was again given up to a pillage more unscrupulous than that of Alaric. The Vandal fleet, waiting at Ostia, was laden with all the wealth which the Goths had spared, and receiving on board the empress Eudoxia and her daughter, made a safe return to Carthage.

250. The Romans were too much paralyzed to appoint a new sovereign.

When the news reached Gaul, Avi′tus, the general of the armies there, was proclaimed, through the influence of Theodoric II., and was acknowledged for more than a year throughout the Western empire. But, A. D. 456, Count Ric′imer, a Goth commanding the foreign auxiliaries in Italy, rebelled, and captured Avitus in a battle near Placentia. He set up Marjo′rian, whose talents and virtues revived some appearance of justice and energy in the government. A fleet was now prepared for the invasion of Africa, in the hope not only of retaliating upon Genseric for his plunder of Rome, but of stopping the ravages of the Vandal pirates upon the coasts of Italy. It was betrayed to the emissaries of Genseric, in the Spanish port of Carthagena.

Ricimer, by this time, was jealous of his *protégé*, and, forcing him to resign, set up a new puppet in the person of Lib′ius Severus, in whose name he hoped to exercise the real power. But the nominal rule of Severus was confined to Italy, while, beyond the Alps, two Roman generals — Marcellinus in Dalmatia, and Ægid′ius in Gaul — possessed the real sovereignty, though without the imperial titles. The coasts of Italy, Spain, and Greece were continually harassed by the Vandals, and Ricimer, two years after the death of Severus (A. D. 467), appealed to the court of Constantinople for aid against the common enemy, promising to accept any sovereign whom the emperor would appoint.

251. Anthe′mius, a Byzantine nobleman, was designated as emperor of the West, and received the allegiance of the Senate, the people, and the barbarian troops. The fidelity of Count Ricimer was thought to be secured by his marriage with the daughter of the new emperor. A formidable attack upon the Vandals was made by the combined forces of the East and the West; but it failed through the weakness or treachery of Bas′ilis′cus, the Greek commander, who lost his immense fleet through the secret management of Genseric. The Vandals recovered Sardinia and became possessed of Sicily, whence they could ravage Italy more constantly than ever.

The Goths, meanwhile, became dissatisfied with the foreign rule. Ricimer retired to Milan, where, in concert with his people, he openly revolted, marched with a Burgundian army to Rome, and forced the Senate to accept a new emperor in the person of Olyb′rius, A. D. 472. Anthemius was slain in the attack upon the city. Ricimer died forty days after his victory, bequeathing his power to his nephew, Gund′obald, a Burgundian. Olybrius died a month or two later, and Gundobald raised a soldier named Glyce′rius to the vacant throne. The emperor of the East interfered again, and appointed Julius Nepos — a nephew of Marcellinus of Dalmatia — who was accepted by the Romans and Gauls, Glycerius being consoled for the loss of his imperial titles by the safer and more peaceful dignity of Bishop of Salo′na.

252. Scarcely was Julius invested with the insignia of his rank, when he was driven from the country by a new sedition led by Ores'tes, master-general of the armies, who placed upon the throne his own son, Romulus Augustus. This last of the Western emperors, who bore, by a curious coincidence, the names of the two founders of Rome and the empire, was more commonly called Augus'tulus, in burlesque of the imperial grandeur which mocked his youth and insignificance.

The mercenaries demanded one-third of the lands of Italy as the reward of their services; and being refused, they sprang to arms again, slew Orestes, deposed Augustulus, and made their own chief, Odo'acer, king of Italy. The Roman Senate, in a letter to Zeno, emperor of the East, surrendered the claim of their country to imperial rank, consented to acknowledge Constantinople as the seat of government for the world, but requested that Odoacer, with the title of "Patrician," should be intrusted with the diocese of Italy.

With the fall of the Western empire, Ancient History ends. But the establishment of kingdoms by the northern nations marks the rise of a new era, which, through centuries of turbulence, will open into the varied and brilliant scenes of Modern History.

RECAPITULATION.

Alaric, invading Italy, is defeated by Stilicho. Gladiatorial combats are forever abolished at Rome. Honorius fixes his capital at Ravenna. Italy and Gaul are overrun by a pagan host. Constantine becomes emperor in the extreme West, A. D. 407–411. Death of Stilicho and massacre of Gothic women and children lead Alaric to a second invasion of Italy, A. D. 408–410. Rome is three times besieged, and finally given up to plunder for six days. Alaric dies, A. D. 410, and is succeeded by Adolphus, who marries the sister of Honorius, and founds a Gothic kingdom in Spain and southern Gaul. Constantius, second husband of Placidia, reigns as colleague of Honorius, A. D. 421; and his son, Valentinian III., succeeds to the whole Western empire, A. D. 425–455. During the regency of Placidia, the general Boniface, deceived by Aëtius, betrays Africa to the Vandals. Gaul is invaded by Attila, king of the Huns, who is defeated by Goths and Romans near Chalons, A. D. 451. He ravages northern Italy; and fugitives from cities which he destroys, found Venice on the Adriatic, A. D. 452. Valentinian III. is assassinated; and his widow, to avenge his death, calls in the Vandals, who plunder Rome fourteen days. Avitus (A. D. 455, 456) is proclaimed emperor in Gaul. Count Ricimer rebels, and sets up first Marjorian (A. D. 457–461), then Severus (A. D. 461–465), and finally applies for an emperor to the Eastern court, which appoints Anthemius (A. D. 467–472). Ricimer revolts again, and crowns Olybrius, who dies in a few months. Glycerius (A. D. 473, 474) soon exchanges the crown for a miter, and Julius Nepos is installed as sovereign. Orestes sets up his own son, Romulus Augustus (A. D. 475, 476), the last Roman emperor of the West. Odoacer becomes king of Italy, and the Western empire is overthrown.

QUESTIONS FOR REVIEW.

Book V.

1. What three successive forms of government in ancient Rome? § 8.
2. What races inhabited Italy? 9–11.
3. Describe, severally, their origin, character, and institutions.
4. Relate the traditions concerning the origin of Rome. 12, 13.
5. Describe the acts and characters of the first three kings. 13–16.
6. What tribes and classes made up the Roman population under Tullus Hostilius? 16.
7. What changes were made by Ancus Martius and Tarquinius Priscus? 17, 18.
8. Describe the constitution under Servius Tullius. 19–21.
9. The reign of Tarquin the Proud. 22.
10. The chief divinities and religious festivals of the Romans. 23–25.
11. The oracles and modes of divination. 26–28.
12. The four sacred colleges. 28–30.
13. The ceremony of lustration. 31.
14. The government and condition of Rome after the expulsion of the kings. 32–34.
15. The causes and effects of the first secession. 35, 36.
16. The Cassian, Publilian, Terentilian, and Hortensian laws. 37, 40, 43, 46, 78.
17. Tell the story of Coriolanus. 42.
18. Of Cincinnatus and his son. 44, 45.
19. Describe the Laws of the Twelve Tables. 46–48.
20. What occasioned the second secession? 49–51.
21. What changes in government resulted from it? 51–54.
22. Describe the Veientine War and its consequences. 56, 57.
23. The invasion of Italy by the Gauls. 57, 58.
24. The sack and siege of Rome. 59, 60.
25. The condition of the Romans after the departure of the Gauls. 61.
26. The treason of Marcus Manlius. 62, 63.
27. The Licinian laws. 64, 65.
28. The final expulsion of the Gauls. 66.
29. The character of the Samnites. 67, 68.
30. The First Samnite War. 69.
31. Relate the incidents of the Latin War. 70–72.
32. Describe the Second Samnite War, and the reduction of the Æqui. 73–75.
33. The Third Samnite War, and the conquest of the Sabines. 76–78.
34. What nations were allied against Rome, B. C. 283? 79, 80.
35. Describe the campaigns of Pyrrhus in Italy and Sicily. 81–85.
36. What changes among the Romans followed their conquest of Italy? 86, 87.
37. Describe the origin and events of the First Punic War. 89–94.
38. What part was taken by Rome in the affairs of Greece? 95.
39. Describe the conquest of the Gauls in northern Italy. 96, 112.
40. The preparations by Carthage for the Second Punic War. 97–99.
41. The invasion of Italy by Hannibal. 100–108.
42. The fate of Hasdrubal. 106, 107.
43. A Roman triumph. 109–111.
44. The wars of Rome in the East and West. 113, 114, 117.
45. The last Punic War. 115, 116.

46. Describe the conquest of Spain. . . . . §§ 118, 119.
47. The condition of Rome after the foreign wars. . . . 120, 121.
48. The policy and death of Tiberius Gracchus. . . . . 122, 123.
49. Of Scipio Æmilianus. Of Caius Gracchus. . . . 124–127.
50. The Jugurthine Wars. . . . . 128–132.
51. Tell the history of Marius. . . . . 130–136, 139–141.
52. Describe the Roman slave-code, and its effects in Sicily. . . . 137.
53. The dictatorship of Sulla. . . . . 142–145.
54. The rebellion of Sertorius. . . . . 146, 147.
55. The War of the Gladiators. . . . . 148–150.
56. Relate the history of Pompey. . . . . 151–153, 155, 166–170.
57. Describe the conspiracy of Catiline. . . . . 154.
58. Relate the history and designs of Cæsar. . . . . 156–177.
59. Of the second triumvirate. . . . . 177–180.
60. Describe the three decisive battles of Pharsalia, Philippi, and Actium. . . . . 169, 179, 180.
61. The city and empire of Rome under Augustus. . . 181, 182, 185.
62. The Roman operations in Germany. . . . . 183, 184.
63. The reign of Tiberius. . . . . 186–188.
64. Caligula. . . . . 189.
65. Claudius. . . . . 190.
66. Nero. . . . . 191–194.
67. How many emperors during A. D. 69? . . . . 195, 196.
68. Describe the reigns of Vespasian and his two sons. . . . . . 197–199.
69. The five good emperors. . . . . 200–206.
70. The reign of the prætorians. . . . . 207.
71. The history of Severus and his sons. . . . . . . 208, 209.
72. The contrasted characters of the two grandsons of Julia Mæsa. . . . . 210–212.
73. How many emperors in A. D. 238? . . . . 213, 214.
74. Describe the reigns of Philip and Decius. . . . . 215, 216.
75. The condition of Rome under Gallus. . . . . 217.
76. What foreign invaders under Valerian? . . . . 217.
77. Describe the reign of the Thirty Tyrants. . . . . 217.
78. What able rulers delayed the fall of the empire? . . . . . 218, 219.
79. Describe the reigns of Carus and his sons. . . . . 220.
80. The new arrangement of the empire under Diocletian and his colleagues. . . . . 221–227.
81. The revolt of Carausius. . . . . 223.
82. The changes in the empire, from Diocletian's abdication to the sole reign of Constantine. . . . . 227–230.
83. The reorganization of the Roman world by Constantine. . 230.
84. What change of religion marked this reign? . . . . 231.
85. What foreign nations obtained settlements within Roman boundaries? . . . . 232.
86. Tell the history of the sons of Constantine. . . . . 234.
87. Describe the character and career of Julian. . . . . 235, 236.
88. Who succeeded Jovian? . . . . 237.
89. Describe the reign of Valentinian. Of Valens. . . . . 238, 239.
90. The reign of Gratian and his brother. . . . . . . 240, 241.
91. The character and reign of Theodosius the Great. . . . 241, 242.
92. What was the comparative duration of the Eastern and Western empires? . . . . 243.
93. What barbarians invaded Italy during the reign of Honorius? . . 243–246.

94. Tell the history of Placidia. . . . . §§ 246, 247.
95. The extent of the Western empire under Valentinian III. 247.
96. Describe the career of Alaric, and the battle of Chalons. . . 248, 249.
97. The successive captures of Rome by Goths and Vandals. . 245, 249.
98. How many sovereigns appointed by Count Ricimer? . . . . 250, 251.
99. How many by the court at Constantinople. . . . . 251.
100. Who was the last Roman emperor of the West? . . . . . . 252.
101. How many centuries had Rome existed from its foundation?

LIST OF BOOKS RECOMMENDED.

The following works are recommended to the student who desires a more complete account of the nations of antiquity.

Rawlinson's History of the Five Great Monarchies of the Ancient Eastern World.

Wilkinson's Manners and Customs of the Ancient Egyptians.

Heeren's Researches into the Politics, Commerce, etc., of the Ancient World.

Niebuhr's Lectures on Ancient History.

Layard's Nineveh.

Milman's History of the Jews.

Stanley's History of the Jewish Church.

Josephus's Jewish Antiquities.

Herodotus. (Rawlinson's translation, with illustrative essays, is incomparably the best.)

Xenophon's Cyropædia, Anabasis, and Memorabilia.

Grote's History of Greece.

Curtius's History of Greece.

Dr. Wm. Smith's History of Greece, in a single volume.

Bulwer's Athens: its Rise and Fall.

St. John's The Hellenes: the Manners and Customs of Ancient Greece.

Creasy's Fifteen Decisive Battles of the World.

Niebuhr's History of Rome.

Arnold's History of Rome.

Mommsen's History of Rome.

Forsyth's Life of Cicero.

Selections from Cicero's Orations.

Cæsar's Commentaries.

Life of Cæsar, by Napoleon III.

Merivale's History of the Romans under the Empire.

Gibbon's History of the Decline and Fall of the Roman Empire.

Among Stories, Poems, and Dramas illustrative of Ancient History, the following are recommended—the first three especially to the youngest readers.

Kingsley's "Heroes."

Hawthorne's "Wonder-book" and "Tanglewood Tales."

Mrs. Child's "Philothea."

Becker's "Charicles" and "Gallus."

Macaulay's "Lays of Ancient Rome."

Ware's "Zenobia," "Aurelian," and "Probus."

Mrs. Charles's "Victory of the Vanquished."

Kingsley's "Hypatia."

Shakespeare's "Coriolanus," "Julius Cæsar," and "Antony and Cleopatra."

Among collections of Engravings, the following should especially be sought.

"Description of Egypt," made by the Commission of *savans* who accompanied the French army in 1797. Commonly called "Napoleon's Egypt." 9 vols. Text, and 14 folio vols. Plates.

Fergusson's "Palaces of Nineveh and Persepolis Restored."

Fergusson's "Illustrated Handbook of Architecture."

Botta's "Monuments of Nineveh."

Layard's "Monuments of Nineveh."

Penrose's "Athenian Architecture."

Stuart's "Antiquities of Athens."

Canina's "Edifices of Ancient Rome."

INDEX.

B

T

FINIS.

www.ingramcontent.com/pod-product-compliance
Lightning Source LLC
LaVergne TN
LVHW010130110826
845151LV00002B/317
9781425541736